A HISTORY OF THE BRITISH CAVALRY
1816 to 1919

VOLUME III
1872 to 1898

By the same author

THE CAPEL LETTERS, 1814–1817 (CAPE, 1955)
ONE-LEG (CAPE, 1961)
SERGEANT PEARMAN'S MEMOIRS (CAPE, 1968)
LITTLE HODGE (LEO COOPER, 1971)
A HISTORY OF THE BRITISH CAVALRY, 1816–1919
VOLUME I: 1816–1850 (LEO COOPER, 1973)
VOLUME II: 1851–1871 (LEO COOPER, 1975)

A HISTORY OF THE BRITISH CAVALRY
1816 to 1919

by

THE MARQUESS OF ANGLESEY
F.S.A.

VOLUME III
1872 to 1898

A LEO COOPER BOOK
SECKER & WARBURG · LONDON

First published in Great Britain, 1982, *by*
Leo Cooper in association with
Martin Secker & Warburg Limited,
54 *Poland Street, London* W1V 3DF

ISBN 0 436 27327 6

Printed in Great Britain by
Western Printing Services Ltd, Bristol

DEDICATED, WITH PERMISSION, TO
BRIAN BOND, ESQ.
WHOSE STUDIES OF THE VICTORIAN ARMY
ARE INDISPENSABLE TO A TRUE APPRECIATION
OF IT

CONTENTS

ILLUSTRATIONS

MAPS

ACKNOWLEDGMENTS

All military historians writing today, whether professional or amateur, must ever be exceedingly grateful to the Chief Librarian of the Ministry of Defence Library and his staff. I am no exception. Mr Andrews and his predecessor, Mr King, have always given me, beside an endless supply of books and documents on loan, speedy and accurate advice as well as copious information, invariably supported by chapter and verse. Their patience has seemed inexhaustible, their wisdom infinite.

Among other institutions without whose help it would have been impossible to complete this volume are the London Library, the India Office Library, the Library of the Royal United Service Institute for Defence Studies, the Society for Army Historical Research, the Household Cavalry Museum, Windsor, and, particularly, the National Army Museum. To their chief officers and staffs I am deeply obliged for a wide variety of help, as also to the Registrar of the Judge Advocate General, the Area Library, Hove, Sussex, and the Home Headquarters of the 5th Inniskilling Dragoon Guards.

Numerous men and women have been importuned by me over the years during which this volume has been taking shape. Some, such as Mr Edmond Combe, Earl Haig of Bemersyde, Colonel Leigh Maxwell, OBE, and Mr John P. Saunders, have allowed me to borrow and keep for unconscionable periods of time, books or manuscripts which I could obtain from no other sources. Others have read parts of the manuscript, thereby helping to put me on the right lines. Prominent among these is Mr Brian Robson, without whose helping hand I should have fallen into erroneous statements of fact connected with the cavalry sword.

The dedication of this volume shows how deeply indebted I am to Mr Brian Bond whose erudite studies of so many aspects of the Victorian military scene never fail to inform and illuminate.

For general encouragement I am indebted to my long-suffering wife, and, among others, to Sir Roger Fulford, Mr Boris Mollo, Mrs Charles Morgan and Miss Jan Morris.

The speedy, painstaking efforts of Mrs H. St G. Saunders of

Acknowledgments

Writer's and Speaker's Research have once again been put at my service without reservation. So have the typing precision and rapidity of Mrs Pat Brayne. To both I proffer my warmest thanks.

My publishers' constant attention and trouble-taking at every stage of this volume's lengthy pregnancy have only been equalled by their resignation and forbearance. They accepted that I was prevented for over a year from working on the volume because of the need to concentrate all my energies on handing over Plas Newydd to the National Trust. My gratitude to them acknowledges no limits.

I am grateful, too, for the excellent maps and plans which have resulted from Mr Patrick Leeson's skilful interpretations of my often obscure sketches.

'The civilian who attempts to write a military history is of necessity guilty of an act of presumption.'

SIR JOHN FORTESCUE,
History of the British Army,
1899, I, v.

'The English try to defend without any compulsion – only by such soldiers as they persuade to serve – territories far surpassing all Europe in magnitude, and situated all over the habitable globe.'

WALTER BAGEHOT,
The English Constitution, 2nd edn.,
1920, 206.

'La cavalerie n'est pas si facile à improviser que l'infanterie.'

GÉNÉRAL FOY,
Histoire de la Guerre de la Péninsule, quoted by Captain Nolan, *Cavalry*, 1853, 39.

'The very noise of the horses galloping has a terrifying effect that frequently goes home to the heart of Infantry.'

COLONEL SIR GARNET WOLSELEY,
The Soldier's Pocket-Book for Field Service, 2nd edn., 1871, 245.

'The stern reality of modern warfare . . . will no longer tolerate useless shams, however graceful and brilliant.'

SIR HENRY HAVELOCK, BT.,
Three Main Military Questions of the Day, 1867, 53–4.

PREFACE

The nearer one gets to the end of the history of cavalry, the harder it is to write definitively about it. It is ironical that within only a few decades of the virtual dissolution of the mounted arm, increasing thought and effort, experimentation and reformation should have been applied to its use. Up to, and indeed beyond, its effective demise, the process of trying to transform the ancient, amateurish art of mounted fighting into a modern science gathered momentum. The trend amongst an increasing number of serious-minded soldiers and others towards a larger degree of professionalism and battle efficiency accelerated as the end drew near. This generated frequent alterations in tactics and training, in weapons and equipment, as well as a spate of books and articles, pamphlets and treatises.

In consequence I have been forced to be much more selective in volume III than I was in volumes I and II. Though it can still be read independently of its predecessors, the present volume is less complete than they are. So as to avoid inflating it unreasonably, I have been compelled to touch much more lightly than I should have liked upon certain questions and aspects of the British cavalry during the last three decades of the nineteenth century. For example, except for occasional allusions, I have reserved for volume IV detailed discussion of such major topics as training methods and the role of cavalry in the face of modern weapons. I have also kept back any but general references to such matters as Mounted Infantry *versus* cavalry proper and the development of such perennial controversies as those about cut *versus* thrust and the best form of cavalry seat, all of which were being vehemently debated, especially in the 1890s. Similarly all discussion of the Yeomanry has also been deferred.

It is perhaps more appropriate to place consideration of these themes in the next volume, since they are vital to an understanding of the Great Boer War of 1899 to 1902 which it will cover. They will serve as a prelude to that conflict which was the first of importance since 1815 in which British mounted troops were really tested on a large scale.

With the consent of my long-suffering publishers I have decided to make the projected final volume into two. The penultimate one will embrace only thirteen years, 1899 to 1913, as opposed to the present one which covers twenty-seven. The fifth and concluding volume will be devoted to the First World War and its aftermath. It will also comprise an epilogue in the shape of an extended *envoi* or denouement and a summing up of the last hundred years of cavalry and cavalrymen in Britain.

* * *

As in the previous volumes of this work I have concentrated upon certain campaigns and battles, describing the cavalry's part in them in considerable detail. This has meant that other comparatively minor campaigns and engagements have been excluded altogether or only touched upon superficially. My intention has been to illustrate by examples what mounted troops experienced in war, not to record every action in which they took part. For instance, the Matabele and Mashonaland campaigns of the 1890s have been omitted altogether, not only because the mounted arm was not largely represented, but also because these small wars against black Africans differed little from others which I have described.

Where I have had to choose between devoting space to relating active service and chronicling peacetime conditions, I have usually come down on the side of the latter. This is because comparatively little has been written about the ordinary social life of officers and men during the period covered, and because there happens to be a wealth of 'Blue Book' material available which throws light upon it.

* * *

Once again I have laid myself open to criticism by mercilessly cutting out all detail about the parts played by the artillery and the infantry in the engagements described, except where it seemed vital to comprehension of what took place.

* * *

My spelling of Indian proper names has been capricious. Sometimes I have used contemporary forms, sometimes modern ones. When quoting from documents or books I have usually retained the original spelling.

* * *

As in the previous volumes the dates of birth and death (where known) of individuals mentioned in the text have been relegated to the index.

A HISTORY OF THE BRITISH CAVALRY

1816–1919

VOLUME III

1872–1898

'What cheaper or less troublesome way of running a great empire could there be than a professional army whose officers all had private incomes, and whose rank-&-file were all paupers?'

CORRELLI BARNETT, *Britain and Her Army*, 1970, p. 314

'There ain't better stuff to make soldiers with than Englishmen; but they're badgered – 'orrible badgered.'

OUIDA, quoted in Featherstone. D.F.
All for a Shilling a Day, 1966, p. 126

'The regimental sentiment and feeling is really the backbone of all our army arrangements.'

THE DUKE OF CAMBRIDGE in 1875 *A.P.R.C.*, 1876, p. 21

'My impression is that the army has done very well and should not be eager to change. An opinion has been expressed that the days of cavalry are over. My own view is exactly to the contrary – that the days of that arm have in fact come in.'

THE DUKE OF CAMBRIDGE in 1890, quoted in
John Walters, *Aldershot Review*, 1970, p. 131

'According to *Punch*, a General inspecting the officers of a cavalry regiment . . . asked a subaltern, "Now, sir, will you please tell me the role of cavalry in war." The subaltern replied: "Well, I suppose to give tone to what would otherwise be a mere vulgar brawl."'

Quoted by GENERAL SIR H. HUDSON in
History of the 19th King George's Own Lancers, 1937, p. 64

'Sir Baker Russell used to say that the duty of cavalry was to look smart in time of peace and to get killed in war.'

LIEUTENANT-GENERAL SIR ROBERT BADEN-POWELL
Memories of India, [1915], p. 113

1

'Years of fitful reform, characterised by commissions or committees of investigation and consequent piecemeal innovations could not counteract a national wave of pacific optimism that believed that the expertise of the army was adequate for the demands made on it.'

GWYN HARRIES-JENKINS, 'The Development of Professionalism in the Victorian Army'

'The creation of a system of short service coupled with reserves was intended to render the Army capable of sudden expansion when necessity so required.'

HON FREDERICK STANLEY, Secretary of State for War, 1879, in appointing the Airey Committee on Army Organization

'John Bull, at seasons, in a panic fright,
Cries out for troops for all the world to fight.
The House of Jaw resounds with long debates,
And votes a huge increase of Estimates.
The British Army, when the talk is o'er,
Remains inadequate as 'twas before.
No stronger force has John his Fleet behind,
But pays his money, and has eased his mind.'

Punch, 1871

'We have always . . . desired to be told . . . what the country expects the Army to do . . . Until that is laid down it is impossible to know what an "adequate reserve" is; we do not know what we are keeping a reserve for.'

GENERAL SIR REDVERS BULLER, Adjutant-General, in 1891.[1]

(i)

The Cardwell reforms: rationalization of authorities; abolition of 'dual control'; the short service system – the Stanhope Memorandum – deferred pay – side effects of short service

Sir John Fortescue, in the Epilogue to the last volume of his monumental *History of the British Army*, wrote that the State 'sent an army out to the Crimea and was somewhat shocked to see it perish of cold and hunger – still more surprised to find that this was its own fault. For the moment Parliament softened towards the Army. It turned it upside down and inside out to discover what could be the matter.'[2] Even though the lessons of the American Civil War of 1861–65 and the European conflicts which followed closely on its heels were avidly studied if not much understood in Britain, little happened in the way of radical reforms until 1868. In that year there came to the War Office a new broom in the shape of Edward Cardwell, appointed Secretary of State for War by Gladstone upon the Liberal Party's sweeping victory at the polls that autumn. In the six years during which he held office he made a valiant attempt to effect his declared aim of increasing efficiency whilst decreasing expenditure. First he speeded up the process, which had been going on in a leisurely fashion since the end of the Crimean War, of reducing the number of overlapping authorities controlling the army. Next, he gradually persuaded the Queen and her cousin, the Duke of Cambridge, who had been at the Horse Guards as General Commanding-in-Chief since 1857, and was to remain there for another twenty-seven years, that 'dual control' must end. This meant acknowledgement by the Duke that his office was to be subordinate to that of the Secretary of State: that Parliament, in other words, was to control the army, not the Sovereign. But the Duke saw to it that the old order in this respect, as in many another, was a long time a-dying.

Other Cardwell reforms included the abolition of the purchase of officers' commissions (see Vol II, 371–81), but the most perplexing of them was an attempt to solve the ancient problem of reserves in a non-conscript army.* An essential part of the 1847 Limited Enlistment Act, which had abolished service for life, (see Vol I, 121) had been the creation, as Earl Grey said twenty years later, 'of a large reserve of trained men who could be taken into the service in time of war'.[3] Since only a derisory number of

* With the concomitant arrangements which chiefly concerned the infantry and the linking of regiments with the militia territorially, (and which, incidentally, depended upon the abolition of purchase), this work is not directly concerned. They included the Localization Act, 1873, by which all battalions were affiliated in pairs and localized, for the purpose of recruiting and training, in brigade areas. One battalion at home, under this scheme, supplied the other abroad with drafts of trained men until, in due course, it relieved its sister battalion overseas. The new element of territorial connection did not apply to Cavalry regiments.

soldiers, on leaving after their first term of service, in fact joined the reserve, the scheme was a conspicuous failure.[4] Cardwell's system of Short Service, enacted in the Army Enlistment Act of 1870, though in theory very superior to anything which had gone before, never, alas, worked very effectively in practice. When the real test came with the opening of the Great Boer War in 1899, it was found, as Hugh Arnold-Forster, a future reforming war minister, wrote in 1900 (with pardonable overstatement) that 'we had returned to the precise position which the country occupied in the Crimean War, where we had a first line of undoubted excellence and behind it nothing but a crowd of unorganized and incompetent recruits.'* The fault was not Cardwell's. It seems likely that, without conscription, with Parliament and people smugly ensconced behind their ironclads and unwilling to pay for a socially respectable army, there was no solution to the problem. Further, until the famous Stanhope Memorandum of 1891, there had never been an authoritative or clear definition of what the army was for. That paper stipulated that after providing support for the civil power at home and garrisons for India and elsewhere overseas, 'the primary duty of the military authorities' was 'to organize our forces efficiently for the defence of this country'. For this purpose two army corps of regulars and one partly regular and partly of militia were to be mobilizable. Beyond these, subject to financial considerations, the aim should be to send abroad two army corps, a cavalry division and line of communication troops. 'But it will be distinctly understood that the probability of the employment of an Army Corps in the field in any European War is sufficiently improbable to make it the primary duty of the military authorities to organize our forces efficiently for the defence of this country.'[5]

The 1870 Act replaced twelve years' long service by six years with the Colours and six in the Reserves. In 1874, two years before the scheme could become fully operative, the terms of service were altered for the cavalry to eight years with the Colours and four with the Reserves. In 1881, under Hugh Childers' reforms (which also created the territorial system proper), these became seven and five respectively for both arms,† the Household Cavalry

* In fact, by the outbreak of the South African war the reserve produced by the short service system numbered some 80,000. It was their quality which was in doubt, not their quantity.

† These could be converted to eight and four if a man's Colour service expired when he was overseas.

being an exception to the short service rule. In the case of the three regiments (1st and 2nd Life Guards and the Royal Horse Guards) service was for twelve years with the Colours and no reserve service.

Men of the line regiments were allowed in certain circumstances to go to the Reserve earlier than the end of their Colour service. Indeed, on occasions they were encouraged to do so. When in 1889, for example, the 6th Dragoon Guards returned from their tour of India, they were 200 men over establishment.* Consequently volunteers were called for to transfer early to the Reserve. How many volunteered is not known, nor is the amount of pressure put upon them to do so.[6]

As Brian Bond, the leading modern authority, has written, the short service system immediately increased 'the annual demand for recruits, since the whole purpose of training changed from keeping a man as long as he was fit to passing him to the Reserve at the earliest moment.'[7] As will be shown (see p. 44), the resulting recruiting crisis came to a head in the early 1890s. Some indication of the increase under the new system is given by the fact that in 1862 only 6,700 recruits joined, while in 1875 the number was 18,500 and in 1885, nine years after the system had come into full force, just under 40,000, the vast majority of them less than twenty years old. The last two decades of the century were not for nothing called 'the Boy-Soldier Period'. In 1881 the 14th Hussars were sent to South Africa from India, where the regiment stayed less than a year before returning whence they came. Since a large number of the men were near to the end of their Colour service, they had to be sent back to England from Natal. Their places, as was constantly the case in all units, had to be taken by volunteers from other regiments. This perpetual disruption undoubtedly affected efficiency because the personnel of troops was always changing and because such a high proportion were semi-trained youngsters. Sergeant-Major Mole remarked that the 14th's nickname, the 'Young Jocks', had never been more apt. The situation became so chronic in 1883 that all time-expired men in India who were due to return home were offered a lump sum of £12 to induce them to extend their service by two years.

From the start there had been two schools of thought amongst senior officers. Typical of the old school's views were those of Field-Marshal Lord Strathnairn, who, as Hugh Rose, had made his

* This was quite normal (see p. 124).

1. Recruiting sergeants, 1875

2. The Riding School, 16th Lancers, 1890

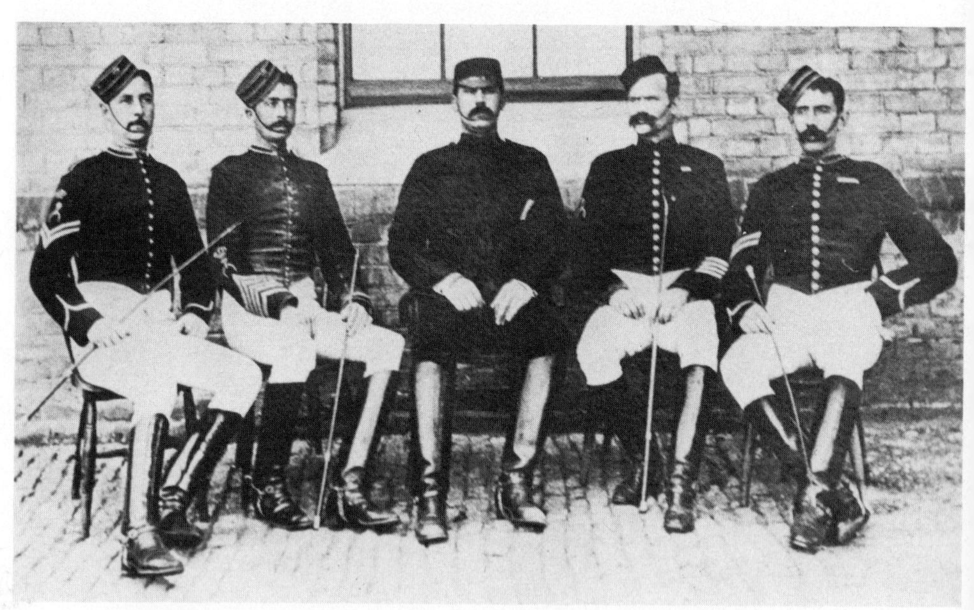

3. The Riding School Establishment, 2nd Life Guards, 1883

name in the suppression of the Indian Mutiny (see Vol II, pp 186–212).

> 'Long service with a pension,' he told the Airey Committee, when he was seventy-eight years of age, 'is the only sure guarantee of good recruiting . . . The longer a man serves the more he looks forward to a pension as the best reward of his services, as freeing him from the dependence of the workhouse, and the solitude and isolation from his friends . . . No pension and uncertain civil employment are the future of the short service soldier, and render him unmilitary.'[8]

Men like Wolseley and Buller, on the other hand, believed that it was the long service man who was unmilitary. 'I think old soldiers are really a fraud, they are not good fighting material,' was Buller's view when he was Adjutant-General. Wolseley held that a cavalry private was 'absolutely useless as a fighting unit' after ten years. The Commander-in-Chief, as so often, in conflict with Wolseley, declared that 'many of the finest soldiers – the older men, the really good men – now go into the Reserve when they ought to be in the ranks.'[9] On the other hand, a senior recruiting officer thought that there was 'not the same dread as there used to be of joining the service. I do not think that there is the same feeling that they are going away from their homes for ever that there used to be.' The same officer, nevertheless, believed that men after their Colour service went back to their homes, not having, in most cases been allowed to re-engage, (see below), saying '"I have lost the six [later seven] best years of my life and I do not like after having been in India to go back to hard work or to revert to the kind of labour that I was taken from when I enlisted." That makes the service unpopular.'[10]

If a man was medically fit, he could *extend* his service with the Colours to twelve years. Warrant Officers* were allowed to extend at any time; non-commissioned officers could claim to do so (which meant, virtually, that they had a right to do so) after one year's probation, while, as a privilege, privates could extend after three years' service, provided they were thoroughly efficient and possessed of one good-conduct badge. No very great numbers did so. In 1890 for example the number was only 4,400.[11] In every case the special assent of the Secretary of State had to be secured. Some

* In 1881, all regimental sergeant-majors, bandmasters and staff sergeants were created Warrant Officers.

sergeants, according to a sergeant-major who gave evidence to the Airey Committee, thought that to extend to twelve years was 'too long . . . to look forward to a pension, and if they extended their service to twelve years with the colours they probably would not be allowed to [re-engage to serve on] to twenty-one years for pension, so that they would throw away the twelve years for nothing.' In fact in the whole cavalry arm only two sergeants who were serving on 1 January, 1879, had extended![12]

Once a man had completed his twelve years he could *re-engage* to serve on to complete twenty-one years. Warrant officers and sergeants had a right to do so after nine years' service. In the cavalry, according to the officer commanding the Cavalry Depot at Canterbury, a good non-commissioned officer was 'almost certain to re-engage for pension at the end of his twelve years'.[13] For instance, 776 sergeants who were serving on 1 January, 1879, had re-engaged.[14] Sergeant-Major Mole's advice to recruits in the cavalry was 'to work away for the sergeant's stripes. These gained,' he added, 'I most emphatically assert they will never regret the step they took, for a sergeant lives a life that is worth living, and while still in the prime of it can leave the service with a pension sufficient for his old age.' For corporals, bandsmen and artificers it was possible, only as a privilege, to re-engage after nine years' service, and for privates after eleven. The numbers who re-engaged to complete twenty-one years' service were small: 1,600 in 1886, and 1,800 in 1890, and very seldom over 2,000 a year.[15] All men (except Warrant Officers) who had passed the twelve-year mark were liable to be discharged at one month's notice, while they could claim their discharge by giving three months' notice. If a recruit could find £10, he could buy his discharge during his first three months' service. After that he had to find £18 and obtain his commanding officer's permission.

One of the effects of short service was a great reduction in the large amount of money which in the past had gone into pensions for old soldiers. Under Cardwell's scheme, however, a new idea was introduced. Short service men, all of whom were ineligible for any sort of pension, received instead 'deferred pay'. This, which ran at the rate of £3 a year, was usually issued to a man only when he was transferred to the Reserve. The purpose of it was to place in the soldier's hands a lump sum to establish him in civil life. In other words, as the Deputy Adjutant-General wrote in 1877, it was introduced to contradict 'the popular notion that soldiers who have served their country are turned adrift without pension or means of support'.[16] Deferred pay, grumbled old Lord Strathnairn, 'notwithstanding all precautions, is like bounty [which Cardwell had abolished] and paying off days, subject to the well known evils of the lump sum of money in the hands of the lower classes'. He was not alone in disliking it. The Commander-in-Chief ('it is absolutely a premium to prevent men re-engaging'), Buller and Evelyn Wood all found fault with it. Nevertheless it continued until 1898. In that year men who wished to were allowed to draw 3d a day 'messing allowance' by agreeing to forego their deferred pay. At the same time it was announced that men enlisting after 1 April would not be eligible for deferred pay.[17]

If suitable, men, once their Colour service was over and so long as they were not over twenty-eight, were sometimes allowed to re-enlist, but they had to pay back their deferred pay. The Inspector-General of Cavalry found that consequently men had to 'enlist fraudulently to get back . . . which unfortunately . . . they are never allowed to do.' Sergeant-Major Mole felt strongly that the attempted re-enlistment of men from the reserve proved 'their real love for a soldiering life'. He thought them 'the very men who ought to be encouraged to serve on, instead of being forced to retire into inactivity before they have reached the early prime of life, and just when they have become efficient cavalry soldiers.' No other employer of labour, he wrote in the 1880s, could command the services of a man in a particular profession for twelve years and then dismiss him 'with a prohibition from following it again.' Mole also knew of 'young fellows invalided but who, loving the Service, managed after a bit to scrape through the medical, and joined another regiment under an assumed name.'[18]

* * *

There were different classes of reserve, but the chief one was known as the Class I, Section B Reserve, and it was to this that short service men were transferred after their Colour service. They could in certain circumstances be called out (but not embodied) to aid the civil power locally. Otherwise they could only be recalled to regular army service by proclamation in case of imminent national danger or an actual state of war. Full mobilization was resorted to only once before the Boer War of 1899. The cause was the Russian scare of 1878 combined with the impending war in Zululand.

Only 470 of the 14,154 summoned to rejoin the Colours failed to report themselves, while 749 were found to be medically or otherwise unfit. On the occasion of the Egyptian War of 1882, partial mobilization produced 10,583 out of 11,649 summoned. On four other occasions volunteers, all unmarried men, were called for. Few turned up. In April, 1885, when it was feared, not for the first time, that the Russians had designs on India, 2,205 reservists, including those of one cavalry regiment, were called up to complete those regiments in India which were below establishment.[19]* In 1895, as an experiment, a single cavalry regiment, the 8th Hussars, was mobilized. Instead of ordering out the regiment's reservists, volunteers from the reserves of all the Hussar regiments were called for. 193 out of the required 202 actually turned up, although 838 'invitations were issued'. Numbers of those who responded were 'not in regular employment. Notwithstanding this,' writes the regimental historian, 'their conduct was exemplary. They rode well, did not appear to have lost their nerve in the least, and there was no cause for the rejection of even one of them.'[20]†

Usually each reservist when embodied would rejoin his previous regiment. In normal times reservists received 4d a day as well as 2d a day deferred pay which they received at the end of each year.

They were liable to be called out annually for twelve days or twenty drills for which they were attached to regular units or to the militia, yeomanry or volunteers. But in practice this did not usually apply to men of the cavalry or artillery. Buller, when Adju-

* The whole question of mobilization plans between 1876 and 1899 in relation to the Boer War will be discussed in the succeeding volume.

† The regimental diary tells what happened during the ten days of the experiment:

'August 1	Drew personal and regimental equipments and carts.
August 2	Altered saddlery, etc.
August 3	Reservists joined, sent to London for horses.
August 4	Registered horses [see p. 390] ridden in school by reservists.
August 5	Each squadron marched to Heath complete in every respect.
August 6	Regiment left Hounslow 9.45 a.m., arrived Chobham 2 p.m.
August 7	Parade in Division Drill under Squadron Leaders first, then under C.O.
August 8	Manoeuvred against force from Aldershot at Lightwater.
August 9	Marched back to Hounslow, 13 miles, in 4¼ hours.
August 10	Registered horses sent back to London at 7.30 a.m., arms, clothing and equipment handed in, reservists settled with and out of Barracks by 2.30 p.m.'

(Murray, II, 503.)

tant-General, was asked why a proportion of these could not be given annual training. He had to reply that it would be too expensive.[21] It was very generally felt that a cavalryman, unlike an infantryman, was not of much use, without considerable re-training, once he had been in the Reserve for more than a year or eighteen months. When, as an experiment in 1882, a few reservists were called out and attached to the 5th Dragoon Guards at Aldershot, it was found that after two years' absence 'a man was no longer a cavalry man. He can look after horses,' said the Commander-in-Chief, 'but I do not think he is a man that an officer would like to have in the ranks.'[22] In 1891 as many as 2,183 of the men in the Cavalry Reserve had been more than two years out of the ranks.[23]

To complete the single Cavalry Division required on mobilization of two Army Corps, the Cavalry Reserve men were essential. Yet, since so many of them would 'have lost their skill as cavalry men,' as the officer commanding the 6th Dragoon Guards put it,[24] from being too long away from regular service, it was not, in fact, possible to create such a Cavalry Division except by using a large number of unsuitable men. Wolseley, whose advocacy of the merits of the short service system which he had been so prominent in preparing was sometimes extravagant, pointed out that this problem could be partially solved by employing the older reservists as part of the 'train'. 'Every cavalry regiment in the field,' he told the Wantage Committee, 'requires thirty-one drivers for regimental purposes alone, all of whom ought to be taken from the regimental reserve men.' He added that he believed that there were more cavalry regiments than would be needed for mobilization; but this was disingenuous, for certainly numbers of regiments would have been required to remain at home, and others would be in India and elsewhere. In the case of invasion, he thought that cavalry would be of little use for home defence 'in our extremely closely enclosed country'.[25] The Duke of Cambridge in his bluff, forthright way summed up the quandary. The men of the Reserve, he told the Wantage Committee,

> 'are a fine body of men but as we never see them we do not know whether they are qualified to take their places in the ranks. I am for having a Reserve, but not for sacrificing the Army for the Reserve . . . I am always asking for the Reserve to be called out but it is impossible owing to the conditions of civil life . . . As a soldier I think they ought to be called

> out, but as a civilian I do not think you can do it, under a system of voluntary enlistment.'

Although in 1879, periodical medical inspections of all reservists were ordered, by 1891 certainly, and probably later, these had never in fact been carried out, probably because of the expense involved. 'We have no supervision', complained the Duke. 'We know the men are alive, though, because they are paid.'[26]

* * *

There were a number of side effects from the short service system which probably did not occur to those who devised it. The proportion of officially married soldiers, for instance, was greatly reduced, which to some degree mitigated the hardship which used to be caused by the small percentage of men who were allowed to be married. Indeed Lieutenant-General (later Field-Marshal) Sir Henry Norman told the Airey Committee that the 12 per cent of the rank and file permitted to be married under short service was 'never anything like approached'.[27] This is not surprising, since no man below the rank of sergeant might marry without at least seven years' service, two good conduct badges and £5 in the Army or Post Office Savings Bank.[28] Of course, in fact, considerable numbers of men were married without leave, as many, on one computation, as six to every one on the 'Married Roll'. In spite of clear regulations, much depended upon the attitude of the commanding officer, but where the married quarters were few, it was difficult for the most humane colonel to exceed the permitted number by much. Discretion was officially given in granting permission to marry 'in anticipation of vacancies occurring', but no privileges could be claimed until the vacancies had been filled.[29] Beside the obvious privilege of being 'taken on the strength', together with her children, and therefore fed and housed free, the most important advantages of being an official wife were her right to accompany her husband to stations overseas, and free education for her children. For the 'unofficials' the old doggerel was still applicable:

> 'Officers' wives having pudding and pies
> And sergeants' wives have skilly,
> But privates' wives have nothing at all
> To fill their poor little bellies.'[30]

* * *

Side effects of short service

The introduction of short service led to great difficulty in inducing young soldiers to become corporals. 'We are only a short time in the Service', they would say, according to the Commander-in-Chief, 'and why should we expose ourselves to be jeered at, and worse, by our comrades who do not like to be spoken to.'[31]

One of the worst aspects of the short service system was the way in which it aggravated the problem of soldiers' return to civil life. Between 1886 and 1891 a private association spent £400,000 in assisting ex-soldiers to find employment. In the same period the government contributed only £1,000. Were its contribution to be increased, argued the War Office, public subscription would decline proportionately![32] In 1682, Thomas Southerne wrote of the common soldiers:

> 'And when they're worn,
> Hacked, hewn with constant service, thrown aside,
> To rust in peace, and rot in hospitals'.[33]

As the nineteenth century drew to a close, things were not quite so bad as that, but it is hard to say that they were significantly better.

Recruits: physical standards

'Our recruiting system is an opprobium to the Army and a great scandal to the country.'

LIEUTENANT-COLONEL REILLY, *Memorandum on the Prussian Army in relation to the campaign of* 1866

'It would pay us well as a nation to obtain men of a better stamp for our Army than those we now enlist, by offering double the pay we now give.'

SIR GARNET WOLSELEY to the Duke of Cambridge, from Egypt, 28 August, 1882

'The ranks were filled with boys . . . who wanted a schoolmaster rather than a sergeant-instructor.'

SERGEANT-MAJOR MOLE, 14th Hussars, of the 1880s

'Clerks and so forth who are better educated go to the cavalry almost entirely.'

THE SURGEON-MAJOR, St George's Barracks, London in 1879

'There are hardly any respects in which [a cavalry soldier's life] does not compare favourably with that of the labouring classes.'

LIEUTENANT-COLONEL W. H. MACGEORGE, commanding the 6th Dragoon Guards, 1891.[1]

(ii)

Rank and file: recruits: physical standards; numbers required annually; types; social status of 'other ranks'; ages – fraudulent enlistments – the recruiting crisis of the early 1890s: less serious in the cavalry – the enlisting process – desertion

In the twenty years up to the Great Boer War about one-third of all recruits for the army had to be rejected because of undernourishment.[2]

'Poor modern Tommy Atkins!' wrote Colonel Sir William Butler from the Nile during the Gordon Relief campaign of 1884. 'What wonder that your capacity for this wild work of cataract navigation should seem doubtful to outside eye! Three years ago you were shuffling along the slums of Whitechapel, almost an outcast among even that terrible "two million of human beings who never smile"; and here today you are doing . . . hero's work. It is no fault of yours . . . if your chest is not deeper and your shoulders are not broader . . . 'Tis but a half or three-quarter century ago since your grandfathers, stout of body, as well as true of heart and spirit, won us dominion under sun as strong and against odds as long as this and these, and if today . . . your body gives out under the strain of sun and service, 'tis [the fault] of those who in their lust of gold and greed of possession forced you from open country life to join that herded multitude of four million beings, of whom half never smile, and the other half know not how to fight.'[3]

In 1879 Surgeon-Major Campbell Fraser, responsible for passing recruits at St George's Barracks, London, told the Army Organization Committee (the Airey Committee*) that he rejected about 1,000 men a year for being below standard chest measurement and weight.

> 'A sergeant brings a man in and weighs him, finds out that he is not up to standard, and sends him away; this man never appears before me. But of those that do appear before me, who are supposed by the recruiting sergeants to be up to standard, from 20 to 30 per cent are rejected.'

At that date no man weighing under 120 lbs, without clothing, was accepted, though a man's weight was often only guessed at, since the War Office was in many places too mean to supply weighing machines! Surgeon-Major Fraser would accept no man of five feet eight inches if he weighed less than 126 lbs.[4]† Dr John

* This Committee, under General Lord Airey's chairmanship, was set up by Frederick Stanley, Secretary of State for War, to try 'to remedy the practical defects . . . in Cardwell's scheme.' (Airey, 3.)

† Very detailed instructions as to how to inspect recruits were devised in the 1870s and 1880s for military medical officers. Those of 1878 include the following:

'The recruit being wholly undressed, the following directions are given *seriatim:* –

a. Walk up and down the room smartly two or three times.
b. Hop across the room on the right foot.
c. Back again on the right foot.
d. Hop across the room on the left foot.
e. Back again on the left foot.
(*The hops should be short and upon the toes*).

[*continued over*

Donald, who had been longer in the recruiting service than any other medical officer, gave the Committee cogent reasons as to why the physical condition of the recruits at the end of the 1870s was

> 'getting very bad indeed, particularly in the manufacturing districts . . . Within the last thirty or forty years our recruiting ground,' he said, 'has been very much curtailed. The increase in the police force (which is composed of the finest men in the country) in England and Wales now amounts to 30,000.'*

Another drain of the 'most muscular men of the country' was the enormous increase in the number of railway employees. Dr Donald added a further point:

> 'The militia used to be raised by ballot, and now they compete with the regular army,† and the volunteers, of the *present time*, belong generally to the class from which the army is recruited.‡
>
> 'Trade has also increased most wonderfully during the last

f. The recruit is halted, standing upright, with his arms extended above his head, while the surgeon walks slowly round him, carefully inspecting the whole surface of his body.'

To detect defects of the voice, the surgeon was told to examine 'the mouth, palate, and fauces [the cavity at the back of the mouth], and then tell the recruit to say loudly, "Who comes there?"' (*Regulations for the Medical Department of H.M.'s Army*, Nov., 1878, 91.)

A disease from which Dr John Donald found a large number of young men suffering was varicocle, a varicose condition of the spermatic veins. 'In winter,' he told the Airey Committee, 'you cannot find it out unless you have the man when he is warm.' To overcome this difficulty he used to place the man in front of the fire. This brought down the scrotum which in the cold got drawn up, enabling the disease to be detected. Dr Donald pointed out that when men went to a hot climate with this disease, they became 'unfit to march'. (Airey, 337.)

* In the 1870s a man on joining the police force was better paid than a sergeant in the army. (Evidence of Lieut-Gen. Arthur J. Herbert, Airey, 349.)

† More than ⅓ of recruits were obtained from the Militia in the 1880s. Each received £1 bounty provided he had done his forty-two days' annual drill. (Airey, 19.)

‡ 'Parents,' said Col. E. A. Wood of the Hounslow depot in 1891, 'will not allow their sons to enlist in the Volunteers, if they think there is going to be any inducement held out to them to join the Army.' (Wantage, 182.)

Robert Blatchford, a 'superior' class recruit who enlisted in the 1870s, found that only four out of the fourteen who joined with him had not been either in the Militia or the Volunteers. (Blatchford, 32.)

thirty or forty years, and the thousands that are employed in it seldom, I think, become soldiers, and those who do are generally unfit for such. Then, too, the introduction of new implements of husbandry moved by horse and steam power has driven most of the agricultural labourers into the towns, and in a short time they become so demoralized and deteriorated in physique that they are not better than the manufacturing population . . .

'I cannot see what inducement there is now for a good man to leave his work and his home, and go and serve in the army for the best six years of his life, and then to be turned adrift.'[5]

The two chief factors which affected the physical standards accepted for recruits, throughout the twenty-seven years covered by this volume, were the degree of urgency with which troops were needed for campaigns overseas and the state of trade, coupled with the current civilian wage rates.

In 1878/9, for example, when the Zulu War and the second Afghan War occurred more or less simultaneously, the increased demand for men entailed a lowering of the height and weight standards. In 1884, again, with the Suakin and Nile campaigns constituting another emergency, there were relaxations for men under twenty years of age. This produced a large and immediate increase in numbers. When, in 1887, the relaxation was stopped because the establishment was being exceeded an equally immediate reduction followed.[6]

On the other hand, in the years between 1884 and 1887, which were ones of severe trade depression, the laid-down standards could be rigorously applied, since there was no shortage of men presenting themselves for enlistment. In spite of this, some 40,000 recruits were obtained in 1886 – the greatest number in any year of the period.

During 1890, trade having much revived from 1888 onwards, the Inspector-General of Recruiting reported to the Committee on Terms and Conditions of the Army (the famous Wantage Committee) that he had been unable to obtain the required number of recruits without accepting 'a very large number of immature lads . . . under the standard'. The previous year there had been only 4,306 sub-standard recruits (known as 'special enlistments'), while in 1890 the number was 7,975. In Ireland alone, in 1890 and 1891, the number increased from 8 per cent to 25 per cent. Should a man have only one disqualification, such as not reaching the height, weight or chest measurements laid down, he was usually accepted so long as he was 'a growing lad'.[7] Even in the cavalry, where the recruiting problem was much less, 'special enlistments' were quite numerous. In 1891, for example, out of 159 recruits for the 20th Hussars, 69 were of this description.[8]

The poor physical quality of recruits was only one aspect of the major problem which recruiting had become in the last decades of the 19th century and which reached crisis proportions in 1891. At a time when the new short service system and the creation of the Reserve were calling for a speedier turnover of men, the 'traditional supply of brawny, illiterate rustics' was diminishing.[9] The reasons for this went beyond the drift to the towns and competition from expanding industry: the emigration of Irishmen to the United States – a process which had started after the great famine of 1847 – was drying up another fruitful source of supply.

Matters were not helped by the parsimony of parliament. It was firmly established that under no circumstances could the numbers of recruits voted for any one year be exceeded during that year. As Sir Redvers Buller, the Adjutant-General, pointed out to the Wantage Committee, 'when you have got recruiting brisk, as long as you keep it brisk, it goes on, but if you check it, it is hard to start again.'[10]*

Of course, when a major emergency came about, as happened in 1878, all normal practices were abandoned. Not only, as we have seen, was recruiting encouraged to the maximum, but every man was ordered to continue in service for the whole term of his enlistment 'until Her Majesty shall otherwise determine', all transfers to the Reserve were suspended and the 1st Class and Militia Reserves were called out (see p. 35).[11]

* * *

There can be no doubt that a large proportion of recruits for the army as a whole were, in the second half of the century, as they had been in the first half, the scum of the populace. At any rate they were some of the poorest. 'No doubt,' said Sir Evelyn Wood in 1879, 'most of the men come starving.'[12] Nevertheless

* In 1870 all recruiting for the cavalry was suspended because the establishment was full. In 1873 for a short time all cavalry enlistments were limited to long service ones, i.e. for twelve years' army service. (Airey, 485, 497.)

General Sir T. Steele, commanding the Aldershot Division, was probably correct in saying that in the late 1870s the 'status of the lower classes is generally improved owing to education; so recruits are as a rule superior in intellect to what they formerly were.'[13] At the same time, it was still painfully true, as was pointed out to the Airey Committee by the Inspector-General of Recruiting, that 'the general impression amongst the respectable classes is that if a son enlists he has brought trouble to his family'.[14] When young John Fraser, the son of an under-gardener, who had joined the Volunteers in 1876, broke the news that he wished to enlist in the regular army, his father exploded.

> 'Never have I seen a man so infuriated,' he wrote sixty years later. 'To him my step was a blow from which he thought he would never recover, for it meant disgrace of the worst type. His son a soldier! He could not believe his ears. Rather would he have had me out of work for the rest of my life than earning a living in such a manner. More than that, he would rather see me in my grave, and he would certainly never have me in his house again.'

Mr Lucas, one of the largest employers in the building trade, giving evidence before the Committee, said that few good men amongst his employees were

> 'in the habit of enlisting . . . Amongst the steady men the mechanics very rarely enlist; the steady labourers also prefer remaining in regular employment. The labourers who leave our employ to go into the army are what we call waifs and strays . . . Men who spend too much of their money on drink, and waste their time in dissipation, frequently, as a last resource, go into the army . . . The men we value do not enlist.'[15]

* * *

One of the more unpleasant deterrents to recruiting a better class of men was that a soldier, as Lord Napier of Magdala pointed out in 1879, was 'under certain civil disabilities. If he goes into a place of public amusement in uniform he is not well received.' But this question had the aspect of a vicious circle. 'You cannot raise the civil condition of men,' a member of Parliament pointed out, 'when a man is obliged to wear a uniform, which rightly or wrongly the public looks down upon . . . The obloquy is of too long standing, and the cause of it, namely, the low class we recruit from, is so clear and distinct that you cannot eradicate it.'[16] Twelve years later, in 1891, Sir Evelyn Wood could say: 'There is many a civilian in company with a non-commissioned officer who would go into a hotel but the non-commissioned officer having more tact stops him at the door and invents some excuse to keep him away.'[17] At the same date the Inspector-General of Cavalry recommended that licensees should be made by law not to refuse a soldier because he was in uniform unless he was improperly dressed.

> 'About three years ago,' he told the Wantage Committee, 'I had a box at the opera, and I gave it to the regiments in London in turn for a week at a time; one night two non-commissioned officers of the Blues went in their tunics and aiguillettes, and properly dressed, but they were refused admittance because they were in uniform.'[18]

* * *

The conditions of enlistment of 1876 laid down that no cavalry recruit must be under eighteen (as had been the case since the beginning of the century). By a General Order of 1877 enlistment over twenty-five was discontinued. In 1881 the minimum age was raised to nineteen. At that date more than half of all recruits were under twenty.[19] A Committee reported in that year that 'a large proportion of the losses from death and from invaliding which occur . . . in the first years of a soldier's service is due to the extreme youth of the men who join, who cannot stand the labour and fatigue to which they are subjected . . . and therefore either die or break down and return to civil life weakened and with diminished powers for earning their livelihood.'[20] A commanding officer, writing in 1883, complained that 'the first six months of a recruit's life is one [sic] of great hardship, and many break down from sheer overwork. From half-past six o'clock in the morning until six o'clock in the evening a recruit has scarcely an hour's relaxation from drill; and when he is thoroughly tired he is expected to concentrate all his energies in mastering the first three rules of arithmetic.'[21] 'In fact,' said the Inspector-General of Cavalry in the early 1890s, recruits 'hardly have time to eat their dinners.'[22]

The minimum age was lowered to eighteen again in 1883, because recruiting fell off so dramatically in the two previous years, and there it stayed. Cavalry officers may have had a hand in this too, for it was generally accepted that a man was easier to teach riding to at eighteen than at a later age.[23]

Most generals preferred young men. Wolseley said in 1870, and reiterated in 1891, that he did not like the old soldier: 'I do not believe in him. Give me young men, they do what they are bid, and they go where they are told.'[24] Surgeon-General W. Munro, however, reflecting progressive medical opinion in the army, thought that no man was really fit for general service under twenty-four. The 6th Dragoon Guards' commanding officer, though, believed that recruits of eighteen and nineteen were 'quite up to their work'. The Surgeon-General also believed that no man should be sent out to India under that age, or remain there after thirty-five.[25]

From 1881 no soldier under twenty years of age, with less than one year's service or with less than four years to serve, was allowed to be sent to India, Egypt or South Africa in peacetime. The immediate results of this compassionate reform (which, incidentally, was imperfectly carried out)* were to increase the number of young, inefficient men in the units at home, and to make more difficult the task of maintaining the numbers of the Indian establishment – at that time between 60,000 and 70,000 Europeans.

In the three years, 1880–1882, 5,500 men under twenty-one were discharged, while 7,177 deserted after less than a year's service. How immensely expensive the wastage was is shown by the fact that one-third of the men who enlisted in the cavalry during an eight-year period in the 1870s had left it before the end of the year after that in which they enlisted; and that another two-fifths had left before the end of the following year. The average service of the whole was about ten months, and they had cost the taxpayer over £450,000.[26]† The wastage in the army as a whole and the full extent of the recruiting crisis can be gauged by the fact that it was calculated that to make good the losses for the three years 1891, 1892 and 1893 alone no less than 102,000 recruits were needed.[27]

* Over 3,500 under twenty were serving in India in 1873. Ten years later the number was still as high as 1,168. (*Army Medical Department Report*, 1876, 200; Aitken, 48.)

† In 1879 the average annual expense caused by cavalrymen who left the army with less than three years' service was £52,627. (Airey, 526.)

The cost of a soldier of the cavalry of the line during his first two years of service at £100 19s 2d was £5 3s 10d more than that of an infantryman. (Airey, 524.)

It was increasingly realized that the physical development of men under twenty, most of whom had been underfed from birth, had too great a strain placed upon it if they were treated as fully grown, fully worked soldiers. Yet there was no question of such recruits being considered as extra to establishment. Consequently, as has been shown, they were subjected to the same 'severe drill-training and hardships of military service'[28] as their elders. More often than not their health was thus permanently broken down. A General Order of 1881 stated that

> 'all soldiers are kept under the observation of medical officers during the first three months of their service, and are reported on once a month . . . Whenever, during this period, a man shows indications of want of stamina or physical inferiority, he is brought before a medical board, and if the board considers that he will not ultimately become fit for military service, he is at once discharged as "not likely to become an efficient soldier".'[29]

* * *

There were, as there had been for many years, great incentives for recruits to pretend that they were older or younger than they actually were. 'In the country,' thought Lieutenant-Colonel Logan, the Superintending Officer of Recruiting in the London District, 'they overstate because they enlist whilst getting boys' wages; in London and large towns many understate when fraudulently enlisting, or because they have not succeeded in other trades or occupations.' By those who understated Colonel Logan found that the age of '$24\frac{11}{12}$' was often given. 'I know what that means; it means any age up to 35 or 40.' On the other hand the same officer told the Airey Committee that although he might think a man only fifteen years of age, he could not act upon his suspicion. 'It would be impolitic to do so.' He added that recruiting 'would fall off very materially' were he to make any close enquiries about recruits' real ages or, indeed, their antecedents. He had been told by friends that they knew that their domestic servants had come to enlist when only fifteen, whilst giving their age as eighteen.[30]* This situation was the same in the early 1890s. In 1891 the Duke of Cambridge, still Commander-in-Chief after thirty-five years, said that recruits

* There were many others who probably did not know their real age. (Rocke, Wantage, 18.)

had to be taken when one could 'catch them, and when they have nothing special to do: you will not find men, unless probably they are bad men, who have nothing special to do; it is only the boys who have no special occupation.'[31]

At the height of the recruiting crisis young men known to be below eighteen were constantly taken because they could be said to have the 'physical equivalents of age'. By that time, indeed, the enlistment of under-age boys had become quite open. One day, for example, Sir Redvers Buller, the Adjutant-General, was accompanying the Commander-in-Chief on an inspection of recruits. 'We looked at one young fellow,' he told the Wantage Committee, 'who seemed very young. His Royal Highness said to him, "What is your age?" He said, "17 years and one month." A serjeant, who was standing near, said, "What is your regulation age?" and the recruit answered, "18 years and 5 months".'[32] Another very human reason for men to say that they were eighteen when they were less was the fact that service under that age was not reckoned if or when a soldier became eligible for a pension. In 1876 the responsibility for detecting the real age of recruits was transferred from 'approving field officers' to army medical officers.[33]

* * *

In cavalry regiments the recruiting crisis was less severe than in the infantry ones. In 1891 Colonel John Russell, commanding the Cavalry Depot at Canterbury, boasted that the Infantry Depot there had great difficulty in getting any men at all, 'whereas I can always get men'. He thought that 'many men are attracted by the uniform and swagger, and this accounts in a great measure for the better class of recruits who join the cavalry.'[34] The ranks of the 11th Hussars and the 17th Lancers were especially easy to fill because of their splendid uniforms. 'There is no doubt,' said Colonel Russell, 'that the colour of the trousers of the 11th Hussars is a great attraction.'[35]* For the heavy cavalry regiments, with much less exciting uniforms, there was the attraction that as a general rule they went overseas less than the light regiments.

A cavalryman was harder worked than an infantryman; indeed as Major J. Stacpole, the Inspector of Rations in the 1890s, pointed out, 'there are so many fatigues that he is called upon to perform

* The 11th Hussars were vulgarly known as the 'Cherry Bums'. This was translated for polite society as 'Cherubims'!

that he never knows when he is done.' In the cavalry many of these fatigues, such as washing up in the barrack room, were undertaken by women employed for the purpose.[36]

Technically, up to the late 1890s, all recruits joined for general service, but in practice most asked for particular regiments and so long as these were 'open for recruiting' they were usually posted to them. Lieutenant-Colonel Egerton Todd of the West London District used to tell the men that they would be 'sent to the regiment they wish, if possible; they have great anxiety on the subject. I say "Recollect you clearly understand you enlist for eight years in the cavalry and four years in the cavalry reserve," but the man nearly always says, "I want to go to a particular regiment, the 16th Lancers or the 8th Hussars", or something of that kind.'[37] Once posted no man, under the regulations, could be transferred to another regiment without his consent.[38] There is evidence, though, that this was not always strictly adhered to. Sergeant-Major Mole, for instance, found that men who had enlisted for the 14th Hussars had to be transferred to other regimental depots because that regiment was so popular. This was 'regarded as a great hardship by those who had enlisted for the "young Jocks" and already learnt what *esprit de corps* meant.' He was often surprised to learn

> 'that youngsters who had only been three months at [the Cavalry Depot at] Canterbury knew everything about the regiment and its traditions, and could quote you, not only the Peninsular battles inscribed upon its colours, but also the Persian, Panjab and Central Indian victories; aye, and Chillianwallah, too, about which they were not only ready to argue, but double their fists and fight if any recruit of another regimental depot, in the heat of discussion, attempted to throw the old unjust slur in their teeth.' (See Vol 1, 279–284)

In the cavalry generally a man's intelligence was more employed than it was in the infantry if only because he had horses and horse equipment to care for. In all regiments, too, by the late 1880s, and in most before then, there were classes for such things as signalling and surveying.

There were various standards of height laid down from time to time for the different classes of cavalry regiment. In the Household Cavalry and the Royals, for instance, the minimum height in the 1890s was 5 feet 10½ inches, while the standard laid down in 1872 for Light Cavalry was from 5 feet 6 inches to 5 feet 8 inches and, in 1886, for Medium Cavalry (except Lancers whose minimum height had to be 5 feet 7 inches) 5 feet 6 inches to 5 feet 9 inches.

* * *

The actual process of enlisting was much the same in the last three decades of the century as it had been for many earlier ones. The Inspector-General of Recruiting in the 1870s put the procedure very clearly:

> 'It commences by a man taking a shilling from the enlister, and he is handed a notice paper that he must appear before the doctor, and the doctor examines him, and if he is fit, after twenty-four hours have elapsed from the time of his enlistment, and within ninety-six hours of that period, he must be attested. During that period he has the power of declining to be attested, and on payment of £1 smart money and any other expenses in the shape of pay or subsistence which he has received he is released. [Otherwise] he is duly attested before a magistrate, and he is then finally approved by the proper field approving officer, and, if not a head-quarter recruit [i.e. if he was recruited by a regiment], he is sent to his corps as a recruit, and on arriving he is again medically examined and inspected by the commanding officer, and if any objection is then taken a report is made to headquarters, and if that objection is found valid the man is released with a protecting certificate to shield him from molestation afterwards as a deserter should he be recognised as a man who had enlisted before.'[40]

Up to 1888, when 'bringing money' was officially put an end to, most enlistments at recruiting headquarters were made through 'bringers'. Some of these were perfectly respectable citizens, old soldiers or pensioners, for anyone could obtain bringing money for introducing men as recruits. But by far the larger number were of the very lowest class, some of them ex-soldiers. They would hang about public house doors and intercept the men when they were coming to enlist (for most enlistments were still made in public houses). Lieutenant-Colonel Logan of the London District told the Airey Committee that 'bringing money is now [in 1879] virtually a bounty to recruits; they will not enlist without being brought', which shows what pressure this class of touts employed. 'It is these men,' continued Colonel Logan, 'who coach intending recruits as regards all the answers they should give as to age, etc, in fact do all the dirty work for which a sergeant would, if discovered, be tried by court-martial.' From the £1 which a recruiting sergeant or other recruiter got for each recruit, he had to give the bringer 10s.[41] The Queen's shilling also came out of the £1, so the recruiter pocketed 9s per man. Should a recruit turn out within six months to be a bad character or a deserter, the recruiting officer had to 'recover the reward'. To do this he stopped it from the recruiting sergeant, who had to try to retrieve it from the bringer. If, which was not always likely, he managed to find him, he would probably be told that the money had been spent.[42]

There were sixty-six recruiting districts in the United Kingdom, of which London was by far the largest. During twenty-one months in 1874/75, out of 140 recruits enlisted for the 5th Lancers fifty-five signed on in London. Only forty-seven were recruited at regimental headquarters. The rest joined up in other parts of the country: thirteen in Belfast, six in Bristol, five in Liverpool, five in Hull, four in Birmingham, three in Portsmouth, one in Halifax and one in Dorchester.[43]

* * *

Large scale desertion was still taking place towards the end of the century. In 1877 something like 7,500 men were reported as deserters, while in 1880 some 5,000 men on the home establishment deserted, though nearly half of these either rejoined or were recaptured. Of the 30,889 desertions which occurred between 1872 and 1879, nearly three-fifths were by men in their first year of service. In the same period, nearly 300 out of every 1,000 men were lost to the army for one reason or another before they had completed three years' service.[44]

In 1891 Lord Wolseley thought that there were 'very few tramps in England who at some time or other have not been in the army. We have men who wander all round the world. They enlist in the winter with the intention of deserting in the summer, and very likely they do that time after time.' On each occasion, of course, these 'professional deserters' got a fresh free kit.[45] The men who effected these fraudulent enlistments were known as 'ignominy men'. Their number decreased speedily as the recruiting crisis developed. In 1891 Colonel Wood of the Hounslow depot gave the reason. 'Recruits join so young now,' he said, 'that any man who enlists above a certain age is always looked upon with a certain amount of suspicion.' Out of the 31,407 enlistments in 1890, there were only 339 convictions for fraudulent enlistment.[46]

Less professional deserters were those young men who, enlisting in despair, gave no thought to the future. When they began to realize that after their term of regular service, followed by their term in the Reserve (on very little pay), they were likely to be thrown out without a pension, they had a great incentive to desert.[47] Desertion took place, too, overseas. General Colley, in 1880, soon after being appointed Governor of Natal and chief of the Army in the Transvaal, reported that the troops were 'deserting very largely . . . The proximity of the Free State offers a strong inducement . . . The desertions among the King's Dragoon Guards have been exceptionally heavy, especially since the regiment was put under orders for India.'[48] (See also p. 205.)

'"By 'Bob's' rattle", said the fat sergeant, "the sun's burnin' holes in your blankets. Rouse about, you insanitary frequenters of the casual ward. Turn out, you gutter rats, you unchristened sons of mendicants. Bless your eyes! Bless your souls!"'

A sergeant waking up recruits in the 1870s.[1]

(iii)

Rank and file: living conditions – health – Christmas in barracks – daily routine – petty restrictions – funerals – care of souls

The post-Crimea reforms affecting the daily life of the soldier ground slowly forwards throughout the last three decades of the century. The provisions which could be bought at regimental canteens, for instance, increased in variety and quality and decreased in price as the years went by. Beer, tobacco, groceries and vegetables, particularly, were sold at a much cheaper rate than was charged in shops outside. Increasing care was taken to see that the rations were of high quality. It would have been almost inconceivable before the 1850s that an officer should have given 'over 200 practical lectures on the subject of meat', as Major Stacpole, one of a number of Inspectors of Rations, did in 1890 and 1891. 'We arrange,' he told the Wantage Committee, 'to have quarters of meat hung up in the barrack rooms and officers, non-commissioned officers and men are asked to be present, so that they all may know what is being done on their behalf.'[2]

All hawkers, who were usually old soldiers, had to be licensed before they could carry on business in barracks. So also had the old apple-women who had 'a large clientele among the drummers and band-boys'. Lockers for each man in barrack rooms were still being introduced in the 1890s,[3] and gas lighting had long since replaced candles, yet at that time the long-standing question of urinals in barrack rooms had not been fully answered. The present author was wrong when in Vol II (p. 328) he stated that the introduction of water urinals in a corner of each barrack room had solved 'one of the great sanitary problems'. It had not been solved, at least, in the Eastern District or at Aldershot, according to Sir Evelyn Wood. 'The little chamber off the barrack room,' he said in 1891, had proved so offensive 'that we could not allow it to be used – the men objected to it.' The loathsome wooden tub, used for urine at night and for washing in the morning, had to come into use again. Another complaint, which had been heard ever since barracks were first built, was the lack of facilities for drying wet clothing. The only way to do this was still around the barrack room fire, 'and,' as Sir Evelyn put it, 'you cannot dry more than about three things at a time.'[4]

As there ever had been, there was a fixed determination amongst the men never to open the barrack room windows if it could possibly be avoided. Consequently there was always, as Horace Wyndham, a popular author of the day, put it, 'an indescribable and subtly all-pervading aroma of pipe-clay, damp clothing, lamp oil, dish cloths, soft soap, and butter and cheese scrapings – for the soldier's food was kept on a shelf in the same apartment in which he eats and sleeps and lives.'

In the forty-five years following the Report of the Army Sanitary Commission of 1857 a steady improvement took place in the health of the army. In that year 13.3 men in the cavalry of the line died out of every 1,000. In 1875 the number had fallen to 6.3 and in

1895 to 4.1. The chief reason for this gratifying progress was the amelioration of living conditions. The diseases which were directly connected with the soldier's environment, such as tuberculosis and respiratory fever, became markedly less common during the period. The incidence of venereal diseases, however, though lower in 1898 than in 1857, remained high. Never less than one man in ten, and more often one in five, underwent treatment each year.[5]

One of the greatest social improvements was the provision of married quarters for warrant officers, non-commissioned officers and those privates who were officially married. In the early 1870s even a regimental sergeant-major of cavalry rarely had more than a single room of no great size. By the mid-1890s, a private could usually command one big room with a kitchen, while a married warrant officer at Aldershot enjoyed 'two good sitting rooms, two good bedrooms, kitchen and scullery, with yard, garden convenience, coal and washhouse.' Some barracks had been improved since the 1850s, but many had not, and these in certain cases had become worse as the years went by. The Royal Barracks at Dublin were notoriously bad, recurring epidemics of enteric fever being caused by the poor sanitation and ventilation. The trouble, of course, was that to bring all barracks up to the standard which had been set by the 1859 Sanitary Committee was a costly business. Lord Wolseley calculated that £13,500,000 would be required to do the job properly. In 1889–90 a comprehensive scheme of demolition, construction and alteration was set in motion. By 1900 £3,809,000 had been spent.[6]

In 1877 there enlisted in the 16th Lancers the only private ever to become a field-marshal. William ('Wully') Robertson, dissatisfied with the life of a footman, gives in his autobiography a fascinating picture of what life was like in the ranks during his time.

> 'Regiments were still composed mainly of old soldiers who, although very admirable comrades in some respects and with a commendable code of honour of their own, were in many cases – not in all – addicted to rough behaviour, heavy drinking, and hard swearing . . . These rugged veterans exacted full deference from the recruit, who was assigned the worst bed in the room, given the smallest amount of food and the least palatable, had to "lend them articles of kit which they had lost or sold", "fag" for them in a variety of ways, and finally, was expected to share with them at the

regimental canteen such cash as he might have in the purchase of beer sold at 3d a quart.

'... Beside the beds, the only other furniture [in the barrack-room] consisted of four benches and two deal tables. The men polished their boots on the former, and the latter were used for cleaning the remaining articles of kit as well as for dining-tables ...

'Uniform was of a very unpractical kind, especially the undress part of it. This comprised skin-tight overalls, an equally tight "shell-jacket" cut off short above the hips, and a forage cap of about the size of a breakfast saucer, and kept in place immediately above the right ear by a narrow chinstrap worn under the lower lip (never under the chin in the cavalry, except on mounted parades). There were no "British-warms" or woollen "jumpers" as to-day [1921], and cloaks were not allowed to be worn when off duty without a regimental order to that effect. This order was never given except when the weather was very inclement ... [See Appendix p. 413 for dress regulations for rank and file, 1898.]

'Riding-school was the terror of most recruits, few of whom had ever before been across a horse. For some weeks no saddle was allowed, no stirrups for some months, and the chief aim of the instructor, or "rough-rider", was not to give his pupil confidence but as many falls as possible. The "rough-rider" deserved his name, for he was as rough with a young horse as with a young recruit. He seldom possessed a decent pair of hands, and his system of training a horse was of the break-down rather than the break-in type ...

'Gymnastics, or physical exercises, were conducted on much the same lines. Every recruit was expected to do the same thing in an equally proficient way, no allowance being made for differences of age, build, or general physical capacity.*

'... When a man "reported sick" he was marched at about nine o'clock in the morning to the medical inspection room of his regiment, and after waiting about in all weathers for an indefinite time was seen by a medical officer. If considered a case for admission he was given an aperient, whether he

* Prince Arthur, Duke of Connaught, was prominent in pointing out the over-harsh methods of gymnastic instructors at this date, but it was some years before they were universally moderated. (Aston, 75.)

> wanted it or not, in the shape of half-a-pint of vile-tasting liquid known as "black-strap". He was next marched off to hospital, which might be anything up to a mile or more away, and there he was interviewed by another doctor before being "admitted" to hospital. Next he was told off to a ward, where he might hope to arrive about mid-day, after having been on the move for some three or four hours. In the afternoon he would put on his hospital clothing, give his own into store, and lie down to await the visit of the medical officer in charge of the ward on the following morning. He was then again examined, treatment was prescribed, and if all went well he received it during the afternoon, or some thirty hours after he first set out from his barrack-room . . . There was no nursing service, at any rate in the hospitals I had the misfortune to visit. Nursing and dressing were the duty of the "orderly" of the ward, and this individual was apt to regulate the amount of attention he gave to his patients by the amount of tips they gave him.
>
> '. . . At night the horses were looked after by a "night guard", which paraded about five or six o'clock in the evening and came off duty at *reveille* on the following morning.
>
> '"Muster parade" was held on the last day of each month, and was the only parade at which every officer and man had to be present. The paymaster was the important person, as he had to satisfy himself that every one for whom he had issued pay was actually serving in the regiment.'[7]

There was no day of the year on which attention to the needs of the horses could be neglected in a cavalry regiment. But Christmas Day came as near to being a full holiday as any. Archibald Forbes, a well-known journalist who had served in the Royal Dragoons between 1859 and 1864, wrote a description of 'Christmas in a Cavalry Regiment' in 1875. Though rather sentimental and patronizing, it is worth quoting at some length.

> 'Christmas Day' he wrote, 'is the great regimental merry-making . . . About a month before, self-deniant fellows busy themselves in constructing "dimmocking bags" for the occasion, such being the barrack-room term for receptacles for money-hoarding purposes. The weak vessels manage to cheat their fragility of "saving grace" by requesting their sergeant-major to put them "on the peg" – that is to say,

place them under stoppages . . . Everybody becomes of a sudden astonishingly sober and steady . . . The guardroom is unwontedly empty – nobody except the utterly reckless will get into trouble just now . . .

'The clever hands of the troop are deep in devising a series of ornamentations for the walls and roof of the common habitation. One fellow spends all his spare time . . . embellishing the wall above the fireplace with a florid design in a variety of colours meant to be an exact copy of the device on the regiment's kettledrums, with the addition of the legend "A Merry Christmas to the old Strawboots", inscribed on a waving scroll below. The skill of another decorator is directed to the clipping of sundry squares of coloured paper into wondrous forms – Prince of Wales's feathers, gorgeous festoons, and the like – with which the gas pendants and the edges of the window-frames are disguised . . .

'A couple of days before "the day", the sergeant-major enters the barrack-room . . . He cannot refrain from the customary short patronising harangue, "Our worthy captain – liberal gent you know – deputed me – what you like for dinner – plum-puddings of course – a quart of beer a man; make up your minds what you'll have – anything but game and venison"; and so he vanishes grinning a saturnine grin . . . The alternative lies between pork and goose . . . Goose *versus* pork is eagerly debated. As regards quantity the question is a level one, since the allowance from time immemorial has been a goose or a leg of pork among three men . . . The sergeant-major is informed of the conclusion arrived at [after the evening stables], and the corporal of each room accompanies him on a marketing expedition into town [taking with him the contents of the "dimmocking bags" and the stoppages in the sergeant-major's hands] . . . He goes direct to the fountain-head. If there is a brewery in the place he finds it out and bestows his order upon it, thus triumphantly securing the pure article at the wholesale price. His purchasing calculation is upon the basis of two gallons per man. [For twelve men] he orders a twenty-four gallon barrel of porter – always porter [a dark brown bitter beer, brewed from partly charred malt] . . .

'It is Christmas Eve. The evening stable-hour is over and all hands are merrily engaged in the composition of the puddings; some stoning fruit, others chopping suet, beating eggs, and so forth . . . [Usually one man is the acknowledged pudding-maker expert. His comrades] pull out their clean towels for pudding-cloths; they run to the canteen enthusiastically for a further supply on a hint from him that there is a deficiency in the ingredient of allspice. And then he artistically gathers together the corners of the cloths and ties up the puddings tightly and securely; whereupon a procession is formed to escort them to the cook-house, and there, having consigned them into the depths of the mighty copper, the "man of the time" remains watching the caldron bubble until morning, a great jorum of beer at his elbow, the ready contribution of his appreciative comrades . . .

'[Christmas Day.] On an ordinary morning the reveille is practically negatived, and nobody thinks of stirring from between the blankets till the "warning" sounds a quarter of an hour before the morning stabletime. But on this morning there is no slothful skulking . . . The soldier's wife who has the cleaning of the room and who does the washing for its inmates – for which services each man pays her a penny a day, has from time immemorial taken upon herself the duty of bestowing a "morning" on the Christmas anniversary upon the men she "does for". Accordingly, about a quarter to six, she enters the room . . . She carries a bottle of whisky – it is always whisky, somehow – in one hand and a glass in the other; and, beginning with the oldest soldier administers a calker [a dram] to every one in the room till she comes to the "cruity", upon whom, if he is a pullet-faced, homesick, bit of a lad, she may bestow a maternal salute in addition, with the advice to consider the regiment as his mother now . . .

'[Church parade follows morning stables] but there are two of the inmates of each room who do not go to church. The clever pudding-maker and a sub of his selection are left to cook the Christmas dinner. This, as regards the exceptional dainties, is done at the barrack-room fire, the cook-house being in use only for the now despised ration meat and for the still simmering puddings. The handy man cunningly improvises a roasting-jack, and erects a screen consisting of bed-quilts spread on a frame of upright forms, for the purpose of retaining and throwing back the heat . . .

'There is a large expanse of table in every barrack-room . . . Bare boards at a Christmas feast are horribly offensive to the eye of taste. Something must be done; something has already been done. Ever since the last issue of clean sheets,* one or two whole-souled fellows have magnanimously abjured these luxuries *pro bono publico*. Spartan-like they have lain in blankets, and saved their sheets in their pristine cleanliness wherewithal to cover the Christmas table . . .

'[After church parade and watering and feeding the horses the men] assemble fully dressed in the barrack-room, hungrily silent. The captain enters the room and *pro forma* asks whether there are "any complaints". A chorus of "No, sir" is his reply; and then the oldest soldier in the room with profuse blushing and stammering takes up the running, thanks the officer kindly in the name of his comrades for his generosity, and wishes him a "Happy Christmas and many of 'em" in return. Under cover of the responsive cheer the captain makes his escape, and a deputation visits the sergeant-major's quarters to fetch the allowance of beer which forms part of the treat. Then they fall to and eat! Ye gods, how they eat! [In twenty minutes of silent eating] be the fare goose or pork, it is, barring the bones, only "a memory of the past". The puddings, turned out of the towels in which they have been boiled, then undergo the brunt of a fierce assault; but the edge of appetite has been blunted by the first course and with most of the men a modicum of pudding goes on the shelf for supper.

'At length dinner is over. Beds are drawn up from the sides of the room so as to form a wide circle of divans round the fire, and the big barrel's time has come at last. A clever hand whips out the bung, draws a pailful, and reinserts the bung till another pailful is wanted, which will be very soon. The pail is placed upon the hearthstone and its contents are decanted into the pint basins, which do duty in the barrack-room for all purposes from containing coffee and soup to mixing chrome-yellow and pipe-clay water. The married soldiers come dropping in with their wives, for whom the corporal has a special drop of "something short" stowed away in reserve on the shelf behind his kit. A song is called for . . . The songs of soldiers are never of the modern music-hall type. You never hear such a ditty as "Champagne Charley" or "Not for Joseph". The soldier takes especial delight in songs of the

* This took place once a month. Blankets were seldom if ever washed and clean straw for the palliasse was issued every three months. (Robertson, 4.)

sentimental pattern; and even when he forsakes the region of sentiment, it is to give vent to such sturdy bacchanalian out-pourings as the "Good Rhine Wine", "Old John Barleycorn" and "Simon the Cellarer". But these are only interludes. "The Soldier's Tear", "The White Squall", "There came a Tale of England", "Ben Bolt", "Shells of the Ocean" and other melodies of a lugubrious type, are the special favourites of the barrack-room . . .

'Songs and beer form the staple of the afternoon's enjoyment . . . There is no speechifying . . .

'It is a lucky thing for a good many that there is no roll-call at the Christmas evening stable-hour. The non-commissioned officers mercifully limit their requirements to seeing the horses watered and bedded down by the most presentable of the roisterers . . . This interruption over, the circle re-forms round the fire, and the cask finally becomes a "dead marine".'

On Christmas Day there was always one man absent from these festivities. This was the private detailed to look after the troop horses out of stable-hours. One of the most recently joined recruits was usually given this 'stable-guard'. Private William Robertson found in 1877 that this was his first military duty. He was 'specially well-cared for . . . The dinner brought to the stable consisted of a huge plateful of miscellaneous food – beef, goose, ham, vegetables, plum-pudding, blancmange – plus a basin of beer, a packet of tobacco and a new clay pipe!'[8]

* * *

Once a recruit had undergone his initial training, he settled down to the routine of regimental life. With variations depending on particular regimental traditions, the cavalry soldier's day at home in the last decades of the nineteenth century started at 6.30 with reveille. Between then and 7.00 he washed, shaved, folded his blankets and laid out his kit for inspection. First stables followed. There he mucked out and cleaned his own horse and saddled it for riding exercise at 7.30. Half an hour later he watered and fed his mount before his own breakfast at 8.00. At 9.00 an hour of mounted or foot drill was followed by fatigues or school. At 10.45 he was back in stables grooming his horse and cleaning saddlery and accoutrements. At one o'clock came dinner; at two musketry or lance practice; at three mounted or foot drill; at 4.30 half-an-hour was allowed for tea, followed by the third stables of the day. Stand down arrived at last at six or seven o'clock.

* * *

In what might be called 'interior economy' respects, cavalrymen were, as always, poorly prepared for conditions in the field. During the Afghan War the 9th Lancers, for instance, found themselves having to bivouac and remain out all night. Some sheep were killed for them, but 'for want of knives, forks, cooking pots, etc.,' wrote the cavalry brigade-major, 'they actually got nothing to eat, starving in the midst of plenty sooner than take the trouble of cutting up the sheep with their swords, and roasting bits of it on sticks, or cleaning rods. Another night's bivouac would probably have effected a marvellous change, but the British soldier, without real campaigning experience, is a very helpless creature; very different to the Native Sowar, who only wants a little flour, water and a few sticks to be quite happy.'[9]

* * *

Petty restrictions, such as would not have been tolerated twenty years later, were still imposed on soldiers right up to 1900. One of these was the regulation which forbade them to smoke in the streets until after 5 p.m. from 1 October to 31 March, and after 6 p.m. from 1 April to 30 September.

When a man's life came to an end, the 'normal cost' of his funeral, which was about £1 15s, was borne as a charge against the public.[10] The form of ceremonial for funerals often varied from one regiment to another. Sergeant-Major Mole describes how it was in the 14th Hussars:

> 'My troop was ordered to parade in full dress without arms, excepting twelve men who carried carbines, and were called the firing party. A black horse, to represent the dead man's trooper, was robed in a costly black velvet pall, embroidered with a white skull and crossbones (this was peculiar to our regiment) with a plume of black ostrich feathers on its bridle. Across the saddle, supported by the collar chains, dangled the dead soldier's spurred boots, toes reversed. The horse was led by two men, cloaked in black, one on each side holding it by a new pocket-handkerchief passed through the rings of its bit. These handkerchiefs, when the ceremony was over, were

always kept by the men as a memento . . . When everything was ready the cortege started forward at a slow march. Contrary to the usual marching order, the shortest and youngest privates led, the older and taller men followed, the non-commissioned officers came next, and the captain brought up the rear. Another curious thing was that the men stepped off by their right, instead of by their left foot, as is customary. When we passed the guard-room the sentry turned the guard out and for once and once only in his career, the poor dead private received a "present arms".'

Mole added that when his commanding officer died his funeral was conducted 'in exactly the same way as that of the trooper'.[11]

* * *

Provision for the care of soldiers' souls in the final decades of the century remained much as it had been for many years, under the direction, so far as Anglicans were concerned, of the great Prebendary Gleig. In 1875, at the age of seventy-eight, he retired from the Chaplain-Generalship which he had held for nearly thirty years. Under his immediate successors, one of whom was a bishop, the chief change that took place was an increase in the number of chaplains. In 1875 there were only sixty. Twenty-four years later there were eighty-two, of which twenty-three were serving overseas.

The first chaplain ever to win the Victoria Cross was from the Bengal Ecclesiastical Department. He gained it in 1879 during the Afghan War on Lord Roberts's recommendation. His citation reads:

'. . . Some men of the 9th Lancers having fallen with their horses into a wide and deep "nullah" . . . and the enemy being close upon them, the Reverend J. W. Adams rushed into the water (which filled the ditch), dragged the horses from off the men, upon whom they were lying, and extricated them, he being at the time under a heavy fire and up to his waist in water. At this time the Afghans were pressing on very rapidly, the leading men getting within a few yards of Mr Adams, who having let go his horse in order to render more effective assistance, had eventually to escape on foot.' (See p. 233).

There retired from the service in 1876 the Reverend H. P. Wright, who had been Principal Chaplain in the Crimean War.

In 1858 he had written a treatise addressed to the Secretary of State, entitled *England's Duty to England's Army* (*Matter affecting the Body, Mind and Soul of the British Soldier*). This work, which was outspoken and very advanced, caused quite a sensation. It urged numerous reforms in living conditions, most of which were in fact adopted before the century came to an end.[12]

Surprisingly large numbers of common soldiers were unselfconsciously religious. The Wesleyan chaplain with Kitchener's army in 1898, for instance, relates how after the Battle of Omdurman he visited the wounded on the field. As he passed on from one to another, numbers 'shouted the Christian soldier's watchword "Four-nine-four".' This referred to Hymn 494 in *Sacred Songs and Solos*, which begins: 'God be with you till we meet again.'[13]

'I do not suppose there are many trades or occupations in which a young man can be certain of having 3s to 5s 6d* a week to spend on his amusements as a soldier can, nor in which a young man can frequently have a day's leave without losing his pay.

'Men when they enlist are frequently deceived by the advertised conditions of the service . . . They are disappointed when they find that a deduction is made from their pay to provide groceries, cleaning things, etc.'

COLONEL J. C. RUSSELL, commanding the Cavalry Depot at Canterbury, in 1891.[1]

(iv)

Rank and file: troopers' pay – stoppages – allowances – good conduct badges – officers' servants – WOs' and NCOs' pay – special gratuities – pensions

The simplest means of resolving the recruiting crisis would have been to make a considerable increase in the soldier's basic pay. But the politicians, believing that the army already cost too much, would never agree to such 'extravagance'. In 1871 Gladstone wrote

* This was almost certainly an exaggeration.

4. Clothing Parade, Aldershot, 1886: 10th Hussars

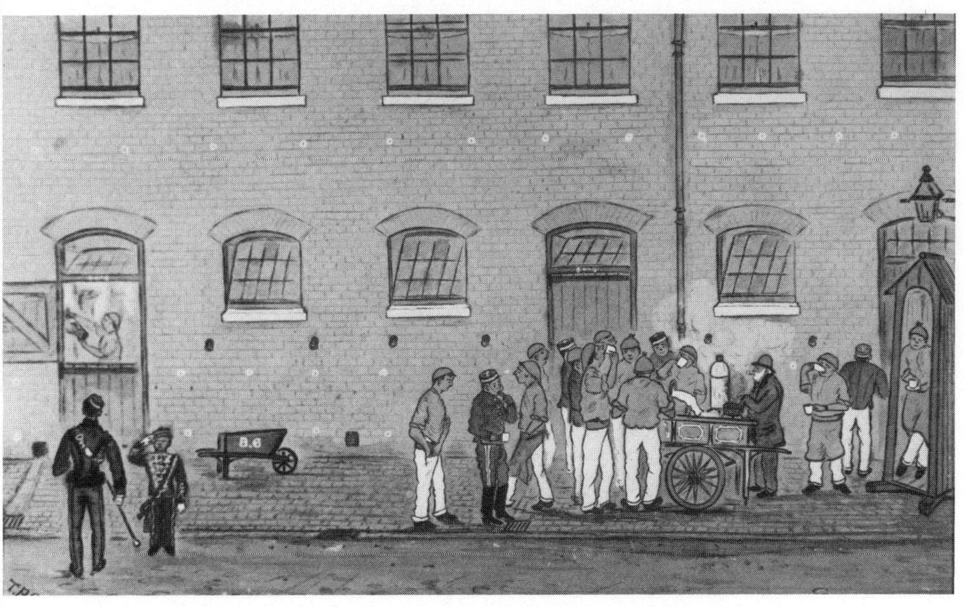

5. Tea-break during Stables, Aldershot, 1886: 10th Hussars

6. Pay Parade, Aldershot, 1886: 10th Hussars

7. The canteen, Aldershot, 1886: members of the 7th Dragoon Guards, Scots Greys, 3rd and 10th Hussars

a long memorandum to Cardwell complaining about the high cost of the army. To show how little the Prime Minister understood the army and the recruiting problem, here is an extract from that memorandum: 'We have at this time a clergy better instructed, and infinitely more laborious, than we had forty years ago, but they are also, man for man, a cheaper clergy.' Could this not be the case in the army, too, he asked?[2]

In fact, there did take place a 'revision' of basic pay. It was *downwards*: from, in the case of the cavalryman, 1s 5d a day (to which it had been raised in 1867), to 1s 2d a day. To more than compensate for this, however, the bread and meat stoppage, calculated at 4½d a day, was converted in 1873 into a free ration, but against this was set the abolition of the old 1d 'beer money' element which had been incorporated into basic pay. A cavalry trooper's *net* pay, therefore, was raised to 1s 2d from 1s 0½d a day.[3] *The Times* went so far as to suggest that the soldier would now be one of the best paid unskilled labourers in the country because beyond his pay he got board, lodging, clothes, education and medical care.[4]

Fourteen years later, Lord Wolseley, in an euphoric eulogy of the army in the Queen's Golden Jubilee year, wrote that

> 'the soldier pays from 2½d to 3d a day for groceries, vegetables, milk and some extra bread, which added to his free rations of bread and meat, gives him three good meals a day. If he wishes for luxuries, he can obtain in his regimental canteen, for a penny or two, butter, cheese, eggs or bacon, and a pint of beer for his dinner, or coffee and bread and butter in his recreation-room for supper before going to bed.'

Wolseley claimed, perhaps a trifle optimistically, that after buying a daily quart of beer and his groceries, the man always had 'from 2s to 2s 6d a week for his pocket money. He has nothing to pay for lodging, coals or candles. Where,' he asked, 'is the labourer or ordinary mechanic who is as well off?'[5] Nevertheless, he pointed out four years later that in the United States, the only other country entirely dependent on voluntary enlistment, privates were paid 1s 9d a day, without any stoppages. He added that he thought the greatest change for the better in the army since the early 1880s had been made 'by trusting the men and by treating them as reasonable human beings . . . The superstition that the more you pay the man the more he will drink is a superstition as much out of date as witchcraft.'[6]

Sergeant-Major Mole, like Wolseley, painting as rosy a picture as possible so as to make the army attractive to recruits, wrote of the 1880s:

> 'Think of the thousands and thousands of lads starting life without a trade in their hands, living from hand to mouth, shunted from pillar to post in an uncertain struggle for existence, who, when their day's work is done, have no comfortable home to return to, and no facilities for improving themselves. Compare this to the benefits a soldier enjoys in the present day . . .
>
> 'A private Hussar in the early sixties was a clever man if he was "on" threepence a day for the last half of each month . . . but now any decently-behaved recruit can walk up to the pay-table once a week and take off three to five shillings certain . . . The modern Hussar has no uniform to replace, as his predecessor had . . . A young fellow who has learnt a good trade may be wise to remain where he is, but the pickers-up of promiscuous livelihoods would do well to take the Queen's shilling.'[7]

Though the ration stoppage was abolished, there were still other regulation stoppages, the top limits of most of which were lessened from 1873 onwards. In 1884 it was estimated that these added up to 14s a month. A man was very canny if he managed to save 12s a month. Nevertheless, except in times of exceptional prosperity when unemployment was low, this probably compared favourably with an unskilled labourer's ability to save.[8]

There were variations from time to time, but by 1898 the items a man had to pay for were his washing and hair cutting (1d per month), while vegetables and groceries were provided by a small stoppage which was not allowed to exceed (including washing) 3s 2½d a week. On joining, the soldier received his regimental clothing and his necessaries free. Replacements of clothing were then supplied annually or biennially.* If he injured, destroyed or

* Except, which was a cause of much discontent, for ankle boots in the mounted arm. Of these there was only an initial issue. (Wantage, 50, 445.)

Another grievance was that men had to pay for saddlery cleaning materials. When, as often happened, a man had to clean saddlery of horses besides his own, his expenses were added to very unfairly. (Maj.-Gen. Fraser's evidence, Wantage, 445.)

lost any articles of clothing between whiles, he had to pay for them. After the initial issue of free kit, he was still required to keep up the supply of necessaries at his own cost. Necessaries included shirts, socks, towels, razors, brushes, combs, sponges, hold-alls, knives, forks, spoons and kit bags. In the cavalry there were additional items, such as gauntlets in regiments which wore them, spurs and horse rubbers.[9] On top of this there were always 'barrack damages' to be paid, either, where attributable, individually, or spread equally amongst the men of a squadron.

When a man went into hospital there was a 'public stoppage' of 7d a day, unless (from 1898) his illness or injury was unavoidably contracted or received on duty. When he went on furlough he received his full pay and an allowance of 6d a day 'in lieu of rations', that is instead of his daily free issue of ¾ lb of meat and 1 lb of bread.

For the enterprising there was a variety of appointments for both non-commissioned officers and privates for which they received 'extra duty pay' varying from 3d to 1s a day. These jobs included gymnastic instructors, sergeant cooks, telegraph clerks, clerks in the staff offices and school assistants. In India, there was an even wider choice (see p. 138). When Mole of the 14th Hussars, during that regiment's tour in India between 1877 and 1886, was promoted to be a rough-riding sergeant-major, he found his pay increased by 1s a day. Beside that there were 'various windfalls incidental to the situation'. He was always tipped when an officer's charger was dismissed riding-school, 'and, again, there were many young officers qualifying for the staff who were obliged to gain an equitation certificate, and these when they got through my school, invariably remembered the schoolmaster. Besides this, a rough-riding sergeant-major was always sure of as much private work as he had time for, such as breaking-in and training horses for civilians and wealthy natives.'

Badges for good conduct, accompanied by extra pay of 1d a day and a chevron worn on the left arm for each badge, were awarded to men after certain terms of good conduct. After two years' they received one badge, after six, two badges, after twelve, three badges and so on.[10]

Officers' 'soldier servants' (who in the cavalry were not meant to be selected until they had completed eighteen months' duty in the ranks) were paid by regulation 2s 6d a week in the cavalry and 1s 6d in the infantry. In each cavalry regiment there were fifty soldier servants, as well as about thirty cooks and mess waiters, most of whom also received some sort of extra pay. Troopers were employed by sergeant-majors, quartermaster-sergeants, sergeants and farriers to look after their horses. They were paid 1s 6d a week [11]

When a man was transferred to the Reserve or was discharged he was given 5s towards providing himself with 'plain clothes'. Sergeants received 7s 6d and warrant officers who were 'entitled to 1st class clothing' 15s. The only items of personal clothing which a man could keep on transfer or discharge were waistcoats (dress and undress), cotton drawers, boots and shoes, gloves and, surprisingly, 'fezzes, turbans, etc.' He had to hand in all tunics, frocks, frock coats, jackets (dress and undress), trousers, trews, pantaloons, kilts, duck gaiters, forage and field service caps, sashes and shoulder pads. He also, of course, had to hand in all items of what was officially called 'public clothing', such as cloaks, greatcoats, full dress head-dresses, haversacks, jack spurs and lancers' girdles, and what was known as 'State clothing' which included, in the case of the Household Cavalry, jack boots and leather breeches.[12]

Warrant Officers and non-commissioned officers received increased pay over the three final decades of the century. For example, regimental sergeant-majors were paid 5s 4d a day in 1893. Ten years earlier they had received only 4s 1d. In the same period a sergeant's pay increased by 3d to 2s 8d and a corporal's by 4½d to 2s.* In 1891 the Inspector-General of Cavalry gave some interesting figures to show that a sergeant of cavalry received at that date less money in the hand than a corporal:

'*Sergeant's Pay*	£	s	d	*Corporal's Pay*	£	s	d
30 days at 2s 8d	4	0	0	30 days at 2s	3	0	0
Deduct as below	2	9	5	Deduct as below	0	18	5
Actually gets about	1	10	7	Actually gets about	2	1	7
Deductions				*Deductions*			
30 days' messing @ 8d	1	0	0	30 days' messing			
Mess subscription	0	1	0	@ 3½d	0	8	9
Grooming horse	0	6	0	Corporal's room	0	0	6
Batman	0	4	0	Washing & sweeper	0	2	6

* See Appendix, p. 408, for comparative rates of daily pay of the rank and file of a cavalry regiment in 1866 and 1893.

Deductions			
Washing	0	3	0
Regimental clubs – cricket, shooting, football and athletic	0	4	0
Sweeper	0	0	4
Library	0	0	6
Hair cutting	0	0	2
Barrack damages	0	0	6
Armourer's bill	0	0	6
Saddler's bill	0	0	6
Tailor's bill (overalls and jacket)	0	3	5
Boot bill	0	3	0
Regimental necessaries	0	2	0
	2	8	11

Deductions			
Library (4d), hair cutting (1d)	0	0	5
Barrack damages	0	0	6
Delf [cesspit digging?]	0	0	3
Armourer's bill	0	0	6
Boot bill	0	1	6
Tailor's bill	0	1	0
Saddler's bill	0	0	6
Necessaries	0	2	0
	0	18	5

From time to time after a campaign special gratuities were given to all ranks. After the 1884 Suakin campaign, for instance, warrant officers received £8 and the humblest private £2.[13]

* * *

Pension regulations were, as always, complicated and constantly altered. That small number of privates who served on to twenty-one years and beyond received, after 1881, 1s 1d a day, with an addition of ½d a day, up to a maximum of 5d for each year beyond twenty-one. The most a Warrant Officer could receive was 5s a day. 'I am not aware,' wrote Wolseley in 1887, 'of any other trade or calling where the man who can neither read nor write can secure such a provision for his old age, nor where the man of very humble education can return into civil life at forty years of age as well off as our non-commissioned officers can do now.'[14] There were also improved disability pensions,* pensions for gallant conduct, 'meritorious service rewards' and Victoria Cross pensions.

The most interesting reform in the pension field was the introduction of 'Compassionate Pensions for Campaign Service'. These were granted to 'necessitous ex-soldiers who had rendered war

* The claim of each man discharged as an invalid was judged from the medical evidence by the Chelsea Commissioners.

service'. In 1874 the Commissioners of Chelsea Hospital were empowered to award, at their discretion, pensions, or increases of pensions, up to 1s 6d a day to destitute survivors of the campaigns culminating in Waterloo, which had been fought fifty-nine years before! It is an extraordinary fact that the total cost of these came in the end to £112,000. The same principle for later campaigns, such as the Crimea and Indian Mutiny, was applied from 1891, but the number of pensions was limited to 100 in any one year. Four years later all veterans with medals for pre-1860 campaigns, aged sixty-five and over, whose total private income did not exceed 10s a week, became eligible for compassionate pensions. Depending on length of service beyond fourteen years, these ranged from 9d to 1s a day. The 1881 reforms instituted pensions for the families of all ranks killed in action or dying of wounds within a year of receiving them. A warrant officer's widow and children automatically received pensions of £20 and £5 respectively upon his death.[15]

> 'It is important that the soldier should be able to read and write and keep his own accounts, as well as be acquainted with his drill.'
>
> *Army General Order*, LXX, of 1871

(v)

Rank and file: increase in literacy – increase in those with 'superior education' – regimental schools – Certificates of Education – Corps of Army Schoolmistresses – the cost of army education

In 1879 there were only four men in the 14th Hussars who could neither read nor write. In 1858 one fifth of the rank and file of the whole army were in that category. In 1863 only about seven in every hundred men were said to possess a 'superior education'. In 1881 the figure had become seventy-one in every hundred.* [1] These startling statistics (which nevertheless may in some respects

* See also p. 86.

be misleadingly optimistic) illustrate the general educational revolution which had taken place in the third quarter of the century, especially since the Education Act of 1870. Wolseley, writing in the year of the Queen's Golden Jubilee, exaggerated only a little when he stated that:

> 'many admirable non-commissioned officers could neither read nor write when they enlisted. They were taught to do so, and well grounded in elementary education in our regimental schools. No matter, therefore, how ignorant a young fellow may be when he enlists, if he is steady, intelligent, and determined to get on in life, he has a career in the army assured to him he can find nowhere else.'[2]

In 1892 a new drill book was issued. It emphasized that soldiers should be 'taught to think and, subject to accepted principles, to act for themselves.'[3] This, too, was revolutionary.

Every soldier, after his first two months, was in theory compelled to attend the regimental school until he had gained a 4th class Certificate of Education.* This was 'at the level of an eight-year-old child – to *copy* a few lines of easy words and to do a few simple sums.'[4] Recruits who could satisfy their commanding officer that they were sufficiently educated were exempted from attending school until the first half-yearly examination. Others – in 1886 as many as 36 per cent – who after two years at school could not even pass the fourth grade, so long as they had proved 'well-behaved and attentive', were excused further attendance. Otherwise until the 4th class certificate had been acquired compulsory attendance for not less than five hours a week was supposed to be mandatory.[5] Yet, in practice, since the claims on the soldier's training time were obviously much greater under the short service system, many of those officers who in the old days had given the schoolmasters strong support, now found it increasingly hard to do so. 'Gradually,' as Colonel White, the historian of army education has put it, 'the recommendations of the [1870] Royal Commission† were undermined, until by 1885 the liability of the recruit to attend school was reduced to his first six months of service.' Two years later regimental schools were replaced by garrison or station ones. The Director-General of Military Education in 1893 complained that, as a result, the direct personal interest of Commanding Officers

* Abolished in 1887.

† See Vol II, 289.

had been lost, since they were reluctant to look into the affairs of a school over which they had no definite authority.

Three years later efforts were being made to overcome the problem of inadequate accommodation.

> 'In order,' wrote the Director-General in 1896, 'to meet modern educational requirements it is becoming more and more evident that every school should have at least one class-room in addition to the large school-room. Progress is greatly hindered when several classes are instructed simultaneously in one room by separate teachers. The noise occasioned by so many voices is very distracting to the pupils, whether adults or children, and imposes a severe strain upon the teachers mentally and physically. All new buildings are abundantly supplied with class-rooms.'

But, of course, the building of new accommodation took time, especially as the annual grants for such work were far from generous.

From 1890 onward compulsory education for adult soldiers was actually discontinued. Commanding officers were now merely 'enjoined' to promote school attendance, though no private could draw his full good conduct pay until he had achieved a 3rd class certificate. It was not until 1913 that recruits were once again obliged to attend school during their first six months or until they had acquired a 3rd class certificate.[6]

The 3rd, 2nd and 1st class certificates were, of course, progressively more difficult to obtain than the 4th class. Before men could be promoted to the various non-commissioned and warrant ranks they usually had to secure one of these certificates. In 1881, for instance, promotion to the rank of colour-sergeant was made to depend upon the possession of a 1st class certificate. In 1892 36.51 per cent of the total rank and file of the army held certificates of one grade or another. By 1899 about 4,000 men held 1st class and 45,000 2nd class certificates.[7] In 1883 the 5th Lancers proudly boasted that it had thirteen men out of its 469 who possessed 1st class certificates, which placed it 'by a long way at the top of the list of cavalry regiments'. From 1890 onwards corporals, before they could rise higher, had to have a 2nd class certificate, and an even harder examination was instituted for regimental sergeant-majors, who had to know an astonishing amount of English history and geography,

> 'requiring,' as the Inspector-General of Cavalry put it

> to the Wantage Committee, 'correct descriptions of perhaps the Pennine Mountains or the river system of Africa, or to explain the terms "Danegelt and Witenagemot", the "Self-Denying Ordinance" and the "Act of Supremacy" etc; that puts promotion out of the question to a great number of troop sergeant-majors, and therefore it is looked upon as a very great grievance by those non-commissioned officers who, just as they come up to the top and think they are going to be sergeant-majors, find it is quite impossible to pass, because, among other reasons, in very many places there are no schools for them to go to.'[8]

The children of soldiers married 'with leave' were compelled to attend school, either, as in most cases, within the regiment, or, on religious grounds, at any 'certified efficient or inspected denominational school' outside, where the father would have to pay the school fees. They had to attend until they were fourteen years old. By the end of the century there had been established in virtually every barracks an 'Infant and Industrial School' under a trained schoolmistress belonging to the Corps of Army Schoolmistresses (later 'the Queen's Royal Army Schoolmistresses').[9]

* * *

The amount of money spent on military education, including officers', was in 1890–1 £112,500, only 0.63 per cent of the total spent on the regular army (excluding India). Of this £33,300 went on libraries, 'charitable institutions', medical schools at Netley and on Kneller Hall (the Royal Military School of Music), and £37,300 on elementary education in the Army Schools.[10]

> 'Military law is the law which governs the soldier in peace and in war, at home and abroad. At all times and in all places, the conduct of officers and soldiers as such is regulated by military law.'
>
> *Manual of Military Law*, 1894, p. 1

(vi)

Rank and file: 'Field Punishment No. 1' substituted for flogging in the field – the commanding officer's powers of punishment – courts-martial – guard rooms – the death penalty – the Curragh 'disturbance', 1877 – the Aldershot 'disturbance', 1893 – the Household Cavalry 'mutiny', 1892

Flogging in peacetime had been abolished in 1868. By the Army Act of 1881, 'Field Punishment No. 1', which consisted in lashing malefactors to a gun wheel for a stated number of hours, was substituted for flogging in the field. This total abolition was the last nail in the coffin of a barbarous practice which had been the staple of military discipline for well over a century. Writing to the Secretary of State for War from Cairo after the Nile campaign of 1884–5, Wolseley attributed the marked improvement which he found in the 'moral tone' as well as in 'the military spirit' of the rank and file 'in no small degree to the abolition of flogging'. He believed that most officers, even those who previously favoured the lash on active service, now fully recognized that many advantages had resulted from its total abolition. 'The soldier,' he added, 'is prouder of himself and of his calling than he used to be.'[1]

There were still those, however, who regretted the new regulations. Colonel Frederick Burnaby of the Blues (see p. 119) wrote home from the Nile on Christmas Eve, 1884:

> 'A soldier stole some stores a few days ago. He has been tried by court-martial and given five years' penal servitude. In the old days he would have escaped with a flogging . . . Poor fellow! I expect he does not bless the sentimentalists who did away with flogging in the army.'[2]

Over all, serious crime declined slightly in the last decades of the century. For example, of every 1,000 men in 1865 there were 109 tried by courts-martial. In 1879, three years after short service had been in full swing, that proportion had fallen to eighty-five.

The number of lesser punishments of the type which had to be entered on a man's crime sheet fell over the same period hardly at all.[3]

The powers of summary punishment which a commanding officer could employ were not much altered during the period, though from 1893 he could award a private fourteen days' imprisonment with hard labour instead of only seven. The commanding officer could also impose a fine of up to 10s for 'simple' drunkenness (as opposed to 'aggravated' drunkenness, which meant being drunk whilst on duty),* and he could deprive a man of pay (for being absent without leave or to make good damage done or loss caused). He could also deprive him of any or all his good conduct badges. When charged with any of these crimes, the soldier was given the option of appealing to a court-martial. There was no appeal against the award of minor punishments. The chief of these were extra guards and pickets and confinement to barracks (for up to twenty-eight days by the commanding officer and up to seven by the officer commanding a squadron). Confinement to barracks normally also entailed punishment drill, having to answer one's name at uncertain hours and, of course, being employed on the least pleasant fatigues. Warrant officers and non-commissioned officers were under no circumstances liable to summary or minor punishments. The only way they could be punished was by reduction in rank and this could only happen as the result of a court-martial or by special order of the Commander-in-Chief.[4]

Punishment drill, according to Private William ('Wully') Robertson of the 16th Lancers,

> 'seemed to have been designed to destroy any shred of self-respect the unfortunate defaulter might possess. The "drill"

* Drunkenness, in the cavalry at any rate, seems to have decreased as the century came to a close. Sergeant-Major Mole found that 'the crime of *drunk* was a rare one and instead of looking in the canteen for a "schemer"' he would 'seek for him in the library, where he was generally to be found assuaging his thirst for knowledge and liquor with magazines and coffee. In short, the lads were sober, eager, willing, and take them for all in all, good stuff for soldiers.' (Mole, 334.)

In 1860 a military branch of the 'National Temperance League' was formed. In 1893 'The Army Temperance Association: Home Organization' was founded. It was in effect an off-shoot of the Indian association which had been created by Lord Roberts in 1888 (see p. 134). ([Anon.] 'A Treatise on the Temperance Movement in H.M. Forces', Supplement to *Bulletin No. 1, vol. 6(114), of the Orders and Medals Research Society*, 1967, 1.)

consisted in being turned and twisted about on the barrack square, in quick time and with only a few short pauses during the hour, the men carrying their full kit, strapped on their shoulders, besides the lance and sword – a total weight of some 40 or 50 lbs. The drill could be made, and frequently was, according to the fancy of the sergeant in charge, extremely exasperating and fatiguing, and in order to escape from such degrading drudgery men would sometimes deliberately commit a second and more serious offence so as to be sent to prison. In the cavalry it was not feasible, as in the infantry, to spare the men for four hours' drill each day . . . As a rule the punishment took the form of one hour's drill and one or two of employment on "fatigue duties"'.

'Wully' Robertson also described the guard room of the cavalry barracks at Aldershot in 1877. It was

'about fifteen feet square, indifferently ventilated, and with the most primitive arrangements for sanitation. No means of lighting it after dark were either provided or permitted. Running along one of its sides was a sloping wooden stage, measuring about six feet from top to bottom, which served as a bed for all the occupants, sometimes a dozen or more in number; at the top was a wooden shelf, slightly raised above the level of the stage, which acted as a pillow; and no blankets (except in very cold weather) or mattresses were allowed, except for prisoners who had been interned for more than seven days . . .

'A man sentenced to undergo imprisonment, even if for some such short period as forty-eight hours, had his hair closely cropped off, and was thus made to look like a convict for several weeks after his discharge.'[5]

On active service, for such offences as 'shamefully abandoning any garrison, place, post or town' and 'misbehaving before an enemy in such a manner as to show cowardice,' death was, of course, still the maximum punishment. So it was, too, for sedition and mutiny.

* * *

On 8 September, 1877, there occurred a 'disturbance' at the Curragh camp outside Dublin, involving men of the 19th Hussars. It is probably the only case of mutiny in the home army recorded during the whole of the century. It was alleged by the mutineers that their commanding officer, Lieutenant-Colonel Henry Cadogan Craigie, was giving them 'a great many more parades' than the other cavalry regiments in the camp. Readers of the second volume of this work may remember that it was Craigie, then a twenty-seven year old captain in the 3rd Bengal Light Cavalry, who unsuccessfully begged his commanding officer to put off the firing parade at Meerut which led to the start of the Indian Mutiny. When those sowars who had refused to fire the suspected cartridges were put in irons they cursed their colonel but blessed Captain Craigie 'and called out that "they hoped he would be a Prince and a Lord".' (See Vol II, 139–142). Now, ironically, twenty years later, it was Craigie, a commanding officer of less than two months' standing, who was being cursed by the white troopers under his command.*

It seems that the unfortunate men, already tired from lasso drill in the morning, received from their sergeants verbal warning for a Saturday afternoon 'General Parade' at 2.30. From this 'none were to be exempt except the servants and the sick.' The object of the parade was to inquire 'after a missing stable jacket'. One report says that sixty-nine men failed to turn up. Private Booth, who was one of the eight so-called ringleaders who were eventually placed on trial, said that he never in fact received the warning. By chance he heard some of the other men mention it. 'I pipeclayed my belts,' he said, 'but found it impossible to have them dry in time. If I had appeared on parade with my belts not dry I should have been punished severely, or turned off parade, and rather than be made a laughing-stock and disgraced I absented myself.' He repaired to the canteen of an infantry regiment where he learned that 'a mob of men' had gone off towards a nearby village. He went to join them. Private Lawton, another of the accused, said that he had just been issued with a new sword belt which had never been pipeclayed. It would have to be pipeclayed three or four times before it was fit for parade. He thought it better, under the circumstances, not to attend 'lest I should be disgraced'. Private

* Craigie, born in 1830, had joined the 3rd Bengal Light Cavalry in 1848. Soon after his regiment mutinied at Meerut, he raised a short-lived body of irregular horse in the North-West Provinces. He then joined the 1st Bengal European Cavalry raised in 1858. Three years later this regiment became the 19th Hussars. In 1863 Craigie was promoted major.

Norton's story, however, was that he had two horses to look after and that he could not get them and their accoutrements ready in time for the parade, 'which I therefore did not attend'.

When it was realized that so many men had failed to appear, a party of mounted military police, followed by two infantry pickets, was sent in pursuit. The men were soon discovered lying in the grass outside the village public house 'drinking porter out of a tub'. As the sergeant of military police approached them they pointed to a pile of stones and threatened that if he came any nearer they would 'take his life'. He begged them to listen to him and advised them to come back. To this they replied that 'they were over-paraded, and all they wanted was an inquiry in order to have Lieutenant-Colonel Craigie shifted.' With sticks in their hands they then told the sergeant that 'if he sent the infantry pickets after them there would be murder'.

At this point there rode up two hastily summoned lieutenants. One of these was twenty-five year old John Denton Pinkstone French, seven years later to start his distinguished fighting career on the Nile (see p. 332), and to end it forty-eight years later as Field-Marshal the Earl of Ypres. 'It is Lieutenant Warde* and Lieutenant French,' shouted some of the men. 'Let us hear what they have got to say'. 'We told them,' said Warde in evidence, 'that they were disgracing the regiment, and the sooner they got back to the lines the better. They began using abusive language towards the colonel, saying "We have come out for the purpose of getting him cashiered. We have tried to do it before. . . . If we do not succeed by this we will do something else that will." . . . They then said they would do what we wanted them to do, so they fell in and marched back to the lines,' all the way shouting abuse.

All the absentees were confined over the week-end. On Monday they asked to talk to the colonel. But Private Booth told the court that he, like the other accused, 'had not a chance to state his case' and that Craigie remanded him for trial 'without hearing a word'. The accused were then kept in prison for six weeks awaiting trial. At the General Court-Martial held in Dublin, neither prosecution nor defence was conducted by counsel. This was normal practice at the time. An infantry major acted as deputy judge advocate.

One of the accused was acquitted, the others were found guilty

* Henry Warde left the 19th Hussars in 1895 as a lieutenant-colonel to become Chief Constable of Kent, a post which he held for twenty-six years. He died aged ninety in 1940.

of 'mutiny by combining to resist and offer violence to the mounted police in the execution of their duty, and by continuing to absent themselves without leave from the parade appointed by the commanding officer, with intent to resist his lawful authority.' One man was sentenced to eight, another to seven, a third to six and the remaining four to five years' penal servitude. These sentences seem very savage, but it is difficult to judge whether this was so because many of the details of the affair are unlikely to come to light. *The Irish Times* nonetheless thought that the extent of the 'insubordination' had been 'greatly exaggerated. Not one of the old, or what may be considered representative, men of the regiment were concerned in the affair, and what did happen is described by every sensible man in the camp as the boyish freaks of a few featherheaded recruits.'[6]

Craigie remained in command of the 19th Hussars another sixteen months. He then at the age of fifty retired on half-pay with the honorary rank of major-general. Two years later he was dead.

* * *

The bearing of grudges between regiments was a characteristic aspect of the regimental system in the British army. Old resentments died hard. Between the 4th and 19th Hussars, for example, there was still anger in the late 1890s over an unfavourable remark alleged to have been made by some private thirty years before about the state of the 4th's barracks when the 19th had taken them over. 'Although,' wrote Winston Churchill in 1896, 'not a single soul remained of those involved in the previous dispute, the sergeants and soldiers were found fully informed about it, and as angry as if it had only taken place the month before.'[7] If quarrels between regiments of the same arm were common, it is not to be wondered at that jealousies and hostility between the infantry and the cavalry were at least equally so. In 1893 a grave disturbance shook the Aldershot command. It was said that the Cameronians (the Scottish Rifles) had a reputation for not getting on with other regiments. They were supposed to have expressed their particular dislike of the men of the Cavalry Brigade then at Aldershot (the 4th and 5th Dragoon Guards and the 20th Hussars) by going about in gangs and picking quarrels with cavalrymen who were alone. One evening a trooper of the 20th Hussars was badly beaten up, it is said, by three Cameronians, taken to hospital and even reported as dead. His 'best girl' is believed to have 'worked up his "pals" to try and avenge him'. What is certain is that on two subsequent evenings large numbers of troopers from the 4th, 5th and 20th repaired to the 'Music Hall' of the brigade canteen where inflammatory speeches were made. On the second occasion a large crowd 'armed with bedposts and other weapons'[8] suddenly surged out of barracks. There was a desperate mêlée at the Cameronians' barrack-gate. A good many men on both sides were injured and numerous windows smashed. Luckily the in-lying picket of the 5th Dragoon Guards was quickly on the scene. Assisted by officers of the Cameronians, including the commanding officer, whose leg was injured by a stone, they restored order before the cavalrymen could force their way into the main barracks. The three cavalry regiments were next day ordered out of barracks into widely separated camps. As a result of a private Court of Inquiry and subsequent Courts-Martial seven men of the three regiments were convicted, one of 'taking part in a military riot' and six of 'inciting other soldiers to take part in a military riot'. Their prison sentences ranged from one year to nine months.

The case which caused the most interest, however, was that of a man of the 5th. Private W. Craven, the 'A' Squadron cook, was charged with endeavouring in the Cavalry Brigade Canteen 'to persuade men of the brigade to make a disturbance'. To assist him in his defence at the District Court-Martial assembled on 25 May, Craven asked for Captain St John Gore,* his squadron commander. This officer insisted upon his right as 'Prisoner's Friend' to have a copy of the whole of the proceedings of the court of inquiry. While he was doing so at headquarters, Sir Evelyn Wood, at that time commanding the Aldershot Division, 'looked into the Office and said "You are quite wrong, Gore, you are quite wrong!" However,' wrote Gore in an unpublished account of the affair, 'I went away sitting on the precious document in my pony trap! It was of very great service.' It was of such good service that he was able to get two witnesses who falsely accused Craven at the enquiry to admit at the court-martial that they had

* St John Corbet Gore, born in 1859, had joined the 5th Dragoon Guards in 1879. He served with the Heavy Camel Regiment in the Sudan, commanded the cavalry at Elandslaagte in 1899, was in the siege of Ladysmith and succeeded to the command of his regiment in 1900. He wrote three books, one of which was an account of *The Green Horse in Ladysmith*. He died in 1913.

lied. Craven was honourably acquitted and Gore was congratulated by the president of the court-martial.

The prosecution witnesses, including the canteen sergeant and corporal, stated that Craven made a provocative speech whilst standing on a table.* 'We are cavalrymen,' he was accused of saying, 'and we will have our rights, and won't be put upon by the Cameronians' and 'bugger the Cameronians, we will go for them yet.'

The only civilian who gave evidence was one Albert Seymour, 'a professional singer'. He was also, surprisingly, a purveyor of flowers to the troopers: 'I took several orders for flowers that afternoon,' he said in evidence, 'the men putting their names on paper. The Provost Marshal took charge of those papers. I don't remember the names of any men on those papers, as I cannot read.' When Seymour entered the canteen on the relevant evening he was at once asked

> 'to stand on my head and sing a song. I did so. I gave a recitation, drank a glass of beer, and gave a toast whilst on my head. I cannot swear to what the toast was, as I know several, and I was under the influence of drink at the time. I then gave a step dance with my teeth by rattling my teeth together; after that a bone solo, by knocking my head with my hands. I represented bells by clapping my hands in front of my face, after which I played a tune in the same way. I believe it was Napoleon's March but I am not sure. After performing these tricks I went round with my hat.'

Seymour's evidence is of little relevance, but it gives a picture of the sort of busker who frequented barracks in the 1890s.

One of the prosecution's star witnesses, Private Henshaw of the 5th Dragoon Guards, was particularly plausible. His evidence would have been very damaging to Craven had not Captain Gore discovered that Henshaw had forty entries on his squadron defaulter sheet. In 1890 he had been awarded seven days C.B. for 'telling a lie to his commanding officer'. Gore was clearly an officer with a sense of humour. In his opening address he said, 'I *liked* the prosecution; and cannot forego the pleasure of hearing its remaining three witnesses who were not called! *I* propose to call them.' This he did with devastating effect.

One of the defence witnesses was Squadron Sergeant-Major

* 'It's a very common thing for men to stand on the tables,' said one witness, 'even to look at a dog fight.'

Easterbrook of the 5th who swore that Craven was 'decidedly not an influential man in the regiment' and that the other men constantly made fun of him. In Dublin four years before, said Easterbrook, Craven 'jumped into a water trough and tried to drown himself. He then came to my quarters with a piece of carpet round him for cape – cried and told me a long story about how badly he was treated; I sent him to bed.' On another occasion Craven, according to the sergeant-major, had 'taken the part of a recruit named Holmes who had been knocked about by a man named Vickers. Vickers struck Craven twice. I shifted Craven to another room [to protect him from the other men] and confined Vickers.'* Corporal Caldwell, also of the 5th, recollected an incident when four privates placed Craven on a table and knocked him about. Craven 'reported the matter to Captain Gore on the following morning.' The four men were very angry at this and 'said they would put [Craven] in a horse trough, hang him, &c.'

Gore's most telling witnesses were Boy Cant and Private Pike, both of the 5th. Young Cant was orderly trumpeter on the relevant evening. At 9.35 p.m., just after he had sounded first post, he saw Craven at the cook-house. Craven said 'good night' and asked him to give him a call next morning at reveille. This he in due course did. Private Pike gave evidence that Craven had left the canteen at about 8.45 p.m., saying that he was going to bed. Pike spent the whole evening in the canteen and never saw Craven return there.

In his opening address, Gore contended that Craven was not the sort to offer 'to lead the Cavalry Brigade' against the Cameronians or anyone else; that he never made any sort of speech, but instead 'ingloriously but prudently' went to bed in the cook-house. He pointed out that on the day after the trouble there appeared the order for transferring Craven to the Reserve after his seven years with the Colours. He had handed in his regimental clothing on 4 May and was actually due to leave barracks next day, when he was arrested.

In his second address for the defence Gore suggested that Craven had been made a scapegoat by spiteful or thoughtless men:

> '"Why not old Daddy Craven?" . . . "Yes, why not Craven? *He* will be clear away out of this, and it will do *him* no harm, and do us a great deal of good: no one need actually say any-

* Vickers was one of the five men of the 5th convicted as a result of the Aldershot affray. He got nine months' imprisonment.

thing – only ask a question about him, or make a suggestion . . ." I ask you to conclude,' pleaded Gore, 'that these careless questions *were* asked, that these suggestions *were* thrown out [at the Court of Inquiry]. I do not think that the gravity of the consequences that might ensue were appreciated at the time, but I ask you to conclude that either maliciously or carelessly . . . was the first slight impetus given to the charge which has at length brought this man before you, face to face with ruin.'

This case has been given at some length because it paints an intriguing picture of some aspects of barrack life. It also illustrates how the provisions of military law could easily be evaded. As Gore pointed out to the court-martial, Rule of Procedure 123(F) was not complied with in Craven's case during the Court of Inquiry. The moment suspicion began to attach to him, he should have been produced so as to be able to confront and cross-examine those who accused him. As it was, Craven was afforded none of the opportunities which 'must be afforded'[9] under the Rule.

* * *

An affair of much the same nature, though of less consequence, occurred in the previous year, 1892. One Saturday morning, it seems, Captain Richard Hamilton Rawson, who was temporarily in command of 'C' Squadron, 1st Life Guards, at Windsor, ordered a kit inspection. With this he expressed himself dissatisfied in the 'most forceful terms'. He therefore ordered the squadron to 'come again' on Monday. Early on Sunday morning it was learned that twenty-four saddle panels, all in the same troop, had been slashed. Consequently, immediately after church parade, the whole troop was confined to barracks. As they had marched to church, men of the other squadrons, looking on from the barrack room verandahs, had loudly cheered them, but Rawson they had hissed. That evening the confined men sang songs in the canteen and when 'Lights Out' sounded gathered on the barrack square signing 'Rule Britannia' and the national anthem.

Monday's papers carried stories of a 'mutiny' in the Life Guards. The second-in-command, in the commanding officer's absence, at once instituted an inquiry. On Monday evening Trooper Horace Marshall, a man who had served eleven years without a stain, cut out and stuck on the canteen wall one of the newspaper headlines containing the word 'mutiny'. Above this he chalked the word 'comrades' and beneath it the words 'stick together'. It appears that Canteen Corporal of Horse* James Bayliss removed the cutting and erased the chalk. Both Marshall and he later faced courts-martial, Bayliss apparently because he had failed to place Marshall in close arrest. But since he had already been reduced to the ranks on this account, he was acquitted. Marshall, on the other hand, was convicted and sentenced to the rather savage period of eighteen months in Brixton goal.

Some time before this Major-General Lord Methuen, commanding the Home District, having received the acting commanding officer's report,† addressed the regiment in the Riding School. He called on the saddle-slashing culprits to step forward. Not surprisingly, not a man moved. As punishment, the whole regiment was moved to Shorncliffe, which was said by the local press to be 'the worst military station in England'. Not until they arrived there were some of the non-commissioned officers, who had broken up their homes in Windsor, informed that their services were no longer required.[10] Captain Rawson, after nine years in the regiment, was retired on half-pay before the year was out. He later commanded the Sussex Yeomanry and became Unionist Member of Parliament for Reigate. He died, aged fifty-five, in 1918.

* In the Household Cavalry, corporal of horse is equivalent to sergeant.

† This was taken so seriously that the Commander-in-Chief interrupted a shooting holiday in Scotland to return to London.

It is very difficult to discover the full story, as the regimental records and diary make no mention of the matter, and there seems to be no record of the court-martial.

> 'Can it be imagined that a man of the class our recruits came from would be comfortable in gentlemen's society, and having to conform to "society manners"? . . . I do not believe there was a man of any rank . . . during my time who would have taken a commission as sub-lieutenant if it had been offered to him.'
>
> J. E. ACLAND-TROYTE, a 'gentleman ranker', in 1880

> 'There was a leaven of educated young fellows, whose parents were well off, and whose one idea in enlisting was to obtain a commission – a phantom prize dangled before their eyes in the vast majority of cases.'
>
> SERGEANT-MAJOR MOLE, 14th Hussars, writing in the 1880s

> 'It is no boon to give commissions to men who are not able to afford them.'
>
> LIEUTENANT H. WILTSHIRE, 20th Hussars, who rose from the ranks, speaking in 1891.[1]

(vii)

Rank and file: 'gentlemen' recruits – promotion from the ranks

Though most recruits were drawn from the lowest classes, there were exceptions. Colonel Logan found that these men usually enlisted in the cavalry.[2] One depot commander always told his sergeant in charge that 'when he got a respectable recruit, he should put him into a room by himself, if possible, and not send him with the lowest that came to sleep there, because it would disgust him with the service at the commencement.'[3] It is difficult to estimate what numbers of 'gentlemen' and men of the middle class served in the ranks. There were certainly more in the cavalry than in the other branches. For instance in 1879 there were seventeen in the 17th Lancers, which was very probably a higher proportion than in any infantry battalion. An officer of the West London district in the same year reported that though most recruits were of the lower class,' he had 'frequently of late had men of superior education. In many cases they have been gentlemen's sons who have enlisted.' Exactly how 'superior education' was defined it is hard to discover, but the General Annual Return of the British Army, 1880, says that the number of recruits of superior education in every 1,000 during 1861 to 1870 varied between fifty-two and sixty-eight, while in 1871 it had risen to 137 and, dramatically by 1879, to 576.[4] (See also p. 70.) This illustrates the great leap forward made by education generally. It does not mean that there was a huge increase of recruits from other than the lowest classes.

The reasons for men of a 'good class' joining up were, amongst others, that they had failed in their examinations for a commission. According to one retired general, they enlisted 'with a view of working their way'.[5] Sergeant-Major Mole of the 14th Hussars, writing in the 1880s, tells of numbers of these who found that

> 'from three to six months seemed to satisfy them, for they nearly always found the game different to what they expected, and purchased their discharges . . . They were not born for the life . . . They soon recognised that without interest at their backs they could hope for nothing, and that in peace time only about one NCO in a hundred gets his commission and then very often by a fluke . . . A commission from the ranks,' he concluded, 'is not always an unmixed blessing.'[6]

'I am strongly opposed,' wrote Buller, the Adjutant-General, in 1893, 'to any scheme which tends to increase the number of candidates for commissions from the ranks . . . The gentleman who has enlisted has lost caste, and it cannot fail that a man who has deliberately adopted as companions men of a lower social and educational standard than himself, must . . . have lowered his own standard by the associations he has cultivated.'[7]

Lord Wolseley, however, writing in 1887, claimed that 'a far larger proportion of well-to-do and educated men enlist now than formerly. Many join now in the hope of obtaining commissions . . . A colonel stated the other day that he had in his regiment some thirty sons of well-to-do gentlemen as privates, corporals, etc., and that they had done much to raise the tone of the men in barracks.' In 1885 twenty-three sergeants received commissions; the following year the number was forty-two. Yet the annual average between 1870 and 1890 of commissions from the ranks, excluding quartermasters and riding masters, was only 3 per cent of the total granted.[8]

Lieutenant H. Wiltshire of the 20th Hussars was produced to the Wantage Committee as an example of a man promoted from the ranks. He had enlisted for twelve years in the 4th Dragoon

Guards in 1876. 'I had nothing to do at the time,' he said, 'and having always had a liking for the Service, I joined.' After fifteen months he became a lance-corporal, after three years' service a lance-sergeant, and after ten years' service obtained his commission.[9]

There were cases, though not many, of men of a not very superior class obtaining commissions because of their service in war. Such a one was Harry Finn who served in the 9th Lancers in the second Afghan War seven years after enlisting. He was awarded a distinguished conduct medal for gallantry and commissioned in the 21st Hussars in 1881. By 1900 he had risen to the command of the 21st Lancers, becoming a Brigadier-General in 1912.[10]

It seems that at times a little underhand dissuasion was applied to warrant officers and non-commissioned officers. Whenever one of these was to be promoted to lieutenant, the allowance of £100 'in aid of his outfit' could only be made 'upon the approval of the Commander-in-Chief'.[11] The Inspector-General of Cavalry in evidence before the Wantage Committee spoke of a 'grievance serjeants have . . . A man is asked whether he will forego the sum of money granted to start him in getting his commission, and if he cannot, he does not get his commission; the rich man has therefore a much greater chance of getting a commission than a poor one.'[12] This seems to imply that the Commander-in-Chief somewhat abused his power of approval, thinking of his action, possibly, as one of charity towards a poor man.

'Wully' Robertson used to say that as Regimental Sergeant-Major of the 16th Lancers he had a full day's work but no worry about mess bills. As a subaltern in the 3rd Dragoon Guards, on the other hand, his work was 'easily got over', but he found it 'hard to meet expenses'.[13]

2

'The Army is all right as long as it is limited to the Mess and the band, but the troops are a damned nuisance.'

Anonymous cavalry officer

'Hitherto our army has been a pleasant home for idle men; generation after generation of officers have been attracted to it by the ease and pleasure it secured to the English gentleman – enjoyment that was only heightened by the opposite extremes of privation and hard work which an occasional campaign afforded. All this must sooner or later be entirely changed by the system of short service: is it, therefore, to be wondered at that short service should be unpopular with many of our regimental officers?'

LIEUTENANT-GENERAL J. GARNET WOLSELEY in 1881

'We live in times when heroism will not do – when all the virtues that adorn the British officers will not do, if not coupled with the most careful professional training.'

EDWARD CARDWELL in the House of Commons, 1871

'In the infantry one has to keep a man; in the cavalry a man and horse as well.'

LORD RANDOLPH CHURCHILL to his son on gaining a cavalry cadetship at Sandhurst

'It was a gay and lordly life that now opened upon me.'

2ND-LIEUTENANT WINSTON SPENCER CHURCHILL on being gazetted to the 4th Hussars in 1895.[1]

Officers: slower promotion after purchase abolition – means of speeding it up – forced and voluntary retirements – pay – allowances – gratuities and pensions – 'seniority tempered by rejection' – Colonel Denne's case – creation of Reserve of Officers – competitive examinations – promotion of full colonels – exchanges – types – mode of life – the mess – marriage – training – 'crammers' – RMC, Sandhurst – the Staff College – quartermasters, paymasters

Officers' promotion

and riding masters – medical and veterinary – Valentine Baker – Hope Grant – Frederick Burnaby

Cardwell's most remarkable reform was the abolition of the system whereby officers bought and sold their commissions. One unsatisfactory consequence of this was the undoubted slowing down of the rate of promotion. For instance, in 1875 there were 360 more officers in the infantry of the line who had served beyond the average periods for each of their ranks than there had been four years earlier at the time of abolition. To provide a partial remedy for this the Regulation of the Forces Act of 1871 had laid down that as a general principle every subsequent appointment to a lieutenant-colonelcy or to a majority was to be vacated every five years. This started to have an effect in 1876, but it would have taken many years before that effect could have been considerable. Further, it was calculated by the Royal Commission on Army Promotion and Retirement, which reported in 1876, that, for many years to come, under the system then existing the average age of an officer on attaining the rank of major would be upwards of forty-nine, and that the command of a regiment would only be acquired on the average at the age of fifty-three and a half.

A number of ways were considered in which this dilatory and unacceptable rate of promotion could be avoided. For example it would have been possible to create, as had been done in the Indian Staff Corps (see below), supernumaries, kept on full pay but not 'required for the needs of the service'. It would also have been possible to make large augmentations of establishments, or to alter the regimental organizations. All these 'exceptional methods and contrivances', designed to speed up promotion, had been resorted to from time to time in the Artillery, Engineers and other non-purchase corps over many years. They were complicated, uncertain in operation, 'based on no sure principle'[2] and inadequate for their purpose. They were also expensive.

The 1876 Royal Commission came to the conclusion, therefore, that what was wanted was a radical reform. Its recommendations were based upon forced as well as induced retirements, not only from the upper ranks but also (and this was the great departure) from the lower. The Commissioners were strengthened in their view by the fact that within the ten years previous to abolition forty-nine lieutenant-colonels, 133 majors, 1,051 captains and no less than 1,623 lieutenants and ensigns had sold out of the infantry alone. The numbers are likely to have been even higher, proportionately, in the cavalry, though figures are difficult to find. However, in 1874 it was calculated that between 1840 and 1870, on average, the rank of lieutenant-colonel in the cavalry of the line was obtained after a little over twenty years' service, that of major after fifteen, of captain after seven and lieutenant after two.[3]

Many and complicated were the Commission's recommendations, most of which were carried out over the next decade or so. The general rules for compulsory retirement included the limitation of regimental command to five years (later to four) and the retirement of majors after twenty-seven and captains after twenty years. But stated thus baldly, the system which followed the abolition of purchase might be thought to be straightforward. This was not so. To illustrate the principles of the reforms and their complexities, a single example, typical of many, may suffice: captains of the cavalry of the line who had attained that rank before the abolition of purchase (and for some years to come pre-abolition officers were, of course, a large majority in the army) became ineligible for promotion after completing twenty-five years' total service. After twenty years' service, however, they were offered two alternative retirement inducements. They could retire *from the army* with a step of honorary rank, as well as with whatever sum they were entitled to as over-regulation money and a pension of £180 a year carrying with it the right to a widow's pension. Alternatively they could retire *from their regiment* 'with unattached majorities, with a right, on accepting the step, to receive the amount of the over-regulation value of their captains' commissions.' Those who accepted this alternative were to 'have the chance of employment other than regimental, and to be entitled on retirement from the army to receive the regulation value of their captain's commission.'[4]

* * *

Ten years after the abolition of purchase, cavalry officers' pay was reduced. This was to compensate for the abolition of the forage stoppage. The new daily rates were:

	£	s	d		£	s	d
Lieutenant-colonel	1	1	6	Old:	1	3	0
Major	0	15	0		0	19	3
after three years' service as such	0	17	0				

	£	s	d		£	s	d
Captain	0	13	0		0	14	7
Lieutenant, on appointment as 2nd-lieutenant	0	6	8		0	9	0
after three years' service	0	7	8	2nd-lieutenant	0	8	0[6]

Adjutants, if captains, which they increasingly were, received extra pay of 2s 6d, or, if they were lieutenants, 3s 6d.[7] The spendable pay of a subaltern was still not all that far from being what it had been in the days of purchase: 'approximately the same as that received by the lowest grade of Government copy clerk.' Officers' pay was certainly not competitive with those of other professions. Winston Churchill's first book *The Malakand Field Force*, published in 1898, earned him in a few months two years' pay as a subaltern.[8]

In the 1890s a mere £4,000 was set aside annually as 'a reward' for proficiency in certain foreign languages. This was reduced to £1,000 in 1898–99.[9] When campaigning, there were various other financial perquisites available to officers. In Cairo, late in 1885, Lieutenant Marling of the Rifle Brigade, as a local captain, drew 'quite a decent screw. In the Mounted Infantry I get a Cavalry Captain's pay'. On top of that he received 5s a day 'command pay' and 3s a day 'Khedival allowance'. He had 'free quarters and rations and light allowance'. He was also 'given three chargers and forage and stabling for three ponies besides.' After the 1884 Suakin campaign, special gratuities were given to all ranks. Lieutenant-colonels drew £64, majors £30, captains £24 and lieutenants £15.[10]

In 1881 it was laid down that both lieutenants and captains, if not selected for promotion, had to retire at forty 'on £200 a year, subject to a deduction of £10 for every year's service less than twenty given'; a major had to retire at forty-eight on £250 or £300 a year 'according to service', and a lieutenant-colonel at fifty-five on £365 a year.* Though most of the regulations regarding forced retirements were to be inflexible, the authorities were to have wide discretion as to accepting or refusing voluntary ones. The inducements for these were standardized and increased

* Colonels retired at fifty-five on £420, major-generals at sixty-two on £700, lieutenant-generals at sixty-seven on £850, and generals at the same age on £1,000 a year.

in 1881. Up to the rank of major, for instance, officers received a gratuity of £1,200 if they retired after twelve years' service, while a major, after twenty years' service, received a pension of £200 a year, and a lieutenant-colonel £250 a year if he retired at any time.[11]* By all these means it was hoped to be able to regulate the promotion rate according to circumstances. On the whole the new system worked moderately well.

Yet it had drawbacks. It was not cheap. The annual cost to the State in officers' pensions was running in the 1890s at about £1,000,000. Efforts were made in 1881 to cut the cost by reorganizing the ranks in such a way that there were more lieutenant-colonels and majors and fewer captains and lieutenants in regimental establishments.[12] (See Appendix, p. 409 for a note on the establishment of cavalry officers.) But, for reasons chiefly connected with the failure to create the intended double companies in infantry regiments, the proportion of seniors to juniors actually worsened. Including general officers, in 1884 it was nearly one to two. Ten years later it had become about one to three. The other chief drawback was that the system failed to discriminate between the efficient and the inefficient. 'Age alone being the criterion, it often happens,' wrote General Sir John Adye in 1895, 'that promising officers who have no wish to retire, are compelled to do so – and this is not only a hardship on individuals, but injurious to the State.'[13]

Of course, it had not been intended by Cardwell in the 1870s or by Childers in the 1880s that age alone should be the criterion, 'seniority tempered by rejection' being the principle. But promotion by selection based on merit to be effective requires a ruthlessness which can too often lead to abuse and to which, at any rate, most men are reluctant to resort. In fact, the Commander-in-Chief's discretion was strictly circumscribed by the actual working of the very scheme which had been designed to allow him to pass over the inefficients. This scheme entailed the furnishing once a year by general officers on the staff of an exhaustive confidential report upon the competency, conduct and character of every officer. To this report there had to be appended a statement by each officer upon the work of those immediately below in rank. This was designed to make it impossible for a commanding officer to assist the interest of a subordinate by favoritism. When an officer was

* If any part of the service had been given before the age of twenty, these rates were subject to deduction.

adversely reported upon, the Military Secretary was required to inform him. This prevented an officer being injured in his fellows' estimation behind his back.[14] Human nature and the sense of loyalty to one's comrades being what they are, an officer had to be extremely and obviously inept and incapable to receive so harmful a report as to make it the clear duty of the Commander-in-Chief to pass him over. As the Duke said in 1857, 'selection is such a very delicate process . . . You virtually by the act of not promoting [an officer] destroy his whole career.'[15] In the first two years of the existence of the new form of confidential report only forty-eight officers in the whole army were reported as unfit for promotion. In the same period only one major, one captain and three lieutenants were actually passed over for promotion.[16] In practice, therefore, promotion was usually tied strictly to age. As late as 1901 a commanding officer declared that promotion was 'practically invariably by seniority. Occasional cases occur in which officers are superseded by their juniors through not having passed the required examination for their next step, but the fact of such examination being passed is no proof that the officer promoted is a bit better than the one over whose head he goes.'[17]

However, there were reasons other than incompetence which sometimes prompted the Commander-in-Chief to promote by selection rather than by seniority. For instance, in 1875, the Duke of Cambridge told the Royal Commission that, where in a cavalry regiment some senior lieutenants had been very young, he had passed them over once, bringing in older lieutenants from other regiments. 'But,' he added, 'I have never stopped the flow of promotion'.

In 1886 much publicity was given to the case of Major and Brevet Lieutenant-Colonel G. R. A. Denne who was twice passed over for promotion in the 4th Dragoon Guards. Denne had been mentioned in despatches and given his brevet after commanding the regiment during the race to Cairo after Tel el-Kebir in 1882 (see p. 304), his senior officer, Lieutenant-Colonel J. B. Shaw Hellier, having been indisposed just before the battle. He was nevertheless, as a result of a confidential report, passed over for promotion to the second lieutenant-colonelcy by a Major Philip A. Pope, who had not done duty with the regiment for eight years. What was suspicious about this 'selection' was the fact that Pope had been aide-de-camp to the general commanding at Aldershot during the last two years, but was now being superseded in that post by the general's own son. Denne's supporters rightly saw this transaction as 'a knavish trick'. So at the time had Shaw Hellier who wrote to Denne to say so. Four years later, when Shaw Hellier was due to give up his command, Denne was again passed over, this time for command of the regiment. The reason given was that Shaw Hellier's confidential report on him stated that his 'intemperate habits' made him unfit for command. Denne demanded an official Court of Inquiry, but was not allowed one. Instead, two senior officers were deputed to make an 'investigation'. A number of the allegations of intemperance were at once disproved as it turned out that Denne had not even been present on the specified occasions! Evidence of drunkenness on two other occasions was pretty inconclusive. More important, much evidence in Denne's favour was disallowed 'by superior instruction'. This included Shaw Hellier's 'knavish trick' letter of 1882 and letters to Denne from very senior officers categorically denying that they had ever, from personal observation or from reports, known him to be, in the words of General Prince Edward of Saxe-Weimar, commanding in Ireland, 'in the slightest degree addicted to drinking'.

Fed up by the way he had been treated, Denne eventually sent in his papers. His friends and relations then made the whole unsavoury business public. A letter to the *Army and Navy Gazette* stated:

> 'Lieutenant-Colonel Denne's success in Egypt could not be forgiven; in time of peace he had been passed over on account of confidential reports as not fit to hold the post of second in command. But in the time of need and danger, before the enemy, when the true man comes out, he fell into command, commanded with credit and distinction, and proved the unreliable nature of the confidential reports which had condemned him. This was the unpardonable offence . . . As long as he should remain in the service he would be [the authorities'] difficulty, a living reproach to them, and it was determined that he must go, and truly every effort has been made to force him to do so . . . Col. Denne has been "*done to death* by slanderous tongues".'

The Duke of Cambridge and Wolseley, as Adjutant-General, appear to come badly out of the case, but whether there was real substance in the charges of Denne's unfitness for command will never be known. The case illustrates the sort of difficulties which, for better or for worse, could hardly have occurred under the purchase system.[18]

* * *

During the Crimean War the demand for officers to replace casualties had proved extraordinarily difficult to meet. Equally, when in the late 1870s the reserves were called out, it became necessary to transfer young officers to regiments (so as to make them up to their increased establishments) before they had completed their full time as cadets at Sandhurst. Further, because in such emergencies the sudden influx of batches of young officers would ultimately produce stagnation in promotion to the higher ranks, the creation of a Reserve of Officers was decided upon. It was reckoned that to complete an Army Corps on mobilization, 450 extra officers would be needed. For each cavalry regiment sixteen extra would be required. This included ten to complete the service troops up to the authorized war establishment and for the depots, leaving six to meet casualties in the field.[19] Officers below the rank of captain remained on the Reserve list until they reached the age of forty; captains till they were forty-five and field officers till they were fifty. All officers who were medically fit and qualified and who had left the army, either by sale of their commissions before 1871, or on pension or gratuity since that year, were liable to serve in an emergency 'whenever the men of the Army Reserve shall have been recalled to the colours'. Other officers, such as captains and majors in the Yeomanry or the Volunteers, could apply to be placed on the Reserve. Any Reserve officer could be employed at other times than those of national emergency if he volunteered his services. All Reserve officers, when their services were no longer needed, received an addition to their pension or gratuity, 'according to the further service they may have given, or the rank to which they may have attained'.[20]

* * *

To obtain a commission in the army there were four main avenues: Sandhurst (see p. 107), Woolwich (for the Artillery and Engineers), the auxiliary forces and the universities. All candidates had to undergo competitive examinations. The small numbers of warrant and non-commissioned officers recommended for commissions by the Commander-in-Chief, and the even smaller numbers of gentlemen nominated by him, such as Queen's Cadets and Pages of Honour, were also generally required to take examinations of some sort. Thereafter, a sub-lieutenant (later second-lieutenant) who could not qualify for a lieutenancy within three years had to quit the army. To obtain each step in rank, examinations had to be passed in regimental duties, drill, military law and 'duties in the field'. Officers patronized 'crammers' (see p. 104) in preparation for these. Dr Maguire, one of the best known crammers (see p. 105), declared that promotion examinations were

> 'the only inducement to study . . . There is absolutely not the slightest chance', he told the Military Education Committee in 1901, 'of any of our officers getting any efficient professional training instruction once they join the Army, except sometimes at Garrison classes, or unless they go to "crammers", who are rapidly diminishing in numbers, as they find teaching does not pay, and as they are the objects of sneers and contempt . . . My lecturers would be much better off in the United States . . .
>
> 'I venture to say that an officer, however rich, who spent £20 a year on Military literature would be laughed at by all his friends, several Generals included . . .
>
> 'Officers should get leave to go to "crammers" as freely as they get leave to go to races, or sports, or balls, or gymkana fêtes. Crammers are encouraged in all the headquarters of the German Army Corps.'[21]

There were grades of certification. Lieutenant L. A. R. M. Bolton of the 13th Hussars, for instance, when in 1890 he 'passed for promotion' to captain was 'granted a special certificate' which stated that he was 'distinguished in Military Law and Tactics.'[22] The boards of examination, assembled twice a year, were appointed by general officers commanding districts at home and stations abroad. They consisted of a president, always a field officer, and two or more other field officers or captains. Officers of a candidate's regiment were not allowed to be members. The written questions were prepared and printed by the department of the Director-General of Military Education; but large parts of all examinations for promotion were conducted *viva voce* and by practical work in the field. When being tested in drill, a candidate, beside giving words of command, had also to explain to men on parade the

8. Indicted before a barrack-room court martial, Royal Horse Guards, c. 1895

9. Saddlers of the 17th Lancers, c. 1895

10. 'Lizzie', the pet bear of the 17th Lancers, c. 1895

11. 'The Stable Call Polka'

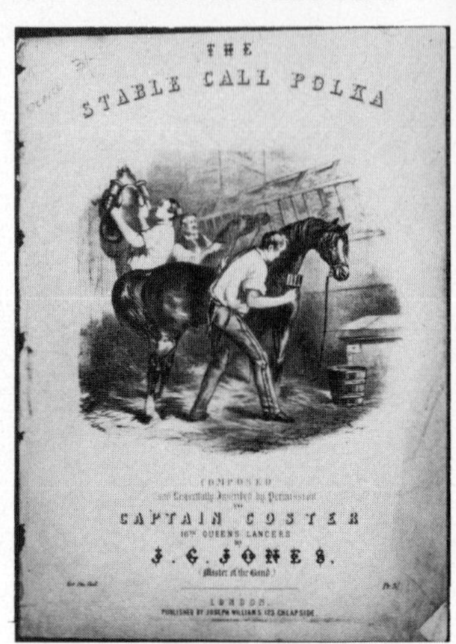

12. Stable duty, 3rd Hussars, c. 1895

exercise or manoeuvre he was about to put them through 'in a clear and audible manner'.[23] To gain the rank of lieutenant-colonel with command of a regiment no examination was required, and the principle of regimental seniority 'tempered by rejection' and 'subject to the power of the Crown to select at will' was meant to apply. After a lieutenant-colonel's actual service, he automatically became a full colonel. He was then eligible for employment during the succeeding five years or until he reached the age of fifty-five. Then, if he had not been promoted to major-general, he had to retire.[24]

* * *

The 1876 Royal Commission also grappled with the thorny question of the promotion of full colonels to the rank of major-general. Its chief recommendation was that all general officers should retire at the age of seventy. The system then in force was that the vacancies thus created were filled by colonels from the 'Amalgamated List', strictly according to seniority. This list had been formed after the Mutiny, upon the amalgamation of the Indian and Royal armies. It consisted of all the colonels in the two armies, arranged according to each individual's seniority. Because the 'Indian' colonels were all from the Indian Staff Corps (see Vol II, p. 250–1) where the system of promotion was quite different from that in the rest of the army, it so happened that for many years to come there would be a large preponderance of 'Indian' colonels, so much so that all vacancies would be filled by them to the exclusion of all others. To overcome this, it was decided, among other measures, to separate the list once more into two parts, Indian and British.[25]

* * *

Exchanges between officers on full pay or transfers from one regiment to another were permitted, but could only be effected through application to the Military Secretary and on the recommendation of the commanding officers concerned. These had to certify 'that the exchange does not originate in any cause affecting the honour or character, or professional efficiency of the officer.' If this meant anything much it referred, presumably, to monetary transactions. These nevertheless unquestionably took place. For instance a certain coolness was said in the 1890s to exist between the 4th Dragoon Guards and the 4th Hussars because a captain of the one telegraphed to a captain of the other: 'Please state your lowest terms for an exchange into 4th Dragoon Guards,' to which the reply was, '£10,000, a peerage and a free kit'. Exchanges and transfers were not allowed when a regiment was ordered abroad, except on health grounds. The medical certificate had to state 'whether the cause of the officer's inability to proceed abroad has or has not arisen subsequently to his having been ordered to embark'.[26]

* * *

The forty-three years between the abolition of purchase and the beginning of the First World War saw no very startling changes in the classes which provided officers. There was a rising but relatively small percentage of middle-class entrants, but most officers continued to come from among the sons of the nobility and gentry, the clergy and the officer corps itself. In the army at home, for example, the percentage of major-generals and above who came from the nobility and landed gentry was in 1830, seventy-eight, and in 1912, fifty-two. However, taking the home army as a whole, the percentage of officers from the aristocracy and the landed gentry was, in 1830, fifty-three; in 1875, fifty, and in 1912, forty-one. It is clear, by comparing these two sets of percentages that the aristocracy and landed gentry maintained their relative monopoly of the top ranks.[27] A stray set of statistics from the magazine of the Royal Military College at Sandhurst throws some interesting light on the parentage of cadets there in 1891. Out of 272, no less than 171 were sons of army officers; forty-five were sons of 'Private Gentlemen'; twenty-eight of clergymen; twenty-four of members of the Indian Civil Service, and seventeen of 'merchants'. Only seven were sons of peers.[28]

Lieutenant-Colonel Hermann Vogt of the German army who was correspondent of the *Kölnische Zeitung* during the Egyptian campaign of 1882, expressed wonder that among the English officers there were 'crowds of lords with £10,000 a year and more (!); but without knowing it beforehand one would not find it out . . .' He noticed that officers had 'almost unlimited liberty as regards uniform when not on duty . . . They appear in yellow leather lace boots and gaiters, comfortable trousers, fancy coats, broad belts, gigantic revolver pockets, scarves, etc. Everything that can be seen in London outfitting shops can be noticed here.' He remarked, too, that there was 'a regular mania among English officers for talking French, though they speak that language in the most abominable manner. Even when an English officer speaks German fluently, and the person to whom he is speaking talks English, he cannot resist the temptation to air his fragments of French.'[29] Another foreigner, Lieutenant-Commander Goodrich of the United States Navy, was deeply impressed during the same campaign by the British officers' 'desire to be in the midst of the work'. He observed 'their cheerful manner under even the most trying circumstances; and a commendable spirit of good-fellowship.' They only needed permission 'to go ahead and do their duty – the execution followed at once, and was marked by intelligence, zeal and perseverance.' They were 'young, active, zealous and capable men, of whom no service, however high its standard, need be ashamed.'[30] Writing in the late 1890s the historian of the British army found that 'nowadays it is nothing for subalterns of the smartest regiment of cavalry to pull off their coats and work with their men at the unshipping of horses from a transport.'[31] Though Churchill was scathing about the philistinism of the officers of the 21st Lancers, he wrote from Egypt in 1898 that he thought them 'a very capable lot . . . quite up to the average.'[32]

* * *

'Henceforth,' wrote Wolseley in 1881, looking to the increase in recruits for training under short service, 'the mode of life of the regimental officer will have to be very different from what it used to be; many hours of idleness daily, the long periods of leave, must be abandoned; he must make up his mind to the constant drudgery of teaching his own men, as the officers of the German army do; and like them he will sooner or later have to content himself with the six weeks' leave which is the maximum allowed.' That time had certainly not come in the 1890s when a cavalry officer at home enjoyed a good two and a half months' leave each year.* This was usually taken during the winter's hunting season.

* Opportunities for leave were, in fact, greater in the infantry. Major Roddy Owen, one of the best-known race-riders of the day and acknowledged as perhaps the most accomplished and daring 'gentleman rider' of the 1880s and 1890s, joined an infantry regiment because leave was so much more generously given than in the mounted arm. In the late 1870s he often got as much as six months. (Bovill, M. and Askwirth, G. R. '*Roddy Owen: A Memoir*, 1897, 8; Bridges, Sir Tom, *Alarms and Excursions*, 1938, 7.)

The historian of the Royal Army Veterinary Corps puts the situation with which post-purchase officers were faced most cogently:

> 'The process of emancipation, as well as the growth of capability to assume the powers now gradually being placed in the hands of unit commanders, was extremely slow; a new generation had to arise. A man who for years had never had a voice in the feeding or management of his horses, whose men were paid by a regimental Paymaster, drilled by an Adjutant or Regimental Sergeant-Major, and who had not the power to take a horse of his own troop out of the stable without permission from his commanding officer, was not likely to embrace with zeal a newly found freedom which he was not trained to use.'[34]

* * *

The gap between the really smart, expensive cavalry regiments and the rest seems to have widened conspicuously as the century drew to a close. In the Household Cavalry regiments the proportion of the landowning aristocracy actually increased, while the 10th Hussars was still the regiment with the highest social position in the cavalry of the line. 'Officers have lived in the 10th Hussars', wrote a snobbish 'British Officer' in an account of social life in the army in 1899, 'with an allowance of only £500 a year in addition to their pay, but they have rarely lasted long, and the average income of the officers is very much higher.' At the other end of the scale were such regiments as the 6th Inniskilling Dragoons which enjoyed the reputation of being one of the most inexpensive cavalry regiments.[34] The agricultural depressions of the 1870s and 1880s affected the pockets of some of the land-owning classes. 'Many men of high social position,' noted the same writer, 'have been unable to afford the expense of maintaining a son in a crack cavalry corps, and in consequence a number of these corps are now mainly recruited . . . from the sons of men who have made fortunes in trade.' Even before an officer had bought his chargers* or polo ponies, he found that in no cavalry regiment could he provide himself with the minimum initial outfit for less than £300. Indeed, as a modern historian of the army has put it, the need for a private income was an

* 'I have to pay £40 for one charger, £35 for the other' – Winston Churchill in 1898. (Churchill: *Companion*, 956.)

excellent substitute for purchase 'as a social filter'.[35] (See Appendix, p. 416 for dress regulations for cavalry officers, 1898.)

On joining a mess, each officer was required to pay an annual contribution to the mess-fund which was by Queen's Regulations limited to thirty days' pay. On promotion he paid a further sum not exceeding thirty days' difference between his old and new rates of pay. Beyond this, 'to defray the ordinary expenses of the mess,' each officer paid quarterly a sum equal to not more than eight days' pay. Numerous official exhortations to try to limit the expenses of messes had only as much attention paid to them as was allowed by the commanding officers. They were not always deterred by an edict of the 1880s which stated that 'any commanding officer who fails to carry out the spirit as well as the letter of these instructions will render himself liable to be removed from his corps'. One of these instructions read: 'The practice which has prevailed in regiments of presents of plate being made by officers on first appointment, on promotion or other occasions, is positively prohibited.' Another new regulation laid down that 'balls and other expensive regimental entertainments' could only be given with the sanction of the general commanding the formation or district. Further, when such an entertainment was contemplated, the commanding officer was supposed to circulate to all officers a paper notifying it. Only those officers who signed this paper were to pay any part of the expense of it. 'Commanding officers are to give their special countenance and protection to those officers who may, from motives of economy, decline to share in the proposed expense.' Commanding officers were enjoined to discountenance all extravagant living among their officers and to 'assist towards the attainment of so important an object by themselves setting an example in this respect.' The custom in some regiments of having luncheon marquees at race meetings was strictly forbidden, so was 'the expensive practice of entertaining regiments on arrival at or departure from a station'. The expenses of all entertainments had to be submitted to the general officer commanding 'at the same time that the mess arrangements are brought under his consideration, and in the confidential reports he will give his opinion whether the spirit of these orders has been loyally carried out.'

The day-to-day running of the mess was usually in the hands of a sergeant. He was known as the mess-man or caterer or 'superintendent of the mess-establishment'. Under him were varying numbers of troopers acting as mess waiters. 'Downstairs' there were the cook, often a Frenchman, receiving as much as £100 a year, the 'kitchen-man' who did the work done by a kitchen-maid in a civilian establishment, and the 'delft-man' who corresponded to the scullery-maid. There were usually two or three troopers for general kitchen fatigues.

Marriage for a young officer was virtually out of the question. Regiments had been known to 'fine' an officer on getting married.* This was because married officers paid only half of the annual mess subscription, which, as they seldom dined in the mess, meant that the cost of maintaining a proper establishment, being divisible into fewer parts, fell more heavily on the bachelor members. 'A married subaltern,' wrote the anonymous 'British Officer', 'is not likely to find himself popular, and, unless a very good chap, may receive a strong hint to remove himself and his bride to some other regiment.'[36]

Except on special mess nights, life in a cavalry mess was likely to be pretty dull. 'Shop' of any sort was generally taboo. So, except in a few untypical regiments, were many other subjects such as women, religion and politics. This left little else but sport and, above all and interminably, *horses*. When the young Winston Churchill was invited from Sandhurst to dine in the 4th Hussars' mess he found

> 'Twenty or thirty officers, all magnificently attired in blue and gold, assembled round a table upon which shone the plate and trophies gathered by the regiment in two hundred years of sport and campaigning. It was like a State banquet. In an all-pervading air of glitter, affluence, ceremony and veiled discipline, an excellent and lengthy dinner was served to the strains of the regimental string band.'[37]

After dinner, such games as billiards, threepenny pool, or sixpenny whist were indulged in. 'Don't lay down the law at whist,' advised a list of 'Don'ts' for young officers of 1888. 'This is simply intolerable to your superiors; besides which, however badly they may play, it is their recognized prerogative.'[38] In the last decades of the century there was a craze for snooker, a game which was invented in 1875 by certain bored officers during the monsoon in Jubbulpore.

* In some regiments the mess fund used to benefit from other fines. These could be imposed when an officer first wore the orderly officer's belt, when he fell off his horse on parade, or should he draw his sword on the mess premises.

On specified nights, all hell was let loose. Horseplay on a massive scale prevailed. 'Debagging' of unpopular officers was common. So was 'high cockalorum', in which one group made a series of arched backs for another to leap astride in an effort to bring them to the floor. Cock fighting consisted of two men, trussed, trying to overpower each other. Sir Hope Grant (see p. 118) had a reputation as a champion cock-fighter even when he was a general. Indeed senior officers often set an example of good fellowship (at the same time, perhaps, seeing that things did not get too far out of hand) by joining in the mess horseplay. During the occupation of Kabul in 1880, for instance, General Roberts dined with eleven 'Eton fellows' and then took part in storming an Harrovian mess. 'Nice sort of conduct on part of Sir Frederick Roberts,' he observed![39]

In London one night in the late 1870s a party of Royal Horse Guards and 9th Lancers made the mistake, while 'painting the town red', of knocking up a police station. They were all run in, fined and worst of all, found their names published in the newspapers![40]

Newly joined subalterns were usually pretty well snubbed till their fellows had had time to sum them up. In the outfit of one very rich young sub-lieutenant in 1880 when he joined the 9th Lancers was 'a solid silver tub! To make quite sure it wasn't merely a show piece of furniture,' wrote a fellow officer, 'his brother subalterns used to carry him home periodically after mess and "tub" him, till he thought proper to have it "melted".'[41]

* * *

No one gives a better description of 'the stiff and arduous training of a Recruit Officer' than the young Churchill.

> 'Every day long hours were passed in the Riding-School, at Stables or on the Barrack Square . . . In those days the principle was that the newly-joined Officer was given recruit's training for the first six months. He rode and drilled afoot with the troopers and received exactly the same instruction and training as they did. At the head of the file in the riding-school, or on the right of the squad on the Square, he had to try to set an example to the men. This was a task not always possible to discharge with conspicuous success. Mounting and dismounting from a bare-backed horse at the trot or canter; jumping a high bar without stirrups or even saddle, sometimes with hands clasped behind one's back; jogging at a

fast trot with nothing but the horses's hide between your knees, brought their inevitable share of mishaps. Many a time did I pick myself up shaken and sore from the riding-school tan and don again my little gold braided pork-pie cap, fastened on the chin by a boot-lace strap, with what appearance of dignity I could command, while twenty recruits grinned furtively but delightedly to see their Officer suffering the same misfortunes which it was their lot so frequently to undergo.'[42]

* * *

Before he reached this stage in his military career, the young Churchill had some difficulty in launching himself upon it at all. 'When,' he wrote, 'I failed for the second time to pass into Sandhurst, I bade farewell to Harrow and was relegated as a forlorn hope to a "crammer". Captain James and his highly competent partners kept an establishment [at 5, Lennox Gardens, off] the Cromwell Road. It was said that no one who was not a congenital idiot could avoid passing thence into the army. The firm had made a scientific study of the mentality of the Civil Service Commissioners. They knew with almost Papal infallibility the sort of questions which that sort of person would be bound on the average to ask on any of the selected subjects.'

At his third attempt, Churchill qualified for a cavalry cadetship at the Royal Military College, Sandhurst. 'The competition for the infantry,' he wrote, 'was keener, as life in the cavalry was so much more expensive. Those who were at the bottom of the list were accordingly offered the easier entry into the cavalry.'[43] Hubert Gough, later to command the 5th Army opposed to the great German offensive of 1918, claimed that he was taught 'more in three or four months' by Captain James than he had learnt in eight years of school.[44]

Another distinguished soldier who was sent to 'Jimmy's' was 'Boney' Fuller, (later Maj-Gen. J. F. C. Fuller), one of the foremost military theorists of the twentieth century. He thought that Captain James was either 'a clairvoyant, or he bought the examination papers from the printers a little in advance. Anyhow a week before our trials were due, each tutor in turn would issue to his students a list of about a dozen likely questions with their answers in full . . . All I can say is that their judgement was unerring. I got at least 50 per cent of the questions which had been given to me, and I had been wise enough to memorize the answers.'

In the 1870s and early 1880s *the* crammer of the day was Captain Lendy of Sunbury-on-Thames who was a Swiss. 'Air you beast,' he used to say to his pupils, 'I will get you een, but you will navair stop een – air – you will be cashiered no doubt.' John Western, who later had a distinguished career in the Punjab Cavalry, remembered that in every subject he took up,

> 'the gist of one or more of the questions actually set in the examination papers had been given to us by Lendy only a day or two before the examination took place. When one considers that there were probably only ten or twelve questions in each paper, and that ten or twenty marks might mean the difference between failure and success, it is easy to understand why parents anxious to place their sons in the Army were ready to pay the considerable fees demanded by such foreseeing teachers as these. How the knowledge was arrived at I know not, but it was arrived at.'[45]

In due course Lendy faded away to give primacy to 'Jimmy' James. 'Jimmy's' best known rival was Dr Thomas Miller Maguire.* He was a great character who defended his profession with outspoken vigour. 'The talk about "cram" is mere nonsense,' he wrote. 'It is never censured in any other professions . . . I never knew a man worth his salt at any subject who did not "cram" himself . . . I say the man who dawdles over books when he can "cram" is an ass.'[46]

There were other crammers whose success rates were almost as high. Two of these were Wolfram of Blackheath and Litchfield of Hampton Court. It was Litchfield who crammed Douglas Haig between his three years at Oxford and his entry into the Royal Military College at Sandhurst in 1884 at the advanced age of twenty-three.[47] Another was 'Old Billy' Northcott who took about forty youths at his establishment at Ealing. Young Percival Marling,

* Dr Maguire, giving evidence to the Military Education Committee of 1902, wrote amongst much else, that

'The influence of ladies on the whole life of the Army is fatal to study. They should be kept out of military life as they are kept out of legal life in the Inns of Court. It is an abomination that the caprices of titled feminine idlers and intriguers, or of the wives of generals, should make or mar an officer's career. The nation should put an end to this monstrosity at once.' (*E.T.O.C.*, 79.)

who was later to win the Victoria Cross at the battle of Tamai (see p. 317), was one of 'Northcott's lambs' in the late 1870s. 'There was no worse place in those days,' he wrote many years later, 'for boys than a crammer's. Most of us were from seventeen to nineteen, and had only just left school. The sole idea of life of quite half of them was to pawn their mathematical instruments and clothes and go up to Town for an orgy, or make love to the local barmaid.'[48]

Other crammers practised their trade abroad. In the 1870s the custom of taking boys away from public schools and sending them to the Continent to prepare for the army entrance examination was common. Colonel Charles à Court Repington, later to become one of *The Times*'s best known military correspondents, left Eton in 1875 for Colonel Roberts' establishment at Freiburg. There he 'forgot a good deal and learnt very little', so he returned home and went to 'Scoones's, then in Garrick Street. . . . It was a good crammer's, and I learnt a good deal in a short time, and, what was better, learnt how to learn, which I had never done at Eton.'[49]

Not all young men went to purely army crammers. The Reverend George Faithfull's establishment at Storrington, for example, also coached boys for the university. Colonel de Sales la Terrière of the 18th Hussars studied with this outstanding clergyman first in 1874 for his matriculation to Oxford, and again in 1887 for the army examinations. With him were four future Household Cavalry officers and numerous others destined for the smartest regiments of both arms. Faithfull's was clearly one of the highest class of crammers.[50]

For those, like Henry Wilson, the future field-marshal, who failed to pass into Sandhurst – he failed for Woolwich twice and Sandhurst thrice – there was a back-door method of obtaining a commission. In 1882 Wilson passed a qualifying test which allowed him to present himself at a competitive examination for a direct regular commission when he had completed two militia trainings. These he underwent as a lieutenant in the Longford Militia. Between them he was crammed, first under a Colonel Wilson (no relation) in Darmstadt, and then in England, eventually passing the competitive examination fifty-eighth in the list.

On occasion, especially if the establishments were low, those who did especially well in the entry examination avoided Sandhurst altogether. Robert Baden-Powell passed amongst the first six in 1876. To his and their surprise all of them were at once gazetted to regiments. Thus he left Charterhouse in June and found himself a full-blown subaltern of the 13th Hussars in India by November.[51]

* * *

After the abolition of purchase there were innumerable changes of establishment at the Royal Military College, Sandhurst. These were bewildering, even demoralizing, for the public schools which supplied so many of the cadets, and for the crammers. By 1889, though, a new mould had been formed. From that year, when the establishment of 360 was fixed, there were six companies of 'Gentlemen Cadets', and the course lasted one year or two terms. Three years later three terms were introduced, with 120 cadets being admitted every half year. At the same time the course was extended, more emphasis being placed on physical training particularly. More time, too, was devoted to riding instruction. For this purpose fifty horses were provided. These replaced the mounts on loan from regiments which had hitherto supplied the 'riding troop'. Musketry instruction seems to have become compulsory only in 1892, while the teaching of German and French, which, in the old days, had been a feature of the course, was only re-introduced in 1897. By the last days of the century the curriculum had become both extensive and detailed.[52]

Most cadets were under twenty. Such a one was Hubert Gough who obtained good marks in the qualifying examination when seventeen.[53] Another was Henry Rawlinson, later General Lord Rawlinson of Trent, who entered aged eighteen on a Queen's India Cadetship. A smaller number who came from the universities, such as Douglas Haig, were well into their twenties. Edmund Allenby, after leaving Haileybury, failed to pass into the Indian Civil Service. So, reluctantly, he sat, in 1880, for the Royal Military College. He was placed fifth out of 110 successful candidates. After only ten months, at the age of nineteen, he passed out twelfth, gaining a commission in the 6th Inniskilling Dragoons.[54]

Charles Repington, who went to Sandhurst in 1877, found there 'a capital staff of officer instructors and professors . . . while the gymnasium was excellent, and the riding school a great delight . . . We lived an open-air life and were savagely hungry after our long mornings in the open. . . . Though we wore tight red tunics, blue trousers with red piping, and shakoes, we were allowed to get into flannels in the afternoons.' Repington, who by today's standards would be condemned as an intolerable snob, lamented that there were

> 'of course, some dreadful outsiders amongst us, as could scarcely be prevented in an open competition[!]. I recall that three or four of these were discovered by us to have dined with the commandant's cook one night, and we decided to punish them in our own way. We took them down to the Lake and threw them in, and if they were not drowned it was not our fault. We ringleaders were put under arrest, and were told that we should certainly be rusticated for our pains. Impenitent but gloomy, we were marched before the commandant, who then and there gave us the deuce of a rowing before all the College and made our flesh creep. We expected the worst, when, to our huge joy, after the rowing was near its end, we saw a twinkle in Colonel Middleton's eye, and he ended by saying "and now that I have told you off and justice is satisfied, I don't mind telling you that I am d-----d glad you did it".'[55]

'Boney' Fuller, when he was admitted in 1897, found that the whole atmosphere

> 'was still Crimean. The Governor and Commandant, Lieutenant-General Sir C. J. East, dated from that war, having joined the Army in 1854. What he governed I have no idea, for the cadets saw him twice a term, when they arrived and when they departed. He was a fine-looking old man, and so was the Sergeant-Major, by name Scudamore, smart, portly, and possessed of a stentorian voice, which he was very much in love with. He would bellow out "Will that cadet stop dancing about like a columbine", and the cadet stopped . . .
>
> 'There were under him several Guards Sergeants, one of them a perfect fiend for smartness. But my drill instructor was of the Line, and bore the appropriate name of Muddle. He was a dear old man who understood boys . . .
>
> 'Our work at this centre of learning was even more archaic than it is today [1936]. We studied Phillip's *Manual of Field Fortifications* and Clery's *Minor Tactics* . . . The first of these books was illustrated with pictures of redans, gabions, wooden fuses, etc., all of which were copied into green-covered note-books, and painted in every imaginable colour. I rather liked this work, but why we were called upon to do it, I have no idea.

'Military law was a jest. Once a week for two hours at a stretch we sat in a classroom and read the Manual, and when we had exhausted those sections dealing with murder, rape and indecency, we either destroyed Her Majesty's property with our penknives or twiddled our thumbs. Fortunately our instructor was as deaf as a post, for this enabled us to keep up a running conversation, broken on occasions by a wild Irishman named Meldon, banging on his desk to make our teacher look up. Then Meldon would solemnly say, "Please, Sir, may I come up and kick your bottom?" and our unsuspecting master, not having heard a word, would invariably reply, "Come to me afterwards, boy, come to me afterwards." '[56]

Churchill's description of Sandhurst life is more flattering.

'I had a new start. I was no longer handicapped by past neglect of Latin, French or Mathematics. We had now to learn fresh things and we all started equal. Tactics, Fortification, Topography (mapmaking), Military Law and Military Administration formed the whole curriculum. In addition were Drill, Gymnastics and Riding. No one need play any game unless he wanted to. Discipline was strict and the hours of study and parade were long. One was very tired at the end of the day. I was deeply interested in my work, especially Tactics and Fortification . . . I did not much like the drill and indeed figured for several months in the "Awkward Squad", formed from those who required special smartening up. But the practical work in field fortifications was most exciting. We dug trenches, constructed breastworks, revetted parapets with sandbags, with heather, with fascines, or with "Jones' iron band gabion". We put up *chevaux de frises* and made *fougasses* (a kind of primitive land mine). We cut railway lines with slabs of guncotton, and learned how to blow up masonry bridges, or make substitutes out of pontoons or timber. We drew contoured maps of all the hills round Camberley, made road reconnaissances in every direction, and set out picket lines and paper plans for advanced guards or rear guards, and even did some very simple tactical schemes. We were never taught anything about bombs or hand-grenades, because of course these weapons were known to be long obsolete. They had gone out of use in the eighteenth century, and would be quite useless in modern war . . .

'I enjoyed the riding-school thoroughly, and got on – and off – as well as most. My father arranged in my holidays for me to go through an additional course of riding-school at Knightsbridge Barracks with the Royal Horse Guards . . .

'Horses were the greatest of my pleasures at Sandhurst. I and the group in which I moved spent all our money on hiring horses from the very excellent local livery stables . . .

'I learned several things at Sandhurst which showed me how to behave and how officers of different ranks were expected to treat one another in the life and discipline of a regiment . . .

'There were only three terms, at the end of which one advanced almost automatically from junior to intermediate, and then to senior. The generations were so short that in a year one was a senior. One could feel oneself growing up almost every week.'[57]

* * *

'A man,' said the Duke of Cambridge in 1875, 'who will stick to his regiment will learn his profession in that regiment much better than in any college'.[58] In view of the Commander-in-Chief's attitude, it is surprising that anything in the way of serious training for high command and staff duties ever got under way while he remained in office. Yet already by the early 1890s, in spite of the army's traditional suspicions of educated officers, considerable advances were being made in the status and in the products of 'the only school of strategy, of organization, of Imperial Defence, in the Queen's dominions',[59] namely the Staff College at Camberley, founded in 1858. Nonetheless the old postures prevailed in many quarters. When in 1889 Count Gleichen told a fellow officer that he thought of competing for entry, he received the following advice: 'Say nothing about it to your brother officers, or you will get yourself jolly well disliked'.[60] In an army where for most officers, as for the Duke, the regiment was everything, to leave it for wider fields, thereby throwing your duties upon your fellows, was still frowned upon. Yet through the indirect influence of Wolseley especially, it slowly became more respectable, and for the ambitious man even desirable, to sport 'p.s.c.' ('passed staff college') after one's name. At least thirty-four officers who had been through the two-year course at Camberley held staff appointments in the 1882

Egyptian campaign, fourteen of them on Wolseley's headquarters staff.

Until the seven-year reign of Colonel Edward Bruce Hamley, who became Commandant of the Staff College in 1870, it was 'in danger of perishing from infantile debility'.[61] Yet in his time there was still no guarantee that a 'p.s.c.' would obtain an officer a place on the staff, although the establishments of staffs were considerably larger than the College's output could fill. All field officers were still considered to be 'qualified for the staff' without having been at the College, for which only captains and subalterns were eligible.[62] Further, numbers of officers were still able to acquire a 'p.s.c.' without attending the course, by passing the terminal examination, which was in many ways the least important part of it. Virtually the only attempt made to teach an officer anything about arms other than his own was represented by two six-weeks' attachments during the course. The usefulness of these depended upon what instruction his hosts gave him. Though in many cases this was minimal, many officers seem to have thought their attachment to other arms the most valuable part of the course.

In 1877 one of the early signs of a move away from parochialism was the admission for the first time of a small proportion of officers from the Indian army. What an advance this was can be appreciated when it is considered that in 1884 young Ian Hamilton could write from Egypt: 'The fact is Indian Service is a thing apart and the Horse Guards take very good care that none of the outsiders come on these sorts of excursions.' Churchill, fourteen years later, wrote home from Wadi Halfa that Kitchener's army had 'a lordly disdain for all Indian tricks here.'[63]

Under Hamley the excessive emphasis placed on pedantic theory and on mathematics was gradually replaced by outdoor reconnaissances and even elementary staff schemes. From the early 1880s two officers, instead of only one as hitherto, from any one regiment were allowed to enter, and the Commander-in-Chief was empowered to nominate two officers, so long as they had passed some sort of qualifying examination. In 1882 applied science entered the curriculum for the first time. This 'also embraced a study of forage and veterinary work.'[64]

A committee of 1880 still found that some candidates appeared 'to be more desirous of escaping regimental duty and disagreeable foreign stations than of qualifying for the Staff service.'[65] Until the early 1880s the numbers competing for entry declined. There were only thirty-three in 1878 and twenty-seven in 1879. As a result of the strong temptation of active service in Egypt and the Sudan in the mid-1880s numbers of competitors for places declined in those years, too, but in 1887 there were seventy-three, the establishment having been fixed the previous year at sixty-four, thirty-two entering annually. From this period one tour of the European battlefields each year was actually financed out of public funds. Though most students entered in their mid-twenties, in 1885 the maximum age for entry was fixed at thirty-seven.

It was difficult to persuade really good instructors to serve at Camberley, for unlike their counterparts in the German army, they were thought of as a breed entirely separate from serving officers. But a few really outstanding men made the sacrifice. Prominent amongst them was Colonel J. F. Maurice, who became Professor of Military Art and History in 1885. A most conscientious teacher, Maurice revolutionized the teaching of military history at the College. He realized that 'for the studious soldier the object was not merely to acquire information about battles "but to improve his judgement as to what ought to be done under the varied conditions of actual war". In the study of military history it was necessary first to ascertain accurately what the facts really were; second, to ascertain the causes that led to the facts; and third, to endeavour to draw sound conclusions for the future.' 'The greatest thing,' Maurice told a War Office Committee in 1888, 'against which I have always to fight is the natural tendency to cram . . . I look upon that as the greatest enemy to education that there is.'[66]

Generally speaking, until the last decade of the century the Staff College, instead of being, in the words of Colonel Frederic Maude, who graduated in 1891, 'a true University, for experimental and original research,' was still 'a kind of repetition school for the backward.'[67] Nevertheless, by 1890 the College was attracting an increasingly large number of outstanding students. At the same time two very remarkable men took over the direction of affairs. General Henry Hildyard became Commandant in 1893. It was he who eventually got rid of the idea that preparation for written examinations was the most important business of the College. For the first time students were classified according to their work throughout their two years. It has been claimed that he 'transformed the College into a "mental gymnasium" for the Army just at a time when the future leaders of the First World War era were passing through.'[68]

In 1892 Maurice was replaced by Colonel George Henderson as Professor of Military Art and History. 'Henders', as he was affectionately known, was possessed of, in the words of Hildyard, 'a practical mind that discarded at once methods impracticable in war, and untiring industry and patience.'[69] To him, under whose spell they fell, many of the chief actors in the awful drama of the First World War attributed a large measure of what successes they enjoyed. Amongst these were Captains Haig and Allenby, both cavalry officers, both made field-marshals and both elevated to the House of Lords. Both, too, were at Camberley in 1896-7. Of their batch of thirty-two, fifteen others became generals, of whom eight were knighted, while only one of the remainder who stayed in the army got no further than colonel.* Haig was thirty-five when he entered. Like Allenby (see below), Haig failed at his first attempt in 1894, largely because in his case it was discovered that he was colour-blind. He eventually entered without a further examination, on the Commander-in-Chief's nomination. Though he made a few lifelong friends he was not widely popular. So much was this so that 'no one would sit next to him at mess if there was a place vacant elsewhere.'[70] But his capacity for hard work, his contempt for empty forms and pedantry, and his concern 'above all else with the elucidation of general principles on which alone right action rested' stood him in very good stead. In after years he used to relate an apocryphal anecdote: An inspecting officer, addressing three students, said, 'Your commandant tells me that you all three show independence of judgment, intelligence, willingness to accept responsibility, and self-reliance: all these drawbacks you will in time learn to correct.'[71]

When Allenby decided to sit for the entrance examination, it was considered an 'almost unique step in the Inniskillings'. His first attempt in 1895 failed, but he got in at his second. Unlike Haig, although both worked extremely hard, Allenby was popular with all. He was elected Master of the Draghounds, 'because,' said a fellow student, 'we did not want Douglas Haig.' The same student, Captain Edmonds, later official historian of the Great War, referring to Allenby's notorious unpunctuality, wrote: 'A cavalryman who had actually passed in by competition could take liberties!'[72]

* One resigned because he had inherited a fortune. Another shot his mother-in-law, her lawyer and himself in *une drame passionelle.* (Edmonds, Sir J. 'Owl Pie' (*Staff College Journal*), 1956, reprinted in Young, F. W. *The Story of the Staff College, 1858–1958,* 1958, p. 18.)

It was during Haig's and Allenby's years that staff tours and war games first really took hold in the curriculum, but in some respects things had not much changed from the previous decade when a student could remark that 'one learnt next to nothing about the duties which a staff officer actually has to perform either in war or in peace'. This was not surprising since very few of the small instructional staff had ever themselves been staff officers. 'Wully' Robertson, who entered a year after Haig and Allenby, and who was probably the first officer promoted from the ranks to do so, thought the course had been a great help to him. Especially was this so when he became Chief of the Imperial General Staff from 1915 to 1918. He claimed that his personal acquaintance with his fellow students, so many of whom were serving under him, and, above all, the fact of having imbibed 'the same basic principles of strategy and tactics' and 'the same methods of administration' as they had, avoided misunderstandings at the highest level.[73]

Nearly all warrant and non-commissioned officers who gained commissions did so as specialist officers. Virtually all quartermasters, paymasters* and riding masters came into this category. Adjutants, however, were being drawn more and more from the ordinary officer class.

In 1870 medical officers, who until then had formed as much an integral part of their regiments as any other officers, were removed from all of them, except those of the Household Cavalry. They came henceforth under the Principal Medical Officers of Districts. Three years later both the regimental and staff branches were united to form one department, serving under their own officers, and

* In the Royals there retired in the late 1890s, after thirty-six years' service, Quartermaster Webb. He was a man of vast bulk and magnificent physique, a great boxer and addicted to hunting. Asked by an inspecting general to what he attributed his success in his job, he replied: 'Well, sir, I never said I couldn't, not I wouldn't, nor as I didn't know 'ow.' (Atkinson, 347.)

Honorary Major John Dyer, Paymaster of the 11th Hussars, was another 'character' of whom many amusing stories were told. Once, in India, he extended hospitality to a young officer, known as 'Chicken Hartopp', infamous for his outrageous behaviour. When the time came for the young hussar to leave Dyer's bungalow, he was sent on his way thus: 'Goodbye, 'Artopps! I'm glad you're going. You've made my 'ouse an 'ell by day, and a brothel by night!'

He was a much sought after speaker at social gatherings. At a dinner presided over by the Viceroy he started a speech thus: 'Your Excellency, my lords, brother hofficers and damned, kiss my arse aides-de-camp.' (May, Maj.-Gen. Sir E. S. *Changes and Chances of a Soldier's Life*, 1925, 59-60.)

wearing their own distinctive uniform. At the same time all regimental hospitals, again with the exception of the Household Cavalry, were abolished at home and gradually replaced by garrison establishments. For obvious reasons this was a long overdue reform of great beneficence, especially in war. Never again, for instance, would the inflexibility of the regimental system lead to the Crimean situation where surgeons of units in action were heavily involved in attending to casualties, while those in units not engaged stood idly by, the Principal Medical Officer having no power to intervene.[74]

Even after numerous improvements were effected in the status and conditions of medical officers, there was nearly always difficulty in completing the establishment. This is not to be wondered at since pay, compared with civilian doctors, was poor. The majority of officers retired as surgeons or surgeon-majors at the age of fifty on £365 a year. In civil life doctors' annual earnings at that age were about £800 to £1,000. Under these circumstances, the likelihood of many really good men entering the service was not great. The ever-present hand of Treasury parsimony in army matters is well illustrated by the fact that when in the 1880s medical officers' pay was increased, the establishment was reduced from 1,050 to 893 in compensation.[75]

In the cases of both medical and veterinary officers, the question of 'relative rank' caused perpetual trouble. Both much resented the fact that they were denied the precedence and other advantages which attached to their relative combatant ranks. Government, as well as most senior generals, resisted the officers' complaints right up to the 1890s, when their reasonable requests were at last granted in some measure.

* * *

Captain Douglas Haig told Sir Evelyn Wood in 1898 that the Egyptian cavalry during Kitchener's campaign was lucky to have an excellent veterinary surgeon. 'He has done wonders . . . in saving camels and horses. Yet, though everyone has been rewarded, the only department ignored in honours is the veterinary.'[76] From this it might be supposed that vets who always hitherto had been treated as inferior to other specialist officers underwent no improvements in their status during the three decades before 1900. In fact this was not so. Particularly under James Collins, who in 1876 became Principal Veterinary Surgeon at home, and his brother who held the same post in India, important reforms both as regards standing and efficiency were forced upon a reluctant War Office. Nevertheless, that they were still regarded as a lower class in some degree cannot be denied. For instance, when a new form of confidential report on vets attached to regiments was introduced in 1882, commanding officers were asked especially 'to report on the officer's strict sobriety', a report which was required in no other case. Ten years later this insulting inquiry came unofficially to the Adjutant-General's ears. He rightly had it expunged. It shows eloquently enough how vets were thought of, but it also, perhaps, indicates that some of them were not of the highest (or at least most sober) character. This would not be surprising since Collins often found difficulty in filling the vacancies on his establishment since 'the emoluments in private life' for vets (as in the case of medical officers) were higher than in the army. Moreover, the prospect of long service in India was a further deterrent. It was easier, for example, in the case of cavalry regiments, to get vets to serve in those 'heavies' which never went to India, such as the Royals and the Scots Greys.[77]

In 1878 vets ceased to be regimental officers and came henceforth directly under the Principal Veterinary Surgeon. At first this did not apply to cavalry regiments because, since each was responsible for providing its own remounts, there fell to regimental vets important remount duties and it was felt that these might have suffered from frequent changes of officers. Nonetheless, in 1881, although the regimental remount system was not abolished till 1887 (see p. 389), vets were withdrawn from cavalry regiments, transferred to the Army Veterinary Service and required to don that service's uniform. The Household Cavalry, however, kept their own vets, and so, until 1911, did yeomanry regiments.

The Egyptian campaign of 1882 was the first in which a Principal Veterinary Surgeon formed part of the headquarters staff. It was also the first which saw a C.B. conferred on a vet and virtually the first in which vets were mentioned in despatches.[78]

* * *

There died in Egypt in 1887, aged sixty, one of the most remarkable cavalrymen of the age. Colonel Valentine Baker, brother of Sir Samuel Baker, the distinguished traveller and sportsman, had commanded the 10th Hussars from 1860 to 1872. Ever inquisitive about military matters, he had been imprisoned for a short time by the French during the Franco-German War of 1870–1, suspected of being a German spy. In 1873 he travelled through Persia collecting and publishing much valuable military information reflecting upon the Russian advance into Central Asia.

In 1875, when he was forty-eight, whilst serving as assistant quartermaster-general at Aldershot, he was sent to prison on a charge of indecently assaulting a young lady in a railway carriage. Whether he was guilty or not, it is certain that even by the standard of the day there was not enough evidence to convict him, since there was only the twenty-two year old girl's evidence to set against his own. There has seldom been a case in which the press and public so crucified and pre-judged a man before his trial. The hearing was a farcical affair held amidst a noisy crowd which besieged the court. The jury was chiefly composed of small Croydon shopkeepers and the judge was blatantly hostile from the start.

On his conviction Baker was dismissed the army, 'Her Majesty having no further occasion for his services'. Her Majesty indeed, like so many of her subjects, had no doubt of his guilt. 'Was there ever a thing,' she wrote to her daughter, the Princess Royal, after the trial, 'and such a position for a poor young girl? And what a disgrace to the Army. No punishment is severe enough . . . Some officers and people tried to excuse him by abusing the poor, unprotected girl but the country are furious with him and he will be disgraced for life . . . What is to happen if officers, high in position, behave as none of the lowest would have dared to do, unless a severe example is made? I own I feel most indignant.'[79]

In the Russo-Turkish war of 1877–8, Colonel Baker took service under the Sultan, soon being given command of a division. In the battle of Tashkessan on 1 January, 1878, in the face of overwhelming Russian superiority, he fought one of the most brilliantly successful rearguard actions on record. He was at once promoted to lieutenant-general. In 1882, Baker Pasha (as he was now known) entered the Egyptian service in command of the police. His subsequent military career is told on p. 309. His earlier career, as one of the few really thoughtful, progressive innovators in the British cavalry, is frequently referred to in Volume II of this work. His influential pamphlet, *The British Cavalry*, published in 1858, together with other publications, marked him as one of the outstanding authorities on mounted tactics and organization.

Whether he was criticizing the poor quality of stable jackets, or, surprisingly, advocating the retention of the sabretache, condemning the cramming system for Sandhurst, deploring the lack of opportunities for officers to fit themselves for war, criticizing the weights carried by troopers, pleading for more rational saddles, pioneering the carriage by train of mounted units, or introducing the squadron system into his regiment, he was always jolting the establishment, questioning the status quo or challenging the fashionable. Had not his career in the British army been cut short, the influence he would have exerted upon the development of the cavalry in the 1870s and 1880s might have been very beneficial. Baker was very far from being the typical cavalry officer.

A slightly more typical cavalry officer of an earlier generation died in 1875 aged sixty-seven. What made General Sir James Hope Grant untypical were his proficiency on the 'cello and his all-pervading religious beliefs. More typical were his passion for all sports, including golf, his skill and daring as a rider and his personal bravery. His uprightness was legendary. He thought nothing when a major of risking his career by exposing the drunken officer commanding the 9th Lancers (see Vol I, 269). When he himself commanded the regiment, he forced the retirement of seven of his officers who were addicted to gambling, having earlier removed the billiard-table upon which they habitually played.[80]

Though devoted to hunting, Grant had no eye for country, was quite useless at map-reading and, indeed, 'could never find his way even in familiar ground, nor even tell the points of the compass'.[81] Further, unlike his brother, Sir Francis, who became President of the Royal Academy, he was incapable of drawing the simplest sketch. His greatest deficiency, however, was his chronic inability to express himself clearly either in speech or on paper. Nevertheless he had an almost uncanny sense of how to fight battles. Wolseley, who was for a long time on his staff and of whose 'advanced views' he was champion, wrote of him that 'the protection of a camp or of an army on the march, and the best mode of attacking an enemy's position, all came as naturally to him as harmony'.[82]

Born in 1808 of a good Scottish family, Grant joined the 9th Lancers as a cornet at the age of eighteen. He served exclusively with that regiment for thirty-two years, until he was promoted major-general in 1858. This was very rare, if not unique, in the days of purchase. It is likely, too, that he was the first cavalry officer ever to attain both his majority and his lieutenant-colonelcy without purchase (see Vol I, 158).

Grant's military career is referred to in the two earlier volumes of this work. His conduct of the China War of 1860, and, above all, his marvellous services, at the age of fifty, in the suppression of the Indian Mutiny, place him high among the British military commanders of the mid-nineteenth-century. After the China War he was appointed Commander-in-Chief of the Madras Army, in 1865 Quartermaster-General and in 1870 commander of the camp at Aldershot. There, during the next three years, against much opposition, he initiated the first autumn manoeuvres and introduced war games and military lectures. His reform of the entire system of outpost duties, based chiefly on his Mutiny experiences, was of enormous benefit to the British cavalry.

On his death bed an aide-de-camp burst into tears. 'What's the matter, Bobby?' asked Grant. 'Why, death is only like going from one room into another.'[83]

* * *

Lieutenant-Colonel Frederick Gustavus Burnaby, who joined the Blues in 1859 and was killed at Abu Klea in 1885 aged forty-three (see p. 336), was one of the small number of cavalry officers who were active politically. He only succeeded, though, in entering parliament (as an extreme conservative) a year before his death. Burnaby, the son of a Leicestershire squarson, was without doubt the most colourful British cavalry officer of his time. Six foot four inches in height and forty-six inches round the chest, he is reliably reported on one occasion to have carried a small pony under his arm, but over-indulgence of his passion for gymnastics seriously weakened both his heart and lungs. One of his other passions was assuaged by his nineteen ascents in balloons, many of them made alone. He actually, in 1882, crossed the Channel from Dover to Envermeu in Normandy, reaching to a height of 10,000 feet. He had a thin, piercing voice, 'dago'-Jewish features and married an Irish lady who was obsessed with Alpine mountaineering in winter.

His exceptional gift for languages – he was fluent in French, German and Italian and nearly so in Spanish, Russian, Turkish and Arabic – served him well on his extensive intrepid travels. These he fitted into his lengthy winter leaves. In 1874 *The Times* appointed him their correspondent first at the Carlist camp in the

Spanish Civil War and later with General Gordon in the Sudan. The exceptionally hard winter of 1875–6 saw him undertaking his famous 300 mile 'Ride to Khiva' across the steppes of Russia. On this, as on all his expeditions, he travelled very light, his baggage never exceeding eighty-five pounds. His racy account of this adventure went into eleven editions in a year. Next season he spent five months looking at the Turks in Armenia and Asia Minor. For his book describing the hazards he faced he received an advance of £2,500. It ran to seven editions.

In 1877 Burnaby joined Valentine Baker and commanded a Turkish brigade under him at Tashkessan (see above). The rest of his short career is told elsewhere in this volume (see p. 336). After his death, Wolseley wrote in his campaign journal: 'How delighted the P. of W. and the D. of C. will be that poor Burnaby is killed. His high military spirit, energy, zeal and remarkable personal courage were not sufficient in the eyes of those Royal tailors to cover up the fact that socially Burnaby was distasteful to them and their set.'[84]

* * *

Another well known if not very distinguished cavalry officer died in 1888. He was Field-Marshal the Earl of Lucan whose command of the cavalry in the Crimea was such a conspicuous failure. (See Vol II, p. 108.) He was eighty-seven. In 1880 there died another Crimean veteran, General Lord George Paget, who, commanding the 4th Light Dragoons, was second-in-command to Cardigan in the charge of the light brigade at Balaklava. He was sixty-two.

3

'The army at home is too weak to supply the army abroad satisfactorily under our present conditions of service.'

'When a cavalry regiment goes abroad, it leaves a depot behind, the only difficulty is to get the regiment fit to go.'

GENERAL SIR REDVERS BULLER, VC,
Adjutant-General in 1891.[1]

(i)

India: size of the Indian army – number of European cavalry regiments in India – the Cavalry Depot at Canterbury – high, medium and low regimental establishments

The annual average size of the army during the ten years 1876–85 was 182,822 men. Of these, 60,503 constituted the European portion of the army in India. For every 66.83 square kilometres of the sub-continent and for every 3,800 native soldiers, there was but one European soldier. Captain Kirchhammer of the Austrian General Staff calculated that this proportion would give as garrison to Paris 483, Vienna 218, Petersburg 174 and Rome 64 men. There were about 126,000 native troops, making the total Indian forces somewhere around 189,000 strong.[2] It was an amazingly small army for such vast tasks as maintaining order in the sub-continent, controlling the North-West Frontier, and, increasingly, supplying troops for campaigns outside India.

Yet the difficulty of keeping up the establishment of European regiments, as well as in South Africa (and since the occupation of Egypt, there too), was even greater under the short service system than it had been before its introduction. Beside the increased rate of turnover inherent in the system, and encouraged on welfare grounds,* which added to expense, there was hardly ever a large enough number of men to complete the establishments. This is demonstrated by the fact that with the Indian establishment remaining the same, annual replacements rose from 5,608 in 1871 to

* 'I think that every commanding officer in India,' said the Inspector-General of Cavalry in 1891, 'advocates that men should be allowed to come home on furlough after five years' service.' (Wantage, 446.)

8,596 in 1878.[3] In 1891 the whole army, at 182,700 men, was 6,400 short of establishment and this figure did not of course include men on the sick list.[4] Lord Wantage, the chairman of the War Office Committee which was set up in 1891 to look into the terms and conditions of service in the army saw 'our army at home' as 'a nursery for supplying men for India and the Colonies'. With this Buller, the Adjutant-General agreed. 'But,' he added, 'it is not a big enough one.'[5]

So far as the cavalry was concerned, there were never less than six, or more than nine regiments in India at a time. Each spent between nine to eleven years on its tour of duty. There were always seven regiments at home meant to be ready to go out of Britain, not only to India, but anywhere they were required. Their total establishment was 4,100 troopers (of whom, in 1891, 956 were fresh recruits). But in fact, after medical examination, there were usually only some 2,900 men actually fit for service. Fit reserve men and volunteers from all the other regiments at home were used to make up the deficiency. Until 1897 each regiment when overseas maintained a depot, generally at Canterbury* and sometimes at Colchester, to which all recruits were sent initially. Two regimental officers were left there to see to the training of their recruits, under the direction of the commandant. The non-commissioned instructors were mostly taken from the individual regimental depots; but the riding establishment was largely manned by warrant and non commissioned officers awaiting commissions as riding masters. 'It not infrequently happened,' wrote Sergeant-Major Mole, stationed at Canterbury, 'that one of them took breakfast in our mess as a non-commissioned officer, and then, the *Gazette* having come to hand, found himself in orders and lunched in the officers' mess.' Mole found the sergeants' mess at Canterbury 'a very fine one . . . It is luxuriously fitted, on its walls in its plate-chest are several handsome presentation articles from non-commissioned officers who have passed through it on their way to a commission.'[6]

The establishment of each regimental depot was altered from time to time. In 1881, for instance, it was eighty-five, but in 1891 it had risen to 119. In neither year was it possible to supply the necessary drafts. A Cavalry Organization Committee reported in

* The staff of the Cavalry Depot at Canterbury consisted of a Commandant (Colonel), Assistant Commandant and Superintendent of the Riding Department (Colonel), Assistant (Major), Paymaster, Riding Master (Hon. Major) and Quartermaster (Hon. Major).

1882 that the average strength of each depot would have to be 135 if the regiments overseas were to be sure of keeping up their strengths.[7] The deficiency came about not only because the depot establishments were not large enough, but also, more fundamentally, because recruits were taken at eighteen but not allowed to go to India until they were twenty (see p. 126). The vagaries of the recruiting system meant that some depots were occasionally over strength but more often that others were under strength. Further, since drafts were generally sent out only once a year, in September, and the time-expired men and invalids returned from India, again only once a year, in May, there were seasonal variations in the numbers of men both in the regiments and in their depots.[8]

In 1897 Canterbury and other depots were abolished, and home regiments from then onwards were required to supply all drafts for those overseas. For this purpose the home establishments were raised. Hussar regiments at home, for instance, which consisted of 603 rank and file in 1895, were augmented to 668 in 1897. The number of horses rose from 350 to 464. Regiments from then on were affiliated or 'brigaded' for the purpose of furnishing drafts. The 4th, 13th and 19th Hussars, for example, were thus incorporated. The 4th and 19th were in India, the 13th at home. So, on the suppression of the depot system, men from the defunct depots of the two regiments in India were sent to the 13th, while men sent home from the other two also joined it.[9] By the early 1890s the classifications of light, medium and heavy cavalry had ceased to have any real meaning, and regiments were affiliated without regard to their classification. From 1889 the old 'heavies' were placed on the roster for service in India. In fact two of them, the 1st King's Dragoon Guards and the 2nd Dragoon Guards, had already gone to India in the early 1880s.

Other complications resulted from the extraordinarily numerous experimental alterations in the establishment of regiments which took place from time to time. (See Appendix, p. 410 for some examples and p. 409 for a note on the establishment of cavalry officers.) In the 1880s and 1890s, for example, there were three types of establishment: lower, medium and higher.* When the 8th Hussars returned from India in 1889 and was joined by its depot, the regiment was 609 strong. It was ordered to transfer fifty men to the Reserve. These were over and above the ordinary time-expired

* The 1898 edition of *Cavalry Drill* laid down that eight regiments of those serving at home were always to be on the higher establishment. (*Cav. Drill*, 19.)

men. When these, too, had departed, the regiment was reduced to 450, which was more or less the medium establishment. On the other hand when the 9th Lancers returned home late in 1885, out of the 434 of all ranks who had gone out to India ten years before, 197 had died or been invalided by reason of disease or wounds. 126 had been discharged or transferred to other corps. Only two officers and 87 rank and file had served continuously with the regiment. To make it up to 429 of all ranks, 109 had to be transferred from other units. It took a regiment about eight years after its return to Britain before it reached the higher establishment and was once again ready to go overseas.[10]*

In 1890 the lower establishment was reduced from 424 to 392 warrant officers, non-commissioned officers and men. This entailed, according to Lieutenant-Colonel MacGeorge, commanding the 6th Dragoon Guards, 'a lot of extra work on the men, especially during the furlough season, when it happens frequently that some men are grooming three horses; I have been obliged,' he told the Wantage Committee, 'to stop the furloughs of all men who become time-expired before 1st June, 1892, otherwise we should have been too short-handed to go on.' One of the troubles was that in the three kinds of establishment the difference between the number of men and the number of horses varied. In the case of the lowest type the difference was 122 and in the highest 259. Why this was so it is hard to say, since in each of the three types of establishment the number of 'employed men' (such as officers' servants, saddlers, cooks, clerks and regimental tradesmen) was usually the same. Lieutenant-Colonel MacGeorge complained that he 'had to make the band groom two horses lately, and they consider that a great grievance, and I think it prevents them re-engaging.' He added that when recruits began to find out that work was harder in regiments on the lower establishment, they would avoid such regiments.[11]

By 1898 the twelve regiments at home were formed into four brigades (or two divisions), with their headquarters at Aldershot, Canterbury, the Curragh and Colchester. Each regiment consisted of three or four squadrons depending upon which class of establishment it was in. The fourth was always to be the 'reserve squadron'. This was to consist of 'the band-serjeant and corporal, the bandsmen, the corporal rough-rider, the clerks, waiters, Maxim gun detachment, and the most backward recruits' – rather a ghostly

* A cavalry regiment in Germany at this time comprised 540 men, in Austria 876, in France 665, in Russia 859. (Wantage, 448.)

unit! Each squadron was composed of three or four troops, again depending upon its strength. 'General Rules' were laid down to guide commanding officers: 'There should never be more than thirty-two nor less than nineteen men in the ranks of a troop; thirty-two to twenty-four men will form a troop of sixteen files [a file consisted of a front rank man and a rear rank man]; while the maximum for a twelve-file troop is twenty-three men, and the minimum nineteen.'[12]*

As in most other respects, the cavalry suffered less from shortage of men than did the infantry. In 1891, for instance, the actual strength of the cavalry establishment at home and overseas, at 17,157, was only 130 short of establishment.[13] Volunteers from all the regiments at home were called for to make up the deficiency. They were called for even from those regiments earmarked for mobilization purposes as part of the 1st Army Corps, as well as from regiments on the higher establishment in which there were the fewest old soldiers. The arbitrariness of the short service system is well illustrated by the fact that some regiments had many more men due to transfer to the Reserve than others. The 19th Hussars, for instance, (an extreme case) whose tour of Indian duty started in 1891, found themselves in 1896 and 1897 with 292 men due for transfer out of 545.[14]

* * *

When the drafts of young soldiers arrived in India, their training was nothing like complete (see below), so that they could hardly

* For a squadron on the higher establishment, where there were ninety-six or more rank and file, four troops of sixteen files each were formed. Under ninety-six and over seventy-five, the four troops were to consist of twelve files each. When seventy-five or under, one troop was to be broken up and distributed among the other three. Seventy-two rank and file equalled three troops of sixteen files each, while less than seventy-two equalled three troops of twelve files each.

For squadrons on the lower establishment (the medium establishment having been abolished late in the 1890s), under seventy-two rank and file and over fifty-seven equalled three troops of twelve files each, while less than fifty-seven entailed breaking up one troop and re-distributing it among the remaining two troops. With forty-eight, two sixteen-file troops, and with less than that, two twelve-file troops were to be formed. Whenever there were a few extra men they were to ride as serrefiles, that is in rear of the squadron or troop. Such men were to be taken from 'the signallers, pioneers, ground scouts and farriers'. (*Cav. Drill,* 20.)

be said to be fully fledged effectives. Further, so as to acclimatize them, they were usually sent off to the hills, particularly during the first hot season following their arrival. As Sir Evelyn Wood pointed out, the consequent want of men meant that soldiers were having to look after three horses each. On one particular day, he told the Wantage Committee, the men of a certain regiment were found to be caring for four horses each. 'The cavalry soldier in England,' he added, 'grumbles if we give him more than two.'[15]

The facilities at Canterbury for training recruits were unbelievably inadequate. Men were sometimes sent out to India who had done no riding at all, though none was normally sent who had not undergone a musketry course on the small 350 yards range. At one moment in the 1880s there were, to use Sergeant-Major Mole's vivid phrasing, 'some four recruits to each horses' leg . . . Whatever other duty was shirked,' he wrote, 'it was more difficult to keep the lads out of the stables than in them, and I had to quell more squabbles over grooming kit than anything else.'[16] The situation had not improved in 1890. That year, out of 404 horses at Canterbury, only 388 were available for riding school work. Yet there were 1,248 rank and file. Further the riding school accommodation was insufficient, nor were there any facilities for teaching reconnoitring and outpost duties. Once their semblance of training, which lasted at the most ten months, was over, recruits, most of whom had enlisted at eighteen, had nothing to do until they reached the age of twenty, deteriorating until they could be legally sent out (see p. 123). In 1891 there were only 549 men old enough to be sent overseas, while there were 700 not yet twenty. The Inspector-General of Cavalry recommended that these should be sent to regiments at home and that when they were twenty they should volunteer for India. But this recommendation seems to have been ignored.[17]

The Indian Army

'[The Horse Guards] thought very little of anyone who had served in India. An Indian victory was not only no grounds for confidence, but it was actually a cause for suspicion.'

THE DUKE OF WELLINGTON

'If Britain was at all to make effective her diplomacy in a world dominated by the nascent military power of America, Prussia and Russia, the overt and explicit symbol of that power was and could only be the Indian Army.'

ADRIAN PRESTON, 'The Indian Army and Indo-British Political and Strategic Relations, 1745–1947'

'The Indian Army is not limited in numbers by an annual vote in Parliament. It is not voted by Parliament at all; its numbers are not enumerated in the Mutiny Act. In fact it may be described as a non-Parliamentary Army, as compared with the Army which is maintained at home.'

THE MARQUESS OF HARTINGTON in 1878

'*Kálapoosh* [service in India] was every young fellow's ambition.'

SERGEANT-MAJOR MOLE, 14th Hussars, in 1886[1]

(ii)

India: state of the Indian Army – European rank and file: high social and economic status – diet – daily life – health – drunkenness and temperance movements – nursing – wives – extra-regimental employment

Though the Indian army was much looked down upon by the officers of the home army, the professional thought and to some degree the types of training and even of equipment of the whole of the British army were largely based on the military experience and needs of the Indian service. After all, something like one third of British strength in peacetime was absorbed by India. Though all this may have had a bad effect upon the creation of a strategic reserve at home against the possibility of European war, the army in India, since its post-Mutiny reorganization, gradually established a high standard of efficiency and readiness for emergencies.

This last was more true of the native regiments than it was of those sent out from home. When, for instance, the Carabiniers in 1879 were ordered to take part in the Afghan War, half their officers were on leave and the regiment was deficient of most of the kit essential for campaigning. They had to go through the red tape of indenting for war stores and securing civil contracts for transport. Until a few years later, khaki uniforms were not normal issue, so the Carabiniers had to arrange regimentally for the dyeing of their white drill. All the laboriously applied pipeclay had to be washed off their belts and other accoutrements, and leather scabbards had to be made in place of the plated issue.[2] Such a state of unpreparedness seems to have been greater in the cavalry than in the other arms. This was partly because, being so expensive an article and one, moreover, which was not actually employable on the North-West Frontier (where action in mountainous country was virtually perrenial), the British cavalry regiment was apt, as Churchill found it, to be 'deprived of any opportunity of seeing active service'.[3]

* * *

The 4th Hussars when they were in India between 1822 and 1833 lost by death 684 of all ranks. During a later tour of the same length, from 1867 to 1878,* they lost only ninety-one. These statistics provide striking evidence of the progress made during the middle of the century in medical science and living conditions. Another significant development during the period was the speed of sea transport. In 1822 the 4th took four and a half months to reach India. In 1867 they took six weeks and in 1896 only twenty-one days. However, in spite of a vast railway network within India, regiments, when moving station, often took as long about it as they had before Queen Victoria came to the throne. The reason for this was partly economy, partly 'flag-waving' and partly to test regiments on the march. The 14th Hussars, for example, in 1881 took six weeks to march from Bombay to Secunderabad. They never marched more than twelve miles a day and on a number of days they rested. They never exceeded an average of three miles per hour, since their pace was regulated by their transport. Most of this was hired from civilian contractors and consisted, as it had done since the beginning of British rule, of bullock wagons, mule

* In Vol II, p. 461, the 4th is erroneously shown as stationed at home between 1867 and 1871. In fact the regiment was in India during those years.

13. Riding school staff, 17th Lancers, c. 1893

14. 'Home, Sweet Home': 11th Hussars, c. 1890

15. Tent-pegging in India, c. 1885; a sergeant of the Bays in the foreground

16. Non-commissioned officers of the 8th, 13th and 21st Hussars, c. 1892

carts, elephants and camels. They generally moved between 3 a.m. and 9 a.m.[4]

* * *

The rank and file of the regiments which went out to India were in many ways better off than those at home. One indication of this was the fact that men, while there, saved about twice as much money as their comrades at home. It was calculated in 1879 that soldiers brought home from India £1 for every shilling they took out.[5]* Sergeant-Major Mole asserted without hesitation that in the 1880s a cavalryman's life at home could not be compared with 'the one he had in India, either for pleasure, for comfort or for profit'.[6] Further, by local standards every European soldier, however much he might be the scum of the slums at home, was, merely by virtue of being white, socially 'superior' to the 'native majority', while his pay made him a rich man by comparison. It was general for men not to consider themselves 'pukka' soldiers until they had served in India, 'eaten rump steaks for breakfast, been shaved in bed and made a two months' march'.[7]

When the 7th Hussars were about to go out to relieve the 14th Hussars in 1886, all the 14th's semi-trained recruits of under three months' service at the Canterbury depot (about 200 in all) were transferred by order to the 7th to try to bring that regiment up to the higher establishment. Those of over three months' service were asked to volunteer. These men, according to Mole, realized that unless they accepted this chance all their soldiering would be likely to be in the United Kingdom. 'Before evening,' he wrote, 'our depot had lost more than half its muster.'[8]

* * *

In India the daily free ration was 1 lb of meat (a ¼ lb more than at home) and 1 lb of bread. 3 lbs of firewood for cooking were also issued free. Nine pice (less than 1½d) were deducted daily for a grocery ration of 4 ozs of rice, 2½ ozs of sugar, 5/7ths oz of tea or 1 3/7ths oz of coffee, 2/3rds oz of salt and 1 lb of vegetables.[9] Other stoppages in the mid-1870s were restricted to 6d a month for cooking, 6d a month for cleaning materials and hair cutting and 1s 6d a month for washing.

* A favourable rate of 2s 0½d to the rupee was allowed to soldiers sending money home. (Airey, 427.)

Breakfast, according to Sergeant-Major Mole, writing of the 1870s and 1880s, was usually at 8 a.m. and consisted of

> 'a great piece of meat, cut off, probably, from an animal killed that morning, fried by the native cooks with onions, or made into a curry. Dinner was at one o'clock, and was served by the four or five table-boys attached to each troop, who always enquired beforehand, "What master have for dinner?", the rations being cooked differently and separately for each man, according to his taste.'

As far back as 1865 Surgeon-General Munro had tried to insist that the men, instead of dining in the middle of the day (even during the hot weather), should do so in the evening, following the example of the natives, but, as he told the Wantage Committee in 1891, 'the men objected to any change so strongly that it was never carried further.'[10]

> 'Tea consisted of a basin of that beverage and anything the men liked to add to it from the coffee-shop; and at supper they could obtain what they wished, ready cooked, from the same place. The food was very plentiful and good, excepting the meat, which, unless stewed and mixed with vegetables, was tough and unpalatable.'[11]

The licensed coffee-shops, kept by native contractors, were attached to the canteens. From them at all hours tea, coffee, stews and 'savoury country dishes' were available. Groceries and, increasingly, tinned provisions could also be bought at the coffee-shops. Prices were usually fixed by a regimental committee and were therefore not exorbitant.

During the Afghan War of 1878–80 the authorized daily ration for European troops was

'Fresh meat, exclusive of bone	1 lb
Bread	$1\frac{1}{4}$ lb
or	
Biscuit	1 lb
Rice or flour	4 ozs
Sugar	3 ozs
Tea	$\frac{3}{4}$ ozs
Salt	$\frac{2}{3}$ ozs
Potatoes	10 ozs
Green vegetables (when procurable)	6 ozs.'

Half an ounce of lime or lemon juice as well as one dram of rum were provided for each man per diem. Half the rum ration was to be drunk 'at dinner' and half 'after sunset'. Salt pork was sometimes necessarily substituted for fresh meat, but it was 'not liked by the men'. Consequently Australian tinned meat was substituted, and 'this was appreciated'. So were pickles, preserved potatoes and compressed vegetables. Among the 'portable foods' which were tried out were 'Edwards Desiccated Soup, Kopf's Food (*Erbswürst*)' which was merely pea soup and 'Company's Mulligatawny and Scotch Broth'.

A report upon the campaign by Surgeon-General Crawford commented that

> 'tobacco should be supplied to troops on service' or that there should be 'the opportunity of purchasing it. The want of tobacco is a sore deprivation to the soldier, who is generally a smoker; it is not advisable in a campaign or epidemic to alter the habit of a life-time, and when there is hard marching and scanty food, tobacco soothes and sustains.'[12]*

* * *

In the cavalry the men's routine work was infinitely less than at home. On 'exercise days' in the cold weather, for instance, when

* The same report gives the 'special scale of clothing and bedding' for the campaign:

'*British troops.*

Waterproof sheet	1
Jersey	1
Warm socks, pair	1
Mittens	1
Poshteen [sheepskin overcoat, worn with the fur inside], or wadded coat, or other suitable garment	1
Boots, pair (on payment)	1
Caps, Balaclava	1
Extra blanket.'	

In addition each soldier was recommended to take from his kit:

'Cholera belt	1
Flannel shirts	2
Forage cap	1
Warm trousers	1
Warm serge coat, lined with flannel	1
Warm socks, pairs	2
Great coat	1
Comforter	1
Blankets	2
Helmet	1
Boots, pairs	2'

Native followers were allowed:

'Blanket, country	1
Puttees, pair	1
Poshteen, or other suitable warm garment	1
Warm pyjamahs, pair	1
Shoes, pair	1
Waterproof sheet	1'

(Crawford, 272–3.)

the men arrived at stables, they 'found their horses already saddled, and nothing for them to do but to mount.'[13]* When in 1878 the natives of Mhow suffered a cholera outbreak which spared the whites, they were hurried out of barracks and cantonment, leaving the men to their own devices. In due course, the scare being past, the divisional commander issued a special order congratulating the men of the 3rd Hussars on the 'most satisfactory and cheerful manner' in which they had performed 'the whole of the stable duties of the corps without any assistance, each man grooming, watering and bedding down from three to four horses daily, sweeping out the stables, keeping the vicinity of them clean and tidy, and removing the litter in hand barrows'![14]

In spite of considerable sanitary reforms over the years, disease was still often rampant. The unsuitable diet, the pernicious drinks which were too often obtainable and, of course, the climate were the chief causes. In 1889 the 5th Lancers suffered severely from enteric fever on their arrival in India. In two months fifty rank and file had died as a result of it.[15] In the mid-1870s at least a quarter of the 3rd Hussars were constantly on the sick list. Annual admissions to hospital always exceeded the regimental strength. In one year forty men of the regiment had to be invalided home, twenty-one for 'general debility', eleven with hepatitis and eight with secondary syphilis. Deaths averaged about six a year.[16] The very young soldiers suffered most. A great many developed heart disease and showed signs of scrofula shortly after arrival in India. Young soldiers were especially prone, too, to typhoid. Infected milk bought in the bazaars was believed to be a chief cause. In an attempt to lesson the risk, the 13th Hussars whilst at Meerut established in their lines during the late 1870s a 'first class dairy'. Whether the incidence of typhoid decreased or not is not known.

Venereal disease was ever present, of course. In 1895 there was a sudden increase in its incidence, especially of a very virulent type of syphilis. A committee which sat two years later decided that this sudden increase was not attributable to increased immorality, and that drunkenness and crime had diminished in recent years. It also declared that the short service system was not responsible 'for any increased tendency to sexual indulgence'. Certain

* There was a fixed establishment of natives in each cantonment, but there was usually a much larger number of them scraping a living in one way or another. From time to time, 'new broom' commanding officers swept these supernumeraries away, much to the resentment of the men.

measures were apparently taken to tighten up on the inspection of prostitutes and to improve medical facilities.[17]

* * *

Sir William Butler once heard a soldier say that India was 'a fine country because you're always thirsty, and there's so much to drink'.[18] Great strides towards reducing drunkenness were taken during the last two decades of the century. The quality of what could be procured in barrack canteens was usually high. Arrack of the best sort was sold there. Mole found it a not very palatable beverage, 'having a sickly taste, but the men tumbled to it in time and liked it mixed with hot coffee at night. It was a pure spirit, and not unwholesome.' In some regiments strenuous efforts, mostly self-defeating, were made to restrict quantities and hours of drinking. Under one commanding officer, men of the 14th Hussars were limited to three pints of beer a day (at 4½d a quart) and two drams of arrack (at ¾d a dram). The canteen was not opened till 11 a.m. 'long before which many men had raised a thirst'. A later commanding officer started a contrasting 'free system'. Under his regime the 14th's canteen remained open from 10 a.m. till evening watch-setting, while rationing and 'pegging up' each drink with the drinker's name loudly announced by the non-commissioned officer in charge were done away with. In the 1880s a regimental temperance club was founded. Further, fifty out of eighty men in one troop alone became, Mole says, total abstainers. There were still, though, numbers of men who could not resist 'flying to the vile country liquor, appropriately named "Billy Stink".' This could be bought in the bazaars at 9d a bottle. Mole said that a quart of the stuff was 'sufficient to drive six men, not used to it, raving mad'.[19]

From the early 1860s onwards sporadic attempts were made by certain officers to provide regimental and other 'institutes' where coffee and other non-alcoholic drinks could be bought in pleasant surroundings, as alternatives to the canteens. By the mid-1880s these had proliferated to almost all stations. One infantry colonel had gone beyond this and, in 1862, founded in Agra 'The Soldiers' Total Abstinence Association, India'. Largely because total abstinence, as opposed to temperance, was too much to ask of most men, the association had only a limited success. It took the active interest of 'Bobs' Roberts to get temperance really going in India. Soon after he became Commander-in-Chief in Madras he wrote to the secretary of the Total Abstinence Association thus:

> '1884 . . . I am making enquiries as to the possibility of meeting your wish to have a recognized room set apart in each set of barracks for the branch society of the association. I quite understand how desirable it is that your temperance work should be placed on a permanent basis . . . I am not an abstainer myself, and if I thought that soldiers could trust themselves to drink in moderation, I would not advocate their taking the pledge.'

Later that year Roberts addressed a temperance meeting in Secunderabad:

> 'Drink and crime,' he said, 'go together; if there were no drunkards in the army there would be little or no crime. A few years ago Lord Napier of Magdala, when commander-in-chief in India, caused a return to be prepared, showing the class of men by whom offences had been committed during a certain number of months. The return proved that total abstainers were wholly guiltless of crime, that partial abstainers were practically equally guiltless, and that drunkards were responsible for the whole of the crime of the army.'

In 1887, to commemorate the Queen's Golden Jubilee, Roberts who by then was Commander-in-Chief, India, united the numerous small societies which had grown up, into 'The Army Temperance Association'. The following year he described a typical institute set up under its aegis:

> 'On entering the building, I found myself in the Temperance room – a spacious, airy department, in which 300 or 400 men were assembled. Some were playing games, others were talking and amusing themselves . . . Waiters were bustling about with tea, coffee and light refreshments. Neither beer nor other intoxicating drinks were, of course, allowed in this room . . . Further on I found myself in the Refreshment, which was much about the same size as the Temperance room. At one end of it was a Coffee shop, where all kinds of oilman stores and regimental necessaries could be purchased at a cheap rate and where very inviting looking suppers were being prepared . . . Those who wished for it could have beer brought to them from the neighbouring canteen.'[20]

* * *

Service in India was subject to the division of the year into cold and hot weather months. From October to March, in most parts, the weather was exceedingly pleasant. During those 'cold' months there sometimes hardly seemed enough of each day for all that had to be done by way of work and recreation. For the rest of the year there was little that could be done during the long hours of daylight. Before the monsoon, men seemed to be living in a furnace night and day; after it, in a boiler.

One of the advantages of the short service system was that the number of soldiers' children in India began to decrease from 1876 onwards. For young children the rigours of life in the plains during the hot season was always debilitating and often fatal. In 1875, for instance, of the 6,643 young children of soldiers in Bengal alone, seventy-six out of every 1,000 died. Similar exceptionally high mortality rates came about every year in spite of the fact that about a third of the children went up during the hot weather to summer homes, asylums and convent schools in the hill stations. That they were able to do so was chiefly due to private philanthropy. One of the chief benefactors in this sphere was Colonel Sir Frederick FitzWygram of the 15th Hussars (see p. 391) who gave £10,000 in 1874 for the construction of summer homes in the Himalayas for the benefit of British cavalry families.[21]

'Homes in the Hills' were also provided for the Indian Nursing Service which was inaugurated in 1883. Lady Roberts, wife of 'Bobs', appealed to all ranks of the army for funds to build these. Not only officers but also many of the rank and file subscribed. Until the first eight trained female nurses landed in India all military nursing had depended upon the tender mercies of 'the orderly on duty' whose training was not just minimal – it was non-existent. Miss Loch, one of the two Lady Superintendents, found that the orderlies at Bangalore were generally

> 'capital fellows, most willing, good to their comrades and ready to learn; but all the same it is unsatisfactory working with them. They volunteer for the sake of change, and as they can throw up their duty whenever they choose one has very little hold over them and there are many changes . . . We have had one or two rows from their not being sober. Then the hospital coolies are frightful thieves, they steal the patients' food out of their dishes if they are too ill to look after it. Then the ward servants . . . are very low caste men,

and dirty, lazy and untruthful. When the doctors come round in the morning everything is straight and spick and span, clean sheets, clean top shirts, and how should they know that only the face and hands have been washed, and the under flannels not taken off for a week.'[22]

* * *

For the voyage to India men were obliged to buy their 'sea kit'. This consisted of such things as 'serge clothing, a wicker and canvas helmet, sea soap for washing clothes in salt water', and an optional pound of tobacco known as 'navy sixes'.[23] On arrival at its Indian station, once the regiment had got itself shaken down and men had become accustomed to their newly acquired mounts, both drills and other duties were much less onerous than at home. One of the first things which had to be attended to was the fitting in the tailor's shop of the two suits of khaki and six of white overalls. These had to be paid for by the men. Together with the other necessaries incidental to Indian service, the cost to each man in a cavalry regiment was, according to General Sir George Luck, India's first Inspector-General of Cavalry, not less than 29½ rupees.[24] This must have kept a man in debt for a considerable time.

On exercise days reveillé would sound at 5 a.m. when the native cooks brought coffee and biscuits to the men's bungalow bedsides. The men would then get dressed and exercise their horses for an hour, after which there came morning stables, followed by breakfast and the cleaning of saddles. After this, on most days, the men were free until evening stables, and after that till watch-setting,

> 'the first post being sounded at 9.30 and the last at 10 p.m. Just before the latter went, the orderly sergeant called the roll in the bungalows . . . and examined the pegs to see that every man's carbine and sword hung in its place. "Lights out" was sounded at a quarter past ten, but this was a nominal call, for they were kept burning in the soldiers' quarters all through the night.'

Occasionally field-days took place, even during the hot weather. In the cold weather divisional parades and field-days could keep the men out from

> 'three hours before day-break till nine or ten o'clock in the morning.

'With the exception of the fifty men or so who were on duty for the day, the others [on most days],' according to Mole, 'had too much time on their hands, and this, broadly speaking, is one of the curses of a soldier's life in India. For five days a week the men had, as a rule, nothing to do between ten in the morning and five in the evening, except eat, drink, sleep and roam about at their own free will over the country. There was no roll-call and no restrictions were placed on their movements or their dress . . . Many of the men took up some pursuit as a hobby, such as keeping pets, training birds to talk, catching cobras, collecting butterflies and the like . . . Every troop started a shooting club, and the men went in for regular practice, and this soon led to shooting competitions, which greatly increased the efficiency of the regiment . . .

'It was the being waited on by so many servants . . . that led to the weary hours of forced idleness that spoilt many a smart man . . . What with being fed up to the chin, and having nothing to do to digest it or work it off, I often fancied the men would have been far healthier and hardier with less of the nigger and more of the sun. The majority of them were of the labouring class, and had for many years regularly done a hard day's work. Suddenly they found their work being done for them, and the result was that soldiers who kept in good condition on English rations grew stale and soft-fleshed on Indian ones . . .

'There is no European in India whose lot is harder than that of the soldier's wife. However good and industrious a cook or housekeeper she may be, she must not put her hands to any of the legitimate duties of her sphere; for if she does, the natives look down upon her at once, and this is fatal to the proper self respect she should have . . . Can one wonder if some of these poor women . . . left for long lonely hours by themselves whilst their husbands are away drinking at the mess canteen, and with no one to give them a word of warning, listen sometimes like their mother Eve to the voice of the tempter and fall? When a case of this kind occurred and was brought to the notice of the colonel by the regimental provosts, the punishment was both severe and effective. The woman's disgrace was published in regimental orders, as follows:

"The wife of ——— having embarked on the troopship ——— for passage to England on the 3rd instant, is struck

> off the strength of the regiment from that date for misconduct."
>
> The punishment fell heavily on the husband too, for not only was his home broken up, but he had to return to barrack-room life, and there amongst men who knew his domestic history, soldier on as a single man till his term of service expired.'[25]

Wives, so long as they behaved themselves, were provided for better in India than at home. They were given a money allowance of eight rupees a month* as well as full rations. These were continued to a widow for a year after her husband's death. Further, her children during their father's lifetime received 2½ rupees each and after his death were maintained until they were grown up or otherwise provided for.[26] 'Fancy,' wrote Captain Combe of the 10th Hussars in 1879, 'one of our widows marrying again already! A very respectable, good-looking woman, rather superior to her class, but it is barely three months since her husband was drowned' in the Kabul River catastrophe (see p. 213). 'The young man put in for a pass to visit her in Barracks within six weeks of the accident.' When the Colonel remonstrated with her, 'she said she must consider her children and the necessity of providing a new home for them ... Such indecent haste!'[27]

* * *

There were numerous appointments 'of a remunerative character' connected with the manifold military departments in India which were filled exclusively from the ranks of the army, mostly by warrant and non-commissioned officers. These departments were, chiefly, the Commissariat, the Barrack, the Ordnance, the Clothing and the Stud and Remount. There were also openings for clerks in headquarter offices, draughtsmen in the quartermaster's offices, and staff-sergeants in garrisons and convalescent depots. Many soldiers were also employed in the vast civilian Department of Public Works. All such men were borne on the army's effective strength, and all were placed on the 'unattached list', to which about 150 men were admitted each year. Promotion to sergeant, if they were not already of that rank, was speedy. Those who proved satisfactory at their jobs could climb a dizzy ladder, starting with such grades as that of sub-conductor and ending up as deputy

* If the wife was not European she received only 6½ rupees a month. (Airey, 425.)

commissaries. This last carried the rank of honorary captain, while deputy and assistant commissaries were honorary lieutenants. In 1879 there were 203 sub-conductors, 211 conductors, 61 honorary lieutenants and 16 honorary captains. All except the honorary officers were liable to be recalled to their regiments at any time.

For most of these appointments it was an advantage to possess some knowledge of native languages. In many regimental schools a man could learn Hindustani. When he passed the 'lower standard' he received £9. If he managed the higher he received £18. Sergeant-Major Mole found that his 'black coach', the *munshi* who was regimental teacher, claimed £3 as his fee for instructing him up to the lower standard.

Men were encouraged, too, to learn trades in the regimental workshops. A '1st class workman' received an annually presented prize of £1 5s. Any such workman who thoroughly taught a trade to an apprentice soldier was given a bonus of £2 5s.[28]

For warrant and non-commissioned officers life in most Indian stations, though very full for much of the time, was peculiarly pleasant. A sergeant might find his married quarters to consist of a sitting room, two bedrooms and a bath room, with a detached kitchen and cook's house behind. His extra expenses were few. They might include 6d a month library subscription and certainly embraced 1s a month for the sergeant's mess.

> 'We kept servants to do our work for us,' wrote Sergeant-Major Mole, who was stationed at Bangalore in 1876, 'Kitty for my wife and a "boy" for myself; and Government provided a native *syce* or groom to look after my horse . . .
>
> 'Nearly all the senior sergeants kept a horse or pony of their own, called in the language of the country *tattoos*, or more briefly *tats*. As soon as we had established our private studs, mounted paperchases were started, and jackal hunts; or failing a Jack in the flesh, we chased him in the spirit in the disguise of a lean, fleet pariah dog, who often led us a merry burst. Our hounds, or "bobbery pack", were made up of drafts from the various barracks, and ran straight and fast when they didn't stop to quarrel amongst themselves.'

When in the 1880s Sergeant-Major Mole found himself one of the oldest non-commissioned officers in the 14th Hussars he could always depend upon a week or ten days' local leave a year.

* * *

If on a man's return home he was lucky enough to land at Portsmouth with the need to spend a night there, he could usually do so in Miss Robinson's Home. This philanthropic lady was known to many grateful men as 'the soldier's friend'.[29]

> 'Princes could live no better than we.'
>
> LIEUTENANT WINSTON CHURCHILL
> on arrival in India, 1896

> 'India is not the place it used was at all!'
>
> CAPTAIN COMBE, 10th Hussars, in 1879[1]

(iii)

India: European officers: servants – cantonments – pay – allowance and expenses – sporting activities: pig-sticking – polo

An American naval officer, observing the Indian Contingent which went to Egypt in 1882, remarked that

> 'the number of servants that the least exacting of European subalterns must retain is simply incredible. One brings the water, another cleans the boots, a third sweeps the house, a fourth waits at table on the master of the house alone, a fifth serves the guest, a sixth is the body-servant, etc.'

He rightly attributed this state of affairs to 'that singular and apparently ineradicable institution "Caste", which limits every man's occupation to one thing and no more.'[2] Young Lieutenant Robert Baden-Powell made the comment that the 'natural trades union of caste in India is far more strict in its slavery than its more artificial imitation in Western countries.' He added that if you managed to acquire good servants, you could trust them with

> 'all your money and trinkets, and, although they may rob others on your behalf, they are entirely honest towards their own masters. They are patient and clever at their work. Your kitmutgar, with three bricks as his kitchen range and a bit of

cow-dung for fuel, will cook you a dinner in camp just as good as you would get in a well-ordered kitchen at home. Your syce will run for miles to take charge of your horse at the end of a ride, and prefers to sleep in its stall to living in a separate house. Your bearer's good qualities shine when you are sick and he proves himself a capable and attentive nurse.'

On Baden-Powell's return to India after an absence of twelve years, his former bearer came on board ship and took charge of his things 'without a word of warning on either side'.[3] Young Winston Churchill used to receive his 'bag of silver' at the end of each month of duty, canter home to his bungalow, throw it to his beaming butler, and then 'in theory' have no further material cares.[4]

A serious attempt to cut down the vast numbers of non-combatants taken on active service was made as a result of the Afghan War. Captain Combe of the 10th Hussars in the autumn of 1878 found

> 'a very reduced establishment of servants; one personal servant to each officer, and one general or mess servant to every three, besides the regulation number of chargers, with a syce and grass cutter to each. Our troop syces are very much cut down,' he wrote home from Kohat. 'Instead of one syce to two horses, only ten percent are allowed, hardly enough to groom the Staff-Sergeants' horses!'[5]

In 1879 a circular issued by the Military Department of the Government of India laid down, in what came to be known as the Kabul Scale, the future field establishment of troops of the Indian Army. The uniform schedule of baggage, camp equipage and of followers came as a necessary shock to officers and men alike.[6]

One of the first things that struck newly arrived officers was that, in the words of Baden-Powell,

> 'the niggers seem to be cringing villians. As you ride or walk along the middle of the road, every cart or carriage has to stop and get out of your way, and every native, as he passes you, gives a salute. If he has an umbrella up he takes it down, if he is riding a horse he gets off and salutes. Moreover they do whatever you tell them. If you meet a man in the road and tell him to dust your boots, he does it.'[7]

* * *

Cantonments were invariably sited five or six miles from the cities. In between lay the lines of the native regiments. The area covered was by European standards immense. Distances were so vast, indeed, that, as Churchill put it, 'walking was impossible. We cantered on hacks from one place to another.' Cantonments were criss-crossed by wide roads, usually lined with double avenues of shady trees. The offices, hospitals, riding-schools and various other institutions were imposing architecturally. Well spaced out around the officers' messes were veritable suburbs of roomy bungalows, each standing in its own grounds, generally walled, with its own spacious garden. These were hired by the officers, there being no official quarters supplied to them.

There were certain allowances, some of which were meant to help with lodging costs. These included horse and tent allowances which, in view of the indispensable costs of Indian living, though adequate, were seldom considered generous. However, officers' pay in India was an increase on home pay of as much as 100 per cent in the case of lieutenant-colonels and about 40 per cent in the case of second-lieutenants. The rate of exchange was officially fixed at 1s 3d, though for special purposes this was sometimes altered. In 1879, for instance, it was raised to 1s 7½d for Family Remittances. Captain Combe of the 10th noted with disgust that this meant that it would cost him 1,230 instead of 1,140 rupees to send home £100; but, he added, 'the bankers, of course, charge more'. In the 1880s the average subaltern of the cavalry of the line in India would probably have to budget for a monthly expenditure of about ninety-two rupees upon those things which were unavoidably connected with his service:

Two chargers requiring two syces and two grass-cutters	Rs 28
One bearer (R.15); 1 khidmutgar (R.10)	25
One-third share of one sweeper (R.6), one water-carrier (R.8), one night-watchman (R.6), one gardener (R.7)	9
One-third share of a bungalow @ R.90	30
	92

On top of that, grain for the chargers had to be provided, though the grass-cutters themselves had to provide bedding and hay or its equivalent. The gardener usually produced lucerne, carrots and similar delicacies, which replaced bran in India.

Though officers did not perhaps find themselves in comparison so well off in India as their men, the life they led was pretty luxurious. 'It was, however, better in a cavalry regiment', as Churchill put it, 'to supplement the generous rewards of the Queen-Empress by an allowance from home three or four times as great.'[8]

* * *

There was a wealth of sporting activities available to officers in India. These ranged from grand tiger shoots and other big-game hunting, involving numerous beaters and elephants, through wild-fowl shooting (especially quail) and horse-racing, to lawn tennis, which spread speedily from the late 1870s onwards. Steeple-chasing and 'paper chases' were particularly popular. So was tent-pegging. But

> 'The sport that beats them o'er and o'er,
> Is that wherein we hunt the boar.'[9]

The pursuit of the wild boar had been a favourite pastime in Europe from time immemorial. But the modern sport seems to be peculiarly Indian in origin. Before 1800 the British speared bears, but as that quarry became ever rarer, wild pigs took their place. Pig-sticking, or hog-hunting, was especially beloved of cavalry officers, for the wild boar is extremely fast moving, courageous and combative. To follow his rapid twists and turns, his endless 'jinks', and then to face him as he suddenly turns in his tracks and charges with his sharp tusks, needs quick thinking and expert horsemanship. There is very real danger to both man and horse. The type of horse required is of medium size with quick wits and exceptional speed. It must have a good shoulder and unusually good balance so as to keep its hold over rough ground.

The season, in most districts, starts in January, as soon as the heavy undergrowth resulting from the monsoon dies down, and continues throughout the hot weather. The sport was strictly controlled on much the same lines as a Hunt in Britain. Private 'expeditions' within the vast tracts of land controlled and hunted by what were known as 'Tent Clubs' were (and still are) as much a sin against etiquette as they would be in fox-hunting country in England. The powers and prestige of a club's honorary secretary were very like those of a Master of Foxhounds at home. Meets generally took place every two weeks and could last up to four days.

The most usual method of hog-hunting was applied where the

jungle was covered with grass and *jhow* (tamarisk) growing girth-high. At intervals in the line of beaters rode the 'spears'. These were divided into 'heats' of three or four horsemen. Only one heat was allowed to follow a boar that was put up, or, to use the jargon, 'reared'. The rider who gained 'first spear', whether he killed or only wounded, was awarded its head and tushes for trophy. Where the jungle, as in many parts of Central India, was impossible to ride through, the heats waited, concealed, for the boars to be driven towards them.

There were different kinds of spear in use. Some were thrown and recovered later, others were used like lances; some were short and javelin-like and used over-hand, others, like the Bombay spear, were up to twelve feet in length and used under-hand. There were also medium-sized spears, about six feet long, well leaded at their butts. These could be used either over- or under-hand. Of the numerous pig-sticking competitions, the most famous was that for the much coveted Kadir Cup, instituted in 1869. There was also the Nagpur Hunt Cup awarded to the Tent Club member with the largest number of first spears in the season.[10]

Pig-sticking was not only recreational; it was also socially useful. The pig-sticker was often warmly welcomed in out-lying villages. Boars on occasion took 'possession of coveted patches of sugar-cane into which the villagers dared not venture.'[11] The arrival of a club in the area was looked upon as a great deliverance.

* * *

Of competitive games both cricket and football were common, but by far and away the most popular game played by officers in India was a newcomer called polo. Though similar games played from horseback with stick and ball seem to have occurred in countries as far apart as China and Turkey in the eighth century, polo, as such, is first heard of in Persia. From there it spread eastwards to, amongst other places, Tibet. There it acquired its name *pulu*, the Tibetan word for ball. The game seems to have flourished in India during the sixteenth century, but for the next 200 years its records there cease. It was re-introduced in 1863 from Manipur.[12] An exhibition match between two teams of Manipuri natives was staged in Calcutta that year. Officers of the 10th Hussars, then at home, read a description of this match in *The Field* and in 1869 they played at Aldershot the first game ever to take place in England.

The officers rode their chargers and used 'golf sticks and billiard balls'. In subsequent games a whitened cricket ball was found more suitable.[13]

The first inter-regimental game was played on Hounslow Heath in 1870 with eight a side, mounted on 'wiry little 12½ hands high ponies'. The 10th Hussars beat the 9th Lancers by three goals to two. A newspaper reported the match under the headline 'Hockey on Horseback':

> 'Posts some twenty yards apart marked the goals. The distance between them was a little under 200 yards. The sticks used were like those used in hockey. Both sides wore mob caps with different coloured tassels attached. The ball, a little sphere of white bone, was thrown up by a sergeant major of the 10th, who then galloped off the ground . . . The game lasted for an hour and a half, with ten minutes interval . . . Though general remarks made it evident the new game is one most fitted for cavalry soldiers it was more remarkable for the language used by the players than anything else.'[14]

The earliest code of rules was drawn up by the Hurlingham Club in 1874 and by 1882 the number of players had been progressively reduced to four a side, where it has stayed ever since. In 1877 the first inter-regimental polo tournament was held in India, the 9th and 10th being among the four competing regiments. The craze soon spread not only to the other arms but also,especially, to the native cavalry and to the rulers of the native States and their forces. Before long there were few regiments whose officers were not playing assiduously three or four evenings a week, even, at times, during the height of the hot weather. The initial cheapness of ponies, the ample flat, hard ground available and 'the suitability of the game to a country where short and good exercise is much required for health'[15] all tended to make the game a lasting success in India. Baden-Powell of the 13th Hussars enthused about 'the natural training involved' in playing polo and 'the practice of quiet, quick decision and dash that are essential' to successful cavalry leading.[16] Lieutenant Winston Churchill of the 4th Hussars talked of 'the serious purpose of life – in one word – Polo.'[17] Over the years innumerable clubs and annual tournaments sprang up, while training of both officers and ponies for the game became at least as important as training for war. Competition between regimental teams grew ever more keen. Injuries and deaths from falls on the iron-hard ground soon mounted so alarmingly that 'Bobs' Roberts, when he was Commander-in-Chief, issued an order that helmets with chin-straps were always to be worn.[18]*

'It was a real satisfaction,' wrote Baden-Powell, 'to a poor man to pick up ponies in all sorts of out-of-the-way places, such as country villages, fairs, etc., and then to break them in, make them handy, balance them and educate them into playing the game.' Polo even invaded the mess where polo pony races took place in the billiard room with jumps made of piled-up furniture.[19]†

* In 1882 Lieutenant George Daly, adjutant of the Central Indian Horse, son of Sir Henry (see Vol II, 151), was killed at polo, wearing no headdress. Steeplechasing was just as dangerous, of course. Two years later his successor as adjutant, Lieutenant Hughes-Buller, was killed in a steeplechase at Mhow. (Watson, 175–7.)

† Baden-Powell also tells of 'musical rides on camels in the ante-room'. (Baden-Powell, 36.)

Native cavalry

'If cavalry be the eyes and ears of an army, it would be difficult to find in any European fighting body sharper eyes or ears than would be supplied by the Indian Cavalry. The Bengal Cavalry in particular is in a highly efficient state, well-drilled, well mounted, and perfectly equipped.'

The Times, 1878

'Our native cavalry in India are, as all the world knows, soldiers by birth and upbringing, and splendid horsemen and swordsmen.'

LIEUTENANT-GENERAL SIR ROBERT BADEN-POWELL

'The 18th Bengal Lancers is beyond all question the finest-looking cavalry regiment that I have ever seen, and, besides our Household Cavalry I know the Austrian cavalry and the Prussian and Russian Guards. I thought them more effective than the Guards of the Second Empire, and of more noble aspect than the Chevalier Guard of Russia.'

SIR CHARLES DILKE in 1888[1]

(iv)

India: the native cavalry: most regiments irregular or silladar – establishments – States forces – extra-regimental employment of British officers – first Inspector-General of Cavalry in India – types of British officers – types of native officers, NCOs and sowars – terms of enlistment – Class regiments and troops – pay – differences between native and British regiments – regimental durbars – swords and swordsmanship – recreations and sports – field training – field duties – abolition of the Presidential Army System

Beside the European Cavalry of the Line regiments stationed in India, the mounted arm there consisted of forty-seven native units of various types. Thirty-three of these were in the Bengal Presidency, nine in Bombay and five in Madras. (For a list of cavalry units as in 1888, see Appendix, p. 418). The Madrasi and the three Bodyguard regiments, as they always had been, were organized on regular lines. All the rest, since the post-Mutiny reorganization, were *silladars* or irregulars. The silladar system was in principle not unlike that of the yeomanry in Britain. Each trooper, or *sowar* as he was called in India, provided his own horse (or its value in cash), his own uniform, saddlery, stable gear, share of tent and mess equipment and indeed virtually everything he needed except generally his arms and ammunition. In effect each regiment did everything for itself, and was therefore by far and away the least expensive mounted force in the world.*

All these units formed the cavalry of the Indian Army proper. They included such regiments as the four of the Hyderabad Contingent, the Deolee and Erinpoorah Irregular Forces (both combining infantry elements), the cavalry of the Corps of Guides and the two regiments of the Central India Horse. Beyond these there were available, chiefly on a local basis, the mounted parts of the Indian State Forces. These comprised some seventeen units, mostly lancers† (See Appendix, p. 422). Their historian, the Maharaja of Jaipur, writes that 'the status accorded to the States Forces by the Government of India and the Indian Army was one of faithful allies.'[2] When many of them served in the First World War, this was indeed the case, as will be proved in a later volume. Even before that holocaust, the rulers of some states had offered their forces for service alongside the Indian Army. It was usual for the Government of India to provide a staff of officers, designated 'Military Advisers', to help the Ruling Princes in organizing and training their troops. In 1888 numbers of States units were incorporated in the Imperial Service Troops Scheme, while others, such as the Jodphur Lancers, were raised especially as part of that scheme.

Excluding the States Forces, the numbers of which are virtually unobtainable and anyway fluctuated enormously, the mounted troops of the Indian Army in the late 1880s amounted to about 26,400.‡ By that period most regiments in Bengal and Bombay

* In some regiments even the carbines were provided at the expense of the men. Such was the case with the Poona Horse, for example, until 1879 when the old muzzle-loaders were replaced by Sniders 'supplied by Government, who took over the old arms at a valuation'. (Anderson and Molloy, I, 239.)

The silladar system was complex, varied from regiment to regiment and was altered as to its details, from time to time. Full descriptions of it up to the early 1870s are given in Vol I, 179–89 and Vol II, 237–42.

† There were many smaller States which maintained squadrons of lancers, not being able to afford complete regiments. For active service and manoeuvres composite regiments of these were formed from time to time.

‡ Bengal, 19,300; Bombay, 4,700; Madras, 2,400.

consisted of eight troops divided into four squadrons and totalled 635 of all ranks, and in Madras of six troops of 562.* The establishments varied from time to time according to the international situation. For instance, in October, 1878, as the war in Afghanistan loomed, Lord Lytton, the Viceroy, ordained that every native cavalry regiment north of the Narbudda should be augmented by ninety-six men. Before that the number of sowars had been only 384 per regiment. To meet the expense of equipping the new recruits 15,000 rupees was advanced to each silladar regiment thus augmented. This loan had to be repaid within two years. There were those who disapproved of this simple means of increasing the cavalry's strength. It was resented by many of the rank and file since it tended to diminish each man's chances of promotion, and it increased the disproportion between native troops and British officers. This disproportion was considered by some old hands as already dangerously large.[3] In 1882, when the Bengal Army was reduced by nine regiments, three of them of cavalry, the strength of each of those retained was fixed at three squadrons (six troops) totalling 500 of all ranks. At the same time one extra British officer was added. Three years later the three disbanded regiments, the 16th and 17th Bengal Cavalry and the 4th Punjab Cavalry, were resuscitated and an extra squadron was added to each regiment.[4] After 1885 the European officer establishment was fixed at ten: a Commandant, four squadron commanders, one of whom was second-in-command, four squadron officers, one of whom was adjutant, and the medical officer.† But in fact, as the Army Lists show, there were seldom less than twelve and often as many as fifteen officers carried on the strength. Many of the more senior officers, such as squadron commanders, were seconded for extra-regimental employment. The historian of The Central India Horse says that in that corps 'the situation became a public joke. Certain pungent verses appeared in *The Pioneer* referring sarcastically to the varied activities of officers of "The Scented Minstrel Horse".'[5] When Lieutenant William (later Field-Marshal Lord) Birdwood of the 11th Bengal Lancers was acting as his regiment's adjutant in 1888, his commandant told him that 'when he had applied for

* For the establishments of all the regiments in 1888 see Appendix p. 418.

† Native cavalry regiments did not have an European veterinary officer on their strength. One of the regimental officers was usually put in charge of the horse hospital, but all veterinary work was entrusted to the local native *salutri*. Some of these men were able veterinary surgeons, others were quacks.

leave in spite of the fact that no British officer but myself, a sub, would be left with the regiment, the General had been inclined to demur – to be told by the Colonel that "a regiment that can't look after itself for ten days can't be worth much!"' Birdwood seldom found 'more than three or four British Officers present with the regiment at any one time.'[6] His commandant, Colonel Arthur Haldimand Prinsep, was a bachelor who had joined the 6th Bengal Light Cavalry eight months before it mutinied at Sealkot in 1857. On that occasion he had been wounded, but he recovered sufficiently to be present at the final siege and capture of Lucknow. He served in the Afghan War of 1878–80 and was present at the capture of Ali Musjid. He was very much, according to Birdwood,

> 'the old type of Indian cavalry officer. He was what is known in India as a great "bahadur" – an extremely handsome man who had absolute faith in his regiment, at the head of which he would gladly have made a Balaklava charge any day. Indeed, his only pace was the gallop, and as for a "steady" regimental parade, such a thing was unknown to him. He had very little use for the drill-book. "Gallop baijao!" (Sound the gallop) seemed his favourite command to his trumpeter.'[7]

Until 1888, when General Sir George Luck became the first Inspector-General of Cavalry in India, commanding officers were very much left to their own devices. Many, perhaps most of them, were like Prinsep, very much of the old school, 'rabid', as one officer puts it, 'on the merits of the *arme blanche* and the *arme blanche* only – in fact I knew one commanding officer who went so far as to discourage marching in step on foot, saying that this infantry device destroyed the cavalry spirit.'[8] Many of the older officers viewed the creation of the new Inspector-Generalship with alarm.

> 'The cry went up,' wrote one young officer, 'that we should be "dragooned", that the traditional characteristics of Irregular Horse would be swept away . . . The alarm was short-lived. "Die-hards" themselves were soon obliged to confess that uniformity of training might possibly be an improvement upon the old individual system, and that there might even be some advantage in the practice of manoeuvre in large bodies . . . Henceforth brigade and divisional manoeuvres were to

become more frequent, and regimental training was to be inspected periodically and regularly by an expert.'

General Luck, whose career had been chiefly in the 15th Hussars, was known as 'a marvellous "drill".' 'He expected precision of movement, and was wont to criticise without sparing men's feelings. Irreverent subalterns might jest about "The Camp of Roaring Luck", but regimental and squadron commanders, with less reason for being light-hearted, were apt to find the joke too grim.'[9] Luck's achievement in securing some degree of uniformity in a short period was very remarkable. Until his appointment even such matters as the pace of cavalry at the walk, trot and gallop depended upon the whim of the commanding officer or the sacred tradition of the regiment. As for drill and equitation, these were just as idiosyncratic and as often as not bore little relation to the drill book. His inspections were extraordinarily searching and detailed, his praise not readily given. That he does not appear to have made many enemies is a tribute to his personality, his professionalism and the feeling of trust which he engendered. It was Luck who began to get subalterns and others interested in such questions as 'attack in line' versus 'attack in echelon'. It was in his time that there broke out a veritable epidemic of letters to the *Pioneer* and the *Civil and Military Gazette* dealing with cavalry questions. He and his successors made it fashionable for cavalry officers in native regiments to take an intelligent interest in their profession. Nevertheless, not even General Luck could eradicate the besetting sin of all British cavalry. 'I wish I could feel sure,' wrote Lord Roberts at a Cavalry Camp in 1893, 'that I should never again see a body of cavalry gallop past me on horses quite beyond control.'[10]

Many of the officers in Indian cavalry regiments were taken from European infantry regiments of the line. It was common practice for a young officer to serve three years in one of these, or partly with it and partly with a native infantry regiment, before he was sent to fill a vacancy in a native cavalry regiment. He then had to pass a course in equitation and, if possible, the higher standard in Hindustani. This took another year. Thus he did not start to learn his work as a cavalry officer until he had served four years. It was five years, therefore, before he could take part in the instruction of his men.[11] There were those who thought this a good idea, but many a cavalry officer thought it a terrible waste of time.

Between the 1880s and the end of the century the age at which officers were required to relinquish command of regiments was progressively reduced. By the late 1890s the age had fallen to fifty-two. The term of command from 1882 onwards was seven years maximum.[12]

* * *

There were normally sixteen native officers to each cavalry regiment. Few of them were actually 'gentlemen' brought in direct, most were promoted from the senior non-commissioned officers. Native officers had often been of vital assistance in raising irregular regiments. They were indispensable links between the men and their British officers whom they guided 'with reference to the public opinion of the native portion of the regiment, and managed those details of interior economy which are unsuited for the interference of the English officers.' Typical of the British officers' views on native officers was that of Captain C. M. Maguire of the 2nd Cavalry, Hyderabad Contingent:

> 'However efficient a native officer may be, he never commands the unquestioning obedience and confidence of his men that a British officer does. The Indian soldiers regard the native officer as one of themselves and do not look up to him as a person of superior class and nationality to themselves.'

To those who tried to induce more 'native gentlemen to qualify themselves for the position of officers', Maguire, who was a thoughtful, professional cavalry officer, could say in 1890 that

> 'the native gentleman is rarely to be met with. He suffers from the same characteristic defects as the native officer, adding as a rule fondness for the palanquin and zenana. He would have no stomach for the mastery, or practice, of the difficult detail required from a troop leader of the present day. Were native gentlemen qualified to be cavalry officers under modern conditions, there would probably be no British supremacy in India.'[13]

It is easy to scoff at all this, but behind Maguire's condescending attitude lay a great deal of truth, and some highly educated Indians today would probably admit to it.

Though from time to time the Government of India stressed the importance of regarding native officers as gentlemen, they were in fact and without exception treated as junior in every way to the youngest of the European second-lieutenants. Their inferior status became the cause of some discontent during the Afghan War. They were not allowed, for instance, even by payment out of their own pockets, and numbers of them were not poor men, to 'obtain the same food as the lowest-graded British private'. At Kabul one staff officer was

> 'more than once asked by old and well-to-do native officers to get them permission to purchase British rations, or even the daily one of tea and sugar, but was always met by the *non possumus* of the Commisariat Department. The native army ration for all alike is, I may remark, almost exactly the same as for the commonest class of camel-driver, and consists chiefly of coarse flour, with a little *dall* (pease) and *ghee* (butter).'

The same staff officer gave another example of how little the native officers were trusted:

> 'When look-out pickets were established upon some of the most commanding peaks [around Kabul], a British officer was, by Headquarters orders, always obliged to be in command, even if the party was only one of a few rank and file. More than one commanding officer vainly urged that he would be personally responsible that this duty could be perfectly well performed by the jemadars [second-lieutenants] he might select – but no! the hard and fast rule must be adhered to. As, by our present native army organization, all units not exceeding a hundred men are supposed to be commanded by natives, we should either adhere to this on service or definitely change it. To employ this in peacetime, and then to evince our disbelief in their capacity when in the field, only humiliates the native officers, and overworks the few British ones, who have their own duties to attend to.'

The historians of the Poona Horse state that 'some of the Indian Officers had to be taught the details of drill by word of mouth as they were unable to read'. How common this was elsewhere it is hard to establish. Of the rank and file, according to the same authorities, 'only a very small percentage could even sign their names'.[14]

However, there were a few native officers who managed to rise to quite exceptional heights. One such was Wurdi-Major Mahommed Afzal, whose services in the Afghan War with the 11th Bengal Cavalry and particularly in the succeeding 'settlement of Afghan affairs', brought him not only rewards in money and land, but also led to his being appointed a Companion of the Star of India. In 1883 he was nominated Agent of the British Government at Kabul with the temporary rank of Lieutenant-Colonel in the Army.[15]

* * *

In illustration of how pampered were the European as compared with the native troops, a staff officer pointed out that during the winter of 1879–80 at Sherpur, all the British troopers were housed in mud-brick buildings, while most of the sowars were under canvas. All the buildings had fireplaces and eighty-two pounds of firewood was allowed for each room every day, while the sowars had, if they could, to provide their own firewood. Further, each European soldier was provided with four blankets, but the luckless natives – and it illustrates their toughness – were allotted only two each.[16]

The regimental establishment of non-commissioned officers was usually eight kot-daffadars (troop sergeant-majors), and fifty-six daffadars, lance-daffadars and acting lance-daffadars (sergeants, corporals and lance-corporals) in each regiment.* Some commanding officers instituted examinations for promotion, but most relied on arbitrary selection, taking into account not only degrees of education, keenness and efficiency, but also social position and respectability.

The Indian army was a long-service army, but men were sometimes permitted to take their discharge after three years (see below). Until the late 1880s the cavalry service was so popular that very few did. The average period of service was somewhere between fifteen and twenty years, and both furloughs and pensions (invalid and ordinary) were not ungenerous. The names of applicants for future vacancies were always kept on a regimental roster. Very often there were long waits before vacancies could be filled. Since the silladar system entailed each recruit making a cash deposit of between £30 and £35 (which was returned on discharge) the service can be seen to have been not unpopular. Nevertheless, on

* For a list of Indian ranks with their British equivalents, see Appendix, p. 424.

at least one occasion, when the drain occasioned by the protracted operations of the Afghan War entailed a continual demand for replacements (chiefly due to sickness) a bounty had to be resorted to. In 1880 fifty rupees were granted to each recruit, while another fifty were given on the completion of three years' service.[17] But this was an exceptional time. Another exceptional time came in 1885, as a result of the Penjdeh incident caused by a boundary dispute between Russia and Afghanistan. The Bombay Cavalry were hastily augumented and the Poona Horse found itself for the first time in its history despatching recruiting parties outside its immediate area.[18]

After his first three years each man had the right to claim his discharge on giving two months' notice, provided his troop was not more than ten men below strength, and, of course, providing the regiment was not on active service.[19]

Generally speaking the majority of cavalry recruits came from the martial races. Most were of good family and respectability, possessing property in their villages. This was especially the case in the north. The best, hardiest and most warlike by instinct were probably the Sikhs, Pathans, Multanis and Baluchis, closely followed by the Punjabi Mussulmans and Tiwanas, the Dogras and Rangurs. Since the Mutiny endless discussions about the Class Composition of the native cavalry had taken place. As a general rule the outcome of them in Bengal had been the principle of Class Troops as opposed to Class Regiments. In Bombay, though, there was a larger degree of mixing of the races in the lowest units. There were strict regulations laid down, some of which were resented as they required certain regiments to maintain troops recruited from races 'who have the character of not being very enthusiastic warriors at the present day, whatever they may have been in days gone by.'[20] (For the class composition of Indian cavalry regiments, see Appendix, p. 423.)

Though the mixing of races within units was a measure thought necessary to make another mutiny more unlikely, it had its disadvantages. Since each race had to be represented by a proportion of native officers and non-commissioned officers, the field for promotion was more limited than it would otherwise have been. Further, the differences between the races as regards food, drink and untensils, made for a quartermaster's nightmare, especially on detached duties. The homogeneous nature of the regiment was adversely affected, too, since men of differing manners and customs came together only to perform their duties. When these were over, close fraternization between the races seldom took place.

* * *

On service, every two (and, later on, three) sowars maintained one follower as groom and servant, and one pony to carry their kits, two days' rations and a thirty-pound canvas tent. The cost of clothing himself and of feeding both himself and his horse was also borne by each man. There were seldom much more than six or seven rupees left out of the ordinary sowar's pay, which started at twenty-seven rupees a month. The most senior of the native officers were paid as much as 300 rupees, while good-conduct pay and various allowances could add as much as an extra sixty. During the Egyptian and Sudanese campaigns of the 1880s, when the supply of grain and forage for the Indian Contingent was undertaken by the Government of India, the rates of pay for the Bengal Cavalry were:

	Rupees		Rupees
Resaldar,		Wurdi Major	150
1st class	300	Jemadar	
2nd class	250	1st class	80
3rd class	200	2nd class	70
Ressaidar,		3rd class	60
1st class	150	Daffadar	30
2nd class	135	Trumpeter	25
3rd class	120	Sowar	20[21]

All soldiers of the native army were, of course, purely mercenary, though there is much evidence that this aspect was often ameliorated by close personal ties between the men and their regiments and the men and their British officers. Nevertheless, as Lieutenant W. W. Norman of the 2nd Punjab Cavalry wrote in 1890,

> 'We cannot expect them to go into battle and fight for British interests with the same feelings of loyalty which actuate British soldiers. There must be essentially "cupboard love", and to keep the cupboard full should be our motto . . . We should look to their interests and see that, not only are they not losers by performing our service, but that they are gainers and content.'

Until the last one and a half decades of the century to be in the army was a comparatively lucrative business, but the prices of provisions and forage increased by about 50 per cent during this period. Further, more efficient and therefore expensive equipment and accoutrements, together with the cost of such things as carbine and fencing clubs and the extra wear and tear of camps of exercise, combined to reduce the financial attractiveness of the silladar sowar's life. By 1890 there was actual difficulty in getting recruits of the right sort. Consequently in 1893 pay was increased. Sowars then received an extra four rupees a month. Another reason for the comparative difficulty in obtaining good recruits at this period was that the field for remunerative employments for natives was ever increasing. Beside more and more purely civil appointments there were posts in such bodies as the Burma, Singapore and Hong Kong police for which pay was higher than for soldiers.[22]

* * *

Writing of the Indian Contingent in Egypt in 1882, one observer found that the troops had

> 'an absolute incapacity to understand that anything wanted by the Queen's soldiers should not be seized at once and as a matter of course. The formality of requisition and payment produces in their minds a feeling of good-humoured contempt. Having the might, they marvel at not being permitted to exert it.'[23]

In other ways, too, the attitude to his profession of the Indian sowar in a silladar regiment was altogether different from that of the European trooper. Since each sowar's horse was his private property, for instance, anything wrong with it was a close, personal matter of intense seriousness. He would always consult his white officer and through the discussions which followed

> 'friendship, leading,' as young Lieutenant Birdwood found, 'to mutual confidence, would spring up between officer and man and endure throughout one's service. As intimacy increased one became familiar with the men's home and family affairs, and even now,' he wrote in 1941, 'though it was well over thirty years since I left my regiment [11th Bengal Lancers], my heart is warmed each Christmas by dozens of letters and

> cards from old soldiers, written in the vernacular, recalling the days when we served together.'*

One of the chief occupations of the good British officer seems to have been to act as a sort of mixture of welfare officer and judge. 'Sahib, word has come that both my bullocks are dead,' said one man to Birdwood when he was acting as adjutant. 'Ruin faces us – what are we do do? It is to be feared that I must "cut my name".' (i.e. take his discharge). After a long amicable discussion, says Birdwood, this very typical problem was solved by a loan from regimental funds.[24]

The officer who acted as adjutant, incidentally, also usually acted as riding master, which meant that he not only had to supervise all foot-drill, riding-school work, recruit training and musketry, but also be responsible for the training of all remounts. These added up to something like seventy a year. There were those who saw the lack of riding masters and of any riding establishments for training riding instructors as very serious deficiencies in Indian cavalry. 'However well the men may ride naturally,' wrote Captain Maguire, 'it is impossible for cavalry soldiers to manoeuvre properly and charge compactly unless they have been thoroughly taught to ride in the riding school on trained horses.' The training of the horses in most regiments was certainly haphazard. Each man trained his own with the minimum of supervision from the adjutant.[25]

A chief difference between sowars and troopers was their method of riding. Sowars depended much less upon balance. They rode with the knees and calves and with less hanging on to the bridle. During the Afghan War Major Walter Ashe, late of the King's Dragoon Guards, noticed that the Bombay Cavalry rode with

> 'a moderately short stirrup, with the knee upon the padded part of the saddle-flap, and rather in front of the stirrup leather, the heel well down and the foot pointing nearly straight forward. The weight of the body was well forward on the saddle – a great point in military equitation – with the fork close on the pommel.'[26]

After their recruit training, native soldiers were given no systematic training. As most of the sowars were not very athletically

* One of these ended thus: 'P.S. – My wife has run away with another fellow. By God, I am annoyed!' (Birdwood, 90.)

minded, only a small number of them competing at military tournaments, there were times during long sojourns in one station when men were not as fit as they might have been.

One of the most marked advantages Indian cavalrymen had over European troopers was in the weight of their equipment. Each sowar carried a flannel shirt, a pair of woollen socks, a clothes brush, a boot brush, a towel, a sponge and a horse-rubber. With his knife and spoon, all this weighed no more than four pounds. Much less formal pampering of the horses took place. Horse blankets were virtually unknown and grooming was seldom more than 'what can be given with a good wisp'. This almost certainly made them better able to withstand both wet and cold.

The wide variety of glamorous uniforms sported by the different native regiments came to be, as with British regiments, more and more confined to formal peacetime occasions. For example, when the 14th Bengal Lancers went to war in Afghanistan in 1879,

> 'blue, scarlet, and gold [were all] discarded, and all were dressed from top to toe in *Khâkee,* or mud colour,' as an officer of that regiment wrote. 'The lances were stripped of their gay scarlet and white pennons (we afterwards resumed these as a distinguishing mark), and the long jackboots replaced by ammunition "high-lows" and *putties*, or bandages of woollen stuff rolled round the leg from knee to ankle after the fashion of Cashmere sportsmen and Italian organ-grinders.'[27]

In Indian regiments there were no permanent regimental depots. These therefore always had to be formed on the outbreak of hostilities for the reception of recruits and remounts and for sick men and horses. They had, of course, to be manned by a certain number of 'efficients' for training and interior economy purposes. Thus it was that, unlike British regiments, the native cavalry's war strength was always and automatically less than its peace strength – an obvious inconvenience.[28]

Another inconvenient peculiarity of silladar cavalry was the fact that the Government of India provided and owned very few of the buildings forming the cavalry lines. Beyond the guard room and the magazines – known as the "bells of arms" where the small arms were kept under lock and key – nearly all other buildings belonged to the regiments occupying them under nebulous tenancy conditions. Until the 1890s 'the frequent excuse, but in reality often no such thing, of a sowar that he must go to his home because his house had fallen down applied equally to the Indian cavalry lines. Made of sun-dried bricks and roofed with tiles on rough wooden rafters which were a ready prey to white ants, they literally either melted away in the rains or collapsed when the ants had eaten through the timber.' The situation became so bad towards the end of the century that Government had to advance 720,000 rupees to bring all the Bengal Cavalry lines up to a decent standard. This loan had to be repaid by monthly instalments from subscriptions levied according to rank.[29] This is an illustration of how inexpensive native cavalry was compared with European!

Another illustration is given by the following extract from the records of the 3rd Bombay Light Cavalry: '1896. The regiment purchased a Maxim rifle machine-gun to fire .303 Lee-Mitford ammunition, mounted on a light cavalry tripod, from the Maxim-Nordenfelt Gun Company, London, at a cost of Rs 5,363-6-11.'[30] It comes as a surprise to learn the extent of the private enterprise existing in silladar regiments only eighteen years before the First World War. One supposes that had the regiment *indented* for a machine-gun it would not have got one!

Most of the men of the native cavalry, at any rate in Northern India, were brought up to their military life from infancy, being the children of men who were themselves the children of men who had served. When a regiment marched through a village in the country where it was recruited, the old men would invariably come out to present an address to the commanding officer. 'There will be few among the old grey-beards,' according to Baden-Powell, 'who have not medals on their breasts showing that they have fought for the Empire. The younger men are generally troopers on leave, or lads who are going to become troopers. They all take charge of the horses of the regiment and proceed to groom and feed them.'[31]

The most astonishing difference between European and native regiments was the regimental durbar. In place of the stiff 'Orderly Room' of regular regiments, with Queen's Regulations and red tape dominating the proceedings, the durbar was wonderfully informal. Every man who chose to attend was at liberty to do so. Beside the giving out of official instructions concerning discipline and interior economy, petitions were heard and considered and all questions connected with the welfare and finances of the regiment were freely discussed. 'In a British regiment', wrote an officer of the Central India Horse in 1890, 'the officer is more of

Tenth Hussar.

X for Tenth, Prince of Wales's own Royal Hussars:
Very gorgeous to view are such bold sons of Mars,
With their jackets o'erlaid
With expensive gold braid,
And their boots and striped overalls perfectly made,
They must feel very proud in such glory arrayed;
But, believe me, the lives of bright beings like these
Are not all enjoyment, good living, and ease;
For in these troubled days of Re-organization,
When our principal *business* would seem *Re-creation,*
What with autumn manœuvres, exams., and long courses,
There isn't much peace for Her Majesty's forces.

17. Tenth Hussar, from *Army and Navy Drolleries* by Major Seccombe, c. 1880.

18. The Duke of Cambridge at the time of his retirement from the office of Commander-in-Chief, 1895

19. Captain Edmund Allenby, Inniskillings (6th Dragoons), c. 1890

20. Lieut Douglas Haig, 7th Hussars, aged 25

21. General Sir George Luck

the strict disciplinarian over an unruly crew of independent spirits; in a Native Regiment he is the patriarch of the flock and guiding spirit that leads them aright.'[32]

Unlike the European troopers the native sowars were allowed and encouraged to keep their swords sharp. They knew the art of always seeing that the cutting edge was as sharp as a razor. Indeed, when something shameful was done, they used to say that it was 'as disgraceful as having a blunt sword'. The young Baden-Powell noticed that the sowars the moment they were off parade removed their swords from their scabbards, carefully wrapping them in oiled muslin. They then hung them up so that nothing should dull their edges.[33] The scabbards in Indian cavalry regiments were made of solid brown leather. They were thinly lined with wood and tipped with metal. Major Ashe thought, as did many others before and after him, that the European steel scabbards were heavy, difficult to clean, glistened in the sun and moon light, blunted the sword and rusted when water got inside them, 'while they make such a rattle that a secret reconnaissance with them is impossible'. He thought that they should be replaced by the Indian model. He thought the same about 'our own troopers' cumbersome sabres, that won't cut and cannot point'. (See also p. 397.) The native tulwar was much preferable. Its keen edge enabled 'its owner to lop off a head or a limb as easily as cutting a cabbage.'[34]

Swordsmanship was, and is, an art much cherished and practised by Indians. Baden-Powell tells us that there were three schools of swordsmanship in Meerut alone. He contrived to get hold of some of their most skilled exponents to come and demonstrate to the men of his regiment, the 13th Hussars.

> 'It was quite an eye-opener to all of us,' he wrote in his excellent autobiographical book, *Indian Memories,* 'to note the various kinds of feints, cuts and guards of which these men were masters. Often and again our men almost boo'd certain hits as being unfair, but when we explained to them that this is what they would meet with if we ever had to fight such men in earnest they realised that the sword exercises laid down for the British soldier were merely a set of general principles . . .
>
> 'There was one favourite cut with the natives in which your opponent seemed to take a slog at your ankle and by a dextrous turn of the wrist he drew his sword through the opposite side of your neck.'

There was another especially dangerous cut at which native cavalrymen became adept. It was only delivered after the adversary had been passed. It dropped a sharp, heavy cut straight down on to the shoulder with fatal effect. It was as a safeguard against this particular cut that the British cavalry in India took to wearing shoulder-scales made of steel rings.[35]

* * *

The Thursday holiday, known affectionately as St Napier's Day after its originator, saw informal mounted sports of an evening: tent-pegging, an essentially Eastern sport, in which the lance was normally used, though sometimes the sword; 'lemon-slicing'; trick-riding (which sometimes included tent-pegging on an absolutely naked horse without saddle or bridle); *gatka-bazi* which was a sword duel between two mounted men; jumping and various forms of *kurtab* (displays of horsemanship), were regularly indulged in. Not only the officers took part but also a small number of the rank and file.[36] From time to time Assaults-at-Arms took place. These were usually inter-regimental affairs, with numerous different competitions taking place. There were prizes, generally presented by the commanding officers, for the best 'Man-at-Arms' and the best trained horse. Obstacle races and 'paper-chases' were also very popular.

Though the chief and much enjoyed recreation of the officers and men, all these sports were also an integral part of the cavalryman's training. More serious forms of it included 'Long Distance Rides', upon which General Luck was especially keen. The Bombay regiments made these a speciality of theirs. The following extracts from the 4th Bombay Cavalry's records are typical of these testing exercises:

> 'Captain Thomas's Party: 1 naik and 4 sowars, accompanied by 3 baggage ponies, 134 miles on the Sholapur road, 67 out and 67 back in 41 hours. The ponies marched 116 miles in 46 hours. No sore backs amongst the horses; one pony's back slightly swollen . . .
>
> 'Captain Young's Party: 1 non-commissioned officer and 4 sowars, 3 baggage ponies and 1 camel; Poona to Malegaon via Ahmednagar, 186 miles in 60 hours and 45 minutes. One horse shod before starting went lame at the fifty-fourth milestone and was left behind; 1 horse was 8 hours and 45 minutes

behind the others in arriving at Malegaon. Baggage ponies marched the 186 miles in 82 hours and 30 minutes; 1 pony slightly galled.

'In all cases, times given include stoppages. Weight carried by ponies, 150 lbs.'[37]

At the conclusion of one of General Luck's earliest Camps of Exercise at which the Sind Cavalry Brigade was showing off its paces, he unexpectedly ordered two of the regiments to march across 118 miles of waterless desert, as a test of endurance. The 7th Bombay Lancers, only recently raised, covered the distance in thirty-six hours. This was thought to be an achievement never before equalled.[38]

Much in vogue in the 1890s were what were known as 'long advances'. These became prominent features of field days, particularly in Bengal. The manoeuvre would start with an advance to a flank in column. The line would then form, and the long-awaited culmination would be a charge made against a skeleton enemy using flags, whose movements were strictly controlled and usually limited to a trot.[39]

A certain keen but not very intelligent commanding officer of one of the Punjab regiments 'became imbued with the idea that cavalry were not sufficiently mobile at night.' He therefore concealed a force of infantry in a secret position. An officer who was with the wretched squadron told off for this unpopular exercise tells what happened.

'[We were] moving more or less together with a few ground scouts in front, whose role in the pitch darkness was markedly useless. Suddenly we stumbled upon the infantry position; these heroes had been armed with blank cartridges, and a sheet of fire and a roll of musketry suddenly spat out of the surrounding darkness. The action of every horse could not with years of practice have been more perfectly concerted. Each and every one started at full gallop in the direction in which his head pointed at the moment. The success of infantry over cavalry in night manoeuvres was clearly demonstrated by the number of casualties that ensued. The language of both officers and men who every moment met in violent collision is not for publication.'[40]

* * *

For the purpose of local law enforcement the native cavalry, by virtue of its superior mobility, was obviously preferable to the European regiments. But some were more mobile than others. The Poona Horse, for example, possessed, according to the Poona Superintendent of Police,

> 'a very great advantage over other corps . . . in being supplied with pony carriage as opposed to mules.* The result is, they can move literally as soon as the horses can be saddled and the baggage packed on the ponies, and they can travel over any country. On one occasion I marched with a detachment over one hundred miles in less than forty hours; but whenever we halted for a few hours, the men's baggage was up, and they were able to get their food for themselves, and to make their horses and selves as comfortable as they would be in their own lines, within an hour of dismounting.'[41]

A great deal of the Bengal native cavalry's time was consumed in minor frontier expeditions, particularly during the 1890s. Their duties included escorting of guns, reconnaissance as much on foot as mounted and, of course, outpost work. None of it was very exciting, though casualties could be considerable. An officer of the 19th Lancers describes a typical engagement against the Orakzai tribes in 1892, with a surprising but not untypical interlude:

> 'On April 17th an early start was made; soon the artillery came into position and began their bombardment, under cover of which the infantry attacked and the cavalry started their movement up the river bed, which became narrower and narrower whilst the mountains became steeper and steeper. At first no one was encountered; at last a small party was seen advancing, two or three tribesmen, unarmed, followed by others. Field-glasses came out. In front was a man in a blue kurta [loose-fitting frock or blouse] and a lungi [headdress, looser than a turban]! Yes; it was the uniform of the 19th Lancers, and the wearer, it turned out, had served in the regiment; he had come out to renew his acquaintanceship, and the baskets on the heads of the men behind him were the

* In 1898 mules were reluctantly taken to replace ponies. This became necessary as a result of the Deccan being denuded of ponies for transport purposes in the Afghan War nineteen years before. Most of the brood mares had been taken at that time, and by 1898 the breed had virtually disappeared, while other suitable ponies had also become scarce. (Anderson and Molloy, I, 258–9.)

usual offerings without which, in the East, no official visit is complete. Compliments were exchanged, no inconvenient questions asked or incriminating replies received, and the cavalry moved on again.

'Next a small hamlet on the hillside. What if it be held? A half-squadron dismounted; the led horses moved away to a flank; the officer drew his sword, the men their carbines, and then forward. Luckily, perhaps, no one was there. So mount and on again, stumbling over rocks and boulders, dismouting sometimes to lead horses over a bad bit. At last a puff of smoke from a crag overhanging the river bed, then a report; evidently only that of a *jezail* [a long Afghan musket], followed by a long raffale on a tom-tom. This was repeated once or twice and then all was quiet. Now the regiment had got right behind the Samana ridge; the enemy ought to be streaming down by this time unless they were too late. At last a movement on the fairly well-wooded hillside, and men appear. Are they Orakzais? No; our own infantry, moving more or less in single file down the precipitious hillside. The enemy had apparently spotted the cavalry and had retreated to the north-west. Nothing more for the cavalry to do but to get back to camp, but not by that nullah bed again; it would be pitch dark by the time camp was reached, to say nothing of the chance of an ambush. Nothing for it but to dismount and lead the horses over the Samana and down the other side.'[42]

Beside the Afghan and Egyptian campaigns, Bengal cavalry regiments or detachments, took part in at least fourteen separate expeditions of one sort of another between 1872 and 1895. During the same period, regiments or detachments of the Bombay cavalry took part in only three expeditions.

* * *

The mobility and readiness of Indian cavalry is well illustrated by the performance of the regiments which formed part of the Indian Contingent for Egypt in 1882. For instance, the very last detachment to arrive in time to take part in the Tel el-Kebir campaign was a troop of the 6th Bengal Cavalry. After a sea voyage of sixteen days this troop landed at Ismailia at 8 p.m. on 11 September. At 11 p.m. it started for Kassassin which it reached the following afternoon. Having joined the cavalry division, it at once marched on Tel el-Kebir, and thence to Cairo. Not a man or horse fell out during those three days of hectic forced marches. As an American observer said: 'Cavalry capable of such a performance is not cavalry to be thought lightly of.'

The same observer noted that the Indian 'mode of packing the equipment is a subject of careful drill . . . In the words of a distinguished British officer, "even the colonel's mustard-pot has its own place".' Comparing the 'dilatoriness' of the British transport service, he commended the Indian practice of shipping all the regimental transport animals, together with two weeks' rations, on the same steamer that carried the troops. But careless stabling aboard the transports, which had to cross the Arabian Sea in the trough of the swell raised by the monsoon, meant that many horses were lost. The 13th Bengal Lancers alone lost more than forty horses from injuries and over-crowding.[43] Yet it is clear that, generally speaking, the arrangements made by the Indian authorities were very superior to those made for the troops coming from Britain.

* * *

In 1895 the Presidential Army System was abolished. Under this the Madras and Bombay armies had come under the Governments of their respective Presidencies, while only the Bengal army had been subject to the Commander-in-Chief, India. At the same time the army of India was now divided into four separate commands, each under a lieutenant-general. These were the Bengal, Punjab, Madras and Bombay commands.

4

'I formed a high estimate of [the Volunteer Cavalry in King William's Town]. Many of the farmers had been non-commissioned officers in our cavalry regiments, and I clearly saw that their influence over the rest would be exercised for good if they were called upon for active service, and that, if only they would pay deference to authority, they would be valuable in war.'

GENERAL SIR ARTHUR CUNYNGHAME, Commander of the Forces in South Africa, in 1874[1]

(i)

South Africa: the nine Kaffir Wars – Cape Mounted Riflemen – Boomplaats, 1848 – 7th Dragoon Guards arrive – Swartkopjes, 1845 – Gwanga river, 1846 – Sir Harry Smith's ride to King William's Town – 12th Lancers arrive – Berea Mountain, 1852 – Volunteer mounted units, 1870s, 1880s

During the period covered by the first two volumes of this history there occurred a number of minor campaigns in southern Africa. Discussion of the mounted arm's part in these has been deferred until now because it was thought sensible to present them as an introduction to the larger conflicts of the 1870s and 1880s.

Fortunately for both reader and author there is no need to enter into the complexities of South African history. It is enough to say here that between 1779 and 1877 there were nine co-called Kaffir (or Bantu) Wars, as well as certain other clashes. The first three Kaffir Wars, the third of which (1799–1802) was the first to involve the British, do not concern us.

Thereafter, until the Zulu War of 1879, the contestants in the first place were the settlers, both Boer and British, in combination against the cattle-stealing depredations of the various fierce and unscrupulous black tribes settled since the middle of the eighteenth-century along the eastern frontier of the Cape of Good Hope. Next, due to the Dutch settlers' increasingly implacable hatred of British rule, no less than to 'relays of meddlesome and ignorant

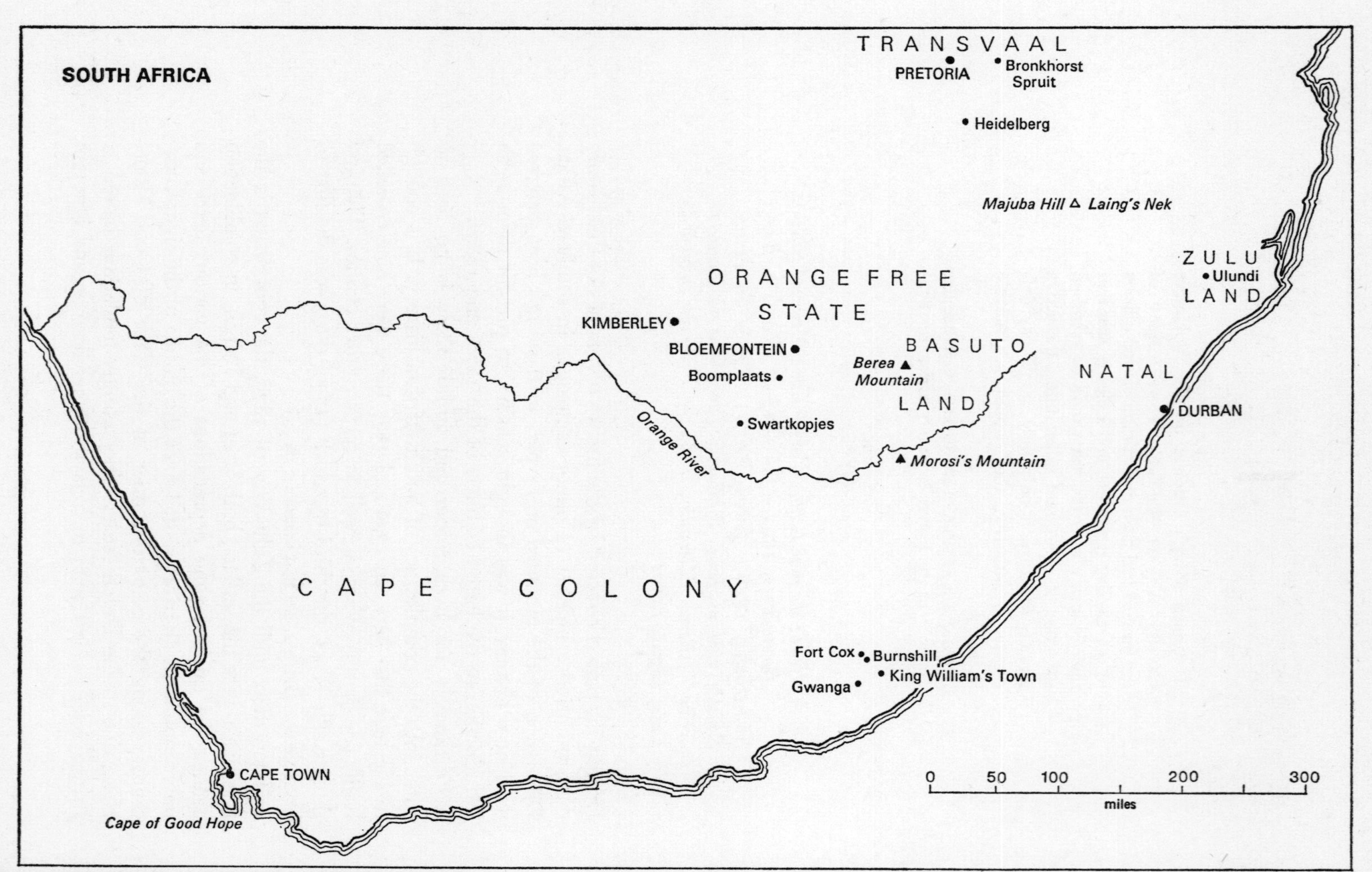
SOUTH AFRICA
TRANSVAAL
PRETORIA
Bronkhorst Spruit
Heidelberg
Majuba Hill
Laing's Nek
ZULU LAND
Ulundi
ORANGE FREE STATE
KIMBERLEY
BLOEMFONTEIN
Boomplaats
BASUTO LAND
Berea Mountain
NATAL
DURBAN
Swartkopjes
Orange River
Morosi's Mountain
CAPE COLONY
Fort Cox
Burnshill
King William's Town
Gwanga
CAPE TOWN
Cape of Good Hope
0
50
100
200
300
miles

politicians in London',[2] fighting began to take place between the two white races.

* * *

For many decades from the first occupation of the Cape in 1796, and indeed to a lesser degree right down to 1918, one of the chief military instruments of the British was the Cape Coloureds, or Hottentots, generally known as Totties. These were descended from 'the first permanent dwellers in the country and the first to be seen by European eyes'.[3] Intelligent, though sometimes lazy and always superstitious, they had, according to Sir Harry Smith, who often had to employ them, 'a natural turn to become soldiers', though he was to find that against an organized enemy they were of little use without the support of white troops.[4] They stood on a lower level of civilization than the Kaffirs, who were 'better armed, of magnificent physique and endurance, and imbued with a warlike spirit and a reckless courage that was entirely lacking among the feebler natives of the west.'[5]

In 1817 the British Government decided to form out of an irregular body which had been raised in 1806 a 'regular' regiment of Hottentots, both cavalry and infantry, under British officers. Ten years later the infantry part was disbanded and the cavalry was converted into three companies of mounted rifles, 250 rank and file strong. Thus was founded one of the most famous of all colonial mounted regiments, and the only one for many years to be composed entirely of mounted infantrymen. It was called the Cape Mounted Riflemen.

The regiment was treated as cavalry, though the officers' and men's pay was at the infantry rates. The men sat upon hussar saddles and their officers wore cavalry moustaches, but for many years their uniform was modelled on that of the Rifle Brigade, with the addition of small plumes to their shakos. In the 1840s an officer who saw them described them as 'little men mounted on small, active horses'. They wore blue forage caps and 'brown buckskin trousers, or *crackers*, as they were called'.[6] In 1856 tunics and 'the cut down shako' were adopted. Eleven years later the uniform was changed from Rifle Brigade green to dark blue.

> 'Some of the NCOs were Europeans, and gradually more Europeans – good-conduct men with two years' service who volunteered from Line regiments – were introduced, until eventually

the regiment became predominantly white. The reason for this,' as Major Tylden, the regiment's most distinguished chronicler, has pointed out, 'was that it was found impossible to keep the Coloureds true to their salt in the face of constant temptation to join the Kaffir tribes, against whom the regiment was constantly employed. Any or no reason was enough to make the unstable, excitable and irrational crossbreeds mutiny or desert . . .

'In 1834 the regiment did well in the Sixth Kaffir War, though one unpleasant incident occurred. Twenty-five riflemen on an outpost plotted to deliver it to the Kaffirs, though nothing came of it. In 1838 a serious mutiny occurred. A party of men, mostly recruits, fired on their officers in the mess room, killing Lieutenant Crowe. The outbreak was easily suppressed.

'In 1839 the regiment was augmented to six companies, each eighty strong, under the command of Colonel Henry Somerset, a most efficient soldier.

'In 1841 a small detachment accompanied the force which was besieged at Durban, and in 1845 a company saw service across the Orange River. This company, under Captain Warden, founded the present city of Bloemfontein . . .

'In April, 1847, the regiment was augmented to twelve companies, which establishment was not altered until 1862, when it was reduced by two companies, and in 1864 by four more.'[7]

One European and three Coloured companies were engaged in an action against rebellious Boers at Boomplaats Farm under Sir Harry Smith. This sharp affair, fought on 29 August, 1848, was largely won, at considerable cost, by the infantry and artillery, but the Cape Mounted Riflemen played a useful part. They lost one officer and a few men. The engagement ended the first of the three chief clashes which took place between the British and the South African Republicans. The next occurred thirty-three years later (see p. 240).

In 1848 it had been laid down for the regiment that twenty of every seventy men on detachment must be Europeans. Five years later more than 200 volunteers were received from regiments of the line. This brought the proportion of Europeans to Coloureds up to two to one. In 1856 a quarter of the men were non-European.

Only one further batch of Coloureds was enlisted after that. During the Indian Mutiny the regiment was treated as a remount depôt for the mounted arm and the artillery in India. To a lesser degree this rôle was continued for some years afterwards. In 1863 a depôt was formed at Canterbury in England and numerous recruits joined, particularly from Yorkshire.

So far as it went, the regiment was, in Fortescue's words, 'a very efficient local constabulary',[8] though always far too weak for the vast extent of frontier which it was supposed to protect. From time to time irregular Hottentot levies were raised to help in this task. One such was commanded by a captain of the 7th Dragoon Guards in the 1840s. He is said to have 'raised it to a wonderful state of efficiency'.[9]

* * *

The great merit of the Cape Mounted Riflemen in the eyes of London was that the regiment's existence largely did away with the costly necessity of maintaining a regular cavalry regiment from home in the South African command. Except for the 21st Light Dragoons, which left the Cape in 1817, only two home regiments served in South Africa before 1879. These were the 7th Dragoon Guards from 1843 to 1848 and the 12th Lancers between 1851 and 1853.

The 7th was the first heavy cavalry regiment ever to be sent on colonial service. Why a heavy regiment was chosen it is difficult to say. Lieutenant Robert Arkwright, the regiment's riding master, believed that 'the 7th were sent to the Cape to spend money: this everyone was aware of.' Certainly many of the officers at that period were very wealthy. Before leaving home they had ordered twenty-one couple of foxhounds to be sent out after them. A further five couple were ordered later. Kennels were built at Fort Beaufort and many of the local settler farmers, mostly British, joined in the jackal hunting. Between October, 1843 and December, 1845, forty-six and a half brace were killed. Other ways in which money was spent by the officers included race meetings 'on a scale hitherto unknown', dinners, balls, concerts and shooting parties. Sporting wagers were very popular. Captain Codrington, for example, backed himself to ride his bay pony from the Drostdy Barrack Gate at Grahamstown to the Inn at Koonap within two hours. The distance was twenty-five miles and he covered it in one hour, fifty minutes. Later Captain Sir Harry Darell, weighing over fourteen stone, won £100 for riding twenty-two and three-quarter miles in one hour, seventeen minutes.[10]

One who saw the men of the 7th soon after their arrival says that there was great difficulty in mounting them. The regiment was compelled to take 'horses as low as fifteen hands. The men in full dress with helmets, carbines and accoutrements looked rather absurd mounted.'[11] The helmets were soon exchanged for forage caps, and from other accounts it seems that the regiment had earlier been given 'a single-barrelled muzzle-loading rifle', probably the Brunswick which was issued to Rifle regiments in 1838. A surgeon of an infantry regiment thought that it was not 'a serviceable weapon for a mounted man, and even when the men were engaged with the enemy on foot I have seen them after several rounds hammering at the ramrods with a stone to get the bullet down.'[12]

One of the first actions in which the regiment took part was a skirmish with some 250 rebel Boers at Swartkopjes on 30 April, 1845. The enemy at one point dismounted and from behind a stone wall and some small mounds opened fire on the pursuing cavalry: ninety-four of the 7th and twenty-four of the Cape Mounted Riflemen under Lieutenant-Colonel Robert Richardson, the 7th's commanding officer. Richardson dismounted one troop of his regiment as well as the Riflemen and fired a volley into the Boers' front. At the same time the rest of the 7th galloped around their flank and attacked them in extended order. So swift was this charge that Lieutenant John Gray of the 7th rushed the enemy's one field piece, a three-pounder. He shot through the head the gunner in charge, who, surprisingly, was a Frenchman. The Boers remounted and fled, leaving two dead. Beside the gun, several wagons and numerous sheep and cattle were captured.[13]

In the following year there broke out the 7th Kaffir War. In this, as in all the other conflicts with the Bantu tribes, to bring the enemy to open action was the hardest task facing the British commanders. Nearly all effort was concentrated upon hunting the elusive cattle stealers over enormous expanses of mountainous, roadless bush country, guarding against ambushes, protecting lines of communication along which travelled heavily escorted convoys of ox-drawn wagons and pack-mules. More often than not the enemy's harassing tactics were successful. When sighted the Kaffirs disappeared, in the words of one young staff officer, 'as savages only can – like needles in straw'.[14]

Very seldom did they become over-confident. Very seldom

did a column move by daylight. One of the very few occasions when they made this mistake occurred at the Gwanga River on 7 June, 1846. A column of some 600 Xosas was surprised and trapped in the narrow valley by two squadrons each of the 7th and the Cape Mounted Riflemen, accompanied by various detachments of infantry and four guns. Captain Sir Harry Darell, in command of the advance guard troop of the 7th, came upon the column as he topped a crest, 'and, without sending to the rear or asking for instruction, he formed troop and charged into the middle of the Kaffirs, and was cutting them down in all directions some time before General Somerset [Major-General Henry Somerset] knew what was going on.'[15] As the rest of the British force came up

> 'the General gave the word to the 7th Dragoon Guards, who were in advance of the guns, to open out and allow the guns to trot through the space, come into action, and fire two rounds: the 7th forming line on each flank of the guns and charging: the Cape Mounted Rifles forming line in extended order and charging in succession to the 7th.
>
> 'The shot and shell did good execution, and the charge,' wrote Lieutenant Bisset of the Staff, 'was the prettiest thing I have ever seen in real fighting. You might have placed a long tablecloth over each troop, they kept in such compact order, and the Cape Mounted Rifles went through the broken mass of Kaffirs in one long line . . . The Cavalry wheeled and came back re-charging the enemy . . . For six or seven miles the troops were mixed up with the running Kaffirs, and deadly slaughter ensued.'[16]

Trooper Buck Adams of the 7th, not the most reliable of sources, says that the Cape Mounted Riflemen did not charge 'as they had no swords. These were lost,' he adds, 'with the baggage at Burns Hill; they had been taken from the Totties as they were to them a useless appendage, and placed in the waggons.' He confirms, however, that the Riflemen 'did considerable execution with their double-barrelled carbines'.[17] Next day 270 dead warriors were counted on the field of battle.

A Rifleman who was looking after two spare horses is said to have taken part in the charges, 'his steed flanked by the two impetuous coursers'. Some of the enemy, armed as usual only with assegais and ancient blunderbusses (from which such things as 'legs of iron pots' would emerge), escaped death by whirling their blankets or robes in the faces of the charging horses, even sometimes completely hooding them.[18]

One officer was killed and three others, as well as seven men, were wounded in this action. Sir Harry Darell was twice wounded by assegais. The first 'struck him on the left arm, and was pulled through from behind as he sat on horseback by the troop-sergeant-major.' The other penetrated deep into the muscles of the hip.[19]

The Gwanga was one of the very few actions in South Africa where the British mounted arm found an opportunity of charging against Kaffirs over really acceptable cavalry country. It was also the last engagement of any importance which the 7th saw in South Africa. The war came to an end in October, 1847, and the regiment left for home in the following April.

* * *

The outbreak of the next – the 8th – Kaffir War followed on soon enough. It found Sir Harry Smith shut up in Fort Cox surrounded by enormous numbers of Kaffirs. Two attempts by Somerset to relieve him were unsuccessful. On 29 December, 1850, he made a dash for King William's Town with 250 of the Cape Mounted Riflemen. He put on the uniform of one of his riflemen

> 'and by this timely incognito,' according to John Montagu, the Cape Colonial Secretary, 'he rode twelve hazardous miles through the desultory fire of the Kaffirs . . . About halfway, a strong attempt was made to intercept the Corps, but Sir Harry Smith and his escort vigorously spurred through their opponents, and after a smart ride reached the town, having eluded six bodies of Kaffirs, who little suspected how great a prize was then in their power.'[20]

The very men who had thus escorted Sir Harry in his epic dash were among the 335 riflemen who, two weeks later, either deserted or had to be disarmed. This left him for a considerable time with virtually no mounted troops. Although some of the disarmed Hottentots were soon re-enlisted, from now onwards the regiment was increasingly made up of European recruits, mostly from home.

At this time the depredations of growing numbers of disaffected Hottentots were added to the increasingly aggressive raids of the Basuto, one of the most powerful Bantu tribes. Every sort of solution was being canvassed except the only really effective one of sending out enough regular troops from home. 'Everybody,' wrote the Duke of Wellington in the last year of his life, 'appears to have discovered some Nostrum for carrying on the War at the Cape.' When the importing of irregular cavalry from India was suggested, he wrote to his friend Miss Angela Burdett-Coutts: 'Indian Cavalry! God help them! Do they know what they are? How are they to be brought from the Continent of Asia to that of Africa? They cannot march. They must come in Transports. Did anybody ever hear of one of them embarked?' To this, showing some ignorance of the needs of the frontier and of the character of the veldt, he added: 'But who ever heard of Cavalry to be used in the Jungle or Bush?'[21]

In mid-October, 1851, two months before the Duke wrote those words, amongst other reinforcements had arrived the 12th Lancers, 480 strong.[22] The regiment was at once involved in Smith's policy of giving the enemies which confronted him no rest. Typical of the numerous small actions undertaken by individual troops was one commanded by Lieutenant Chandos Clifton. 'He pursued two herds of cattle,' wrote Smith, 'swam with his party the rapid river by which they endeavoured to escape, and succeeded in capturing 527 head of cattle, and not without resistance of the enemy.'[23] As in all the Kaffir wars the fighting consisted chiefly in sudden ambushes, often skilfully laid, in the cutting off of stragglers and in night assaults. Above all, endless marching and counter-marching required exceptional stamina from both men and horses. Numerous horses – they were all tough little Capes – died of starvation or exhaustion. 'We applied for money to replace them,' wrote a lieutenant of the 12th many years later, '. . . but the War Office said that they only replaced horses which died of Glanders or were destroyed on that account. After that no horse died of anything but Glanders. I certified them all!'[24]

At the end of 1852, after Smith had been replaced as Governor, High Commissioner and Commander-in-Chief, his successor, Major-General Sir George Cathcart, having put an end to the 8th Kaffir War, moved against the Basuto chief, Moshesh. The Basuto tribesmen, for the most part, had abandoned 'the traditional native style of fighting on foot with shield and assegai . . . By 1852 they could put in the field 7,000 well-mounted men.'[25] Cathcart, not trusting to native levies and auxiliaries, used nothing but regular British troops. He was fortunate in possessing enough.

At the affair of the Berea Mountain on 20 December, a rather messy engagement fought in intense heat, his force of just over 2,000 of all arms persuaded Moshesh to give up the struggle. As usual, the trouble centred around cattle. Cathcart had demanded a fine of 10,000 head as compensation for continued depredations upon the Boer settlers' farms. The Basuto decided to fight rather than pay the fine. The British mounted column, commanded by Lieutenant-Colonel G. T. C. Napier of the Cape Mounted Riflemen, consisted of 114 of the 12th Lancers and 191 of his own regiment. As the men of this column, one of three approaching from different directions, reached the northern end of the Berea, 'a long, scarped table-land',[26] they saw many thousands of Moshesh's cattle grazing on its slopes. In the course of the morning the cavalrymen ascended the hill and began rounding up a 'magnificent herd' which they came across on the plateau. 'After a hard gallop,' wrote a cavalry officer who was present, 'a few of us managed to head the herd and turn them back to Napier, though not without danger of being hurled over a krantz [overhanging rock]. I cannot describe to you the force of the stream of cattle which would have escaped, had we not luckily shot an ox or two in a narrow opening between two stones, the only outlet; this stopped the torrent rushing forward.'[27] Soon after midday the lancers and riflemen succeeded in driving this herd of over 4,000 beasts and some fifty horses* down the hillside. Suddenly some 700 Basuto horsemen and a few footmen, who had been skilfully concealed in dead ground,

> 'attacked the rear guard who were forced to retire in order to save themselves from being cut off. I at once sounded the assembly,' wrote Napier in his official report, 'and collecting as many Lancers and C.M.R. as I could, formed up in support of the rear guard, and kept the enemy in check until they had time to form again, which they did as soon as they got clear of the rocky ground. The enemy then tried to outflank me on both sides, but the steady front presented by the troops prevented them doing so.'[28]

This attack on the weak rearguard, commanded by Major William Tottenham of the 12th, was the most critical moment of the action, for the main body of the cavalry had gone on a mile and a half ahead quite unsuspecting of the perils behind it.

* After the action these captured horses were put up for sale. They were mostly young colts and they fetched prices varying from eight shillings to £12. (King, Capt. W. R., *Campaigning in Kaffirland . . . in 1851–2*, 1853, 321.)

> 'We did our best,' wrote an officer of the rearguard. 'We drove one squadron in, and then another at our best pace, and then confronted their main body . . . We now re-dressed our line at 300 yards from their centre, which was three deep, their flanks advanced in an attitude to surround us. We charged, and received at 70 yards' distance a concentric fire from the whole line, after which the semicircle closed its horns upon us, and we were surrounded and cut off. We were therefore compelled to dash back and re-form close to them, but their regular and overwhelming advance pushed us on and we were obliged at last to gallop for our lives.
>
> 'Our retreat was headlong, for the enemy had headed us and pursued us with good speed . . . Tottenham behaved like a hero; the last to turn, he remained almost the last in the retreat, and by cool courage and good riding managed to save a sergeant-major by shooting a Basuto while just about to stab him. After a mile we were pulled up by a stone wall, and here many fell . . .'

It seems that several of the lancers foolishly, or perhaps unavoidably, faced with this obstacle, dismounted so as to lead their horses over the wall, with the result that they could not mount again in time to avoid being overtaken. The Riflemen seem to have jumped the wall.[29]

> 'At length,' continues the rearguard officer's account, 'some Cape Mounted Riflemen came back to our support, and their carbine shots checked our pursuers . . .
>
> 'Our captured cattle were now driven on as fast as possible, and though Kafirs [Basutos] collected on our flank, yet they would not face Tottenham's little rear guard commanded by himself on foot, and hampered with a wounded man upon his horse.'[30]

A company of the 74th Foot now arrived from base camp and covered the retirement of Napier's column and his 4,000 cattle.

Twenty-seven other ranks of the 12th lost their lives. So did five of the Mounted Riflemen. Some of the former had ridden into a morass during the retreat and had been butchered before the eyes of their comrades. Others were cut off and battle-axed. Wearing very tight overalls and carrying nine-foot lances, the men were at a very real disadvantage. The light axe, in close-quarter work, was fully a match for both lance and sword, both of which were carried by the 12th. The flint-lock horse-pistol which they also carried was pretty useless. The double-barrelled carbine, one barrel of which was normally loaded with buckshot, was carried by the Riflemen in addition to their swords. So it was by some of the lancers, but once they were dismounted, since carbines were attached to the horse and not to the man,* they were not available.

It seems clear that Napier, whom Cathcart intended should cooperate with the two infantry columns, got himself separated and 'disorganized in pursuit of cattle'.[31] Cathcart later stated that Napier disobeyed orders in going on to the Berea and climbing to its top. It was not intended, he said, that time should be wasted in driving cattle.[32] When, later on in the engagement, cavalry support would have been welcome, there was no sign of Napier. He had shot his bolt. Colonel G. F. R. Henderson, writing after the end of the Great Boer War, groups the Berea with Isandhlwana, Inhlobane Mountain and Laing's Nek, as an example of 'how often in South Africa alone, even with small forces, the bad work of the staff was responsible for failure.'[33]

Among the officers who distinguished themselves in this engagement was the twenty-five year old Lieutenant Valentine Baker of the 12th (see p. 116). It was his first important taste of action. By it his eyes were opened to some of the more glaring imperfections of the regular cavalry. These he sought to correct through the pungent criticisms which he included in his 1858 pamphlet on the practical organization of the mounted arm. (See Vol II, 426).

Comparative peace having been restored to southern Africa, the 12th Lancers sailed for India at the end of 1853. Fifteen years were to pass before another cavalry regiment arrived in South Africa.

* * *

In 1870 the regiment of Cape Mounted Riflemen was disbanded. By that date there were only ten Totties left in it. No replacement was sent from home, nor was another regiment raised in South Africa to take its place. Fifteen years earlier various small detachments of European mounted police which had been raised in Cape Colony were amalgamated and given the name of the Frontier

* See p. 235 for General Roberts's views on this matter more than a quarter of a century later.

Armed and Mounted Police. On the Cape Mounted Riflemen's demise these were the only mounted men left on the Frontier. Consequently they 'tended to become more and more soldiers rather than police'.[34] In 1878 they were reorganized on a military basis and the name as well as the regular status of the Cape Mounted Riflemen were revived for them. The chief difference between the old and the new regiments was that the new was a Colonial corps whereas the old had been an Imperial one. Further, the new regiment unlike the old one was organized on a version of the *silladar* system. (See p. 148.) This meant that Government supplied nothing except arms and ammunition.

At the same time there were constituted on a militia basis three regiments of Cape Mounted Yeomanry. 'The idea was to recruit well-to-do young farmers and to call out half the men at a time to serve probably for three months' active service.' Enlistment was for three years. Arms (chiefly Snider carbines), ammunition, uniform and all equipment were provided by Government. An initial £25 capitation grant for each man's horse and saddlery and a further £15 each year after the first for upkeep were also to be paid. The pay of the privates was 4s. a day. One of the attractions to Government was the cheapness of the yeomanry. Whereas a Cape Mounted Rifleman cost £134 a head per annum, a yeoman, in peace time, cost only £20. 'The scheme was a failure, the numbers wanted never being attained, and in many cases recruits had to be sought in the towns, often at the expense of the volunteer units, already short of men.'[35] The authorized strength was 3,000. The highest number actually achieved was 600. Some of these saw action in the Basutoland Rebellion of 1880–1; others were included in the attack on Morosi's Mountain in 1879, both minor campaigns in which the mounted arm as such took little part.* The three regiments were disbanded in 1881.

During the late 1850s, the 1860s and up to the late 1870s there took place eight distinct military operations, five of them in Natal and three in Cape Colony. None of them was on a large scale; all of them involved some measure of mounted action. During the

* The Cape Mounted Riflemen, however, acting as infantry, played an important part in the three assaults on Morosi's Mountain in April, June and November, 1879, gaining two Victoria Crosses. Morosi was the chief of the Baphuti Basutos. He was finally captured in the third assault upon his stronghold. (Tylden, Maj. G. 'The Capture of Morosi's Mountain, 1879' *J.A.H.R.*, XV (1936), 208–15.)

same period there began that trickle of new, mostly ephemeral, volunteer units which was to become such an extraordinary torrent in the late 1870s and the 1880s. Some fifteen of those which were raised between 1855 and 1876 were mounted units. Amongst these were the famous Royal Natal Carbineers, the Victoria Mounted Rifles of Natal and the Diamond Fields Horse. Less well known and not quite so long-lasting were such bodies as the Ixopa Mounted Rifles, Prince Alfred's Own Volunteer Cape Town Cavalry, known as 'the Sparklers',* the Murraysberg Volunteer Cavalry and the Aliwal North Mounted Volunteers.[36] Nearly all units of this sort came into being because of some crisis on the frontiers. Word would come through

> 'that men were wanted: meetings were called in courthouse or farmstead; the Magistrate, the Field-Cornet or some popular local man took the chair. Often,' writes Major Tylden, the great authority on South African military history, 'money was raised; uniforms, sometimes rather incongruous ones, were chosen . . .; a badge was designed, and in some cases a pagri of a particular colour selected. There are instances where men found their own arms, and nearly always their own horses; officers were elected, and the unit was duly proclaimed in the *Government Gazette* and came into being. Sometimes it was little more than a rifle club, it faded away, was re-raised, amalgamated with a few others, changed its name, disappeared. Or else it marched away, fought, suffered casualties, failed only too often to get recruits, was drafted out, was reconstituted and in some cases, exists today with a history of many years' service.'[37]

In 1877 there broke out the 9th and final Kaffir War, sometimes called, from the tribes engaged, the Galeka-Gaika War. In the course of it British soldiers for the first time used the Martini-Henry rifle in action. One musketry sergeant-instructor managed to kill a Kaffir at the unprecedented range of 1,800 yards. An initial shortage of horsemen was partly overcome by turning a detachment of the 24th Foot and another of the 88th Foot into two weak companies

* Well mounted and smartly turned out, this regiment wore blue and silver or white lace, white belts and white metal helmets with white plumes. Founded in 1857 and disbanded thirty-two years later, the regiment carried out escort and other ceremonial duties in the capital. (Tylden, G. 'The First Four Volunteer Units of the Cape', *J.A.H.R.*, XXXIV (1956), 14–15.)

of mounted infantry. Before the war ended ten months after it had begun, twenty-four mounted volunteer units had taken part in it. These ranged from such small units as the Chalumna Volunteer Cavalry, thirteen strong, and the Buffalo Volunteer Horse, numbering 105, to the Frontier Light Horse of over 270 of all ranks.

In 1878 there were three further conflicts, the Pokwane Expedition in January, the Second Sekukuni War in February and the Northern Border Rebellion in May. The scale and importance of these were small compared with the invasion of Zululand which followed in January, 1879, and precipitated the Zulu War.

> 'I must say that I should like to have just one little shy at the Zulus. People say that they will attack us in the open, and if they do that it would be great fun.'
>
> MAJOR REDVERS BULLER, 13 August, 1878[1]

(ii)

Zulu War, 1879: the first invasion – Isandhlwana – Rorke's Drift

The causes and the rights and wrongs of the Zulu war need not be closely examined here. The Zulus were made into a powerful nation by King Shaka early in the nineteenth century. Since then they had been, like the other Bantu tribes, frequently involved in hostilities with their neighbours – not least with the Boers who had emigrated north-eastwards from Cape Colony. In 1877 the Transvaal was annexed by the British. Zululand from then onwards was encompassed to the west as well as to the south by subjects of the Queen. 'It was plain,' says the official account of the war, 'that the Zulu warriors could gain distinction only by coming into collision with British subjects.'[2]

There were those, then and later, who believed that peaceful co-existence with the Zulus could have been established. The assumption that King Cetshwayo, Shaka's nephew, with his formidable army, must constitute an unacceptable threat to Natal and the Transvaal was, and still is, in doubt. Nevertheless a few minor unfriendly acts by the Zulus, committed whilst a commission which had been accepted by the King, was sitting to determine border disputes, were the pretext for Sir Bartle Frere, the High Commissioner, to decide upon the invasion of Zululand. His line

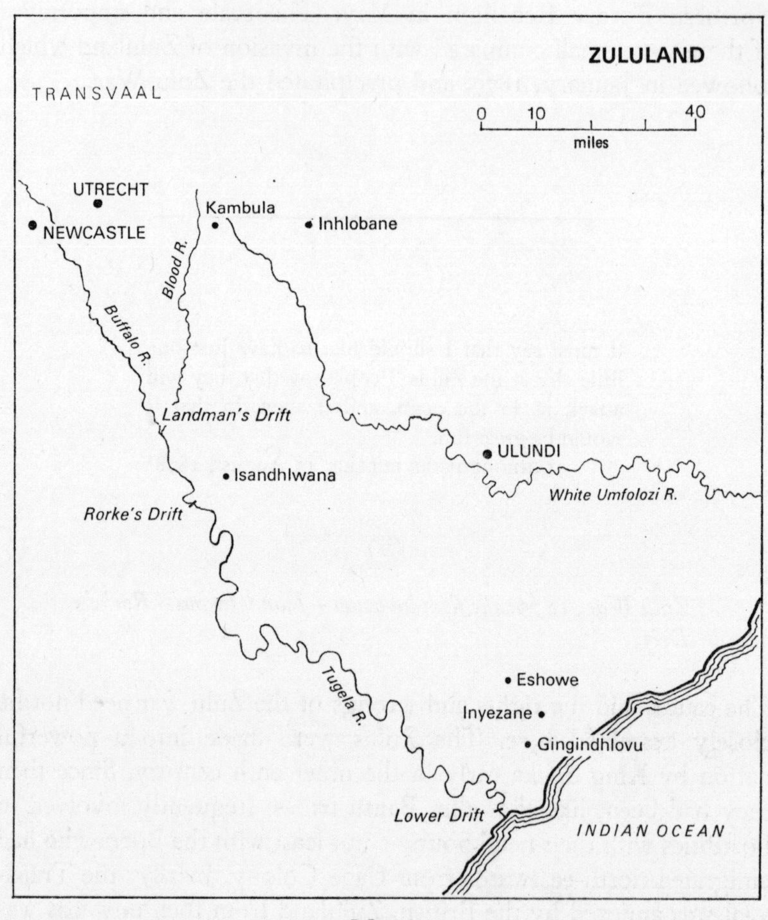

Map 2

was that there was no quarrel with the Zulu nation, only with its warlike monarch. It was necessary, therefore, to capture the King, occupy the royal kraal at Ulundi, and destroy his army.

This was an oversimplification. To a large degree Cetshwayo was a prisoner of the army which he had inherited. This massive military machine consisted in the late 1870s of over 40,000 men under the age of sixty, over half of whom were thirty or younger. There were twenty-six active regiments. Enlistment was in effect compulsory and discipline was severe. It included enforced celibacy. This bar to marriage was normally removed only when the warriors had 'washed their spears' in blood. Since Cetshwayo's coronation in 1873 few opportunities for action had occurred. In consequence, the men of considerable numbers of regiments, most of them nearly forty years old, were long overdue for marriage. Naturally they were impatient to display their prowess in battle. The king's freedom of action, as Donald R. Morris has put it in his brilliant book, *The Washing of the Spears*, 'was more and more dominated by the warlike spirit of the regiments.'[3]

The warriors were trained athletes carrying large cowhide shields and assegais – light six-foot throwing spears with six-inch steel tips. These could be hurled more or less accurately up to seventy yards. A handful was usually carried, the last one being kept as a stabbing weapon. Knobkerries were also carried. A proportion of the warriors, never very great, carried firearms. The 'tip and run' tactics characteristic of most African tribes were foreign to the Zulus. 'The commander pitted against them,' points out Major Tylden, 'could always count on a set battle and a quick decision . . . The Zulu warrior, certain of death at the hands of the executioner if he failed in an attack, made little or no effort to defend himself against pursuit, and was most vulnerable to cavalry or mounted riflemen. The former he especially dreaded.'[4]

* * *

The army collected for the invasion, commanded by Lieutenant-General Lord Chelmsford, numbered 16,800 men in five columns, two of which were in reserve. There was a singular deficiency of mounted troops. No regular cavalry was of course available, but there were three other sources of horse soldiers. The white volunteer units mustered 660 officers and men, many of them good horsemen and crack shots. Only about 290 of these were available at the start of the campaign. Then there were men taken from every regular infantry regiment in the South African command and mounted on locally purchased horses. These were formed into 'squadrons' of mounted infantry. The other ranks were armed initially with regulation rifle and bayonet. Later on they received

Swinburn-Martini carbines with a bowie knife as bayonet. Even later, No 2 Squadron was armed with swords.[5] Though their horsemanship was not of the first order these mounted infantrymen, mostly grooms, cooks, bandsmen and privates with some experience of riding, were usually more reliable than the colonials. Their uniform, according to one who saw them later on in the campaign, was 'a red coat, more or less tattered, trousers and leggings ditto, with a battered helmet. They looked like a cross between a groom out of place and a soldier after a night in cells and a big drink.' One of the colonial volunteer officers thought that 'this sort of cavalry will be the force of the future for Africa, as they are as good as any others and far cheaper.'[6]

The third source was the Natal Mounted Police which had been founded in 1874. At first, recruits, paid no more than common labourers, were 'social failures of all ages and physical descriptions'.[7] By 1878 there were 110 men, each providing his own uniform and board and required to repay an advance for his horse and equipment. He also had to provide his own food, quarters and forage.

In the three columns which formed the initial invading force there were thirteen miscellaneous bodies of horsemen. The right column, commanded by Colonel Charles Pearson, entered Zululand by the Lower Drift of the Tugela. It was 4,750 strong, only 312 of that number being mounted. The central column which entered at Rorke's Drift, commanded by Colonel Richard Glyn, contained another 300 mounted troops out of a total of 4,709. The left column which was to move southeast from the headwaters of the Blood River, consisted of 2,278 of all ranks, including some 660 horse. It was commanded by Brevet Colonel Evelyn Wood, VC, who was to acquire the nickname of *Lakuni* from the Zulus. The word describes the hard wood from which the Zulu knobkerries or bludgeons were made.[8]

* * *

On 20 January the centre column, with which Lord Chelmsford himself travelled, made camp under the great hill of Isandhlwana. The elaborate process of laagering was not gone through because of the inordinate time and labour which it always entailed and because the General placed his trust in the fire power of his infantry. The risk, as Donald Morris has suggested, was probably only justified 'as long as his scouting arrangements afforded him adequate notice of an impending attack'.[9] These they did not do. An enormous impi of about 13,700 Zulus managed to conceal its movements completely. On 21 January it was established, totally hidden and silent, in a deep ravine a short distance from Isandhlwana. It was only detected, by chance, in the morning of 22 January by a stunned Basuto horseman of Durnford's Horse (sometimes known as Durnford's Basutos).

At dawn that day Lord Chelmsford had marched out of camp with a mixed force to deal with a body of Zulus which had been discovered the previous day some miles away. With these he fought an indecisive engagement. On his return to camp just as dark was falling, he saw that the tents were still standing, but around them lay the disembowelled bodies of virtually all the troops he had left behind that fateful morning: some eight hundred whites and nine hundred natives.

In the interval the main Zulu impi, immediately on being discovered, had swooped down on the camp, encircled it and wiped out the whole force except for some fifty-five mounted officers and men who managed to escape across the Buffalo River. What exactly happened and why will never be known. It is certain, though, that enormous numbers of Zulus, possibly as many as 5,000, were mown down by the disciplined volleys of the regular infantrymen before these, in turn, were overcome. It is probable that the ammunition ran out, and that this was the chief cause of the catastrophe.

There were numerous instances of extreme bravery. It appears, for instance, that the very last organized resistance, headed by Brevet Colonel Anthony Durnford,* who commanded the camp, was put up by fourteen of the Natal Carbineers together with some twenty of the Natal Mounted Policemen, after they had run out of ammunition. All of these brave men could have attempted to get away on their horses, but they chose to fight to the death dismounted. According to a Zulu who saw them 'they threw down their guns when their ammunition was done, and then commenced with their pistols, which they fired as long as their ammunition

* Colonel Durnford, with a spare (fourth) column, consisting of some 250 mounted natives (including Sikali's Native Horse), 300 native infantry and a rocket battery, had arrived at Isandhlwana from Rorke's Drift not long before the Zulu attack. Since he was the senior officer in camp he automatically took command.

lasted; and then formed a line, shoulder to shoulder, and back to back, and fought with their knives.'[10]

Most of the men of the victorious impi, having 'washed their spears', returned to their homes. However, the right 'horn', which had seen virtually no action, swept on seven miles to Rorke's Drift, where the Swedish mission station was being used as a hospital. There, outnumbered by forty-five to one, the 104 able-bodied defenders, mostly infantrymen, held out all night until the Zulus, after fearful casualties, called off their attack. Soon afterwards Chelmsford arrived with the survivors of his central column.

> 'Buller's irregulars, from beginning to end of the campaign, may be said to have been on the chronic scout . . . [They] never took much pains about parading . . . When they got ready, they mounted; when he found around him a reasonable number of mounted men, the leader of the corps started; his fellows followed in files, and and the men who were late overtook the detachment at a canter.'
>
> ARCHIBALD FORBES, war correspondent[1]

(iii)

Zulu War, 1879: Inyezane – Wood and Buller – Inhlobane Mountain – Kambula – Gingindhlovu

Colonel Pearson's right column, meanwhile, on the same day as the disaster at Isandhlwana, fought an action against some 6,000 Zulus at Inyezane. Having dispersed them, not without casualties of his own, Pearson pushed on the following morning to Eshowe, thirty-seven miles inside Zululand. There, on hearing the awful news of the destruction of the central column, he quickly constructed a fort. Pearson now found himself cut off and in a state of siege. He sent back most of his mounted volunteers and the men of the Natal Native Contingent, all of whom got safely home to Natal.

He held on, with dwindling supplies, but mostly untroubled by the enemy, until he was relieved at the beginning of April.*

* * *

The news of Isandhlwana found Colonel Wood's left column deep into northern Zululand without any means of support. On 31 January it arrived at Kambula where a strong laager was constructed on top of a hill, 'whence he could cover both Newcastle and Utrecht, giving confidence to both the Natal and Transvaal borders.'[2] Chelmsford gave Wood a completely free hand and warned him that there was a chance of his having to face the full weight of the Zulu army.

For nearly two months Wood remained alert, his mounted men engaged in patrolling some 160 square miles of country and in raiding into Zululand. Of the newly raised colonial volunteers thus employed, 'recruited for the campaign at the pay of five shillings a day',[3] one of their officers has this to say:

> 'They appeared to be rough, undisciplined and disrespectful to their officers, fearfully slovenly and the veriest drunkards and winebibbers that ever took carbine in hand. On the other hand, they looked what they eventually were, just the rough and hardy men to wage a partisan warfare against an active enemy. The steeds they bestrode were as hardy as themselves . . . It needed a thoroughly masterful man, like Colonel Redvers Buller, to bring these desperadoes into subjection.'[4]

Buller, a captain in the 60th Rifles, described by a newspaper correspondent as 'a silent, saturnine, blood-thirsty man' and known to the Zulus as 'the steam engine',[5] was in some respects the perfect leader of irregular horse, without fear, absolutely tireless. 'If we were lying in the mud and rain,' wrote one of his youngest recruits, 'so was Buller. If we were hungry, so was he. All of the hardships he shared equally with his men. Never did Buller, as commander, have a patrol tent to sleep under, while his men were in the open.

* It seems certain that after Isandhlwana there was hardly anything to stop Zulu raids into Natal. Why these did not take place it is hard to say. Certainly in February and March the Buffalo and Tugela were in full flood which partly accounts for the Zulus' inaction. Further, Cetshwayo was horrified by the losses incurred at his great victory. He was probably anxious, too, not to precipitate the British retribution which he must have known was bound to come.

He was . . . the idol of all.' However, he was apt to be reckless, had a 'very frank tongue'[6] and his orders were not always models of clarity. But he ruled his men of the Frontier Light Horse,* Baker's Horse, the Transvaal Rangers and the Border Horse with a rod of iron, making into an effective force a motley bunch, consisting of 'broken gentlemen, of runagate sailors, of fugitives from justice, of the scum of the South African towns, of stolid Africanders'. There were even 'a few Americans . . .; a Chilian; several Australians; and a couple of Canadian voyageurs from somewhere in the Arctic regions.' They wore no uniform, most of them wearing their own leather-patched patrol jackets dyed mimosa colour, open-necked flannel shirts, brown cord breeches and a slouch hat around which was wound a strip of coloured cloth to distinguish the regiment. 'We had', wrote a new, seventeen-year-old recruit to the Frontier Light Horse, 'no overcoats or raincoats, only one blanket, strapped to the saddle.' They carried no swords and were armed for the most part with revolvers and Martini-Henry carbines. Their ammunition bandoliers were about the only uniform item of their equipment.[7]

On 26 March, hearing that Chelmsford's relief of Pearson at Eshowe was likely to be hindered by a large Zulu force (see below), and determined that his column should no longer remain idle, Wood decided to attack Inhlobane mountain, 'a great lozenge five miles long and a mile across, rising a thousand feet above the plain'.[8] This was some eleven miles from Kambula. On its flat top were 2,000 head of cattle, protected by about 1,000 Zulus. 'I am not very sanguine of success, but I think,' he wrote to Chelmsford, 'we ought to make a stir here, to divert attention from you, although . . . by our latest reports it is asserted that you have only Coast tribes against you, and that all Cetshwayo's people are coming here.'[9]

At first light on 28 March Buller, with 392 European horsemen and 277 'friendly' Zulus, (known as Wood's Irregulars), forced his way to the top of the mountain, his irregulars 'leading their horses

* This corps had been raised in 1877 by Lieutenant F. Carrington at King William's Town, Cape Colony. Buller soon took over command, serving with it in the Ninth Kaffir War, where it suffered casualties. In July, 1878, it numbered 276 of all ranks. When Buller took over all Wood's mounted troops, the command went to Captain Barton of the Coldstream Guards, who was killed at Inhlobane. Captain C. D'Arcy succeeded him. He and Sergeant O'Toole were awarded the Victoria Cross for their part in a reconnaissance on 3 July, the day before the battle of Ulundi. The regiment was disbanded in December, 1879. (Tylden: *AFSA*, 85–6.)

up'[10] one of the steep sides. He suffered some casualties, particularly horses, from snipers as well as from the roughness of the ascent. Once on top he began to round up the cattle. Meanwhile another force, including 190 horsemen, under Lieutenant-Colonel John C. Russell, 12th Lancers, Buller's second-in-command, had also reached the top from the other end, virtually unopposed.

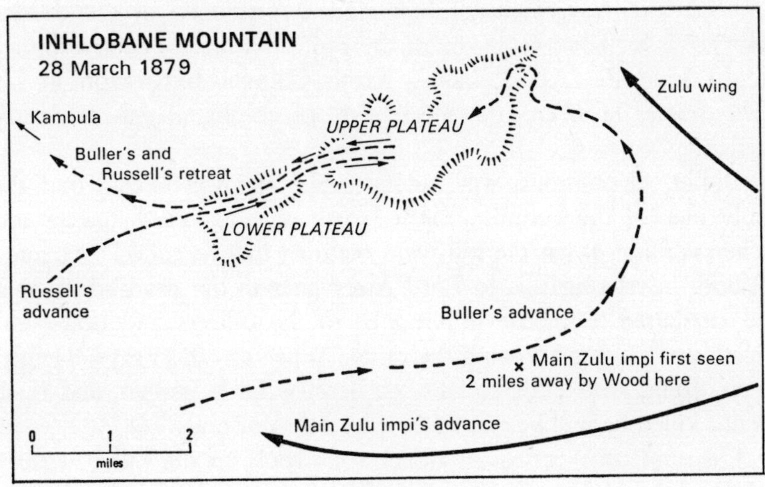

Map 3

The operation seemed to have been successfully concluded when to the south the long-expected impi, calculated by some to number 20,000, was seen advancing towards Kambula. A dramatic race now developed. Buller and Russell and their by now rather scattered sub-units had to be got down from the mountain or they would be trapped by the right horn of the impi, and the whole force must reach the laager at Kambula before the Zulus did. Unfortunately neither Wood's nor Buller's orders were very clear. Consequently a series of misunderstandings as to directions to be taken led to the Zulu right horn combining with the mountain's defenders to enjoy a regular field day. The column's Director of Transports watched Buller's 'regular scramble to get down to where Colonel Russell should have been . . . The place, however, was quite impracticable for horses. How any got down was a mystery, with the horses plunging madly, while the Kaffirs [*sic*] were shooting and assegaieing the poor fellows.' Lieutenant Alfred Blaine of the Frontier Light Horse found it 'just possible for men to go down with horses in single file; but the Kaffirs were behind us in hundreds, and everyone was so anxious to get down that we got all jammed up . . . We could not hit [the Zulus] even with our carbines . . . The officers could not use their swords . . . The Hlobane retreat was a most awful affair . . . No men ever fought more pluckily than the Zulus, they are brave men indeed.' They assegaied or shot twelve officers and 160 men, among them eighty Zulu 'friendlies'. These unnecessarily severe casualties included forty men of the Border Horse* as well as twenty-six of the 156 of all ranks of the Frontier Light Horse.[11] 'At Hlobane', wrote Colonel Henderson in his *The Science of War*, 'the mechanism of command was evidently defective.'

Buller, throughout, was indefatigable. He told Wood that the only men of the Frontier Light Horse 'that he could make stand when coming down the hill were the men that he called by name'. Wood, in relating this to Lord Airey later in the year, added that he attributed 'immense importance to the officers and non-commissioned officers knowing their men. When an officer says "Heigh! You, John, stop", his word tells, because he is known, and if he is not killed he will hear it again if he does not obey.'[12]

On numerous occasions Buller rode back up the hill to rescue men who had lost their horses. The moment he reached camp, although he had been in the saddle for almost two days with little rest, he set forth in pouring rain with fresh horses and managed to rescue at least seven more of the survivors. For his gallant conduct he received the Victoria Cross. Before long he became known as 'the Bayard of South Africa'.[13]

The Zulus, short of sleep after forced marches from Ulundi, went into bivouac for the night. The following day, 29 March, as expected and as intended by Wood, the men of the impi, many of them supplied with Martini-Henry rifles and ammunition captured at Isandhlwana, attacked the laager at Kambula. There followed a British victory which was almost the exact opposite in every respect

* This corps was only sixty-one strong. It had been raised for the second expedition against Sekukuni, and seems to have been armed with lances. Its founder was Lieutenant-Colonel Frederick Weatherley, a Canadian, who was among those killed at Inhlobane. His career had started in the Austrian cavalry. Later he bought a commission in the 4th Light Dragoons, with which regiment he claimed to have charged at Balaklava. He soon exchanged into the 6th Inniskilling Dragoons in India. Weatherley finally sold out and acquired property near Lydenburg where he farmed and prospected for gold. (Tylden: *AFSA*, 43; Morris, 303.)

to the disaster at Isandhlwana. It lasted for four hours. At the beginning Wood, at Buller's suggestion, ordered some of his mounted men to sting the Zulu right horn into attacking prematurely. This they did by, in the first place, dismounting half a mile from the Zulus.

> 'The Umbonambi regiment,' wrote Wood, 'suffered a galling fire for some time, and then, losing patience, rushed forward to attack, when the horsemen, remounting, retired 400 yards, and, repeating their tactics, eventually brought on a determined attack from the Zulu flank. The Umbonambi followed up the horsemen until they were within 300 yards of the laager.'[14]

It seems that some of the horsemen employed other tactics. These rode to within 100 yards of the black horde and fired into it from the saddle.* Trooper Mossop of the Frontier Light Horse remembered many years later that this first volley was the signal for every tent in camp to be struck. 'The Zulus, seeing the camp a moment before white with tents, and then seeing them all disappear, would imagine that the defenders were deserting it, and, as we would be retreating at the same time, their excitement (it was hoped) would induce them to rush the camp before the other wings had time to close in.'[15] From then on, skilfully directed shell fire combined with repeated infantry volleys frustrated the Zulus' persistent attempts to close. Finally, after two bayonet attacks against them,

> 'a shiver seemed to run through the enemy, and all in a moment they broke and fled. The relics of the irregular horse now sallied out in pursuit,' wrote the adjutant of the Frontier Light Horse. 'The horses were so thoroughly done up by the fatigues of the previous day, that the pursuit was not so ruinous as it would otherwise have been. Nevertheless under the vigorous direction of Colonel Buller, it was well sustained

* Among Buller's mounted troops were seventy of the Natal Native Horse, all Basutos. Some of these were men who had escaped from Isandhlwana. These refused to stop in the laager and spent the whole battle skirmishing outside, 'annoying the rear of the enemy.' (Tylden, *Inhlobane,* 8; Tomasson, 183; Norris-Newman, 165.)

These Basutos were invaluable as scouts. 'They were courageous and possessed the merit of being cheap, finding their own horses and getting £3 per month. Their ponies were hardy little brutes, in fact they seemed to be untirable.' (Tomasson, 125.) The Basutos' chief faults were 'their excitability and their random shooting'. (Tomasson, 71.)

till nightfall. The enemy were so exhausted that they made no fight of it, but were shot down.'[16]

The horsemen, apparently, 'used their carbines from the saddle one-handed, like pistols, or else picked up discarded assegais and used them like boar spears.' 'When we overtook small bodies,' wrote Trooper Mossop, 'they made no attempt to resist. They were beaten, and that was the end. Many a man just turned, exposing his broad chest, saying, "Dubula M'Lungu" ("Shoot, white man") – and the white man shot. The Zulu gave no quarter, and expected none.' An infantry private wrote home: 'I can tell you some murdering went on . . . I only wish it had been a cavalry regiment from home, in which case not one of them would have got away. As it was, some escaped into the mountains, it being too dark to follow them further.'[17] The British casualties were twenty-one killed and sixty-five wounded.

Throughout the months which followed the battle, until the second invasion began, Buller's mounted men were employed in constant patrolling. Their other duties 'consisted of the usual regimental guards, cattle-guards, vedettes, night pickets . . . but the worst duty of all was the wood-fatigue. The nearest wood was some six miles off on the summit of a mountain. We had to go every day with the infantry to cut and carry it.'[18]

* * *

The first trickle of what was soon to become a flood of reinforcements, sent from home and elsewhere after the news of Isandhlwana, began to arrive in Durban in mid-March. Lord Chelmsford now decided that he was strong enough to go to the relief of Pearson at Eshowe. He was not unopposed, for Cetshwayo sent an impi of some 10,000 warriors to try to prevent him. On 2 April this impi was decisively defeated in a battle lasting an hour and a half at Gingindhlovu. Foolishly the Zulus attacked Chelmsford's 5,600 men not when they were strung out on the line of march but when they were securely established in an entrenched laager. Early on in the fight the Zulu attack (similar in most respects to that at Kambula four days before) seemed to falter. Chelmsford therefore ordered Major Percy Barrow, 19th Hussars, who commanded the small mounted force,* to leave the laager and push the

* Sir Henry Bulwer, the Governor of Natal, strongly opposed the war. Among the many ways in which he obstructed Chelmsford was the imposition

22. Sir Evelyn Wood, VC

23. Sir Redvers Buller, VC

24. Lieut-Colonel Arthur Prinsep, 11th Bengal Lancers

25. Sir Donald Stewart

26. Lieut-Colonel Robert Baden-Powell

27. Sir Gerald Graham

28. 'Bobs' Roberts: watercolour for *Vanity Fair*, 1880.

29. Lieut-General Sir Samuel J. Browne, VC

left horn back. The Zulu left horn, however, quickly recovered, forcing some of the horsemen to fight their way back. Three of these, including Barrow, were wounded and six horses were killed or injured.* Otherwise, the mounted men were not used till the pursuit. In this the mounted infantry experienced great difficulty in employing effectively the swords with which they had recently been issued and in the use of which they had been inadequately trained. One man severed the ear of his own horse, while another's sabre was snatched from his grasp by a fierce Zulu suddenly turning at bay. Chelmsford's aide-de-camp relates that there was another fierce

> 'warrior who would not fly, but set his back to a thorn bush and defied his foes. "Leave him to me," said a sergeant of the Greys who was instructor in the Mounted Infantry. A ring was formed and at it they went, sword mounted, against assegai and shield dismounted. The soldier was the more skilful, but the Zulu was in better condition. Cutting was tried at first, but it was turned by the shield invariably; at last a point went through shield and man, and the hero found the death he courted.'[19]

Next day Pearson was relieved and everyone returned to the border. The aftermath of the first abortive invasion of Zululand had been dealt with. Now the second invasion had to be planned and launched.

after Isandhlwana of a veto against Natal mounted rifle units entering Zululand. Many of the men quit their regiments in disgust and formed a new unit called the Natal Volunteer Guides. There were fifty of these under Barrow's command at Gingindhlovu. There were also seventy mounted infantry and 160 mounted natives and oddments.

For later references to Barrow, see p. 313.

* The total British casualties were nine killed and fifty-two wounded. The Zulus were believed to have lost 1,200 men.

'"Why is it that the men of Lord Chelmsford's column cannot be regarded as Christians?" Answer: "Because they made an idol of Wood and did not believe in the Lord".'

Riddle current in camp[1]

(iv)

Zulu War, 1879: the second invasion

What to do with the unnecessarily massive reinforcements which were daily arriving at Durban, and how to provide transport and supplies for them, were Chelmsford's chief worries during the months of April and May. Among the 10,500 officers and men (including five infantry battalions) were two regular cavalry regiments: the 1st (King's) Dragoon Guards and the 17th Lancers. The K.D.G.s, 649 strong, had last seen service in China, nineteen years before (see Vol II, p. 223). Of the officers only the lieutenant-colonel commanding (Henry Alexander) had had any previous experience in the field. The 17th, which had last been in action during the chase of Tantia Topi in 1859 (see Vol II, p. 217), had had to take sixty-five men and horses from the 5th Lancers and the 16th Lancers so as to make up its numbers to 622 officers and men. It was commanded by Colonel Drury Curzon Drury-Lowe, of whom we shall hear a good deal more (see p. 273 and p. 286).*

Both regiments brought their horses out with them, the King's Dragoon Guards, 537, and the 17th, 527. Four steamships, hired from the National Line, transported them. These left London and Southampton between 24 and 28 February and all were disembarked at Durban between 6 and 14 April. When landed the horses looked like 'tucked-up whippets'[2] after their long incarceration aboard ship. For about a week they were encamped near Durban recovering. At first they refused to touch the rank grass of Natal,

* Drury-Lowe had entered the regiment as a cornet aged twenty-four in 1854. He had commanded it from 1867 to 1878. His successor, Lieutenant-Colonel Thomas Gonne, on the very day that the embarkation orders arrived, was accidentally shot while superintending the practice of the non-commissioned officers with the newly issued revolver. He was so severely wounded as to be unable to proceed on active service. Drury-Lowe was therefore gazetted as supernumerary lieutenant-colonel and re-assumed command, 'his return', according to the regimental historian, 'being joyfully welcomed by all ranks, without exception, from the second in command downwards'. (Fortescue: *17L*, 174.)

but gradually they became acclimatized. Both regiments carried Martini-Henry carbines. The Lancers were armed with swords as well as their lances.

The colonists were filled with wonder at the size of the horses and at the uniforms and equipment of the men. They were startled at the heavy load each horse was expected to carry, amounting to some 260 lbs. An officer of irregulars found that 'the question here most asked was, would the English horses stand the same amount of work as our hardy little beasts on the same amount of grain.'[3]

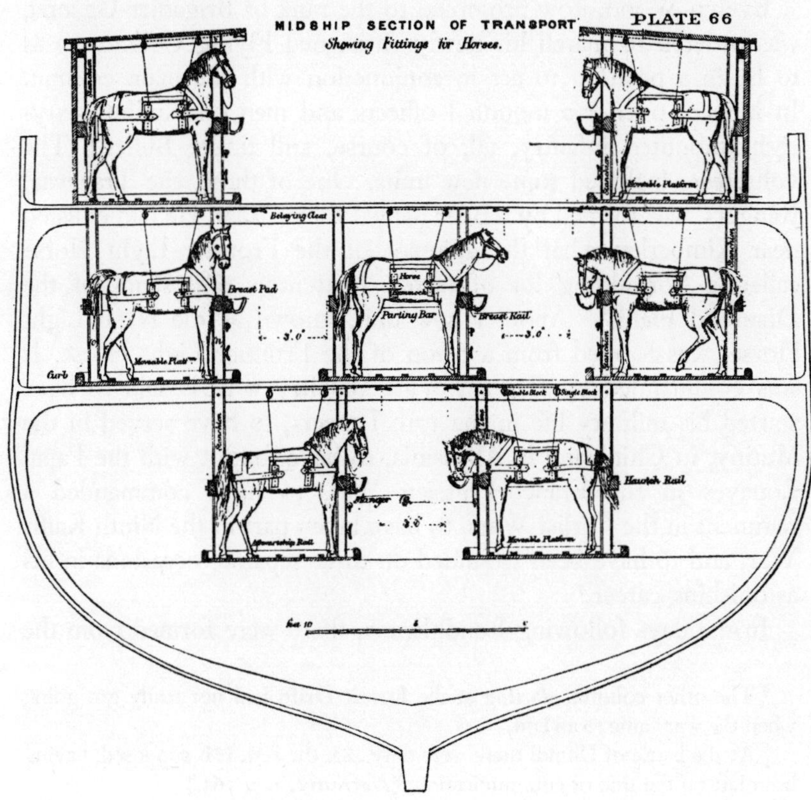

On 17 April the advance elements of both regiments began their long march inland. So weak were the horses that the daily average was only ten miles, and every third or fourth day a complete halt was necessary. Accompanying the column were detachments of the Army Service Corps carrying forage. This consisted chiefly, throughout the campaign, of mealies [maize], 'mouldy oats and compressed-hay chaff'.[4] During mid-May, two and a half months

after leaving England, the two regiments had arrived at Landman's Drift on the frontier, ready to form a brigade in one of the two main columns formed for the second invasion.*

On 21 May the field of Isandhlwana was visited by a strong mounted force. Many bodies were buried and many wagons brought away. No hostile Zulus were encountered. Five days later, 'in consequence of the great difficulty of transporting the requisite forage',[5] it was decided that of the King's Dragoon Guards, all but a handful should remain on the frontier and take no part in the march to Ulundi.

Evelyn Wood, now promoted to the rank of Brigadier-General, was ordered to march his newly christened Flying Column so as to be in a position to act in conjunction with the main column. In it were over 700 mounted officers and men,† including sixty-eight mounted infantry, all, of course, still under Buller.‡ The volunteers included some new units. One of these, the Transvaal Rangers, was formed by a Boer named Pieter Raaf. He had enlisted near Kimberley what the adjutant of the Frontier Light Horse called a 'forbidding lot of mixed Hottentots and scum of the Diamond Fields'.[6] Another new unit, known as the Natal Light Horse, was formed from a troop of the Frontier Light Horse. It was commanded by Captain Watt Whalley who is said to have started his military life in the 17th Lancers, to have served in the Mutiny, in China and in Abyssinia, to have fought with the Papal Zouaves in the Franco-Prussian War, to have commanded a regiment in the Carlist Wars, to have taken part in the Ninth Kaffir War, and to have been wounded on three separate occasions in his astonishing career.[7]

In the days following Isandhlwana, there were formed from the

* The other column, starting at the Lower Drift, had not really got going when the war came to an end.

† At the battle of Ulundi there were only 482, the rest, it is supposed, having been left on the line of communication. (*Narrative*, 102, 165.)

‡ Among the infantry reinforcements for Wood's Flying Column were parts of the 80th Regiment. 'Buller came to me,' wrote Wood, 'and asked if a protecting certificate might be given to his Regimental Sergeant-Major. "What do you mean?", I asked. "Well, he is about the best man in the Frontier Light Horse," he replied, "but he has just been to me to say that he is a deserter from the 80th, and as he is sure to be recognized tomorrow, he intends to be off tonight, unless you will condone his offence, and give him a protecting certificate." This I did and the man served with credit until the end of the war.' (Wood, 390.)

white non-commissioned officers of the disbanded 3rd Regiment of the Natal Native Contingent (infantry), three troops of Natal Horse. One of these was commanded by another of those shadowy figures who flash momentarily across the Victorian military scene as leaders of mounted men. Major Claude Bettington, described as a first-class fighting man, was 'very strong, a fine horseman, good-looking and a good fellow'. A young Engineer officer once saw him in the course of a kit inspection knock down two of his troopers 'quite easily. I was told that they were all in great awe of him.'[8] *

As always, Buller was extremely active in patrolling. Captain Tomasson of the Frontier Light Horse describes the Colonel's method. He

> 'always made a point of encamping in the dark, and invariably moved a few miles after sundown. The enemy then never knew where we were at night, so could not surround and attack us. The most perfect silence was always strictly enjoined. The horses were put in rings of some thirty or so each, fastened to each other, the men slept at their heads in a circle. Sentries paced round the rings all night to see that no horse broke loose. One blanket only was carried, and the nights were most bitterly cold. The guards had to be visited hourly, and the vedettes also looked to. Smoking was not allowed. About two in the morning the men were roused, and silently loosed the horses and fell in. The saddles were never removed at night when on patrol. Then came the work of counting and whispering over the roll call. All was done in most perfect quiet. The orders, short and to the point, were given in a low tone to the men.'[9]

Throughout June the main column and the Flying Column

* The young Prince Louis Napoleon, the Crown Prince Imperial of France, who had insisted upon being allowed to join Chelmsford's headquarters as 'a spectator', was killed by Zulus on 1 June. He had gone with a party to choose the column's camp site for the following night. He was accompanied by Captain Carey of the quartermaster's department and escorted by an inadequate number of Bettington's troop of the Natal Horse. Two of these, as well as the Prince, were assegaied by some thirty Zulus who surprised them, while Carey and the rest managed to gallop off. Part of the Prince's saddlery broke as he grabbed at it in trying to mount his horse. The scandal of the Prince Imperial's death caused a greater furore in Britain than had the disaster of Isandhlwana. It was another piece of bad luck for Chelmsford and did not enhance his reputation.

moved ponderously forward, gradually getting nearer to the great royal kraal at Ulundi. At every halt the laborious business of laagering was religiously gone through. The regular cavalry joined Buller's men in intensive patrolling. Seldom was any enemy activity encountered, but in a trifling skirmish on 5 June Lieutenant Frith, adjutant of the 17th Lancers, was shot dead by a Zulu marksman. Cetshwayo from time to time sent emissaries asking on what terms the white invaders would agree to withdraw from his country. Chelmsford's terms were impossible for the King to fulfil and the final time limit ended on 3 July. On that day, as the ultimatum expired, Buller crossed the White Umfolozi River with his irregulars. His reconnaissance in force discovered the whereabouts of a large Zulu impi 'posted in horse-shoe form'. He noted, too, 'an excellent position for the next day's fight'.[10] On his return it looked at one moment as if the gallant Colonel's men had fallen into a trap and that all of them would be cut off by a force of 5,000 Zulus. This he just managed to avoid, though he lost three killed and four wounded.

> 'The black cloud hanging over South Africa was removed by the Battle of Ulundi and the burning of the royal kraal . . . The Zulus . . . bowed to the supremacy of the white race.'
>
> TROOPER MOSSOP, Frontier Light Horse[1]

(v)

Zulu War, 1879: the battle of Ulundi – end of the war

Next day, early in the morning, Chelmsford's and Wood's columns slowly moved up to the chosen site of the battle of Ulundi, leaving behind them a strong entrenched base. The combined columns were formed into a hollow rectangle containing some 4,400 souls, mostly regular infantrymen, twelve pieces of artillery and two Gatling machine guns. To one young mounted volunteer it looked like 'a little red matchbox about to be trampled to dust by the feet of the Zulu army'.[2] To its front and sides were Buller's mounted

Ulundi, 4 July 1879

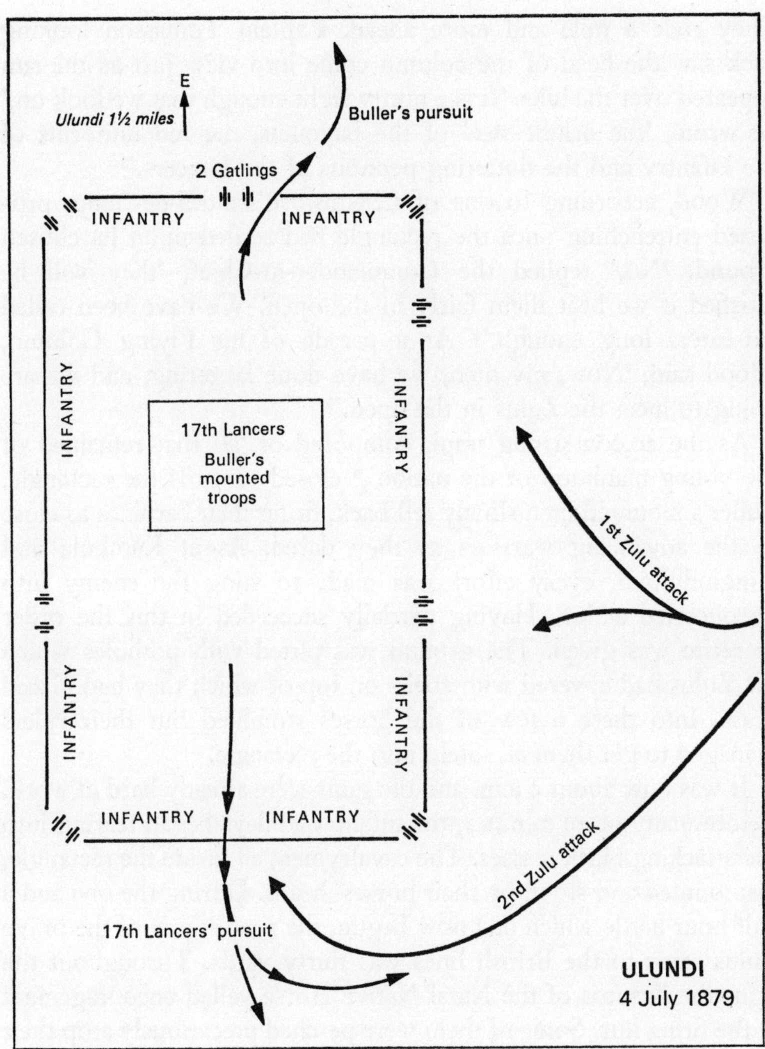

Map 4

men; behind it rode three squadrons of the 17th Lancers and a troop of the King's Dragoon Guards, flanked by Bettington's troop of Natal Horse and Shepstone's mounted Basutos.*

The most advanced of the cavalry was the Frontier Light Horse.

* These had been recruited after Isandhlwana by Theophilus Shepstone jr in the Orange Free State. They were armed with modern breech-loading carbines.

Altogether at the battle of Ulundi there were 899 mounted officers and men, including 260 of the 17th Lancers.

They rode a mile and more ahead. Captain Tomasson looking back saw the head of the column come into view just as the sun appeared over the hills. 'It is a pretty sight enough that we look on,' he wrote, 'the bright steel of the bayonets, the red uniforms of the infantry and the fluttering pennons of the Lancers.'[3]

Wood, according to one of Chelmsford's aides-de-camp, proposed entrenching once the rectangle had settled upon its chosen ground. 'No,' replied the Commander-in-Chief, 'they will be satisfied if we beat them fairly in the open. We have been called ant-eaters long enough.'[4] At a parade of his Flying Column, Wood said, 'Now, my men, we have done laagering, and we are going to meet the Zulus in the open.'[5]

As the 20,000 strong impi, composed of 'all that remained of the young manhood of the nation',[6] closed towards the rectangle, Buller's mounted men slowly fell back, firing their carbines as close to the advancing warriors as they dared. As at Kambula and Gingindhlovu, every effort was made to sting the enemy into unconcerted action. Having partially succeeded in this the order to retire was given. The ground was pitted with potholes which the Zulus had covered with sticks on top of which they had placed grass. Into these a few of the horses stumbled but their riders managed to get them all safely into the rectangle.

It was now about 9 a.m. and the guns were already hard at work. Before many more minutes, the infantry volleys began tearing into the attacking black masses. The cavalrymen, all inside the rectangle, dismounted and stood by their horses' heads. During the one and a half hour battle which had now begun, the nearest any of the brave Zulus came to the British lines was thirty yards. Throughout the fight the Basutos of the Natal Native Horse yelled encouragement at the firing line. Some of them were perched precariously atop their mounts, firing their carbines for all they were worth.

Chelmsford soon decided that the moment had arrived for the cavalry to leave the rectangle and complete his victory. He gave the order 'Lancers out,' to which Drury-Lowe added: 'Stand to your horses. Prepare to mount. Mount.' But almost at once the last of the Zulu reserves made a final rush, and down again from their horses came the lancers. A few minutes later the Zulu reserve gave up the unequal struggle and Chelmsford, waving his helmet, shouted, 'Go at them, Lowe!'

'"Lancers out" comes again,' wrote Captain Tomasson of the

> Frontier Light Horse, 'this time in earnest. The Lancers spring onto the saddle, the infantry open and let them out. Down comes General Wood looking as pleased as possible to us. "*All mounted men out*", and in an instant we are off.'[7]

As the lancers, followed by the troop of King's Dragoon Guards and the irregulars, debouched from the rectangle, Captain Edmund Wyatt Edgell was shot dead leading his squadron out. At the same instant his troop farrier was also killed. When the rectangle had been cleared, the lancers formed in echelon of wings.[8] They then charged the still unbroken part of the Zulu right horn, their front covering a little over 300 yards. The noise of the impact, 'when horse met foot', was so great that it was heard by the men inside the rectangle.[9] At this moment Lieutenant and Acting-Adjutant Herbert Jenkins' jaw was shattered by a bullet. Determined not to miss the charge, he rode to one side, took out his handkerchief, bound up his face and galloped off to join his troop. Drury-Lowe, too, was hit, a spent bullet catching him in the back and causing him to fall from his horse. In consequence, though he was not in fact badly hurt, it was his second-in-command, Major Samuel Boulderson, who now led the charge. Trooper Mossop of the Frontier Light Horse describes how it looked to him.

> 'On their great imported horses they sat bolt upright, their long lances held perfectly erect, the lance heads glittering in the sunshine.
>
> '. . . In one movement the lances dropped to the right side of the horses' necks, a long line of poles, stretching out a distance in front of the horses, the steel heads pointing straight at the mass of retreating Zulus. As the big horses bounded forward and thundered into them, each lance point pierced the Zulu in front of it; the man fell, and as the horse passed on beyond him the lance was withdrawn, lifted and thrust forward into another Zulu in front.
>
> 'The movement of withdrawing the lance and again getting it into position was very rapid; I could not quite understand how it was done. It was such a mix up for us riding behind the Lancers, with our horses jumping over dead Zulus, and having to deal with those who were knocked down by the Lancer horses but not pierced, that we did not have the opportunity to study the work. I suppose we were sent out as a support in case the Zulus rounded on them; but I reckon that any body

of men who were on the run, and saw that line of long spears [lances] making for them, would not think of turning but would run the harder. It was a grand sight to see them at work, but they did not appear to me to be humans and horses – just a huge machine. A handle was turned – and it shot forward; a button was pressed – up went the spears, and it reformed into line; another button was pressed – down went those awful spears, and again it shot forward. They were soon prevented from making more charges by the deep dongas.'[10]

At this point some 500 Zulus, hidden in the long grass, suddenly rose up, those with rifles firing at their attackers. These, re-forming where they could, pushed forward, trying to get at the Zulus, some of whom grabbed the lances and stabbed at the horses' bellies. A series of individual combats now followed. In these most of the lancers housed their lances, employing their sabres instead. The rest of the mounted men soon overtook them, fanned out and began firing at the remnants of the once formidable Zulu army.

The British casualties at Ulundi amounted to twelve dead and eighty-eight wounded. The 17th Lancers lost one officer and two men killed and three officers and five men wounded, as well as twenty-six horses killed or wounded. The Zulus may have lost as many as 1,500.

'We had a glorious go in, old boy,' wrote a non-commissioned officer of the 17th Lancers. 'Pig-sticking was a fool to it. After all the humbugging, marching, reconnoitring, short grub, and very bad what there was, rain, frost, heat, and the thousand annoyances of a campaign, especially such a one as this, we had a day that made up for the lot . . .

'The enemy were not long in showing, and we saw as had been anticipated that we were entirely surrounded. In the mean time we had set fire to their kraals. This seemed to get their "daner riz", and we were sent to draw them on; they did not want much drawing on, you bet. We retired on to the square and went inside, not a moment too soon for the infantry to fire. The action now became general, except for us who had to stand still at our horses' heads, and get popped without the chance of returning a shot. They advanced yelling like madmen . . . Men and horses were dropping all round, and it was hardly a place for a nervous old gentleman to take a stroll . . .

'As we left the square the infantry ceased firing, and gave us a rattling cheer, then we were off and amongst the Zulus. You should have seen us,' he wrote to his brother in Barnstaple. 'With tremendous shouts of "Death, Death!" we were on them. They tried lying down to escape, but it was no use, we had them anyhow, no mercy or quarter from the "Old Tots". We only stopped when we could go no further and the horses were completely done up . . . The fellows we charged were all young men, splendidly-made fellows, and all stripped for fighting.'[11]

Before the day was done, the 1,500 huts which formed the capital city had been fired. The war was now over. There remained only the capture of Cetshwayo, who had fled the field of battle. This task took some months of hunting and was achieved at last by one of many patrols sent out by Sir Garnet Wolseley who had succeeded Chelmsford. It included a squadron of King's Dragoon Guards, some mounted infantry and men of Lonsdale's Mounted Rifles.

The King was sent into exile and Zululand divided into thirteen separate kingdoms. In 1883, Cetshwayo was restored to rule over half his former realm, but his power was negligible. He died a year later.

'The Boers are merely fighting because they hate us, who buy their land, develop their country, and do not let them whip their own niggers at will.'

An officer of colonial horse in 1881

'Major Brownlow's charge, which I had counted upon to support infantry and free their flank, came off too soon, owing to some mistake.'

'Had Major Brownlow's force consisted of trained cavalry, I have hardly a doubt but that the position would have been ours, and without much loss. But one cannot blame mounted infantry and untrained horses for not doing all that trained cavalry might have done.'

MAJOR-GENERAL COLLEY after his defeat at Laing's Nek, 28 January, 1881[1]

(vi)

First Boer War, 1880–1881: Laing's Nek – peace

The end of the Zulu War saw a massive reduction of British forces in South Africa. Of the regular mounted troops, for instance, the 17th Lancers sailed for India in October, 1879, leaving their horses behind for the King's Dragoon Guards. With Cetshwayo's capture, there did not seem likely to be any further great threat to peace. The Boers of the Transvaal, it is true, gave signs of restiveness under British rule, but it was remembered that they had been soundly defeated before the stronghold of the Bapedi chief, Sekukuni ('Cetshwayo's Dog'), on more than one occasion. Further, the British annexation in 1877 had been effected peacefully by a handful of police.* No great alarm was therefore felt when in December,

* The Transvaal Republic set up by the trekking Boers in 1848 was annexed by the British in 1877 as the only means of restoring order in a country whose treasury was insolvent and whose frontiers were unprotected against the Zulus, and within whose borders was the mountain stronghold of Sekukuni. Annexation was an arbitrary measure of protection 'alike to Boer and native, and to the few straggling British subjects who had made their homes in that country'. To try to escape from the 'civilizing' restraints of benevolent British rule, many Boers attempted a further trek; but it ended in disaster, for the limit of healthy Africa did not extend beyond the Limpopo. The Boer, therefore, 'turned at bay to face his pursuer, civilization'. ([Anon.] 'The Boer War of 1881. By an English Officer who fought in it.' *Forum,* Jan, 1900, 600–1.)

1879, the Boers held a series of armed mass meetings, demanding a return of their independence. Indeed when a troop of the King's Dragoon Guards was used for the first time in aid of the civil power in Pretoria, there was no resistance.[2]

In that same month there was formed in the capital a moveable column consisting of the King's Dragoon Guards, 120 mounted infantry, four guns and thirteen infantry companies, a force believed to be 'amply sufficient to destroy any force' the Boers could collect.[3]

In October, 1880, further reductions took place. The King's Dragoon Guards, leaving behind two troops, embarked for India, their horses being sold to the Boers. This reduction was described by Rider Haggard as 'a piece of economy that was one of the immediate causes of the [Boer] revolt'.[4] At the same time 300 mounted volunteers 'mostly, if not altogether, drawn from among the loyalists',[5] were raised near Pretoria by Major Ignatius Ferreira. These became the third 'regiment' of Ferreira's Horse and were known as the Transvaal Horse.* They were now sent to Basutoland to assist the Cape Government in their repression of the Basuto rebellion. This left only two weak squadrons of mounted infantry in the whole of the Transvaal.

Numbers were further reduced by desertion. The boredom, the monotony of diet, 'the trying climate, the dearness of necessities and the entire absence of luxuries,' which made the Transvaal one of the least popular stations in the army, were among the causes which pushed up the desertion rate alarmingly. Another more compelling cause was the fact that the nearby Boers of the Free State welcomed anyone with a firearm or horse. The temptation was therefore great. One bright and 'patriotic' female claimed to have incited more British soldiers to desert than any person in history. She used her brothel to smuggle out deserters lending them civilian clothes as well as money. Had she started earlier, she claimed, 'there would not have been a private left in the King's Dragoon Guards'.[6] Altogether in 1880, 260 men deserted from the

* Ferreira was of mixed Portuguese, French and Dutch ancestry. Born in Cape Colony, he started as a trooper in the Northern Border Police. He raised the first 'regiment' of Ferreira's Horse in 1877. It served against Sekukuni the following year. The second 'regiment', 115 strong, served under Buller during the Zulu War and was also present at the capture of Sekukuni's stronghold.

The Transvaal Horse took with it to Basutoland two 9-pounder field guns. It saw action at Leribe in December, 1880, and was disbanded in 1881 with a strength of 450. (Tylden: *AFSA*, 80.)

small force which was all that was available when the First Boer War broke out in December.

On 16 December the Boers seized Heidelburg and next day established a republic. Four days later they virtually destroyed a column of the 94th Foot at Bronkhorst Spruit. Small garrisons found themselves beleaguered at Pretoria and at six other towns.

Reinforcements were at once set in motion from home and from India.* The 15th Hussars came complete with their horses from Meerut; the 14th Hussars followed from Bangalore; the 7th Hussars came close on their heels from Ireland, and the 6th (Inniskilling) Dragoons, as well as a scratch squadron of mounted infantry, were sent from England. In the event none of these saw much service in South Africa, for the war was over before most of them could be ready, in spite of the driving force exerted by Sir Evelyn Wood who was sent out in command of them.

In the meantime, Major-General Sir George Pomeroy Colley, who had succeeded Wolseley as Governor, High Commissioner and Commander-in-Chief in South-East Africa, decided that he could not wait for the reinforcements to arrive. With no more than 1,200 troops, all European, he advanced to the relief of the beleagured garrisons.

At Laing's Nek, on 28 January, 1881, Colley attacked a Boer force of about 2,000 men. He was decisively repulsed and his 'dangerously high idea of what a few British soldiers' could do[7] was rudely shattered. After shelling the Boer position with his six guns, Colley sent his mounted squadron charging uphill as a protection to the exposed right flank of his simultaneous infantry attack. The squadron, commanded by Major Brownlow of the King's Dragoon Guards, was made up of details of that regiment, mostly time-expired and convalescent troopers, a number of drivers from the Army Service Corps and some mounted infantry composed of volunteers from the 58th and 60th Foot: 191 in all. The careful synchronization between the mounted and foot attacks which had been intended went wrong when Brownlow, as Colley wrote to Wolseley,

* The speed of communications had vastly increased in the last year or two. Whereas the news of Isandhlwana took twenty days to reach London, the telegram sent from Durban announcing Bronkhorst Spruit was on the Secretary of State's desk four days after the disaster took place. In 1880 telegrams asking for reinforcements, and from London offering them, were received at their destinations the day after they were sent. (*Correspondence relative to Military Affairs in South Africa . . . War Office, 1881*, 1882, *3 et seq.*)

'bore more to the right than I had intended, and came under fire, and, drawing up his men facing the steep part of the hill, charged right up it before the infantry had even begun the ascent . . . Of course, in action, the man on the spot must often decide the ground and the moment for a charge and Brownlow's was most gallantly made. Brownlow and a part of his leading troop, consisting principally of KDGs, actually crested the ridge . . . Brownlow's horse and that of his subaltern [being] shot dead . . . The Boers had received the order to retire, and were running to their horses, and the hill was actually won, when the supporting troop, seeing, as they thought, all their leaders down, turned and galloped down the hill – I believe, before a man was shot; and the Boers, seeing them turn, immediately ran forward to the ridge again and slated them. Brownlow, who was on foot, got off by a miracle; the whole lot went headlong down the hill, and although their losses were not very heavy (four killed and thirteen wounded, almost all out of the leading troop) the mounted men were practically out of action for the rest of the day.

'. . . In justice to Brownlow's second troop, it must be remembered they consisted only of mounted infantry very recently organized – it was a steep and bold charge, and some of their horses with little training could not be brought to face the fire, and they had seen, as they believed, nearly all their leaders down.'[8]

'Poor Brownlow who behaved *splendidly*,' wrote Colley to his wife two days after the defeat, 'is quite broken-hearted, and when he came down the hill refused to speak to his men or go near them. I have been comforting him, however, and telling him we must make allowances for untrained men with untrained horses.'[9]

Troop Sergeant-Major Lunny of the KDGs is believed to have been the first man on the ridge and the only man to actually get to grips with the mostly well-concealed Boer marksmen. He killed one and wounded another with his revolver before falling dead with six bullets in his body. Thirty-two horses were hit. Lieutenant H. J. Lermitte, a thrifty Scot of the 21st Foot, had his mount shot under him. He was the last man down from the hill. 'I got up,' he said later, 'and, seeing no one about, I turned and legged it down the hill. My helmet had fallen off, my sword dropped out of my hand, and I lost my field glasses. It was a dashed expensive day.'[10]

Laing's Nek, though a minor engagement, was the first since the Crimean War in which British troops found themselves opposed to an enemy of European blood. It was the first time, too, that the formidable fighting capacities of the Boers were clearly demonstrated. The lesson was not well learned. Whether the engagement was militarily justified is open to doubt. Wolseley and General Sir Frederick Maurice, according to Lady Colley, held that it was. Others believed that even if Colley had forced the Nek, he could never have operated with any success in the Transvaal with such a small column without regular cavalry and with his large wagon train.[11]

Laing's Nek was also the only time during the first Boer War that mounted troops took part in a regular engagement. In the Pretoria garrison, however, were about 100 of the Pretoria Carbineers, also known as D'Arcy's Horse, as well as some sixty of Captain Henry Nourse's Horse ('Nourse's 'Orses'), both corps raised for the emergency. These patrolled the areas for miles around during the 100 days of the siege. They also took part in three sorties which were made from the town. The Carbineers alone lost nearly a third of their strength as casualties.

At Colley's second defeat in the action at the Ingogo on 8 February, there were a few Mounted Infantry (again under Major Brownlow), but they did not play an important part. At the disastrous battle of Majuba Hill on 27 February, where Colley was killed, some of the recently arrived 15th Hussars helped to cover the retreat of the defeated infantry as they poured down the hill, and to bring in the wounded.

As in no other instance during the nineteenth century, retribution was not exacted following British military defeats. Gladstone, before coming to power, had condemned the annexation of the Transvaal. On taking over the government, he had supported British rule. But now, after three military humiliations at the hands of the Boer rebels, he gave to men with arms in their hands what had been earlier denied to them in their peaceful prayers. The reluctant but highly competent Evelyn Wood was employed as negotiator. He made peace with the Boers. The outcome was the Pretoria Convention of 1881, which, modified in 1884, gave back virtual independence to the Transvaal. Such a result, arrived at in such a manner, bore within itself the seeds of future conflict.

5

'Afghanistan merits the character given to Spain by the first Henry of France: Invade with a large force, and you are destroyed by starvation; invade with a small force and you are overwhelmed by a hostile people.'

SIR HENRY DURAND

'The whole question is one of commissariat; that of commissariat, one of means of transport.'

THE DUKE OF WELLINGTON

'By that time I dare say we shall have possession of Cabul. With such a government as we have now thank God! the Russians will have been turned pretty nearly out of Asia by this time next year'.*

SIR THOMAS TRINGLE, a rich business man in Trollope's *Ayala's Angel*[1]

(i)

The Second Afghan War: first phase, 1878–1879; three column invasion – action at Mausam – Kabul river disaster – battle of Fatehabad – actions at Matun, Shahjui, Saif-u-din and Khuskh-i-nakhud

Towards the end of 1838 two British columns had invaded Afghanistan (see Vol I, p. 213), thus launching the First Afghan War. On the morning of 21 November, 1878, almost exactly forty years later, three columns repeated the process. The 'Eastern Question' had once again come to the fore. With the special tensions which in the late 1870s brought Britain and Russia to the brink of war this book is not concerned. Nor need be discussed in detail the specific events which led up to the Second Afghan War. It is enough here to quote the words of Maurice Cowling, a singularly unbiased modern historian. The three columns, he says,

> 'were making their advances in one sense because they were weapons of coercion to be used against Sher Ali, the emir of Kabul and ruler of Afghanistan. They were there in another

* 'It has to be stated that this story was written in 1878.'

sense because a minister in England [Gathorne-Hardy, first Lord Cranbrook] was lazy or tired or forgetful and because a viceroy in India [second Baron and, later, first Earl of Lytton] was enthusiastic and disobedient, an imperfect instrument for the enforcement of the foreign policy of the British cabinet and ignorant, or careless, of its parliamentary commitments.'[2]

The essential facts of the final drift into war are that Sher Ali very unwillingly received a temporary Russian mission in Kabul, having earlier thwarted Lytton's efforts to establish permanent British observers in Afghanistan. Lytton, thereupon, most rashly sent forward a mission under Sir Neville Chamberlain, which was turned back at the frontier. Such a rebuff being intolerable, war was inevitable. Put thus bluntly, the complexity of the situation is conveyed not at all. Now that most of the facts are known, it seems that the war was unnecessary and that Lytton's execution of a 'forward' policy, only sanctioned with profound reluctance by Disraeli's cabinet, was at least as much to blame for it as were the actions of the emir or the Russians.*

* * *

The northernmost column, known as the Peshawar Valley Field Force, under Lieutenant-General Sir Samuel Browne, VC, left Jamrud on 21 November, 1878. It numbered over 16,000 officers and men with nearly fifty guns and innumerable followers. Its cavalry brigade, which brought up the rear, consisted of two squadrons of the 10th Hussars, two of the 11th Bengal Lancers, two of the Guides Cavalry and four horse artillery guns. In command of it was another holder of the Victoria Cross from Mutiny days, Brigadier-General Charles Gough.

The column's first task was to capture the fort of Ali Masjid at the entrance to the Khyber Pass. Once that was achieved – against determined opposition – no further resistance was encountered. By 20 December the whole force except those troops guarding the lines of communication was assembled at Jalalabad. Here the officers and men settled down for a lengthy stay. Among the 'long list of stores' indented for from Peshawar by the 10th Hussars were 'lawn tennis balls, which looks,' wrote Captain Boyce Combe, the

* But see Lutyens, Mary *The Lyttons in India*, 1979, for a convincing defence of Lord Lytton based on unpublished letters.

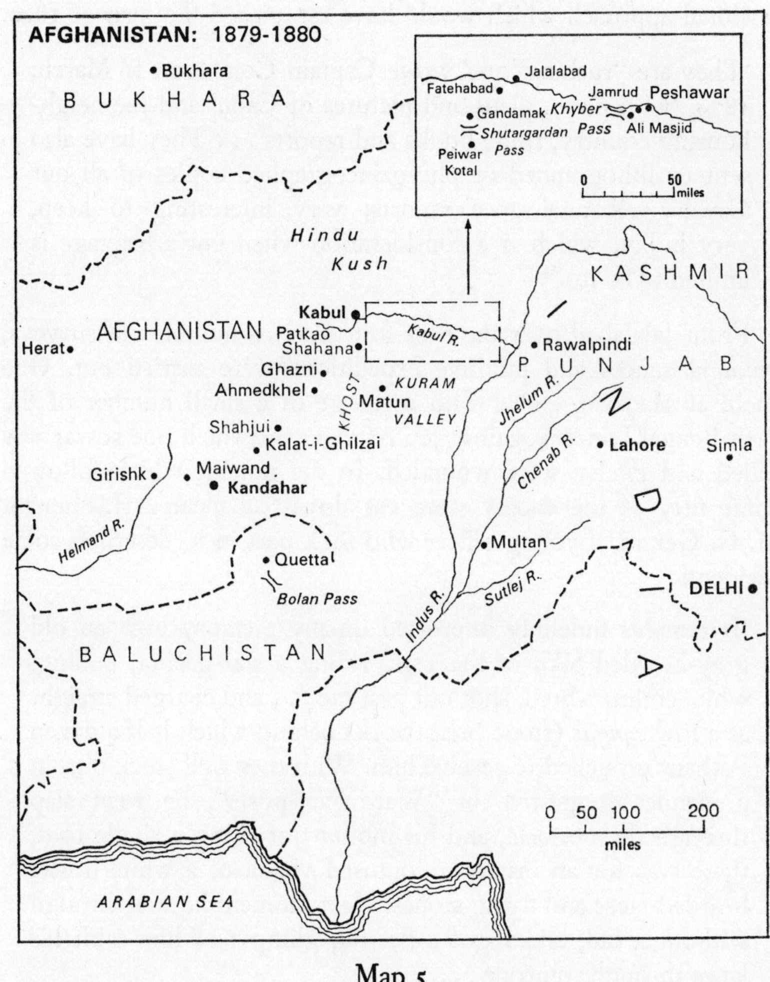

Map 5

cavalry brigade-major, 'as if they anticipated a long halt'.[3] Even the regimental band, which had been broken up and its instruments put in store at Rawalpindi, was sent for. 'It is so miserable,' complained Combe, 'without music on the march, on parade, etc'. In February the instruments arrived, having run the gauntlet of the Khyber Pass – 'full of lawless individuals . . . who are friends or foes according to the strength of the escort. The bandsmen,' wrote Combe, 'are already blowing dust out of them and getting their lips in order.'[4]

The similarities between the first and second Afghan wars were numerous, but there was increasing evidence now of a new professional approach which would have astonished the men of 1840.

> 'They are "rushing" us,' wrote Captain Combe on 16 March, 1879, 'with maps, plans and pictures of Cabul and the neighbouring country, route books and reports . . . They have also sent us lithographed or photozincographed copies of all our Cavalry reconnaissance reports; very interesting to keep, very bulky, which is a consideration when one's baggage is limited to 80 lbs.'[5]

From Jalalabad over the next four months numbers of surveys, reconnaissances and punitive expeditions were carried out. One such, at Mausam, ended with a charge of a small number of the 11th Bengal Lancers against 300 Afghans, in which one sowar was killed and twelve were wounded. In the pursuit which followed some fifty of the enemy were cut down or speared. Lieutenant M. G. Gerard, a young officer who took part in it, describes some incidents:

> 'It remains indelibly impressed on my memory how an old grey-bearded Sikh of the 11th, riding a star-gazing, pulling, white country-bred, shot out past me . . . and charged straight at a low *sangar* (stone breastwork) behind which half a dozen Pathans crouched to receive him. With toes well stuck out, in a manner suggestive of "Ware gate-posts", he went slap through the obstacle, and his mount not rising a single foot, there was for an instant a confused vision of a white horse, bearded faces and flying stones. Next moment he was through without a fall, and I got a fleeting glimpse of him with his lance through someone . . .

During the aftermath of the charge – ('it was a regular case of "disperse and pursue"') – the hillmen

> 'turned and fought like tiger-cats when we closed on them. Not one in three had a firearm, and when they had blazed off at you, they took this crosswise to guard the head . . ., the skull being the sole point they appeared to think vulnerable. One had but to make a feint of employing the obsolete cut No. 7, and up would fly their guard over the the face, when dropping your point you went clean through your man . . .
>
> 'The fourth man I tackled fired at me just as I closed, and I felt a blow on my side, but next moment my sword went

through something hard, and the weapon was twisted out of my hand and hung by the sword-knot. The blade, which was a straight rapier one by Wilkinson, got a slight but permanent wave in it, and I can only account for it receiving such a wrench by having taken my opponent through the head-piece as he crouched and tried to stab the horse from below . . . I do not suppose the whole melee lasted three minutes.'

One non-commissioned officer was awarded the Order of Merit, third class, and three other ranks were specially promoted, for gallantry in this action.[6]

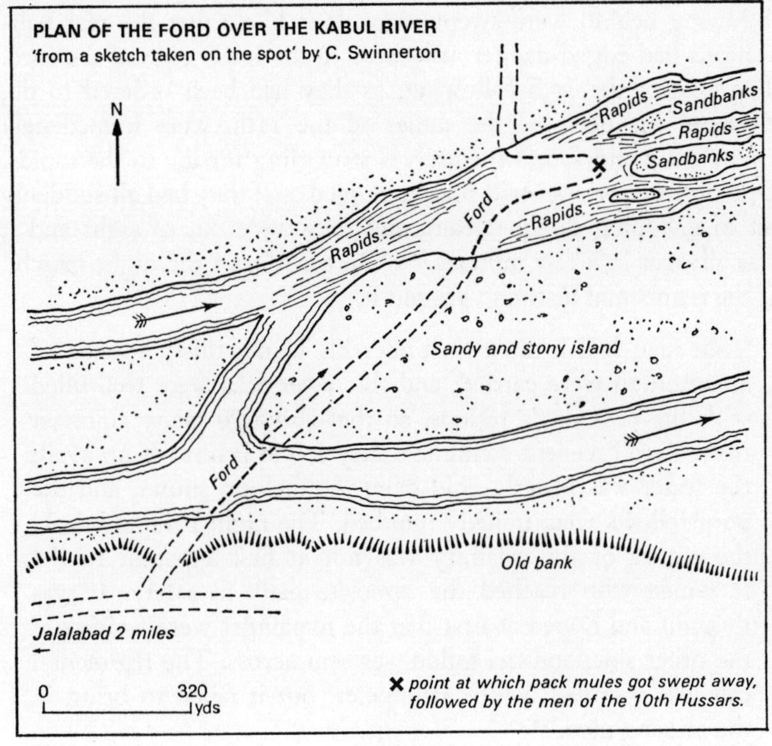

Map 6

Another of these punitive expeditions involved a squadron each of the 10th Hussars and the 11th Bengal Lancers, which formed one or two small columns sent against the Khugianis. The two squadrons started to cross the Kabul river at 9.30 in dim moonlight on 31 March, 1879, at a ford just below where a trestle bridge had recently been removed because of the swollen state of the river. It seems that the S-shaped ford was known by the Staff to be very dangerous at all times, for both above and below it were 'rapids, broken by sandbanks and rocks'.[7] A report to this effect had been overlooked in the haste with which the expedition was got up. Further, the passage had been staked out soon after the British had arrived at Jalalabad, but the stakes had recently been removed at the request of the local friendly inhabitants 'to whom the difficulty of the ford had been an effective defence from the raids of the hillmen'.[8] The 11th, 'composed of men accustomed from youth up to the treacherous rivers of the Punjab,'[9] led by a single Afghan guide, managed to cross without mishap, but some pack mules following behind were swept away. It is likely that the rear half-sections had edged dangerously near to the lower side of the ford. The men of the 10th following, as they had been ordered to do, close on the heels of the mules of the 11th, were immediately swept away and found themselves struggling for life in the rapids. One of the survivors said that 'it seemed as if they had all suddenly set to galloping down stream, and they were out of sight and it was all over in a few minutes.'[10] 'On account of the night march,' as the regimental historian has put it,

> 'each man had a tunic on under his khaki; thirty rounds of ammunition were carried, and the haversacks were well filled with the next day's rations, so that although many amongst them were excellent swimmers they found it now of no avail; the water was bitterly cold from the melting snows, and the poor fellows were quickly numbed. The night being so dark, the nature of the calamity was not at first apparent to the few men who reached the opposite bank in safety. It was thought and hoped at first that the remainder were waiting at the other side, and the guide was sent across. The regimental call was sounded by the trumpeter, but it failed to bring in the missing men.'[11]

Five troopers, being able to rid themselves of their belts and arms, escaped to the far bank. Two others managed to make the near bank. Of the seventy who set out, one officer and forty-six other ranks were drowned or kicked to death by their struggling horses.

The cause of the disaster was the failure of the squadron to incline upstream. The need to make a conscious effort to do this had probably not formed a part of the 10th's training. The men should have been taught that when crossing a fast-flowing stream it is a natural thing with your eyes resting on the running water to suppose that you are crossing it at right angles, whereas in fact you are tending to drift downstream.

The disaster inspired Kipling to write a famous poem, 'Ford o' Kabul River'. Part of the first verse runs thus:

'There I lef' my mate for ever,
  Wet an' drippin' by the ford.
    Ford, ford, ford o' Kabul river,
      Ford o' Kabul river in the dark!
    There's the river up and brimmin', and there's
        'arf a squadron swimmin',
      'Cross the ford o' Kabul river in the dark.'

The final verse ends:

' 'Im an' 'arf my troop is down,
  Down an' drownded by the ford.
    Ford, ford, ford o' Kabul river,
      Ford o' Kabul river in the dark!
    There's the river low an' fallin', but it
        ain't no use o' callin'
      'Cross the ford o' Kabul river in the dark.'[12]

* * *

Two days later, on 2 April, 1879, near Fatehabad, a numerous body of Khugianis* was found by Brigadier-General Charles Gough's main body in a strong position on the crest of some gently sloping hills protected by stone breastworks. By sending forward the four guns of I Battery, C Brigade, Royal Horse Artillery, which twice fired a few rounds of shrapnel and then limbered up and retired, Gough skilfully tempted the enemy out into the plain below. The British infantry now attacked on the left and met with stiff resistance. At the same time the cavalry, barely 200 all told, led by Lord Ralph Kerr of the 10th Hussars, charged into a large mass of tribesmen on the right. In a letter home Captain Combe describes what happened:

* Some were armed with Enfield rifles, more with the long native rifles known as jezails, and all with 'the formidable Afghan sword-knife'. (Swinnerton, 26.)

'The cavalry were having a good time of it; the enemy coming into the open gave them a great chance, and the Guides Cavalry [part of two squadrons], especially, got well home and pursued a long way. Altogether it was a Cavalry day and the brunt of the loss fell on them – the Guides Cavalry losing their Commanding Officer, a very nice, good fellow, Wigram Battye . . . Their only other officer was also slightly wounded, and two of our young fellows were just touched, but will probably not be returned as wounded.*

Everyone is full of the pluck of these fellows [the Khugianis], who, in all cases when overtaken, stood at bay and fought like men. It was rather curious to see a fellow, armed only with a large knife, dancing round and round and keeping off three or four Hussars, who could not get their horses to face him, though it always ended in his being cut or shot down. One of our Troops was detached and came across some fellows in a hollow, so the Captain dismounted twenty men and went in at them on foot; they at once charged out and one fellow caught him a cut over the head, which knocked him down: he would soon have been killed but for his "Sub" [subaltern], who clubbed a carbine and brained his opponent.'[13]

After the initial charge other groups of cavalrymen also dismounted and used their carbines, pistols or revolvers to dislodge small bodies of the enemy. The 10th Hussars alone expended 1,022 rounds of ammunition in the course of what has been called the most successful engagement of the war.[14]

The men of the 10th, incidentally, had found their double-barrelled pistols 'so heavy that they were at a discount'. Some of them 'gave theirs away to the Sergeant-Majors sooner than carry them.' But, wrote Captain Combe, several men also found their newly issued revolvers useless. They fired all the barrels 'into the men without the slightest effect'. Consequently 'directly we got back here, the double-barrelled pistols were in great demand' again.[15]

When Major Battye of the Guides fell, 'first receiving two bullets in his hip and shortly after another in the chest,'[16] Lieutenant W. R. P. Hamilton, 'then the only officer left with the Regiment,

* The total cavalry casualties were: Guides: seven killed or died of wounds, twenty-seven wounded; seven horses killed and thirty-seven wounded. 10th Hussars: seven wounded; one horse killed, eleven wounded and one missing. (Guides, 87; Liddell, 407.) These figures are likely to be more accurate than the official ones given in Hanna, II, 292.

assumed command, and, in the words of the citation for the Victoria Cross which he won that day, 'cheered on his men to avenge Major Battye's death. In this charge Lieutenant Hamilton, seeing Sowar Dowlut Ram down and attacked by three of the enemy whilst entangled with his horse (which had been killed) rushed to the rescue, and, followed by a few of his men, cut down all three and saved the life of Sowar Dowlut Ram.'[17]

By all accounts some hundreds of flying Khugianis were cut down in the pursuit. This seems to have been started promptly and to have been followed through with determination. One account points out the contrasting behaviour of the 10th and the Guides during the pursuit.

> 'The English horsemen charged *en masse*, in their ranks, and many of the active mountaineers opposed to them easily escaped the rush on the one side or the other. The Guides, on the other hand, charged in loose order, hunting the enemy wherever a man could be seen. It was observed, also, that the narrow edges of the long straight swords of the 10th rebounded harmlessly from the thick leathern *postheens* [sheepskin coats] which clothed the bodies of the enemy and from the heavy folds of the turbans which covered their heads. I was informed,' wrote the divisional chaplain, 'by one of the men engaged that he found the thrust infinitely more effective than the cut; while by the Guides, with their broad keen sabres, the thrust was hardly ever resorted to at all . . . It was a remark commonly made at the time that if a few Lancers had been present the loss of the enemy would have been much more severe, the ground being so rough that many of the fugitives were able to ply their rifles under shelter of rocks or hollow places, almost with impunity.'[18]

A day or two later, according to Captain Combe,

> 'some of the men who fought against us came in to salaam and spoke about it openly . . . They say they don't care a bit for "guns" or the infantry, but the swords of the cavalry are awful! They declared they only lost ten from the artillery, and very few from the infantry, fire; but that the cavalry killed 1,000! or more; (probably half this number is nearer the mark) [or even less].'[19]

* * *

The central and smallest column of the three which crossed the frontier on 21 November, 1878, was commanded by Major-General Frederick ("Bobs") Roberts, VC. Named the Kuram Valley Field Force, it numbered to start with some 5,300 officers and men with thirteen guns. Two troops of the 10th Hussars, the 5th Punjab Cavalry and the 12th Bengal Cavalry formed the cavalry brigade, commanded by Colonel Hugh Gough, VC, commanding officer of the 12th Bengal Cavalry and brother of Charles Gough.

By a skilful deception plan combined with a night march of the chief part of his force, Roberts captured the strongly held and almost impregnable mountain position of the Peiwar Kotal. The cavalry was not much employed, except in a reconnaissance role.

In the New Year about 2,000 men of the force made a reconnaissance in force into the district of Khost. The mounted element consisted of seventy-eight sabres of the 10th and 155 of the 5th. These distinguished themselves at Matun on 7 January, 1879. Hearing rumours that the tribesmen, hitherto believed to be most friendly, were about to attack him, Roberts sent out a troop of the 5th to reconnoitre.

> 'They had scarcely gone three miles from camp,' wrote Gough, 'when they came across a body of infantry, about fifteen hundred or two thousand men, with some cavalry. Being so outnumbered, they were forced to retire, which they did well, sending in information. The General ordered me to take out the remainder of the cavalry . . . Moving at a good pace, we came up with the troop of the 5th retiring steadily. The tribesmen in the flush of victory were advancing with a flourish of swords and banners . . . Seeing our reinforcements, they retired, skirting the foot of the hills. The ground was awful, so getting my men under as much cover as available, the 10th Hussars opened a heavy dismounted fire on the enemy, and the 5th P.C., making a charge, got well into them. There was really no ground for cavalry to act, but the 10th Hussars and the 5th P.C. worked splendidly – charged up mounds under fire, took up good positions, and then dismounted and opened fire on their enemy, who had not time to get away. In about an hour or so they were flying in confusion towards the hills . . .
>
> 'In the meantime our camp itself had been suddenly attacked and surrounded by some four thousand men, our own force

being about eighteen hundred . . . Captain Stewart, whom I had sent back by the General's orders with thirty sabres of the 5th P.C., arriving in the nick of time, made a gallant charge and cut up some thirty of them. They lost over a hundred, whilst our losses were two killed and five wounded, and one or two horses killed.'[20]

Gough's official report specially mentioned a charge made by Major B. Williams, Commandant of the 5th. 'It struck me,' he wrote, 'as one of the most gallant episodes in Cavalry warfare I had ever seen.'[21] Major Williams' own report ran as follows:

'. . . On arrival . . . I immediately took advantage of a low detached hill . . . We dismounted a troop and opened fire at 400 yards, on which the enemy retired towards the high hills, keeping possession of one or two low hills at their base on which they planted their standards.

'Leaving a few men in this position to protect our right, I moved the remainder round to the left and taking advantage of some broken ground under fire of dismounted men, attempted to drive the enemy from the low hill. Aided by the fire of the 10th Hussars, the enemy were driven to the far side of it, but seeing their standards still flying there, I collected together the 4th Troop and went up the hill at a gallop, and rapidly dismounting half the men drove the enemy with a quick fire off the hill towards the high range.'[22]

This minor affair has been described at some length because it has the elements of numerous similar actions which took place during the war and to describe which there is no space. It shows, too, how readily even the least irregular of cavalry regiments, such as the 10th Hussars, took to the role of mounted infantry. Forty years earlier this sort of half mounted, half dismounted action would have been rare – even looked down upon. By the 1880s it had become normal practice.

Another good example of its use occurred later in the war when 150 sabres of the 2nd Punjab Cavalry, forming part of a small mixed force, fought a highly successful action on 24 October at Shahjui. In the course of it the men alternated mounted and dismounted action a considerable number of times. This engagement was also one of the very few occasions on which the Afghan cavalry really stood against British cavalry. In the resulting straight fight the 2nd lost one man killed and no less than twenty-seven wounded, mostly by sabre cuts.[23]

* * *

The third column used in the invasion of Afghanistan was named the South Afghanistan Field Force, and its objective was Kandahar. Commanded by Lieutenant-General Donald Stewart, it numbered nearly 13,000 of all ranks, with seventy-eight guns. The 15th Hussars (397 of all ranks), with the 8th and 19th Bengal Cavalry, the 1st and 2nd Punjab Cavalry, and, from the Bombay Army, the 3rd Scinde Horse, formed the two cavalry brigades.

To reach Afghanistan proper it was necessary for this column to traverse the friendly state of Baluchistan. As early as the beginning of October, 1878, in readiness for the coming war, reinforcements had been sent towards Quetta, where since 1876, a British Resident with a small military force had been settled. Some days before the frontier was crossed on the declaration of war, General Stewart was writing that his supplies had 'to be carried over 200 miles by routes almost destitute of water, and in many places without grass or firewood. It requires 30,000 camels to keep up my supplies.'[24] Worst of all, as it also had been in 1839 (see Vol I, p. 216), was the crossing of the Bolan Pass. During the six days which the 15th Hussars took to accomplish this, they had to cross and recross the river as many as twelve times a day. The regiment carried with it six days' supply of grass and *jawari* (millet grain).

> 'The track was so narrow and stony,' says the regimental historian, 'that occasionally an advance could only be made in single file; the ground so hard that pegs could not be driven into it and tents had to be fastened down with, and horses, picketed to, large stones; the cold so intense that the men could not remain for many minutes at a time in the saddle, and, crossing the famous Dasht-i-Bedaulat, or "Plain without Wealth", "the bread and meat were frozen rigid, and even the tea and rum that some carried in the water-bottles were almost solid ice."[25]
>
> 'The horses of the Hussars lived from Saturday afternoon, the 14th, till Monday afternoon, December 16, on one quart of what was little better than liquid mud; and the ponies, camels and bullocks did not get even that, while travelling during this time some forty-six miles heavily laden. On the

last march into Quetta, which was reached on the 17th, the Hussars passed a native follower . . . sitting dead and frozen stiff by the embers of a tiny fire.'[26]

Many another miserable follower died from the cold. The wastage in transport animals was appalling. Just under 12,000 dead camels, for instance, were counted along the last seventy miles of the route.[27]

Virtually no opposition was encountered by Stewart's force. The only engagement of the whole march – a minor one[28] – was fought against considerable odds by a squadron of the 15th Hussars, led most valiantly by Major George Luck (later to become the first Inspector-General of Cavalry in India (see p. 150)), with part of the 1st Punjab Cavalry, on 4 January, 1879, near Saif-u-din. Its chief interest lies in the fact that it proved difficult to distinguish the Afghan regular cavalrymen from the British sowars.

'When close they could only be known by a peculiar fur cap, like a small bearskin with a red scollop of cloth in front over the forehead. Their postins [sheepskin coats] were the same as those worn by the native cavalry, the carbine was slung, they wore swords and long boots, and the very horse accoutrements were in the same style as our own cavalry.

'The whole scene,' wrote an eye-witness, 'can be described, or, rather, best imagined, as a scrimmage, knots of men and single horsemen circling and pursuing in every direction, with here and there a prisoner standing beside the man who had captured him, and now and again a heap of clothes on the grass to mark the spot of some Afghan who had fulfilled his days.

'. . . One man of the 15th was out as a scout and actually, for a time, did left flanker to a party of the enemy!'[29]

A corporal of the baggage guard had a good time of it that day. He left his duty, 'ran an Afghan through after a long chase, acted as No. 6 to an R.H.A. gun, and then returned to baggage guard.'[30]*

After the peaceful occupation of Kandahar four days later, numerous reconnaissances were sent out, mostly for gathering forage and for surveying unexplored areas. Some of these encountered opposition. Such a one was that which ended at Khushk-

* The 15th Hussars had seven men wounded and the 1st Punjab Cavalry four in this engagement. The enemy was said to have lost 100 men.

i-nakhud on 26 February, 1879. 266 sabres of the 3rd Scinde Horse, after being surprised whilst a saddlery inspection was in progress, charged a large body of Afghans, including a number of *ghazis* (religious fanatics). Colonel Maunsell, a later Commandant and the regimental historian, says:

> 'The actual formation the charge was made in is not known, but it was, in all probability, a slap-dash affair and consisted merely in riding hard at the enemy anyhow. For this type of attack the more lines it can be made in the better, not merely for the purpose of inflicting loss, but for getting wounded men out of difficulties.'[31]

Part of the regiment now pursued the flying enemy under Major William Reynolds who 'early in the affair received a bullet wound, but still led his squadron to the attack, and so became engaged,' according to the official account of the war, 'in personal encounters with several of the enemy, when his horse fell with him in a *karez*,* and before he could recover himself he was cut down and hacked to pieces.'[32]

The day's casualties were 'pretty severe for a fight with Afghans': four killed, twenty-three wounded and twenty-eight horses killed. The enemy were from a tribe called the Zemandawaris. 163 of their bodies were counted in the open. They seem to have been led by chiefs possessed of considerable military skill, whose men showed stubborn valour and that contempt for death almost invariably displayed by Afghans. They later formed a large part of the irregulars in Ayub Khan's army at Maiwand. (See p. 254).

* An irrigation channel 'cut underground with shafts rising from [it] at every thirty or forty yards'. (Le Messurier, 33.)

'It is a great political triumph, getting Yakoob Khan to come in, but the Afghans will always believe we did not go to Cabul because we couldn't.'

CAPTAIN COMBE, 10th Hussars, 4 May 1879

'The transport train was, as usual, the weakest link in the chain, and everything had to be made subservient to it.'

HOWARD HENSMAN, *Daily News* special correspondent[1]

(ii)

The Second Afghan War: second phase, 1879; Treaty of Gandamak – massacre of Cavagnari – Roberts's march on Kabul – battle of Charasia

On 21 February, 1879, Sher Ali died. His son and successor, Yakub Khan, was prepared to negotiate. On 26 May the Treaty of Gandamak was signed. Its provisions included the cession of some territory to the British and the right to send a representative, with a suitable escort, to reside permanently in Kabul.

The Peshawar Valley Field Force was ordered to return to India. During what came to be remembered as 'the Death March', the 10th Hussars alone, marching in daytime temperatures of as much as 118°F in the shade, lost thirty-eight men from cholera.

'One night,' wrote the cavalry brigade-major, 'we sent on fourteen or fifteen cases, to travel in the cool; next morning, on arrival, the General and I went to the shed set apart as cholera hospital and saw ten of our men laid out in a row, with just a blanket thrown over them. The Doctor would not let us look at them, as he said it was impossible to recognise them and it was no use running the risk of the shock the sight might give us. The number of deaths was kept secret from the men, only an officer being sent to read the service over them as they were buried in a trench, and the only way we had of finding out the names of the dead was by checking the survivors with the lists of men sent to Hospital, and striking out the absentees as dead. At every station we left cases, and the only report we got was perhaps "three deaths – two Hussars, one artillery".'

Thus ended the war for the 10th Hussars.

Surgeon-General Ker Innes reported how the men of the Force looked on the march:

> 'Their clothes were stiff with profuse perspiration and dust. Their countenance betokened great nervous exhaustion combined with a wild expression difficult to describe. The eyes injected and even sunken; a burning skin, black with the effects of sun and dirt, a dry tongue, a weak voice, a thirst which no amount of liquid seemed to relieve. Many of the men staggered rather than marched into their tents and threw themselves down utterly incapable of further exertion until refreshed by sleep and food.'

The base hospital at Peshawar soon became grossly overcrowded and the city resembled a charnel house. Between mid-June and September there were 350 deaths among British troops. This represented a rate of seventy-four per 1,000 of strength.[2]

Captain Combe summed up affairs thus: 'A curious campaign, which cost us over 100 men, not one of whom was killed or even died of wounds! The widows,' he added, 'are providing for themselves pretty freely, one already married, two more engaged, and a third besieged by applications and only undecided as to which to choose.' Sir Samuel Browne 'could never ascertain the reason why the 10th Hussars suffered as they did. They suffered a great deal from pneumonia and bronchitis.' It was, he thought, that the 'number of young men amongst them' was the cause, but he stressed that they were 'a very fine, splendid regiment'.

Six months' *batta* [field allowance] was granted for the campaign. Combe reckoned that this meant 'about £120' for him.[3]

* * *

After the treaty of Gandamak Stewart's force at Kandahar was also ordered to withdraw to India; but a small number of its regiments were still there when the news of the massacre of Sir Louis Cavagnari, the British 'Envoy and Plenipotentiary' at Kabul, was received. He had arrived there on 24 July. On 3 September the men of several Afghan regiments, demanding their back-pay from the emir without success, mutinied and attacked the neighbouring Residency. Cavagnari, his staff and seventy-one of the eighty of all ranks of the Guides forming his escort were killed after putting up a

30. Valentine Baker Pasha

31. Lieut-Colonel John French, commanding the 19th Hussars

32. Lieut-Colonel Percy Barrow, 19th Hussars

33. Osman Digna

34. General Sir Garnet (later Viscount) Wolseley

35. Lieut Percival Marling, VC, at the time of the battle of Abu Klea, January 1885

36. Colonel Frederick Gustavus Burnaby, Royal Horse Guards

37. Lieut-General Sir Drury Curzon Drury-Lowe

prolonged and most gallant defence. Lieutenant Hamilton, who had gained the Victoria Cross at Fatehabad (see p. 217), and twenty-two of the Guides cavalry were among those massacred. Whether this catastrophe could have been prevented by the Emir is still an open question. It is certain that Cavagnari had been too sanguine in over-estimating Yakub Khan's power.

Since, by the terms of the treaty, the Kuram district was to be under British control, Roberts's Kuram Valley Field Force, unlike the other two to north and south of it, had not been broken up and sent back to India. Thus it was the nearest body of troops available and ready to undertake the retributory march on Kabul which was the obvious reaction to the massacre.

Major R. C. W. Mitford, the second-in-command of the 14th Bengal Lancers, found that

> 'a very short time sufficed for the officers' preparations, few of us having more than the authorized weight of "kit", consisting of a tiny double-roofed tent, 7 ft sq, weighing 80 pounds; personal baggage restricted to the same weight (this required much consideration, even to the possibility of taking an extra toothbrush!); 25 lbs of baggage for each camp follower, and a like amount for each charger . . . The arrangements for the men took more consideration and a longer time.'

As always in Indian campaigns, the chief obstacle to a speedy advance was lack of transport. Private B. P. Crane of the 9th Lancers, the First Squadron of which had joined Roberts's force earlier in the year, wrote in his diary: 'We are carrying mostly all our baggage on our spare horses and grass cutters' tats [native ponies]; there is only 25 lbs a man allowed to carry.'[5] The squadron had had to give up sixty of their eighty regimental camels for general transport purposes. The 14th Bengal Lancers marched most of the way to Kabul on foot, the horses carrying supplies for both themselves and their riders, while the men of the 5th Punjab Cavalry were also dismounted 'and carried the Commissariat grain slung across their saddles'.[5]

Forced, because of supply difficulties, to split his force into two parts, thereby taking considerable risks, Roberts managed to reach his destination in a little over a month after the massacre, a remarkable achievement especially as his 'tail' consisted of about 6,000 followers and some 3,500 baggage animals. On two occasions he met with opposition.* The first small fight took place at the foot of the 11,000 foot Shutargardan Pass, when 2,000 tribesmen were easily dispersed. Some of the men of the 9th came into action. Private Crane tells what happened:

> 'The trumpet sounded to stand-to and mount; we advanced about a hundred yards, when they fired a volley from behind the trees on the top of the hills into our advanced guard, but the bullets luckily went over their heads. We immediately got the order for even numbers to dismount with carbines, the odd numbers holding their horses; the same the Native Cavalry, it being a very awkward place for cavalry to work, between two very high hills, where it would be impossible for horses to climb up.'[6]

* * *

At Charasia, six miles from Kabul, a large regular force, supported by thousands of tribesmen, held an extremely strong mountain position. On 6 October, before they could complete their defences, Roberts attacked them with the artillery and infantry of that part of his force which had come up, having carefully deceived the enemy as to where the main blow would fall. From the cavalry point of view, there are two points of interest which emerge from this battle, one of Roberts's finest: the efficiency of the mounted patrols which gained vital information about the exact dispositions of the enemy, and the failure to effect a proper pursuit over excellent cavalry country. This last came about because it was essential for Roberts to keep much of his mounted arm for the defence of his camp. All around it masses of Afghans were poised on the hill tops, prepared to swoop should the British suffer a check. Further, most of the rest of his small cavalry brigade, which consisted of only 1,202 of all ranks, was needed to keep open communications with the troops which had not yet come up, and with his supplies.[7]

The battle of Charasia is also interesting because his conduct in it gained for Colour-Sergeant Hector MacDonald, later to become a general, his commission; while Major George White, later to become a Field-Marshal, won his Victoria Cross there.

* The Emir, who found himself crushed between his 'hawks' at Kabul and the avenging British, decided to throw in his lot with Roberts. Much to that general's embarrassment he came out to his headquarters and stayed there, with a considerable retinue.

Also taking part was the twenty-six year old Ian Hamilton who, though an infantry subaltern, found himself with the cavalry. In old age he wrote,

> 'It was in "the cavalry pursuit" – still to my credit in the War Service records in which I led a troop of the 5th Punjab Cavalry in a charge – that I first learnt that the sword is no good against an Afghan lying on his back and twirling a heavy knife. The dust clouds of the Chardeh Valley – the 5th Punjab Cavalry – red pugarees – blue swords flashing; the galloping line, and I also galloping with that sensation of speed which the swiftest motor car can never impart . . . Afghans in little knots, or else lying on their backs whirling their big knives to cut off the legs of our horses, a hell of a scrimmage in fact, until the *sowars* got to work in couples, one with sword uplifted, the other pulling his carbine out of the bucket and making the enemy spring to their feet and be cut down or be shot as they lay. Dust, shouts, shots, clash of steel . . .'[8]

Roberts, having captured seventy-eight of the Afghans' guns, made his formal entry into Kabul on 13 October, the cavalry brigade heading the procession. The previous day Yakub Khan had told him that he wished to abdicate, declaring that he had been most miserable and would rather be a grass-cutter in the English camp than ruler of Afghanistan. Before long he was bundled off to India where he spent the rest of his days in comfortable exile.[9]

Roberts now decided that his line of communication with India should become that which passed through the Khyber Pass. He also decided to quarter the whole of his force in the vast cantonment of Sherpur, a rectangle of four-and-a-half miles circumference just north of the city. Amongst reinforcements which arrived there early in November were the headquarters and two squadrons of the 9th Lancers. Hugh Gough confessed to 'being rather staggered by the amount of their baggage (they had even their full-dress uniform with them), and still more when I saw camels in the rear toiling along with machinery which turned out to be the regimental soda-water factory.' So ill-prepared was the regiment – or, rather, so besotted were the authorities with the need for lancers to possess no firearms beside a virtually useless horse-pistol – that when ordered for service, the regiment had no carbines. These had to be served out in a rush and the men put through a hurried course in musketry. Captain Combe was amazed that the men were 'all shaved and pipe-clayed as in cantonments! Looks very smart and nice,' he added, 'but I should like to see them after some of these trips we have been on lately.'[10] The First Squadron, whose men were now nicknamed 'Apperley's Irregulars', after their much loved commander, had been separated from the rest of the regiment for nine months. The reunion with their comrades was warmly welcomed. 'They brought a coffee-shop with them,' wrote Private Crane, 'which was very acceptable, as we have been without tobacco for some time; could not get any here. We have not been able to get our ration of rum, waiting for the convoy to come in; been getting half-dram of country drink.'[11]

Mir Karez, 10 December 1879

'Ninety years old, and so infirm that he had to be carried from village to village on a bed, Mushk-i-Alam might well be accounted no formidable foe; . . . but facts soon proved that his power extended far beyond the district in which he had first been heard of . . . Chief and peasant answered to the call which summoned them to destroy Roberts and his army, as their fathers had wiped out the forces of Elphinstone.'

COLONEL H. B. HANNA[1]

(iii)

The Second Afghan War: third phase, 1879–1880; action at Mir Karez – actions in the Chardeh Valley – siege of Sherpur

Roberts soon learned the lesson which had been taught to his predecessors in 1841–2 and to all but the strongest of the emirs from the earliest times, namely that to control the capital was not necessarily to control Afghanistan. In the beginning of December, 1879, what may well have numbered as many as 100,000 Afghan troops of one sort or another, fired by religious and national hatred of the invaders and for once more or less united in the desire to wage a holy war against the invading infidels, began to converge on Kabul from all directions. It was vital that Roberts should strike before the various bodies could concentrate. To achieve this and at the same time defend the cantonment he possessed some 8,000 of all ranks.

On 8 and 9 December two columns were sent off from Sherpur towards Argandeh, fifteen and a half miles to the west, the larger under Brigadier-General H. T. Macpherson, VC, the smaller under Brigadier-General T. D. Baker. Macpherson was 'to meet the enemy and force him back on Maidan'. Baker, after making a lengthy detour to the south, was 'to place himself across the line by which the enemy, after defeat by Macpherson, would have to retire'[2] on the road to Ghazni.

Whilst Baker was working his way round, Macpherson was ordered on 10 December to attack and disperse 5,000 Kohistanis assembling near Mir Karez, ten miles to the north-east of Sherpur. This he achieved in a smart little action with his 1,300 infantry, four mountain guns and seventy-five of the 14th Bengal Lancers. Because of the hilly nature of the terrain, he had left behind at

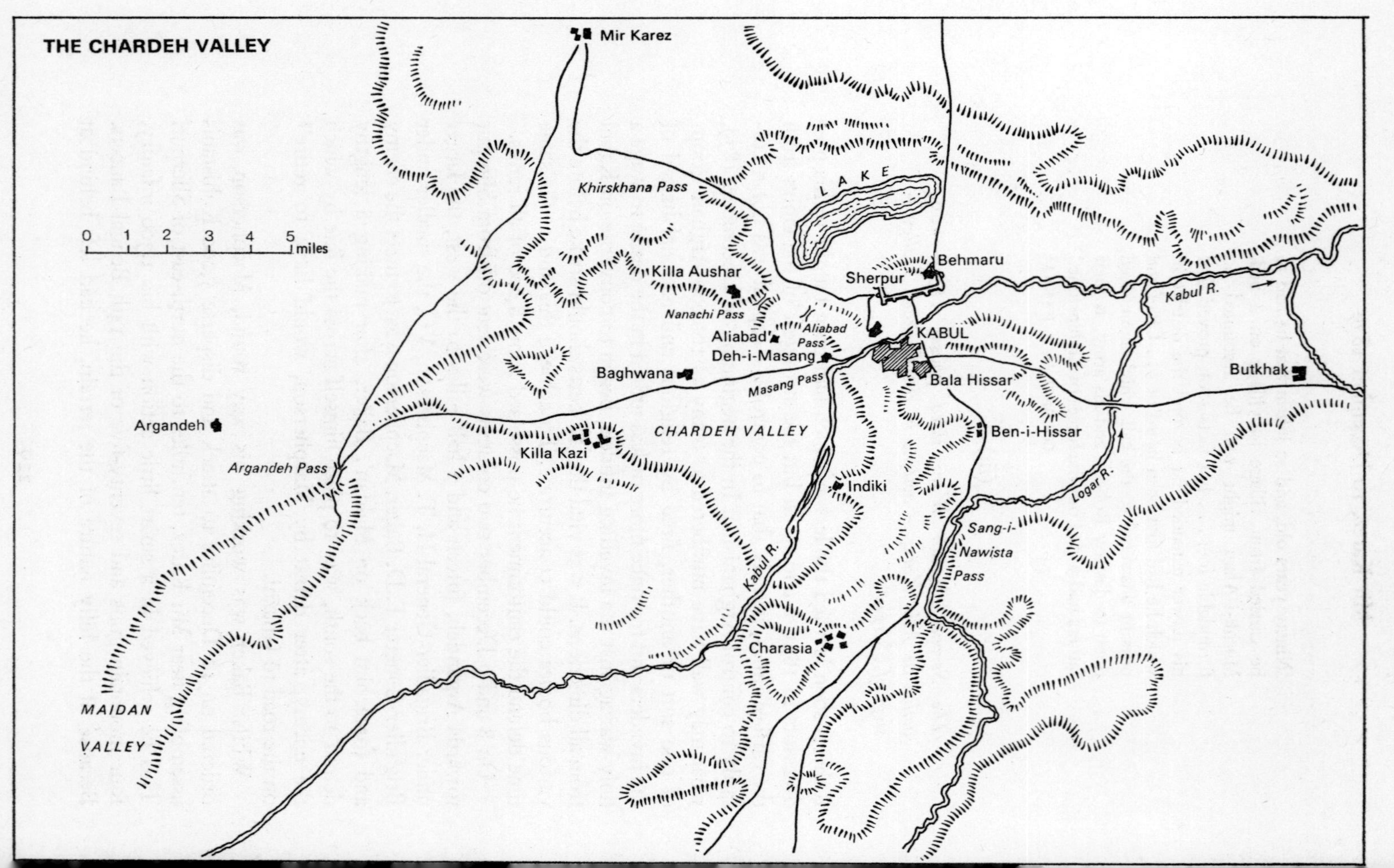
THE CHARDEH VALLEY
0 1 2 3 4 5 miles
Mir Karez
Khirskhana Pass
LAKE
Behmaru
Sherpur
Killa Aushar
Nanachi Pass
Aliabad
Aliabad Pass
KABUL
Deh-i-Masang
Baghwana
Masang Pass
Bala Hissar
Kabul R.
Butkhak
Argandeh
CHARDEH VALLEY
Ben-i-Hissar
Killa Kazi
Argandeh Pass
Indiki
Logar R.
Sang-i-Nawista Pass
Kabul R.
Charasia
MAIDAN VALLEY

Killa Aushar, three and a half miles from Sherpur, his four horse artillery guns and 180 lances of the 9th Lancers and the 14th. Next morning these were reinforced by more men of the 9th and 14th. Brigadier-General W. G. D. Massy, an infantry officer who was Roberts's cavalry brigade commander, took command of the four guns and the 257 lancers. Massy's orders, according to Roberts who gave them to him in person, were 'to advance from Killa Aushar by the road leading directly from the city of Kabul towards Arghandi and Ghazni; to proceed cautiously and quietly, feeling for the enemy; to communicate with General Macpherson, and to act in conformity with that officer's movements, but on no account to commit himself to an action until General Macpherson had engaged the enemy.'[3] Massy at once sent off one troop of the 9th (forty-three strong) to open communication with Macpherson. He himself set off, not, as Roberts had apparently ordered him to, by the *road*, which would have meant his moving round two sides of a parallelogram, but straight *across country*. His small force had advanced about three miles when Captain Bloomfield Gough's troop of the 9th, acting as advance guard, caught sight of the enemy 'advancing over some low hills in dense masses, like,' according to Private Crane, 'a swarm of bees'.[4]

Massy to his astonishment had come into the presence of some 9,000 of the main Afghan army, 'all on foot save a small body of Cavalry on their left flank', covering an unbroken frontage of nearly two miles. About 3,000 of them were extended in the shape of a crescent, 'developing two horns, quite *à la Zulu*'. Behind was an irregular body, numbering 6,000 or more.[5] The astute Afghan leader, Mahomed Jan, with far better intelligence than was at Roberts's disposal, had concluded that the three British columns were sufficiently far from each other and from their base for him to be able to attack that base with safety. Having started off earlier than Massy had done, his men were now within seven and a half miles of Sherpur.

> 'With any number of standards, white, red and black, they seemed,' Captain J. A. Stewart-Mackenzie of the 9th wrote home next day, 'to be making straight for us. The R.H.A. opened fire,* but as they were in such straggling order, only a

* Roberts makes the point in his MS marginal note to Duke (222) that 'Massy's guns crossed and came into action to the south of the Ghazni road without his knowing of the fact – a very important one as this road offered a secure line of retreat for artillery.'

few were killed; we could see them through our glasses picking them up. We then went on and again opened fire. Their bullets now began to drop in among us, so the Colonel [Lieutenant-Colonel Robert Cleland] ordered me to dismount my troop, and open fire to try to check them. This I did, but our fire had little or no effect on them. After firing a few rounds, we were ordered to mount and follow the guns, who had retired some 300 yards. This we did, and on arriving at the guns they opened fire, but don't seem to have done much harm. The bullets were now coming in like hail, and knocking the horses down both in the squadron and also the R.H.A. horses.

'General Massy, who was in command, now ordered Cleland to charge . . . I heard Cleland say, "How far am I to go?" and Massy said, "Use your own discretion." We were now about 500 yards from the enemy, who were advancing in skirmishing order, the ground intersected with nullahs and watercourses. The Colonel gave the order to charge in extended order. Off we went, opening out as we went, the Colonel right ahead of us. It did not take us long to open out, and before we knew where we were, we were among them. The ground we had to get over was awful ground for cavalry, deep watercourses and nullahs . . . The enemy were scattered all over the place in small bodies, some behind hillocks, some on horses, but all firing like the devil into us, dropping men and horses all over the place. I must tell you we were only 126 in the ranks, so may imagine that when we got among them, that it was all we could do to hold our own; they were all round us, and the ones in rear of them coming up firing as they came.

'In the melee I found myself next the Colonel, who was on his horse supported by two men. I saw that he was badly wounded, so I told them to take him to the rear. I then as senior assumed command, and finding that the men were falling fast and that we were surrounded on all sides, I ordered the retirement.'[6]

Private Crane in his diary described how the lancers 'retired, rallied again, and charged again; but only to be repulsed. Checking their advance for a short time, everyone had now to gallop for his life.'[7] Captain Stewart-Mackenzie takes up the story:

'On our way back we picked up many men who had their horses shot, and many wounded men. The enemy, those that were mounted, kept following us, riding round and firing, and then cutting at us with their swords, shouting at the top of their voices, "Allah, Allah!"

'On arriving at the guns, we rallied, and then I received an order to charge on the left flank; the guns were now lumbering up.'[8]

The fleeing lancers were soon faced by 'a very broad, deep nullah' over which there was only one possible crossing place.

'Many of them,' wrote Crane, 'lost their lives. Horses and riders were lying on top of each other, and they were cruelly hacked by the murderous Afghans. There were riderless horses galloping over the field, and men, who had their horses shot from under them, running in all directions . . .* And what made things worse, the treacherous villagers fired on ours as they passed their villages.'[9]

By this time Roberts and some of his staff had galloped from Sherpur to the scene of action. 'The engagement,' he wrote, 'had now become a question of time. If Mahomed Jan could close with and overwhelm our small force, Kabul would be his.'[10]

Roberts's Chief of Staff, Brigadier-General C. M. MacGregor, writing in his diary that night, was scathing about the 9th's performance: 'The 9th Lancers did make a sort of a charge, but not a good one, then retired . . . 9th Lancers were quite out of hand, would not face them, and went back.'[11] Roberts, on the other hand, goes out of his way to praise both the 9th and the forty-four men of the 14th Bengal Lancers who were acting in support.

'The effort,' he wrote later, 'was worthy of the best traditions of our British and Indian Cavalry . . . To assist them in their extremity, I ordered two of Smyth-Windham's four guns to halt and come into action while the other two continued to retire, but these had not gone far before they got into such difficult ground that one had to be spiked and abandoned in a water-cut, where Smyth-Windham found it when he came up after having fired a few rounds at the fast-advancing foe. I now ordered Smyth-Windham to make for the village of Baghwana with his three remaining guns, as the only chance left of saving them. This he did, and having reached the village, he again opened fire from behind a low wall which

* The first army chaplain to gain the Victoria Cross did so by helping these men. For his citation see p. 63.

enclosed the houses; but the ammunition being nearly expended, and the enemy close at hand, there was nothing for it but to limber up again and continue the retirement through the village. At the further side, however, and forming part of its defences, was a formidable obstacle in the shape of a ditch fully twelve feet deep, narrowing towards the bottom; across this Smyth-Windham tried to take his guns, and the leading horses had just begun to scramble up the further bank, when one of the wheelers stumbled and fell, with the result that the shafts broke and the gun stuck fast, blocking the only point at which there was any possibility of getting the others across.'[12]

MacGregor was now told by Roberts 'to go and rally 9th Lancers. I went,' he wrote, 'got a squadron [!] together, and told them to get out to enemy's right flank and charge, but they would not; then they began bolting; I went after them, shouted and swore at them, but to no purpose.'[13]

Stewart-Mackenzie found that

> 'After this it was *sauve qui peut*, and you never saw such a scene of confusion. We were all jammed into a corner of a small field at the side of a village, only one place that we could get over, the enemy close behind pouring volleys into us. At last we all got over somehow, and on clearing the village I dismounted some men to cover the retreat, which they kept on doing till the 72nd [200 of the 72nd Highlanders sent for from Sherpur by Roberts] took up the fighting.'[14]

It seems that during all this time Captain Bloomfield Gough's troop of the 9th, which, it will be remembered, had been Massy's advance guard, was acting more or less independently, charging on more than one occasion into the mounted part of the enemy line on the British right. Unlike the rest of the 9th, this troop suffered few casualties and managed to keep in some sort of order. It served to a certain extent as a rallying point for the others, all of whose officers were put out of action, either from being themselves hit, or from losing their mounts.

The men of the 9th suffered from their carbines being attached to their horses, while their swords (which they carried as well as lances) were attached to their person. Since the firearm was needed chiefly on foot and the sword on horseback, this arrangement was highly dangerous. In this engagement the troopers, once their horses had fallen, had no time to disengage their carbines from their buckets before the enemy was upon them. 'It was a sorry spectacle,' wrote Roberts nearly a quarter of a century later, 'to behold these men, with their swords dangling between their legs and impeding their movements while they vainly endeavoured to defend themselves with their lances.' More than forty carbines were lost by the regiment in this affair. Writing in 1897, Roberts recalled that Lieutenant-Colonel Bushman, Cleland's successor in command of the 9th, had brought with him from England a sling which permitted the carbines to be slung on the man's back when going into action,

> 'and also of the carbine being carried in the bucket on all ordinary occasions. This pattern was adopted, and during the remainder of the campaign the men of the 9th Lancers placed their carbines on their backs whenever the enemy were reported to be in sight. At the same time I authorized the adoption of an arrangement – also brought to my notice by Colonel Bushman, by which the sword was fastened to the saddle instead of round the man's body. This mode of wearing the sword was for some time strenuously opposed in this country [England], but its utility could not fail to be recognized, and in 1891 an order was issued sanctioning its adoption by all mounted troops.'

However, eleven more years had to pass before *officers* were authorized to have their swords similarly carried.[15]

What, meanwhile, of Macpherson? By a stroke of luck his column, having encamped overnight near the scene of his action at Mir Karez, had started its south-westward march at 7.50 a.m. instead of at 7 a.m. as intended. For this Roberts later blamed him, but had he been on time he would in fact have been even further away from Massy's little force in its hour of need.* As it was

* Roberts most unfairly blamed Massy for the débâcle. 'Every possible care was taken,' he wrote, 'to prevent the small body of cavalry and four H.A. guns coming into collision with the enemy until they had rejoined the infantry of Macpherson's Brigade; the officer in command [i.e. Massy] was ordered to wait upon Macpherson's and to keep well to the rear until Macpherson had got clear of the hills and debouched in the plain near Killa Kazi – unfortunately these orders were [not attended to ?].' (Marginal note to Duke, 231). As a glance at the Map on p. 236 will show, this just does not fit the actual situation, for Macpherson would have been well to the west of Killa Kazi and therefore of the enemy. The truth is that Roberts and everyone on the British side had supposed Mahomed Jan to be much further to the west than he actually was

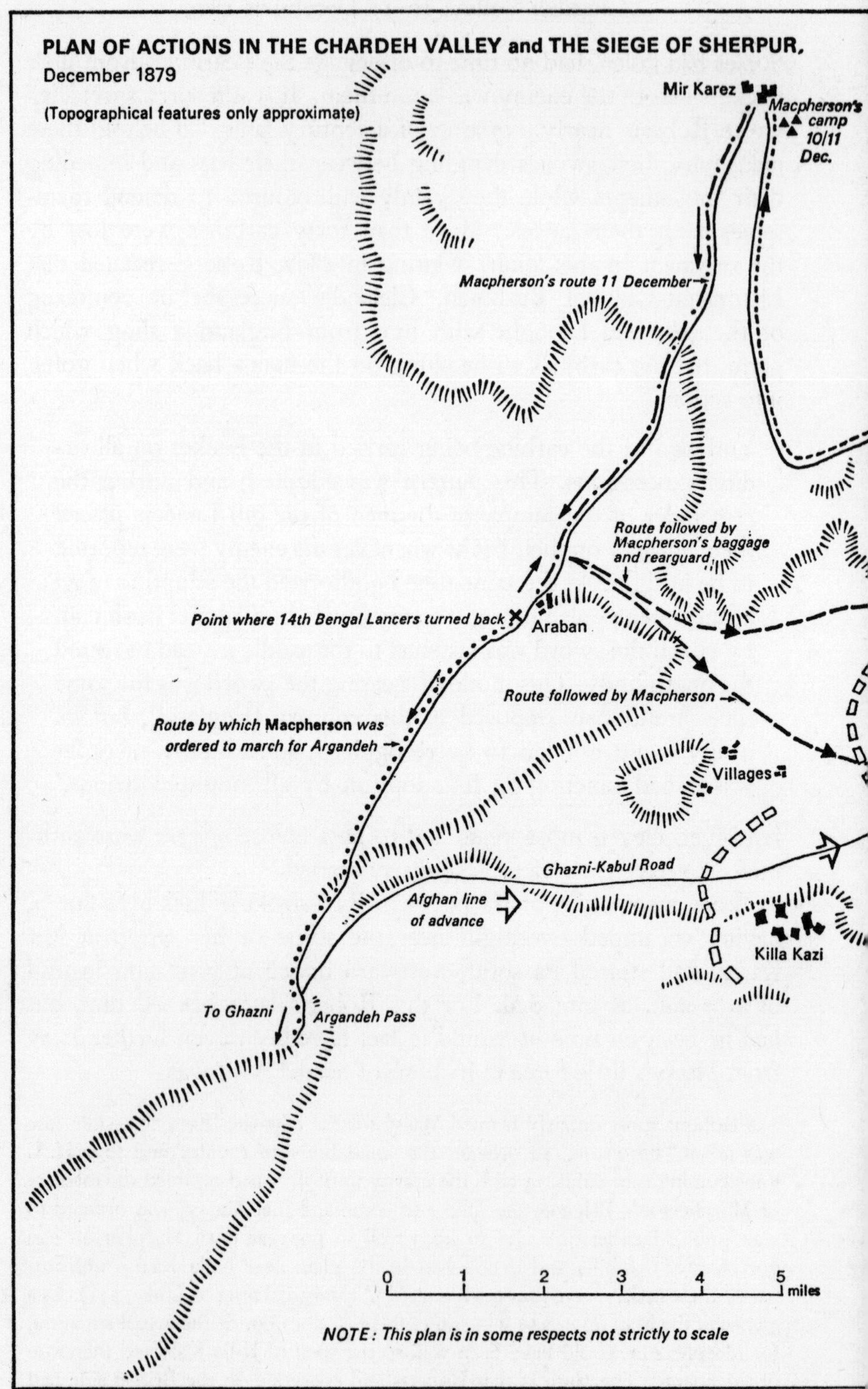
PLAN OF ACTIONS IN THE CHARDEH VALLEY and THE SIEGE OF SHERPUR,
December 1879
(Topographical features only approximate)
Mir Karez
Macpherson's camp 10/11 Dec.
Macpherson's route 11 December
Route followed by Macpherson's baggage and rearguard
Point where 14th Bengal Lancers turned back
Araban
Route followed by Macpherson
Route by which Macpherson was ordered to march for Argandeh
Villages
Ghazni-Kabul Road
Afghan line of advance
Killa Kazi
To Ghazni
Argandeh Pass
0 1 2 3 4 5 miles
NOTE: This plan is in some respects not strictly to scale

Map 8

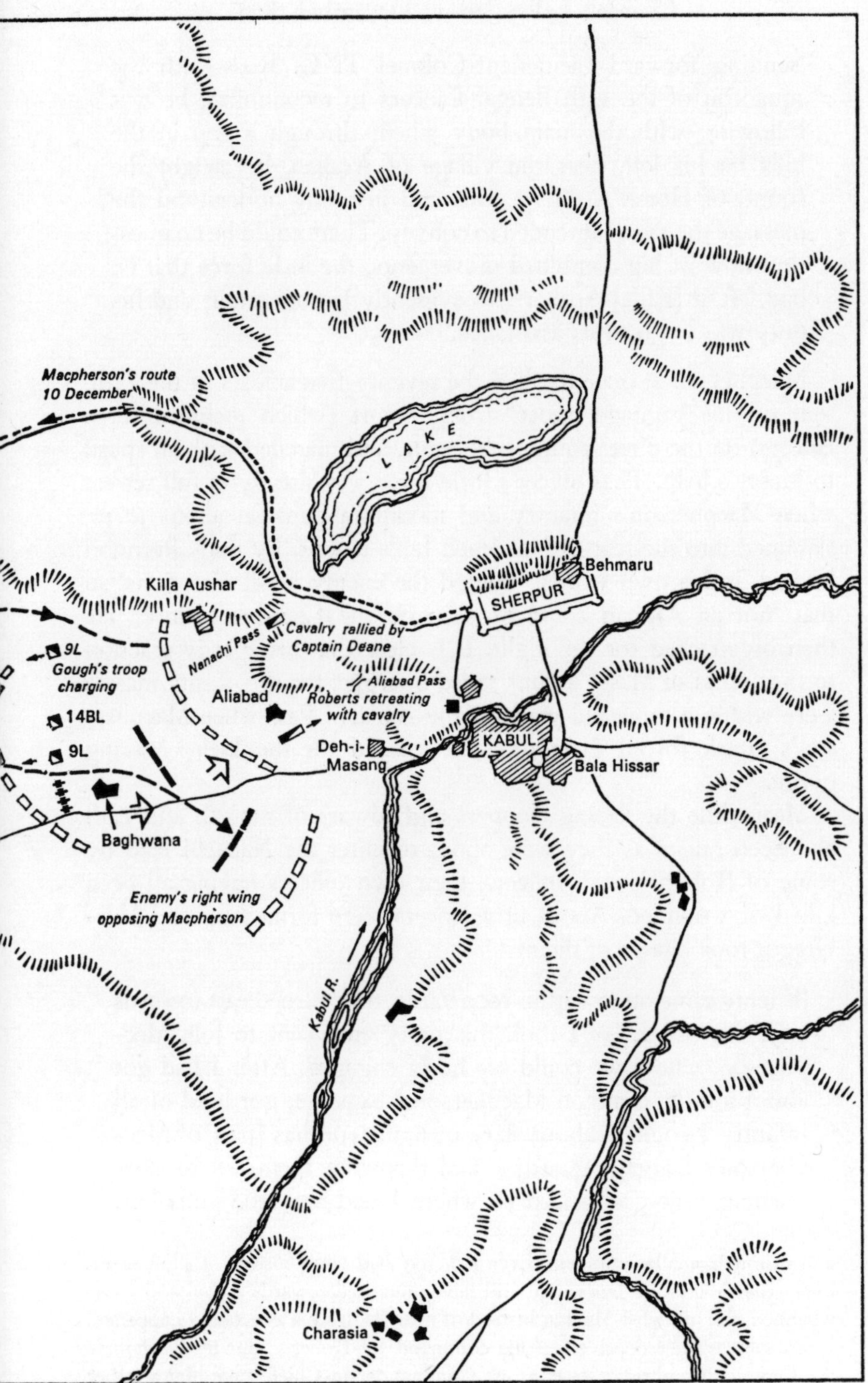

Macpherson's route
10 December
LAKE
Behmaru
SHERPUR
Killa Aushar
Nanachi Pass
Cavalry rallied by
Captain Deane
9L
Gough's troop
charging
Aliabad Pass
Aliabad
Roberts retreating
with cavalry
14BL
9L
Deh-i-
Masang
KABUL
Bala Hissar
Baghwana
Enemy's right wing
opposing Macpherson
Kabul R.
Charasia

'sending forward Lieutenant-Colonel T. G. Ross with the squadron of the 14th Bengal Lancers to reconnoitre, he was following with the main body when, through a gap in the hills on his left, near the village of Araban, he caught the sound of Horse Artillery guns and instantly understood the message they were intended to convey. There could be no question now of big combined movements; the little force that he had left at [Killa] Aushar was evidently in sore straits and his duty was to go to its assistance.'[16]

Macpherson at once recalled the seventy-five lancers of the 14th, sent off his baggage under strong escort (which included these lancers) on the direct route to Sherpur, and marched with all speed to Massy's help. That officer's little force was already in full retreat when Macpherson's infantry and mountain guns, at about 12.30, slammed into the rear of Mahomed Jan's troops. By mid-afternoon he had, in his own words, 'hunted the enemy in all directions' so that 'not an Afghan could be seen on the Chardeh plain.'[17] He then bivouacked for the night. It is clear that his speedy reaction to the sound of Massy's guns saved Sherpur, for the enemy masses were within a thousand yards of the Nanachi Pass when Macpherson's attack forced them to make instead for the Deh-i-Masang gorge.

Meanwhile the fleeing troopers and sowars of the 9th and 14th had been rallied as they were about to enter the Nanachi Pass by some of Roberts's staff officers, their own officers having all been killed or wounded. About fifty lancers were formed up and MacGregor took charge of them:

'Enemy came on to within 1000 yards, then turned east towards city,' he wrote, 'so I took this party and went to join Macpherson, whom we could see hotly engaged. After I had got about a mile, came on Macphersons' baggage; got hold of all infantry I could – about sixty of 67th Gurkhas [part of Macpherson's baggage guard] – and throwing them out in skirmishing order, advanced to where I had seen the guns left.

and in much smaller numbers. Even if Massy had never moved at all, it seems likely that Mahomed Jan would still have advanced towards Kabul and overwhelmed him at Deh-i-Masang instead of near Baghwana as actually happened.

Massy was later deprived of his command by Roberts, but in due course the Duke of Cambridge, ever a just Commander-in-Chief, gave him another command suitable to his rank.

Found three guns; got them out and sent to rear, then advanced again, and got the fourth; took it off.'[18]

The guns were quickly repaired and were ready for use next day. Thus the disaster of 11 December was partially retrieved.

The casualties suffered by Massy's force that day were heavy: twenty-seven killed and twenty-five wounded. Two officers and sixteen men of the 9th were among those that lost their lives, as were one officer and seven men of the 14th. Lieutenant-Colonel Cleland later died of his wounds. The officer of the 14th, Lieutenant Forbes, 'had been twice wounded and had been put for *safety* on one of the gun limbers; when the guns were abandoned he was left, and young [Lieutenant] Hardy [of the Royal Horse Artillery] refused to abandon him or his guns, and was last seen standing over him with his revolver.'[19] Fifty-one horses were killed, thirty-six of them belonging to the 9th and eight to the 14th.

Baker's brigade, meanwhile, had reached the Maidan Valley as intended and had had some quite serious fighting. The absence of news of Macpherson made him very anxious and it was not till late in the morning of 12 December that he learned by heliograph what had happened to Massy the day before. Slowly, being harassed all the way, Baker made his way through the Chardeh Valley back towards the threatened base.

* * *

As early as 7 December Roberts had sent for the Corps of Guides from Jalalabad. He was relieved to see them come into Sherpur early on the morning of 12 December, after having made a forced march of thirty miles the day before. That morning also saw the enemy occupying the heights overlooking Kabul. Part of the day was spent by Macpherson in trying to dislodge them. This he finally did on 13 December with the help of Baker's column which attacked the enemy from the rear. While the infantry and artillery were thus engaged, the cavalry was occupied in breaking up large bodies of tribesmen pressing towards the cantonment from north and east. At one point virtually all the men of the cavalry brigade were pitted against a numerous mass of Kohistanis directly threatening Sherpur. Second-Lieutenant M. O. Little of the 9th tells how Massy

'went to the top of a small hill about half a mile from camp;

we then saw a few of the enemy on the next knoll, so he dismounted a troop and fired at them, whereupon they retired to the bottom of the hill. There were now about 500 of these fellows down in a big plain, yet General Massy with the squadrons of cavalry could not be persuaded to move us from the top of the hill, where, of course, we were utterly useless. The Guides cavalry, who had gone out before on their own hook,* charged first. General Massy then gave poor [Captain] Butson leave to take on his squadron, which he did, and charged the enemy just after the Guides . . . Poor Jim Butson, it appears, was shot dead, and [Captain] Chisholm received a bad bullet wound through the thigh.'[20]

Private Crane, who charged in Butson's troop, wrote in his diary that

'the enemy were caught at the end of the hills, where we charged into their midst, cutting them down right and left. [Captain Butson] was the first to fall, a bullet going right through him, he fell from his horse and instantly expired. The enemy retired on to the plains. A troop of ours caught them on the flank, killing a great many of them.'[21]

Captain Butson was shot, according to Sir Charles Wolseley's diary, 'in the act of shouting to his men to follow him "for the honour of the 9th".'[22] A fellow officer described him as 'a nice cheery, young fellow . . . the best polo player in the regiment'.[23]

Part of the regiment, with the 5th Punjab Cavalry in support, now

'came across some Afghans who were lying in a nullah . . . Where they were it was very difficult to get at them, as we could only advance into the nullah in single file. Serjeant-Major Spittle, leading the way, was shot from his horse and killed directly. The other men following up, soon laid them all low . . .'

Spittle, described as 'very stout', was a 'favourite with all the Force'. He often 'used to say that he "would like to see the *H'*Afghans who would stand before me and my Black 'Orse".'[24] Crane continues the story: 'We mounted, and our dead were placed on the back of horses, no dhoolies having yet come up . . . General

* 'The Guides Cavalry were an independent command'. (Roberts: *Desp.* 15.)

Roberts came and inspected us . . . He glanced at the points of our lances, for a great many of them were smothered with the blood of the enemy.'[25]

Brigadier-General Hugh Gough, left in command of the cantonment, watched 'one bit of fighting' that was

> 'very pretty: the enemy, who from their disciplined movements appeared to be the "regular troops", were drawn up on the far end of one of these plateaux in open column, when suddenly a body of Native Cavalry, whom from their red puggerees I judged to be the 5th Punjab Cavalry, rapidly getting into formation, advanced at the charge, whereupon the Afghans losing heart, and with it all further discipline, broke and fled, being pursued down the slopes with all speed by our sowars.
>
> 'Almost simultaneously with this incident I saw the Guides Cavalry coming round the foot of the hills at a trot, and as they turned the corner they met a body of Afghans retreating, probably the same that had fled before the 5th Punjab Cavalry. In a minute the Guides were on them – a sight to see! They splashed through the small *jheel* (or pond) which lay between them and their foes, and all we could then see was the flash, flash of steel as the sabre did its work. A few musket-shots from the demoralised mob of Afghans and all was over.'[26]

Roberts's hopes that his successes of 13 December had broken up the tribal combination were dashed next morning. Greater numbers than ever were then seen to be crowning the heights to the west of Kabul. Efforts made by the infantry and artillery to dislodge them were decisively defeated. Far larger masses of the enemy than Roberts had ever imagined likely were advancing upon him from the north, south and east. 'The crowds of Afghans in the Chardeh Valley,' signalled the officer in charge of one heliograph station, 'remind me of Epsom on the Derby day.'[27]

At about 1 p.m. some 200 or 300 Afghans were seen to be advancing along the north bank of the Kabul river between the city and Sherpur. Captain W. J. Vousden, quartered with his troop of the 5th Punjab Cavalry just outside the cantonment walls, suddenly saw a favourable opportunity for a charge. In the words of Roberts's despatch, Vousden

> 'most gallantly charged into the middle of them, and notwithstanding that only [eleven] of his men were able to follow

him, six of whom were wounded (the remainder being stopped by a heavy fire which was opened on them from behind some low walls), he succeeded in dispersing the enemy, and in inflicting severe loss upon them, killing five men with his own hand.'[28]

An infantry colonel who witnessed this brilliant little cavalry action had never in his life seen

'anything more gallant than the behaviour of this little band. The leaders, whose conduct was imitated by the others, never looked behind to see if they were supported, but just went in for the enemy, cutting down man after man. There were at least two hundred firing at them, but they seemed to bear charmed lives. I fancy they owed their safety to their activity, for they wheeled and dashed about in such a way it would have been difficult to hit them.'[29]

Three of the wounded died of their wounds and three horses were killed. All the surviving native officers and men received the Order of Merit for Bravery, and Vousden was awarded the Victoria Cross.[30]

Not long after this dashing little affair Roberts decided that he must abandon the city and everything outside Sherpur and retire within the cantonment walls. By a miracle the telegraph lines had not yet been cut, so he was able to order Brigadier-General Charles Gough to push on with his brigade from Gandamak as fast as he could.

'By Jove!' wrote Combe that night, 'and really that is all one has breath to say. A change has indeed come over the vision of our dream – last night we were all cock-a-hoop, thinking ourselves fine fellows, and that all we now had to do was to walk round and burn some villages; and within twenty-four hours we are locked up, closely besieged, after a jolly good licking and all communication with the outer world cut off!'[31]

The siege lasted for ten days. The cavalry was very hard worked during that time. Every day vedettes were thrown out, and the men shared with the infantry the daily duty of patrolling the miles of ramparts. At night, in bitterly cold weather, the cavalry formed the outlying picquets. 'At one period,' according to Howard Hensman, the *Daily News* correspondent, 'the saddles were never taken off the horses of the 5th Punjab Cavalry for sixty hours, and the other regiments have been nearly in the same condition.'[32]

On 23 December Mahomed Jan made his final grand effort. After some hours of severe fighting he was totally repulsed. Every available cavalryman was sent out in pursuit, 'and before nightfall all the open ground in the neighbourhood of Sherpur was cleared of the enemy.' The following morning Roberts 'realized that not only had the assault been abandoned, but that the great tribal combination had dissolved.'[33] The same day Charles Gough's brigade entered the cantonment and Kabul and the surrounding districts were re-occupied.

During the rest of the winter Roberts strove to consolidate his position. To relieve the strain on food supplies and because the horses were 'done up and required rest',[34] he sent back to India the 12th Bengal Cavalry and the 14th Bengal Lancers. To take their place in some degree a Mounted Infantry Corps was formed 'and, with some difficulty, furnished with mounts'.[35] It consisted of three officers and 120 other ranks. In late March substantial reinforcements arrived from India, including the 3rd and the 17th Bengal Cavalry. In early April there arrived the 3rd Punjab Cavalry.

> 'In an incredibly short space of time two long lines of swordsmen seemed to spring from the hill, extending so as to envelop our right and left.'
>
> GENERAL E. F. CHAPMAN, describing the crisis of the battle of Ahmedkhel[1]

(iv)

The Second Afghan War: fourth phase, 1879–1880; Stewart's march to Kabul – battle of Ahmedkhel – action at Patkao Shahana

Sir Donald Stewart at Kandahar, as soon as he learned of Cavagnari's murder, cancelled the withdrawal of his troops to India. During the autumn and winter he managed to keep Southern

Afghanistan more or less quiet. On 30 March, 1880, his force left for Ghazni, some 230 miles distant, on its way to Kabul, 'to take part,' in Roberts's words, 'in the pacification of Northern Afghanistan.'[2] It consisted of six battalions of infantry, fifteen guns and a cavalry brigade under Brigadier-General C. H. Palliser, comprising the 1st and 2nd Punjab Cavalry, the 19th Bengal Lancers and 'A/B' Battery, Royal Horse Artillery with six nine-pounder guns. This division was replaced at Kandahar by troops from the Bombay Presidency. Of these more will be heard later.

As usual, the difficulties of moving troops over large distances in a totally inhospitable country were enormous.

> 'During the preceding winter,' wrote an officer with the force, 'the mortality among the camels had been so severe, and the market was so badly supplied, that efforts almost superhuman were needed to get the requisite number of animals together for the march . . . Some idea of this number may be formed from the fact that the baggage train when in single file extended over nine miles.'[3]

On 19 April there took place an important engagement near the village of Ahmedkhel. For some days before, cavalry reconnaissances had observed large bodies of horse and foot moving parallel to the line of advance. In the morning of the 19th these showed themselves in great force, perhaps 12,000 in number,* and in a very formidable position. Sir Donald decided to attack, although he had but half his force up with him.

His advance guard, commanded by Palliser, consisted of about 690 infantrymen, some 300 of the 19th Bengal Lancers, of which fifty formed part of Stewart's escort, and the six horse artillery guns. These guns, as well as those of the field batteries of the main body, when within a mile and a half of the enemy, moved out to take up positions from which to shell the ridge in front where the main mass of the enemy footmen was assembled. The horse artillery were escorted by one squadron of the 19th and by 349 sabres of the 2nd Punjab Cavalry who had come up from the main body. Protecting the left flank of the infantry were the rest of the 19th.

At about 9 a.m. the artillery came speedily into action, but the infantry, including some who had been rushed up from the main body, were still deploying when, instead of being the attackers as

* It is probable that not more than 5,000 actually took part in the three assaults.

intended, they found themselves furiously attacked. The enormous masses of the enemy, covering a front of nearly two miles, moved forward. At first the advance was

> 'so gradual that their next movement,' according to an eye-witness, 'took every one by surprise. Suddenly, with a tremendous shout, beating of tom-toms, brandishing of swords, and waving of standards, more than 3,000 Ghazis, horse and foot, detached themselves from the main body and came down the hill right into the thin line of British troops with a fury and determination that nothing could surpass . . . They never turned or wavered for an instant, and before one could draw one's breath the more advanced among them were among the troops and fighting hand to hand; while others, better mounted, who had outstripped the rest, had succeeded in . . . bearing down on Sir Donald Stewart and the headquarter staff who occupied a low hillock in rear of the advanced line . . . Some of the Ghazis were actually killed within twenty yards of the general commanding, and they were at one time so close that Sir Donald Stewart himself and the headquarter staff had to draw their swords in self-defence.'[4]

The sudden attack of these two or three thousand fanatics broke with the greatest violence upon the lancers of the 19th on the left flank. These were still moving into position when the enemy, a large proportion of them being Ghazis, rushed in among them, driving them 'right down first upon the 3rd Gurkhas, who . . . swiftly formed squares, then upon the 19th Punjab Infantry.' Both these infantry regiments then poured 'a succession of deadly volleys into the rear of the struggling mass of friends and foes, who, interspersed with ammunition mules, swept over the medical officers at their dressing stations.'[5] According to the 19th Bengal Lancers' regimental history, Colonel P. S. Yorke, commanding the regiment,

> 'saw that he was, or was likely to be, in a mess and that the only thing to do was to charge and get out of it as quickly as he could; charge, to give the infantry, whose flank he was protecting, time to get into a suitable formation; then get away, to give them a fair field of fire, which they could not have so long as the enemy were mixed up with our own men. No one likes retiring; it is specially difficult after charging.

> It speaks a great deal for the discipline of the regiment that they were able to rally so soon and in such good order as to be able within a few minutes to re-form and, with two squadrons of the 1st Punjab Cavalry [316 sabres of which had been rushed forward from the rear-guard], make a fresh attack on the enemy operating on our right flank.'[6]

Sir Donald Stewart is less flattering. 'Some of the cavalry,' he wrote, 'did not do well. There was a stampede of a part of the cavalry, and everything was swept before it.'[7] General Hudson, the regimental historian, on the other hand, points out that the 19th 'had lances and pistols only, no tulwars [sabres], and that once you have made a successful point with your lance it has an unpleasant knack of detaching itself.'[8] It is clear, nevertheless, that some of the men panicked for a time, since the headquarters' chaplain, according to Stewart 'distinguished himself by stopping some runaway sowars who lost their heads. The Padre's stick,' he added, 'had the desired effect, however, and they pulled up.'[9]

At the same time as this was happening on the British left, successive waves of white-robed men on foot issued forth from the hillsides opposite the British centre. These were held by the infantry and by the guns, though the latter were for a time forced to withdraw 200 yards to the rear. Simultaneously a mass of horsemen charged down on the British right. These were checked in part by a spirited charge of the 2nd Punjab Cavalry, and in part by further charges of small bodies of the 19th and of the 1st Punjab Cavalry.

Before long the ill-armed masses were mown down by the British breech-loading rifles and the case shot of the artillery firing at short range. Within an hour of the start of the action the Afghan hordes were in full retreat. For a few anxious moments, though, the courage, speed of movement and numbers of the enemy had looked as if they were about to triumph over Stewart's disciplined troops.

There seems to have been hardly any attempt at a pursuit. An officer who later inspected the battlefield wrote that it was difficult to 'imagine more perfect ground for horse artillery and cavalry'. He was told by officers who had been present that 'after the fight, the enemy streamed across a lovely plain without being pursued, or they must have lost twice as many as they did. However,' he added, 'it would never do to publish the whole truth.'[10]

More than 700 enemy bodies were counted on the field, and it was estimated that as many as 2,000 were wounded. Seventeen British other ranks were killed and 118 wounded. Of the twelve officers wounded, four were of the 19th and two of the 2nd. Of the dead non-commissioned officers and men, five came from the 19th and three from the 2nd. Forty-one of the lancers were wounded and so were twenty men of the 2nd and nineteen of the 1st. The three regiments lost eighty-nine horses of which eight were killed, sixty-eight wounded and thirteen reported as missing.

Lieutenant E. A. Young, the adjutant of the 19th, received thirteen wounds.

> 'When the regiment charged,' he wrote later, 'I was riding immediately behind Colonel Yorke . . . When my horse was shot in the shoulder and reared, I couldn't get him to move from the spot and was soon surrounded by the enemy horsemen. One of them managed to spit himself on my sword, right up to the hilt, and before I could disengage I had sword cuts rained on me and was knocked off my horse. When I was lying on my face on the ground, a man tugged at my silver pouch belt, but failing to get it fired into my back. The bullet mercifully glanced off my spine, ran round my ribs and came out in front. Another man tried to get my sword, which was fastened to my wrist by the sword knot, which he severed with his tulwar and nearly cut my hand off at the same time. After this I became unconscious till I was roused by one of our Sikh sowars who had come to search for me. He found me among a heap of enemy's corpses who had been killed by the fire of the Gurkha battalion. I had received twelve sword cuts and a bullet wound!'

Young was engaged to be married at the time, and it is said that he wrote offering to release his intended. She at once wired back to say that she 'would marry the bits'! Two of her sons grew up to be distinguished officers.[11]

* * *

Stewart reached Kabul on 5 May after a remarkably speedy march during which not a single camp follower was lost. Being senior to Roberts he at once took over command of what now became the Northern Afghanistan Field Force. Beside his own division this of course included Roberts's Kabul Field Force which alone now numbered some 14,000 men and thirty-eight guns with a further thirty guns and nearly 15,000 men on the Khyber line of communication. Among these last were the best part of at least eleven cavalry regiments, including two European ones, the 6th Dragoon Guards (Carabiniers) and the 8th Hussars. All these were usually broken up into small detachments used for patrolling the road. They also protected reinforcements going forward, the sick going to the rear and the constant stream of supplies. At other times they were employed in pursuing gangs of tribesmen who tried to cut the telegraph lines and ambush the supply columns.

Seventy-five men of the Carabiniers on one such occasion (5 January, 1880), following an equal number of the 3rd Bengal Cavalry across what appeared to be a perfectly straightforward ford over the Kabul river in broad daylight, came to grief in almost exactly the same way as the 10th Hussars had done nine months earlier. (See p. 213.) This time only five men were drowned. Aware of these two accidents, part of the Central India Horse on 22 May, 1880, when faced with crossing the Kabul in full flood at a place 400 yards in width, constructed rafts made of skins to ferry their equipment across. Most of the men swam alongside their horses. 'Some of the men crossed as often as ten times this day to swim horses and ponies over.'[12] On 6 June another crossing of the river by 200 of the regiment 'continued without intermission' from 4 a.m. until 9 p.m.[13]

On the whole the tribes in the Kabul area gave little trouble during the summer. One exception was when a gathering of some 1,500 Ghazis in the Maidan Valley was dispersed on 1 July 1880 near the village of Patkao Shahana. A purely mounted force consisting of 577 men of the 19th Bengal Lancers and the 1st and 2nd Punjab Cavalry under Palliser managed for once to sneak up on the enemy and to pursue them for two hours over seven or eight miles, cutting down as many, it is said, as 200 of them. In the course of the day this little flying column travelled forty miles. Three men were killed and twenty-nine wounded. The dead were carried back to camp on horses and the severely wounded on litters constructed by tying lances together with the men's turbans.[14]

* * *

For some months the almost desperate search for a more or less acceptable ruler for northern Afghanistan had been going on. It seemed to have ended on 22 July when Stewart proclaimed Abdur Rahman, a grandson of the famous Dost Muhammad, Emir of Kabul.* Immediately afterwards orders were issued for the early retirement of the British forces throughout the country. It was fervently hoped that the war was over.

> 'The [Bombay] Native Cavalry have been severely censured. What can be expected from so small and sorely tried a force? They had been kept divided up, idle and inactive all the day, simply moving from one place to another . . . exposed quite unnecessarily to an extremely severe and converging fire of rifles and round shot . . . At the final rush in of the Ghazies [when] the line had gone, the cavalry were again called upon to charge, no direction given. They did so . . . and cleared the ground . . . They were again formed up and faced the pursuing enemy, retiring slowly, but ever facing the Afghans . . . They should receive some credit for their conduct in unquestionably checking the pursuit at first.'
>
> MAJOR-GENERAL SIR JOHN HILLS, RE
> regarding the battle of Maiwand[1]

(v)

The Second Afghan War: fifth and final phase, 1880; battle of Maiwand – seige and battle of Kandahar – end of war

In fact the war was far from over. A final, agonizing stage lay ahead. Abdur Rahman had an uncle, Ayub Khan. He was a son of the late Emir, Sher Ali, and controlled the province of Herat, the only one still free from British occupation. Ambitious and competent, Ayub gathered together a formidable army with which to

* At this time the Government believed in establishing separate rulers for each of the three chief provinces.

put into effect his declared object of driving the infidel from Afghanistan. His first aim seemed to be to unseat the Governor (or Wali) of Kandahar district, a puppet of the British. Alternatively or subsequently he intended to make direct for Kabul via Ghazni.

In the early summer of 1880 rumours of Ayub's westward advance from Herat were rife. Consequently the Wali became alarmed lest the peasantry around the Helmand river area should rise in Ayub's support. On 1 June, 1880, he marched for Girishk with 6,000 men, whom the Government had recently armed with rifles and guns. Finding himself cold-shouldered by the tribes, he begged Lieutenant-General J. M. Primrose, who had succeeded Stewart in command at Kandahar, for the support of British troops. Though the garrison of Kandahar was already weak and though the troops on the enormously long lines of communication could ill be spared, it was decided in Simla, after permission had been received from London, but without the wholehearted approval of the Commander-in-Chief in India, to send a column to support the Wali. This column would almost certainly have to fight Ayub's army. It was under no circumstances to cross the Helmand river and was to prevent the enemy making either for Ghazni or Kandahar.

On the approach of this British force, commanded by Brigadier-General G. R. S. Burrows, who had never seen active service in his thirty-six years in the Bombay army, the Wali's troops mutinied and made off to join Ayub, leaving their six smooth-bore guns behind them.

Burrows's column, which Primrose, relying on promised reinforcements for Kandahar from up the line, made as strong as he dared (though nothing like strong enough), was formed from the small number of Bombay troops which, it will be remembered, had replaced Stewart's Bengal force in Kandahar. (See p. 244.) It marched out from that place on 4 July, and consisted of about 1,750 infantry (66th Foot, 1st Bombay Native Infantry (Grenadiers) and 30th Bombay Native Infantry (Jacob's Rifles)), 477 cavalry and six nine-pounder muzzle-loading rifled guns of 'E' Battery, 'B' Brigade, Royal Horse Artillery, as well as the Wali's six smooth-bore guns, now largely manned by men from the 66th. The cavalry and horse artillery were brigaded under Colonel (acting Brigadier-General) Thomas Nuttall, who, though he had seen active service in the Mutiny, had spent much of his time in recent years in civil police appointments. He had lately been commandant of the Sind frontier force. He had never been in the cavalry nor had he ever commanded it before. The 3rd Bombay Light Cavalry, commanded by Major P. A. Currie, provided 267 effective officers and men and the 3rd Scinde Horse* commanded by Lieutenant-Colonel J. H. P. Malcolmson, provided 210. (See Appendix, p. 427.) Of these, 146 men were on baggage guard, under Malcolmson, throughout the disastrous battle of Maiwand which followed.

Ayub's army was much more numerous than Burrows's. Of regular foot soldiers he had some 6,500. His horsemen numbered 1,000 regulars and perhaps 1,500 irregulars. Over and above these he 'had attracted a vast horde of tribesmen, on horse and on foot, ghazi and peasant . . . every male capable of bearing arms'[2] from a large area around. The Ghazis, particularly, being fanatics ready to die for their faith and their country, were at least as formidable as any of the regulars. The total probably came to something like 15,000. In artillery Ayub was overwhelmingly superior, bringing to the battle thirty pieces, mostly six-pounders but including three modern fourteen-pounder Armstrong guns.

As nearly always during the war – for example before the Chardeh Valley disaster on 11 December (see p. 231) – the Political Officer and his 'spies' were ill-informed or over-sanguine.

> 'The remaining method of procuring information,' as a modern historian of Maiwand has put it, 'was the use of cavalry patrols, but Burrows was confronted with a situation where the unsettled state of the country made it impossible to send out single horsemen, or even small groups. The minimum safe strength of a patrol had to be a troop of cavalry, whose range and speed were limited. Although contemporary doctrine claimed that single horsemen with a thorough knowledge of the work, and with mounts in the pink of condition might be able to travel forty or fifty miles at the rate of twelve or fourteen miles an hour, and continue to do so for several days, it was ruled that this could not be expected of a body of horsemen; and a normal cavalry patrol was expected to keep up a rate for any ordinary distance of only six miles in the hour.
>
> 'Burrows was not in patrol contact with Ayub Khan . . . But he was sending out daily reconnaissance parties [up to sixteen miles distant] . . . Unfortunately the system on which these patrols were conducted was faulty. No permanent out-

* This regiment, it will be remembered, had distinguished itself at Khushk-i-nakhud in this very area eighteen months earlier (see p. 232).

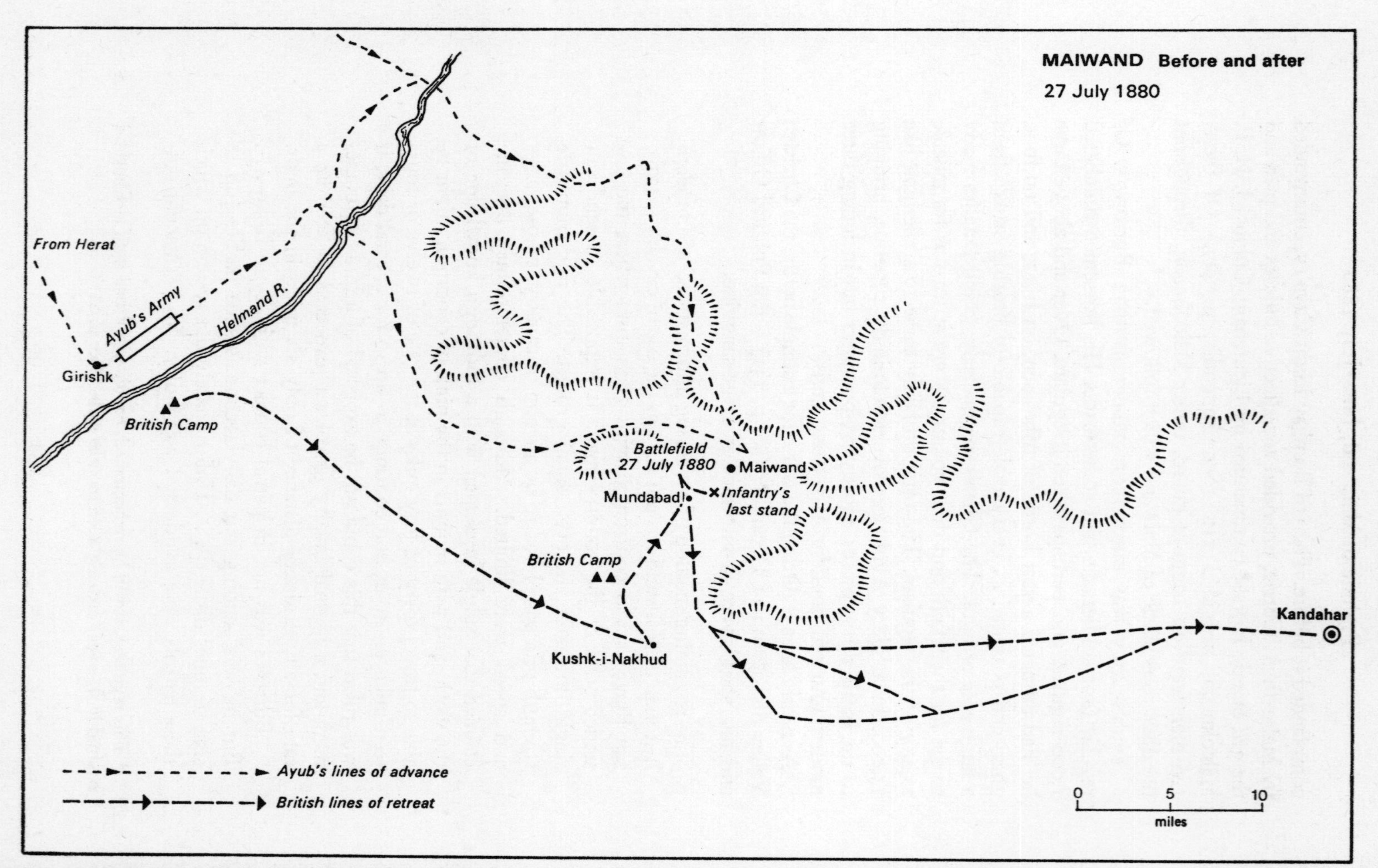
MAIWAND Before and after
27 July 1880
From Herat
Ayub's Army
Helmand R.
Girishk
British Camp
Battlefield
27 July 1880
Maiwand
Mundabad
Infantry's
last stand
British Camp
Kushk-i-Nakhud
Kandahar
Ayub's lines of advance
British lines of retreat
0
5
10
miles

posts were maintained; the daily patrols, instead of relieving each other, returned to camp; the same roads were followed, the same times were observed. The routine became easily predictable, patrols could be avoided and secrets kept; during the twenty-four hours that elapsed between successive arrivals of the cavalry troops the enemy were free to move in any direction. And as the attitude of the country generally was hostile, whereas any movements by Burrows were fully reported to Ayub Khan, little or no information about the Sirdar was brought into the British camp.'[3]

In fact a patrol of the Scinde Horse did bring in, on 25 July, information that Ayub was expected at Maiwand on the 27th – a report which turned out to be correct.[4] But the Political Officer, ever contemptuous of intelligence produced by the cavalry, seems to have persuaded Burrows that his own reports were more correct. These indicated that if the British marched from their camp at Khushk-i-Nakhud on 27 July, they would forestall Ayub by at least a day. The chief importance of trying to achieve this lay in the fact that just north of Maiwand was the entrance to the valley through which Ayub could, if that were his intention, give Burrows the slip and march for Ghazni and Kabul. Burrows had strict orders to prevent this happening.

On 27 July, long before first light of what was to be a day of appalling heat, cavalry patrols moved out to provide protection while the baggage was being loaded. This 'weary process of unravelling the closely packed camp'[5] took many hours and the main body, led and flanked by much of the cavalry with four of the horse artillery guns, did not make a start till about 7 a.m. Progress was extremely slow, for the baggage, carried by 3,000 animals, marched with the infantry. Soon after 10 a.m., cavalry patrol reports confirmed that Ayub's main forces were marching across the British front. It was clear that Ayub had won the race to the entrance of the valley. Burrows's only hope was now to bring him to battle immediately, though he realized that the disproportion between the two forces was 'as one to eleven, and all the advantages of position were on the Afghan side.'[6]

His horse artillery, escorted by cavalry, at once went forward to open fire on the enemy. At much the same time the baggage, with a strong guard, including ninety-six of the Scinde Horse and fifty of the Light Cavalry, was placed in the enclosures of the village of Mundabad, while the three infantry regiments, together with the smooth-bore guns, were ordered forward.

> 'On their arrival,' according to Major G. C. Hogg, the cavalry brigade major, who was one of many officers who were later ordered to give personal accounts of the battle, '... the infantry were ordered to lie down 150 yards in rear of the guns. The ground was tolerably level and quite open, and there was no protection in the position which was taken up for our front, flanks or rear ... Ayub's army and position were now distinctly visible, in spite of the mist. He was about 2,500 yards distant ... in irregular formation, extending for about three or four miles, with his right, after he had faced our brigade, much thrown back.
>
> 'The enemy at first took no notice of our artillery fire, and for twenty-five minutes did not return a shot in reply, the interval being employed in bringing up their right shoulders ... At 11.15 the enemy's batteries were in position, and one by one opened fire ... An artillery duel then commenced, and was continued till about 12 noon ... After the artillery on both sides had been engaged a short time, the enemy developed turning movements on both our flanks. On our left he sent the bulk of his cavalry, and on our right some *ghazis* and a few horsemen. To meet these movements, Lieutenant A. M. Monteith's troop of the 3rd Sind Horse and Lieutenant Reid's troop of the 3rd Light Cavalry were wheeled outwards to the left, and on our right a small portion of Major Currie's men, about 40 sabres under a Native officer, were wheeled outwards to the right. Lieutenant Smith [Scinde Horse], with his 50 sabres, who on first coming up from right flanking party duty, had taken up a position on our left rear, was also ordered to move to the right, and face his men in the same direction. These movements on the part of our cavalry did not in any way prevent the enemy carrying out their turning movements; but the threatening position taken up made them keep their distance.'[7]

This extract has been quoted to show in what a piecemeal way the small number of cavalry was used.

Ayub's inexorable enveloping movement now went slowly forward. The infantry kept firing away, killing many hundreds of Afghans, but there were always more to take their place. Part of

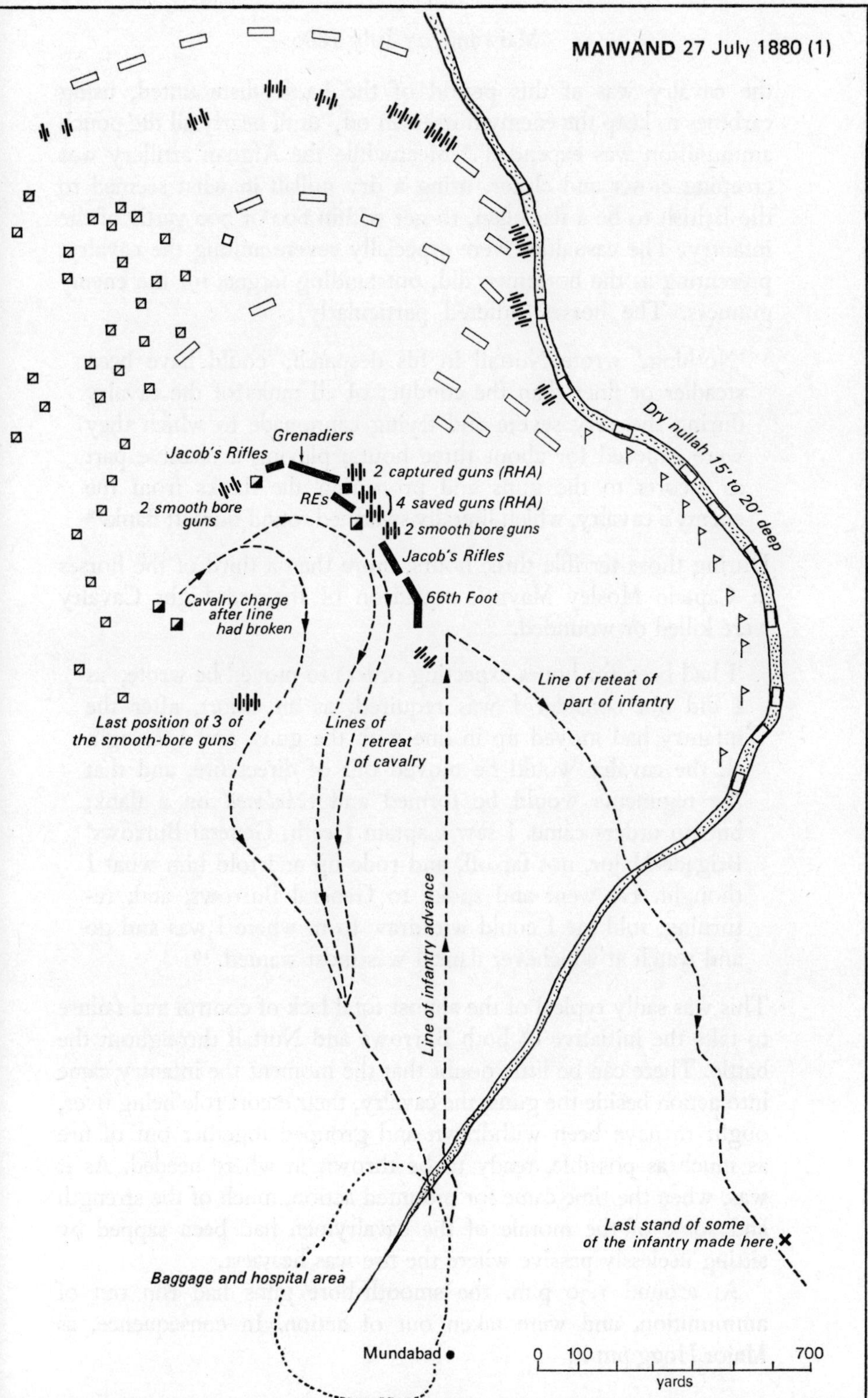
MAIWAND 27 July 1880 (1)
Dry nullah 15' to 20' deep
Grenadiers
Jacob's Rifles
2 captured guns (RHA)
REs
4 saved guns (RHA)
2 smooth bore guns
2 smooth bore guns
Jacob's Rifles
66th Foot
Cavalry charge after line had broken
Line of reteat of part of infantry
Last position of 3 of the smooth-bore guns
Lines of retreat of cavalry
Line of infantry advance
Last stand of some of the infantry made here
Baggage and hospital area
Mundabad
0
100
700
yards

Map 10

the cavalry was at this period of the battle dismounted, using carbines to keep the enemy horsemen off, 'until nearly all the pouch ammunition was expended'.[8] Meanwhile the Afghan artillery was creeping closer and closer, using a dry nullah in what seemed to the British to be a flat plain, to get within 600 or 700 yards of the infantry. The casualties were especially severe among the cavalry, presenting as the horsemen did, outstanding targets for the enemy gunners. The horses suffered particularly.

> 'Nothing,' wrote Nuttall in his despatch, 'could have been steadier or finer than the conduct of all ranks of the cavalry during the very severe and trying cannonade to which they were exposed for about three hours; playing a massive part as escorts to the guns and protecting the flanks from the enemy's cavalry, which literally swarmed round our left flank.'[9]

During those terrible three hours, more than a third of the horses in Captain Mosley Mayne's squadron of the 3rd Light Cavalry were killed or wounded.

> 'I had been for hours expecting orders to move,' he wrote, 'as I did not consider I was required, as an escort, after the infantry had moved up in line with the guns, and I thought all the cavalry would be moved out of direct fire, and that the regiments would be formed and *echeloned* on a flank; but no orders came. I saw Captain Heath, General Burrows' Brigade-Major, not far off, and rode up and told him what I thought. He went and spoke to General Burrows, and, returning, told me I could withdraw from where I was and go and watch at whichever flank I was most wanted.'[10]

This was sadly typical of the almost total lack of control and failure to take the initiative of both Burrows and Nuttall throughout the battle. There can be little doubt that the moment the infantry came into action beside the guns, the cavalry, their escort role being over, ought to have been withdrawn and grouped together out of fire as much as possible, ready to be thrown in where needed. As it was, when the time came for mounted action, much of the strength and some of the morale of the cavalrymen had been sapped by sitting uselessly passive where the fire was heaviest.

At around 1.30 p.m. the smooth-bore guns had run out of ammunition, and were taken out of action. In consequence, as Major Hogg put it,

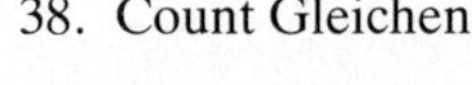
38. Count Gleichen

39. Lieut-General Sir Herbert Stewart

40. Lieut-Colonel Talbot

41. A trooper of the Sind Horse at the time of the Second Afghan War, 1880

42. 'A Wounded Comrade'. A private of the 17th Lancers attending to his wounded horse after the Regiment's charge at Ulundi, 1879

'some *ghazis*, probably about 100, who had hitherto kept a respectful distance, were seen pressing in towards the right rear of our line. General Nuttall discussed the advisability of attacking them with our cavalry posted on that flank; and, under instruction from him, I directed Lieutenant Smith, 3rd Sind Horse, to charge with his troop, and to take with him the half-troop of the 3rd Light Cavalry who were on his left flank close by. Observing that there was some delay in carrying out the orders, I rode up to Lieutenant Smith, and asked

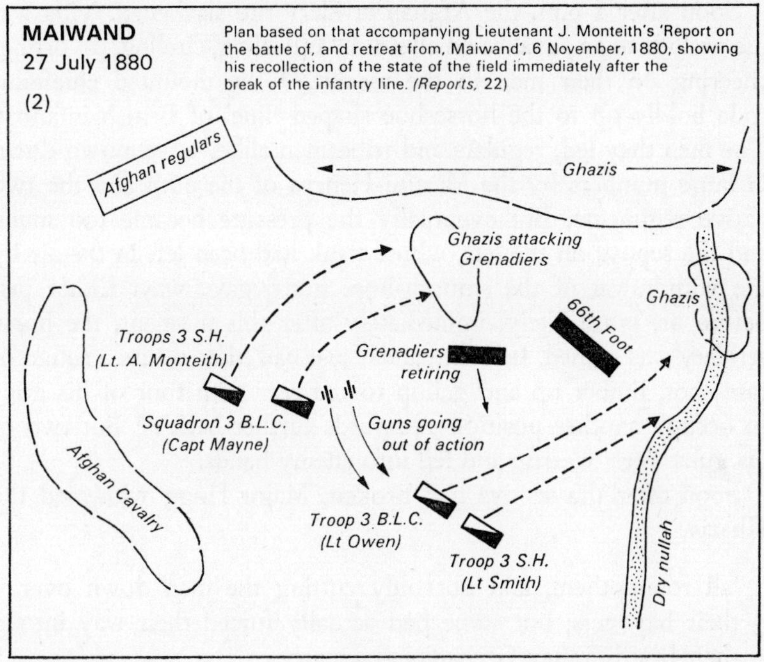

Map 11

him the cause of it. He said his men were out of hand, and asked me to help him. I observed that most of the men had carbines in their hands instead of drawn swords. I spoke to them severely, and got them to return carbines and draw swords; and at the same time I ordered Lieutenant Owen, 3rd Light Cavalry, who was passing by with some message, to take command of the half-troop of his regiment which had been ordered to charge, as it did not appear to me that the Native officers had any control over the men. After this Lieutenant Smith advanced at a gallop towards the enemy; but before the charge could be delivered, the word "halt" was shouted from the rear by General Nuttall, who told me on my return that he had halted the men as there was a *nullah* in front of them. The enemy appeared to me to gain confidence when they saw the cavalry halt, and our men retired hastily, and in confusion, till they got in rear of about the centre of our line, when they pulled up. I observed, as they were re-forming, that swords had again been returned and carbines drawn.'[11]

Soon after 2 p.m. the Afghan artillery fire slackened. This was the prelude to an advance on all sides. 'Wheeling, circling, cavorting, cheering on their men to the assault,'[12] the mounted chieftains rode boldly up to the horseshoe shaped 'line' of British infantry. The men they led, regulars and tribesmen alike, were mown down in large numbers by the Martini-Henrys of the 66th and the two native regiments. But eventually the pressure became too much and the sepoys on the left, whose flank had been left in the air by the withdrawal of the smooth-bore guns, gave way. Either just before or, more likely, immediately after this moment, the horse artillery was rushed. Its commander just had 'time to fire a round of case-shot, limber up and gallop to the rear with four of his guns to occupy another position 150 yards further back'.[13] But two of his guns were overrun and fell into enemy hands.

Soon after the sepoys had broken, Major Hogg witnessed the Ghazis

'all round them, and not only cutting the men down over their bayonets, but some had actually forced their way into their [the Bombay Grenadiers'] square.

'General Burrows now [at about 2.35 p.m.] rode up at a gallop to General Nuttall, and said – "Nuttall, the infantry has given way; our only chance is a cavalry charge; do you think you could get the cavalry to charge the line of ghazis in rear of the infantry, and they might perhaps then be induced to re-form?" . . .

'There was no time to wait for a well-dressed line, and General Nuttall ordered the cavalry* to advance and charge, placing himself with his staff in front of the line. The men, in-

* Possibly about 130 sabres: Mayne's squadron, Geoghegan's troop, 3rd Light Cavalry, and A. M. Monteith's troop, 3rd Scinde Horse.

stead of advancing straight to their front, inclined to the right,* and fell on the ghazis who were attacking the Grenadiers, which regiment was undoubtedly saved by the cavalry charge from heavy loss. After doing this much, the cavalry, instead of advancing straight on into the mass of the enemy, seeing the infantry all retreating, and the guns all gone, wheeled about and retired, to the very best of my belief, without orders. I certainly heard no orders, but . . . whilst personally engaged in combat with the enemy, I turned round to see if the men were following, and found they had gone.

'After wheeling about, the cavalry retired steadily . . . As they were retiring, General Burrows came up a second time to General Nuttall.'

According to Captain E. D. N. Smith of the 3rd Scinde Horse, Burrows said to Nuttall at this moment: '"What do you propose next?" General Nuttall said: "I don't know, Sir," and pointing to the cavalry said, "You see, they are out of hand," or words to that effect.'[14]

Lieutenant T. P. Geoghegan of the 3rd Light Cavalry, whose troop was part of the baggage guard, described in his report how the battle seemed from the rear. The enclosures and gardens around the baggage area were early

'seized by the enemy, who swarmed into them in large numbers, and kept up a constant fire on the baggage all day . . .

'About 2 o'clock two smooth-bore guns came back to the baggage and fired on large masses of men who had out-flanked the fighting line on both sides and were closing in on the baggage.

'Colonel Malcolmson [commanding the baggage guard] ordered me to watch a mass of *ghazis* who had out-flanked the right of the fighting line, and were threatening to take it

* It seems likely that Nuttall was responsible for this incline to the right, which threw the whole line into disorder. Unaware, apparently, that in the absence of instructions to the contrary, the men would naturally follow where he led, he wheeled to the right 'to clear the front', expecting them to carry straight on. No officer who had served in the cavalry would have been likely to make such an error. On the other hand Major Currie, commanding the 3rd Bombay Light Cavalry, was charged at his court-martial with responsibility for the right incline, (see Appendix, p. 426). This charge, which was not sustained by the Court, would seem to have been instigated by Nuttall so as to throw the blame on shoulders other than his. (see p. 261 below).

in rear. They were about 250 or 300 yards from me. I was ordered to charge them if they made a rush. The fire of the 66th seemed to keep them in check, as while I watched them they made no progress. Suddenly I saw a team of horse-artillery horses galloping towards me from the fighting line, without guns or drivers.

'Immediately afterwards, as well as I remember, four guns of the Horse Artillery came to the rear. I asked a trumpeter what had happened, and he said they had lost two guns, and that all the gunners of those two guns had been killed. Colonel Malcolmson then shouted to me from behind to take my troop up and do what I could.

'I galloped up as hard as I could, and met on the way all the infantry retreating in confusion. I found General Nuttall forming up the remnants of the cavalry for a charge . . .

'As I was wheeling my troop to get them into line with the rest, my horse had his near fore-leg shot off, and I was thrown. When I got up, the line of cavalry was gone, and I was left behind.

'When the cavalry was forming up before the charge they were surrounded on all sides. In fact, there was a line of men on foot and on horseback not forty yards in rear of them, who could have ham-strung every horse if they had come on.'[15]

Lieutenant Geoghegan managed to get a stray horse and to rejoin his regiment.

During the first stages of the retreat 'the cavalry', according to the surgeon of the 3rd Light Cavalry, 'formed on either side of the guns, and every now and then the latter unlimbered and fired a shot, the cavalry in the meantime halting.'[16]

A considerable part of the hard-pressed infantry, thoroughly exhausted and desperate for water, got hopelessly separated from the main body which was making for the road to Kandahar, some forty miles distant. Efforts to get them to close on to the cavalry and guns were fruitless, and many died in making valiant last stands.

The pursuit of the main body was not very vigorous and after about seven miles ceased altogether. 'What saved the defeated brigade from destruction,' wrote Major Hogg, 'was the plunder.' Lieutenant E. V. P. Monteith (not to be confused with A. M. Monteith), with about fifty sabres of the Scinde Horse, formed a rear-guard and checked what enemy cavalry managed to resist the lure of the loot. These 'fortunately made no attempt to head us, but confined their movements to our rear.'[17] Both Monteith and Geoghegan (who later relieved him) did a great deal to save stragglers throughout the retreat. 'The gun teams,' according to Major E. P. Leach, VC, who was with Burrows, 'were by this time completely exhausted, and had some difficulty in keeping pace with the cavalry.'[18] Major Currie and Lieutenant-Colonel Malcolmson, the commanding officers of the two regiments, were later court-martialled. Both were honourably acquitted. A preliminary Court of Inquiry was held in early September at Kandahar, to inquire, as Combe put it, into the conduct

> 'of two Cavalry Officers, both of whom are accused by the Generals of behaving very badly; refusing, or neglecting, to charge, being in too great a hurry to leave, refusing to sound the "straggler's call" after dark, when they themselves had found water, "lest they should bring the enemy on them"—one of them appears to have completely lost his head, and the other, I believe, has taken to drink. Pity it was not hushed up and both made to go quietly.'[19]

These full courts-martial were held in Bombay in March and April, 1881. The charges are given in the Appendix at p. 426.

A careful reading of the voluminous proceedings leaves no doubt whatever that Combe's second-hand opinion given above is nonsense. Both Burrows and Nuttall emerge as not only alarmingly incompetent, but also extraordinarily vindictive in their efforts to shift the blame from themselves at any cost, including straight lying. The evidence upon which they based all their charges of cowardice failed most dismally to stand up to cross-examination. It seems clear that Nuttall was completely non-plussed and that even at the start of the retreat Burrows was quite non-compos. Indeed, long before dark, Malcolmson had to send the Wordie Major of the 3rd Scinde Horse to collect him. The Wordie Major was seen by the acting adjutant of the regiment with his arms around the 'insensible' general's stomach.[20]

After splitting up into various groups, searching for and eventually finding water, the main body, including all the cavalry, came together at about 1 a.m. on 28 July. The horrors of that night, punctuated as it was by continual but groundless fears that the enemy was close behind, were not lessened when another scorching day dawned. From every village through which the brigade passed came harassing fire, and the pangs of hunger were now added to the agonies of swollen tongues and parched throats. Many of the sowars gave up their long-suffering mounts to the infantrymen, while such baggage-animals as had survived provided mounts for others. In the course of the early afternoon the weary cavalcade entered Kandahar.

Mercifully it had been met in the morning by a force sent out to succour it. According to one account the garrison had learned of the catastrophe in the small hours, when a jemadar of the Scinde Horse with twenty-five men had ridden in straight from the field of battle. These men had apparently been on baggage duty 'when a badly wounded major of artillery seeing the ghazis' rush and the break-up of the British line, had bidden them ride hard for Kandahar and warn Primrose of the disaster, and had given [the jemadar] a pair of binoculars to produce as a proof of the genuineness of his story.'[21]

* * *

The total British casualties amounted to over 1,120, about 43 per cent of the force. The 3rd Bombay Light Cavalry had twenty-seven men killed and eighteen wounded (about 14 per cent). The total cavalry casualties were sixty-four. Nearly 2,700 animals were killed, destroyed or wounded. Most of these were transport animals. The two cavalry regiments lost 156 horses. In the 3rd Scinde Horse alone no less than nine native officers, non-commissioned officers and sowars were awarded the Order of Merit.

Ayub is said to have admitted a loss of 1,500 of his regulars, while according to one authority 'the losses inflicted upon the Ghazis were summed up by themselves as "beshumar" (countless) – 3,000 to 4,000 – and they added that it took them seven days to bury their dead.'[22]

The disaster of Maiwand, the worst ever suffered in battle by the old Anglo-Indian army, was in part due to poor generalship. Yet even a Roberts or a Stewart might well have found it difficult against such overwhelming numbers to have prevented defeat. The chief responsibility probably lies with Simla and London for forcing such an inadequate force into so untenable a position. Bigger men than Primrose and Burrows would almost certainly have insisted on their orders being modified or their strength increased.

Burrows's employment of his mounted arm was feeble. Yet once the infantry had given way, even had all his cavalry been concentrated, it is unlikely that he could have averted defeat; but the complete rout which followed it might well have been avoided.[23]

Maiwand dealt a blow to the prestige of the Bombay army from which it took a long time to recover. 'I am sure,' wrote Roberts, 'that but few Bombay regiments are able to cope with Afghans.'[24] The superior martial qualities of the northern races such as the Pathans and Sikhs were everywhere and often proclaimed for many years to come, yet in fact the regiments at Maiwand included few Bombay-enlisted men. The men of the two cavalry regiments, for instance, came chiefly from the Rohtak and Delhi districts.

* * *

The siege of Kandahar which now followed lasted nearly four weeks, but Ayub does not seem to have prosecuted it with much vigour. On 16 August Primrose ordered a sortie against Deh Khojah, a village outside the walls. It was an ill-managed affair in which there were 223 casualties out of 1,556 men engaged. 200 sabres of the 3rd Bombay Light Cavalry as well as the Poona Horse (which had arrived at Kandahar in July), all under Nuttall, played their part sufficiently well. They made two charges against large numbers of tribesmen, supported by 100 men of the 3rd Scinde Horse. They suffered badly during the disastrous retirement. Their casualties numbered thirty-one men and seventy-two horses.

* * *

On 3 August, 1880, the viceroy authorized Roberts to march from Kabul to the relief of Kandahar. Six days later the Kabul-Kandahar Field Force, nearly 10,000 strong, set out on what one of the little general's staff officers called 'The Race for the Peerage'.[25] There were three infantry brigades, eighteen mountain guns (but no wheeled artillery) and a brigade of cavalry. This last, commanded by Brigadier-General Hugh Gough, VC, consisted of 337 officers and men of the 9th Lancers, 401 of the 3rd Bengal Cavalry and 417 of the 3rd Punjab Cavalry. It was reinforced by the Central India Horse, 505 strong, which had made forced marches from Jellalabad so as to join the brigade. Even with much reduced scales, the followers numbered over 8,000, and, in all, over 18,000 men and 11,000 animals had to be fed.

As a rule, two of the four cavalry regiments marched five or six miles ahead, while the other two marched on the flanks. A squadron was usually told off to form the rearguard. The chief occupation of the flanking regiments was the collecting of forage. They would take with them 300 or 400 baggage animals on which to bring in the provisions. Sometimes they were out as much as fourteen hours a day on this duty.[26] The squadron on rearguard had a very different task to perform. It often 'had to deploy a troop in extended order to "whip in" stragglers, who, if left behind, were doomed to certain death, a fact which they either did not realize or disregarded.'[27] Lieutenant James Hunter of the 9th Lancers noticed how 'the natives used to go off the road and hide themselves where they could escape the eyes of the rearguard, that they might be left to die in peace.'[28] In fact, according to Roberts, only twenty camp followers perished.[29] How dangerous it was to leave the main column is illustrated by the fact that, according to one staff officer, 'in two instances a mounted *sowar* disappeared, horse and man, when carrying a message between two squadrons within sight of one another.'[30]

Beside the exhaustion induced by the gruelling pace set by Roberts, the chief hardships suffered by his men were the extremes of temperature, 'at times as much as 80° between day and night,'[31] the scarcity of water, the constant sand storms and the suffocating dust raised by the movement of the column. Trooper Crane of the 9th Lancers has left a graphic description of a typical day:

> 'Tuesday, 10 [August]. – Reveille sounded at 3.30 [a.m.]. No one, except men who have . . . marched with a division, could hardly picture to themselves the bustle and shouting of the native followers; the shining glare from the fires that have been lit to show a light to saddle our horses and pack the tents; the neighing of the horses, the dismal moan of the camel as a load is being packed on his back, the mules kicking their loads off just as we have packed them on their backs; some mules getting loose and running amongst the troop horses, causing some of them to break loose; then the packing the baggage on the saddles; when we have formed up on parade, the time it takes before we get on the move, sometimes having to wait to let all the baggage get on in front; and times out of

number the loads fall off the mules' backs when on baggage guard (the mule drivers going along half asleep), having to dismount to stack it on again; the tedious marching along the hot, dusty roads, sometimes parched with thirst . . . ; the one continual line of camels, mules, donkeys, the loads on their backs almost bearing them down; the shouting of the native drivers, most of whom get on top of a load, and pretty nearly break the poor animals' backs; the long line of infantry tramping along the hot, dusty roads, with the sun peeling the skin off our faces – all tramping on to the next camping ground.

'The pleasure of it is when you sight the flags of the camp colourmen who have gone on before to mark the ground out for the different regiments. Then there is water to be found to water the horses; then, when we get into lines, the horses to be picquetted, the tents to be pitched, the horses to be groomed, and saddles and arms to clean. Then the native cooks who cook our dinner – it is mostly dusk at evening before we can get any dinner; then the meat is not half done and very tough, it only having been killed a few hours before it is cooked; then it is late at evening before we can get any tea. Sometimes not being able to get bread, the commissariat not having time to bake, so they serve us out with japaties – that is, coarse flour made into a round flat cake, but is enjoyed because we have a sauce to help it down . . . By the time the trumpet sounds the last post we get under the blankets and sleep pretty soundly for the few hours we get until reveille sounds, and the quietude of the night is broken again with the bustle and shouting, with the getting ready for another day's march.'

Ten days later Crane describes how food, forage and baggage animal replacements were come by:

'[20 August] Came to a village where a number of sheep, camels and oxen were grazing. We surrounded them and drove them into the village where the headman of the village was forced to sell them. Got a lot of corn and grain here; found a number of sacks of grain hidden in a nullah, which was taken and given over to the commissariat stores . . .

'[21 August] Scarcity of grain for horses; feed them on the fields of fresh [standing] Indian corn that we come across . . .

'[24 August] We get some beautiful fruit as we go along, from the fields, such as water melons and fine grapes, which are very refreshing to us when marching in the hot sun. We have two drams of rum daily the last three days, which is very acceptable, not being able to get any beer here . . .

'[27 August] Very hot marching; when dismounted glad to lay down in shade from our horses, where many of us ofttimes fall to sleep.'[32]

One of the passes which had to be negotiated was immensely steep and rose to 8,100 feet. In other places, as noted by Combe, the DAQMG of the Cavalry Brigade, 'working parties at the heads of the columns make ramps, etc., where necessary, but it is a wonderfully open country, though now and then much cut up by ravines.'[33]

On 27 August the 3rd Bengal Cavalry and the 3rd Punjab Cavalry marched thirty-five miles to Robat, seventeen miles from Kandahar, 'with all our baggage complete,' as Combe boasted. 'Starting at 1 a.m. our camp was pitched before 12 noon, and the Rear Guard in half an hour later. A very creditable performance, showing what we can do when not hampered with infantry.'[34] At Robat direct heliographic communication was established with Kandahar, and on 31 August the town was entered. The famous march was over. It had not been as risky, perhaps, as Stewart's march over the same ground in the opposite direction three months earlier. Nor, certainly, had it been as hazardous as Roberts's first advance on Kabul, but it had covered 313 miles at the height of summer in twenty-two days – a remarkable achievement by any standard.

When, on 24 August, Ayub heard of the approach of Roberts, he raised the siege and took up a strong defensive position in the hills. It has been suggested that he believed that the relieving force would take Primrose's garrison with it and return at once to India. Whether this is really what he believed or not, by midday on 1 September he had been totally routed by Roberts in the brilliant battle of Kandahar in which the cavalry scarcely took part. 'We arrived as usual just an hour too late,' wrote Lieutenant Hunter of the 9th. 'However, we did a great advance across the plain in echelon of squadrons against what turned out to be a party consisting of women and children, donkeys, cows and camels, which presented a most formidable appearance at a distance.'[35]

* * *

The war, at long last, really was over. It had been immensely more lengthy than had ever been envisaged when it started. Originally thought likely to cost a couple of million pounds, it had in fact cost £23½ millions, of which India had to find £18½ millions at a time of near-famine over large areas.[36] The war, too, had drawn from the Indian army a very large part of its total strength. For example, thirty-two cavalry regiments, including one from the Madras army, had been involved in one way or another, most of them being engaged exclusively on keeping open the long lines of communication.

The British abandoned the idea of fragmentation and decided to entrust the whole country to the rule of Abdur Rahman, an experiment which, surprisingly, succeeded sufficiently well. The armies marched back to India and peaceful relations with Afghanistan were once again established. They were to last for another thirty-nine years.

6

'A victory is twice itself when the achiever brings home full numbers.'

Shakespeare, *Much Ado About Nothing*, Act i, sc. 1, l.8.

'The real reason why the Horse Guards are being sent to Egypt is that the present Minister of War wishes to abolish them altogether and that, being well aware of the unsuitability of heavy cavalry operations in Egypt, he expects to be provided with an argument as to their uselessness in time of war.'

Vanity Fair

(i)

The Egyptian campaign, 1882: causes – nationalist revolt under Arabi – bombardment of Alexandria – preparations for expeditionary force: mounted element – Sir Garnet Wolseley's plan

A year and a half after its humiliation at the hands of the Boers in southern Africa, the limited military capacity of the Empire was employed in northern Africa against a far less formidable foe with outstanding success. In the summer of 1882 there arrived in Egypt that British military presence which was to remain for the next seventy-four years.

When, in April, 1880, Gladstone formed his second administration, Egypt, nominally a Khedivate under the shadowy suzerainty of Turkey, was on the verge of anarchy. The Khedive Tewfik had fallen effectively under Anglo-French control. The national bankruptcy which had arisen in part from the extravagances of his predecessor, Ismail, who had been overthrown in 1879, was only temporarily staved off by Disraeli's purchase of his Suez Canal shares in that same year. Now, as expenditure far outran income, 'the Khedive came to live from loan to loan. As his credit in London and Paris dwindled, the interest rates became more and more exorbitant.'[1] By 1881, with British and French Debt Commissioners in charge of the country's finances 'and of much else too',[2] the Khedivate

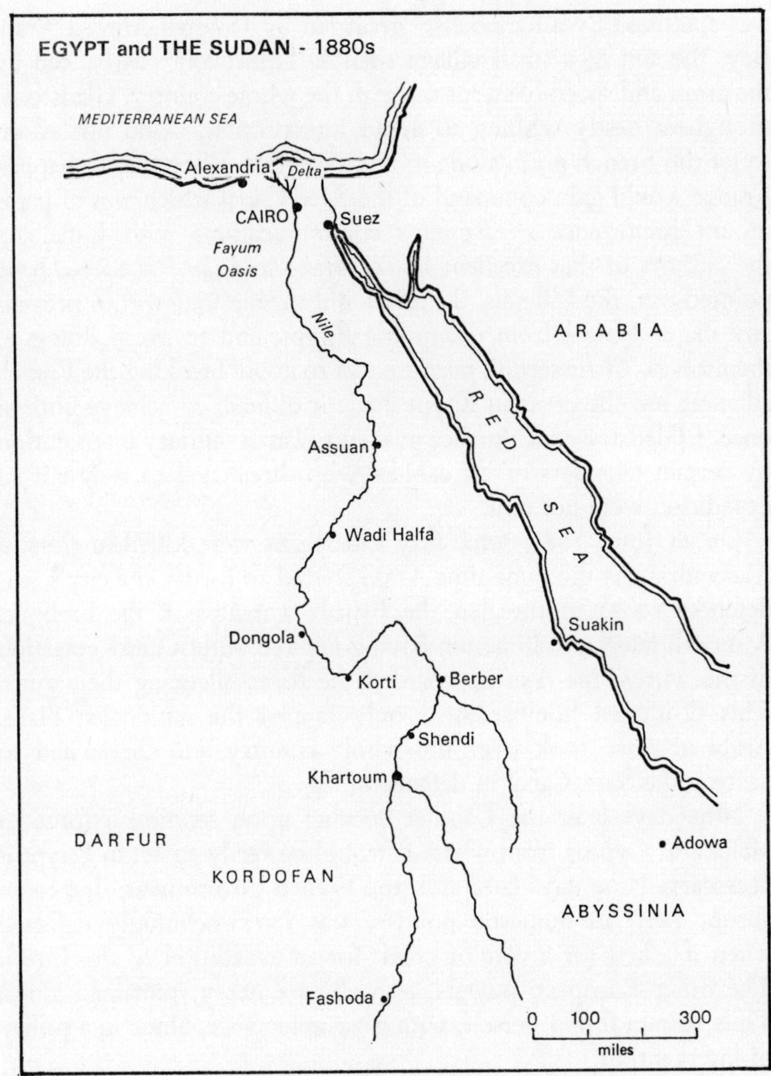

Map 12

'was going the way of many Oriental *régimes* eroded by penetration of European influences . . . The symptoms [of imminent anarchy] were unmistakable: the restless peasantry, the discontented landlords, the immature liberal opposition, the broad movements against the foreigner, the collapse of traditional authority leading to a military *Putsch*.'[3]

That *putsch* came about in September, when Anglo-French control was shattered by a nationalist revolt led by Colonel Ahmed Arabi Bey, the son of a small village sheikh. The revolt was backed by the army and speedily swept through the whole country. Gladstone, though earnestly wishing to avoid intervention, could not afford to let the French go in alone to restore order. Were that to happen France would gain command of the Suez Canal which was of paramount importance to Britain's communications with India. As the authors of that excellent book, *Africa and the Victorians*, have pointed out, the Liberals' '. . . first aim throughout was to prevent any major Power from occupying Egypt, and to avoid doing so themselves. Their second purpose was to avoid breaking the French alliance; but the crisis in Egypt made it difficult to achieve both at once.'[4] Gladstone was further pushed towards military intervention by certain members of his cabinet who threatened to resign if an expedition were not sent.

On 11 June, 1882, some fifty Europeans were killed in riots in Alexandria. At the same time Arabi started to fortify the city's sea-defences so as to threaten the British warships in the harbour. A month later, an ultimatum having expired without any cessation of the works, the fleet bombarded the forts, silencing their guns. This ill-judged bombardment only fanned the nationalist blaze. Arabi at once took over the whole country and threatened to destroy the Suez Canal in defence of Egypt.[5]

Nine days later the Cabinet decided upon sending a force to Malta and Cyprus from where it would be ready to act in Egypt if necessary. Nine days later still, the French government, due to an abrupt twist in domestic politics, was overwhelmingly defeated when it asked for a vote of credit for an expedition to the Canal. The other European powers, as well as Turkey, remained aloof. Thus Britain found herself, with great reluctance, alone in a policy of intervention.

* * *

The possibility of the need for an expedition had been taken into account by the War Office some months previously. Various papers had been prepared, but the first important official step was not taken till 28 June when the Commissary-General was asked to make a a return of transport animals available and to calculate the number of transports necessary for a first-line corps of 24,000 men. On 4 July secret instructions were issued to officers commanding those regiments which it had been decided to include in the expeditionary force. Since numbers of troops had been detailed for manoeuvres in England, it was possible, in the words of the official historian of the campaign, 'to order the cavalry regiments to organize "*for the manoeuvres*" the regimental transport that would be necessary.'[6]* Lieutenant-General Sir Garnet Wolseley, Gilbert's 'very model of a modern Major-General', dubbed by Disraeli 'our only General', who had crushed the Canadian revolt of 1870 and conducted the Ashanti campaign with brilliant success, was, as Adjutant-General, in charge of all these preliminary arrangements. Now he was appointed to command the Egyptian expeditionary force. Hugh Childers, the Secretary of State for War, gave him a virtually free hand.

He assembled a total of nearly 35,000 troops† in the course of the campaign, but this figure includes some 4,000 drafts and depôt troops. The actual force available in the field amounted, as a German officer pointed out contemptuously, 'to little over the strength of a German division'.[7]

The mounted element numbered some 3,700. There were 477 officers and men of a composite regiment of the Household Cavalry commanded by Lieutenant-Colonel H. P. Ewart. This was made up of a full service squadron from each of the three regiments: the 1st and 2nd Life Guards and the Royal Horse Guards (Blues). The Household Cavalry had not seen service overseas since the Waterloo campaign, sixty-seven years before. For the last campaign in which they were to be dressed in coloured uniforms, the men wore red (Life Guards) and blue (Royal Horse Guards) 'serge mediterranean frocks', 'dark pants', blue puttees wrapped round their calves and laced ankle boots, known as 'high-lows'.[8] On their heads they wore pith helmets without their spikes and wound round with puggarees. So as to make them less visible in the bright light,

* On 21 July that portion of the reserves which had left the colours in the previous two years was called out. 11,030 out of 11,650 answered the call. 135 of the balance were satisfactorily accounted for. In the event only about 1,500 of these reservists were actually required to join their regiments. (Maurice, 16; Goodrich, 336–7.)

† *From home*: cavalry, 2,292 officers and men; ten infantry battalions, 8,169; eight artillery batteries (54 guns), 1,881; Royal Engineers, commissariat, transport, ordnance, police, medical, railway staff and telegraphists, etc., 3,851. *From Gibraltar and Malta*: nine infantry battalions, etc, 7,592. *From India*: cavalry, 1,497; two European and three native infantry regiments and other troops, 5,829, (plus 6,518 native followers). Drafts and depot troops, about 4,000.

all helmets 'were stained a light brown with tea or umber'. Each man was also issued, as were the rest of the force, with cholera belts and with blue-tinted goggles against the desert glare. These were 'very generally discarded' during the course of the campaign, but the green and blue 'veils' issued against mosquitoes were 'habitually used during sleep'. The horses were provided with eye-fringes, which were invaluable against the swarms of flies. 'To do justice to these pests,' an American observer wrote, 'requires a fund of objurgation not at the command of the average mortal.' On board ship every man and, according to Wolseley, 'nearly every officer', had his hair cut 'as short as that of a rat'. Also in the course of the 3,000-mile sea journey, all swords were first sharpened and then 'browned by burning blade, hilt and scabbard'. Each cavalryman was armed with a Martini-Henry carbine, carried as usual in a leather bucket at the right side of the saddle. The Household Cavalry troopers were also issued with revolvers. All trappings made of metal were allowed to rust, so as to avoid reflecting the sunlight.[9]

Two full heavy regiments were also included: the 4th Dragoon Guards (605)* which had not been away from home since the Crimean War, and the 7th Dragoon Guards (605) which had last seen active service in South Africa in 1848 (see p. 173). In addition there were the 19th Hussars, employed as 'Divisional Troops', which meant that beside providing generals' and other escorts and various guards, varying proportions of the regiment were attached to each of the two infantry divisions. In the contingent which came from India were the 2nd Bengal Cavalry (431), the 6th Bengal Cavalry (483) and the 13th Bengal Lancers (492). In command of the Cavalry Division was Major-General Sir Drury Curzon Drury-Lowe, aged fifty-two, late of the 17th Lancers. As a captain he had

* To make up this number as many as seventy-five men and no less than 172 horses, with a captain and two lieutenants, had to be taken from the 5th Dragoon Guards. 'Although the men returned,' wrote the 5th's historian, 'recruits had had to be trained, in place of them while they were away, and remained on the establishment afterwards . . . The difficulties of simultaneously training seventy-five recruits and 172 remounts and at the same time carrying on the ordinary work of the regiment, can well be imagined. Luckily the regiment was at York at the time, with no out-stations, or it would have been impossible.'

The 4th's commanding officer went sick just before Tel el-Kebir. The regiment was commanded during the race to Cairo by Major Denne, the subject of a promotion scandal four years later, (see p. 93–4). (Pomeroy, I, 206.)

captured four of Tantia Topi's elephants in 1858 (see Vol II, 217). In the Zulu War he had commanded his regiment (see p. 194) and in the First Boer War all the cavalry. Under him, in command of the 1st Brigade was Colonel Sir Baker Creed Russell, aged forty-five. He was described by one of Wolseley's aides-de-camp as 'a cavalry leader of the old type,' who 'always looked the typical heavy dragoon, although, as a matter of fact, he had done his regimental soldiering in the 13th Hussars. A very big man, with a loud voice, a long drooping moustache and extremely long legs, he loved fighting for fighting's sake.'[10]* The 2nd (Indian) Brigade was commanded by Brigadier-General (half-pay) Henry Clement Wilkinson, also aged forty-five, late 16th Lancers. He had commanded a cavalry brigade in the Second Afghan War.

The very first troops to land at Alexandria, where the Khedive had placed himself under the protection of the fleet, were two infantry battalions. From these a body of mounted infantry was immediately formed. It consisted at first of only two officers and thirty men, some of whom were volunteers who had been employed in South Africa as mounted riflemen but many were only slightly acquainted with riding. 'A somewhat motley detachment' is how Sir Evelyn Wood described them. Excellent ponies and saddles were commandeered for them from the Khedive's own stables.[11] In the course of the campaign the numbers fluctuated, rising at one time to 150, but falling at another, due chiefly to illness, to about forty.[12] They were mounted on ponies bought in Cyprus. One officer wrote that 'Mounted Infantry was the coveted service of the moment, for it was on its trial; we had every opportunity of showing what could be made of it.'[13]† The organization was by squadrons consisting in principle of two troops of seventy men each.[14]

The first cavalry to leave England were the Household Cavalry. Their embarkation at the Albert Docks in London took place amid scenes of 'great enthusiasm'. As their leading transport passed through Cowes Road on 2 August, the Queen took 'the opportunity of communicating a farewell'. Thirteen days later they arrived at Alexandria. One who saw their horses picketed along

* Lieutenant-Colonel Ewart was actually senior to Sir Baker, but he waived his right to command the brigade so as to retain immediate command of the Household Cavalry regiment. (Arthur, II, 670.)

† There were at least two civilian volunteers acting as Mounted Infantry officers. (Dawson, Brig.-Gen. Sir Douglas *A Soldier-Diplomat*, 1927, 75.)

the waterside thought them 'sadly pulled down after the tumble and tossing of the sea to which they had been subjected'.[15] By 10 August all the cavalry had left home.

* * *

Wolseley's plan was to concentrate all his troops, except the Indian contingent, in the Alexandria area so as to make Arabi believe that he meant to march upon Cairo from there. In fact he intended to seize the Suez Canal, make Ismailia his base and then to crush the Egyptian army in the desert before taking Cairo from the north-east. This route, which was some forty-five miles shorter, had in fact been reconnoitred by an officer of the Intelligence Department as long ago as the beginning of the year. The deception plan worked well. The secrecy was so great that not even Lieutenant-General Sir Edward Hamley (see p. 111), one of the two infantry divisional commanders, knew of Wolseley's real intentions. As the troops arrived at Alexandria, they were engaged in keeping Arabi in a state of constant alarm. In consequence much of the Egyptian army was drawn to the region. Wolseley's concentration was complete by 22 August.

> 'It was a magnificent scene when the enemy's camp lay in front of us. . . . This action at Mahsama was a brilliant success.'
>
> The Brigade Major of the 1st Cavalry Brigade[1]

(ii)

The Egyptian campaign, 1882: actions at Magfar and Mahsama, 24 and 25 August

On 19 August Sir Garnet sailed from Alexandria with about half his force, as if to make a forced landing at Aboukir Bay. There the seventeen transports and the eight ironclads which were escorting them anchored, while some small craft went close in shore to open fire on the forts. The rest of the fleet, as soon as it was dark, slipped away towards Port Said. Very early next morning the Navy seized the Suez Canal, both Port Said and Ismailia being occupied without significant resistance. In fact, as early as 2 August 450 sailors and marines had seized Suez, encountering no opposition. Some days later the first troops of the Indian contingent arrived there. Arabi, amazingly enough, neither defended nor blocked the Canal.

It was vital to Wolseley's operations that the sweetwater canal which was the sole source of fresh water for Ismailia and Suez should be secured before the enemy could damage it. The same applied to the single-line railway, which in roadless desert was indispensable to the whole plan of campaign. By 22 August the railway and fresh-water canal between Suez and Ismailia were in Wolseley's hands. The previous day he had pushed forward the very first infantry landed at Ismailia to occupy the rail and canal junction at Nefisha. But further west Arabi's massed labourers were constructing dams. In consequence 'a gradual but continuous decrease of level in the canal . . .', wrote Sir Garnet, 'induced me to risk a cavalry movement with horses which had been less than two days on shore after a long sea voyage . . .'[2] Thus began on 24 August the action of Magfar – the first and most risky of the campaign.

The 2nd Life Guards and Blues squadrons* and a company of mounted infantry, followed later by the only two 13-pounder horse artillery guns which had been disembarked, marched from Ismailia soon after 4 a.m. The going was extremely difficult, the sand in this part of the desert being 'very heavy and soft' and 'in many parts fetlock deep'.[3]†

At about 9 a.m. the leading cavalrymen drove in the enemy's outposts and were advancing further when masses of enemy infantry began to threaten to attack. These, who for the next hour or so were reinforced by the train load, before long opened a distant but heavy musketry fire. The British infantry on the left

* One troop of the 1st Life Guards was detached as escort to the guns. The other acted as baggage guard. (Talbot, 2 Sep, 1882). A troop of the 19th Hussars provided an escort for Sir Garnet and his Staff.

† The 'old Artillery horses' which had been provided for drawing the Household Cavalry's regimental carts, proved 'practically useless, being old and weak, and, in any case, were too few in number.' (There were forty-four.) Consequently each cart was only half loaded, and the officer's belongings had to be left behind. 'The troop horses carried 20 lbs of forage, but the men's kits were reduced to nothing but their cloaks; not even water-decks [painted canvas covering for equipment].' (Talbot, 2 Sep, 1882, 1.)

near the canal, not 1,000 in number, partially protected by sandy hillocks, returned it. So, later, did the two horse artillery guns. Almost immediately large numbers of Egyptians, some of them mounted, threatened to overlap the right of the small British force. Here, nearly a mile north of the railway, the cavalry and mounted infantry were preparing to thwart this outflanking movement when they came under the extremely accurate fire of four (and later twelve) artillery pieces.* Fortunately, all through the campaign, the Egyptians used 'common shells with percussion fuzes, which sank so deep in the very soft sand before bursting that few splinters flew upwards' and when, occasionally, shrapnel was employed 'the time-fuzes were badly cut'.[4] Consequently, far less damage was done than would have been expected from what was generally agreed was excellent gun practice.

As a staff officer noted, the two Household Cavalry squadrons were now 'kept moving slowly on the desert in open column in order to distract the aim of the enemy's gun-layers.' One shell killed a horse. 'Its rider was on his feet in a moment, calling out "Three cheers for the first charger in the Life Guards killed since Waterloo!" '[5]

To a squadron commander of the Life Guards it seemed impossible that the ground should have been held by such a diminutive force. 'If the enemy had had ordinary courage,' he wrote, '*they had nothing to do but to walk us off the ground*. We saw,' he added, 'Bedouin Cavalry come right round the flank, but, as we faced them and prepared to charge, they retired.'[6]† For nearly an hour, a vastly superior number of enemy was held off. The horses soon became completely exhausted, and before long cavalry and mounted infantry both took to their feet. 'As soon as any of the enemy more bold than the rest,' wrote the official historian, 'ventured to attempt an advance they were instantly picked off by the men of the Mounted Infantry . . . Their effective shooting for a time entirely stopped all movement on that side.'[7]

At about 12 a.m., on what was an exceptionally hot day even

* The first four were 'bronze rifled muzzle-loaders'; the later eight were Krupp guns.

† Early in the action, a Staff Officer noticed that the cavalrymen had 'disencumbered themselves of their hay nets; these lay in the desert . . . all in a row, two and two, looking in the mirage for all the world like an extended battalion of soldiers, and so deceived the Egyptians that many a volley was fired at them.' (Molyneux, 233.)

for that time of year, the Egyptians set in motion further encircling movements on the British right. At much the same moment the squadron of the 1st Life Guards which had originally escorted the guns was ordered by General Drury-Lowe to take the place of the mounted infantry, two of whose officers had been wounded.

> 'I dismounted half the men,' wrote Captain the Hon. R. A. J. Talbot, who was commanding the squadron, 'and occupied a line with small groups of men, facing from N.W. to N.E. alternately, advancing and retiring a few hundred yards. The men were very steady, firing, as ordered, occasional shots. My horse had a lot of work to do, as the Squadron occupied ground enough for a Brigade.
>
> 'After the Mounted Infantry had watered and fed, they came out again and joined me, and were under my orders, which were to hold the position, if possible, till after dark. The rest of the Regiment [went into] reserve about three-quarters to a mile off. There was a desultory fire of shell occasionally, waxing hot if we advanced, and long range rifle fire. I confess I was very glad when the sunset came, and when dark I withdrew. We were ordered to fall back three miles . . . We watered our horses by about 9 o'clock, having been hard at work seventeen hours.'[8]

Early in the day, though he had so puny a force, Wolseley had decided that 'it would not be in consonance with the traditions of Her Majesty's army that we should retire, even temporarily, before Egyptian troops, no matter what their numbers might be.'[9] He had therefore sent back messenger after messenger with orders to bring up reinforcements. However, nothing substantial had arrived before about 5.20 p.m., when Sir Baker Russell came up with 350 sabres of the 4th and the 7th Dragoon Guards, who had only disembarked that very day. They arrived just as the enemy was threatening a further advance. Their presence put an end to it. Further infantry, including the Guards Brigade, commanded by the Queen's favourite son, the Duke of Connaught, arrived at dusk and later. So did the remaining four guns of the Horse Artillery battery, as well as a battery of 16-pounders.

Both men and horses spent a hungry, comfortless night in a much lowered temperature. No supplies had come up from Ismailia. This was partly because some of the rails had been removed by the enemy, and because the canal level had sunk too low for water transport. But the chief cause was the total inadequacy of the regulation service carts and wagons. Most of these were useless in the desert. As early as March an authoritative report had pointed this out. 'Maltese carts fitted for two mules, with wheels not less than five feet in diameter and with extra broad tyres' had been recommended, but only the Indian authorities had paid attention. The Indian contingent therefore had few transport difficulties. For some days the route westwards from Ismailia was 'a very painful sight with abandoned and broken-down vehicles and horses and scattered stores – to say nothing of men being dead-beat owing to their exertions in the heat and heavy sand to help the transport animals.' Driver James Wickenden of the Royal Horse Artillery records that the men 'were only allowed a pint and a half of water each day, and that seemed to disappear by magic. Now and then we had some tinned meat and a few potatoes, but I don't believe I had a hatful of these delicacies all the time.' An infantry surgeon commented on the types of rations issued during the campaign:

> 'Sour, black, underbaked bread, such as we had so much of in Egypt, should never again be issued to British troops. The Egyptians had good bread, which we gladly picked up wherever we found it; and the Indian troops being excellently well off in this respect, it is therefore reasonable to say that British soldiers should have been equally well provided.
>
> 'Australian tinned beef is useful on a hurried march, though it might well be made more palatable. The Australian tinned mutton should never again be issued; it is a vile rancid mixture, resembling chopped up strings floating in oil. The hungriest man with the strongest stomach recoils at the mere look of it.
>
> 'As regards "Erbswurst", it is nourishing so far as the pea flour is concerned; and chemists say it is also partly composed of animal matters . . . It is most unpalatable, soldiers don't like it, a mere washy pea soup.
>
> '. . . Many soldiers told me that they had gone without dinners for some days, as they actually turned against the daily unchanging stews. Altogether, our cooking on active service is far from what it might be; and from all I have read, it is much about the same as in the old Peninsular and Crimean wars.'

The men soon learned to make 'capital beds by scraping holes in the sand, rolling ourselves in our blankets', as Wickenden described it, 'with our helmets for pillows, and then raking the sand over us so that we were almost buried.'[10] Lieutenant-Colonel Coghill of the 19th Hussars described how his regiment tied their horses 'to sacks which we fill with sand from a hole we dig and bury the sack using the mound as our pillow.'[11] The horses, when they had consumed the ten pounds of oats and hay which they had carried with them from Ismailia, had nothing to eat but a few rushes cut from the canal banks.[12]

At the first gleam of dawn on 25 August, the cavalry, the rest of which had joined in the night, led the advance over the ground which had been held the previous day by the enemy's extreme left. The movement was 'in echelon of Regiments, from the right, in squadron columns'. The Household Cavalry formed the second line, while the guns were between the cavalry and the infantry.

> 'We saw no signs of the enemy for some time,' wrote Captain Talbot. 'They had evidently retired from yesterday's position, which is unaccountable, as it was a very strong one, and had taken up a fresh one on the ridge above Mahsummeh [Mahsama] station.* I don't exactly know what happened to the 4th and 7th Dragoon Guards, but I fancy they had misunderstood their orders, the 7th getting miles away to the right and the 4th to the left, where they charged an entrenchment somewhere near Rameses and got slated.†
>
> '. . . However, when we came in front of the enemy's position, there were only one Battery of R.H.A., ourselves, and the Mounted Infantry. The enemy opened shell-fire upon us from guns to our front and from our left front down the [canal] from the Camp at Mahsummeh Station. The fire was admirably directed; one shell fell in the midst of Simon Lockhart's troop, killing Candy and wounding Shepherd and Magee severely, Corporal Rice and Matthews slightly. There were no stretchers or ambulances or assistance of any kind, either on the 24th or 25th, only what was afforded by Hamilton [the

* Wolseley reckoned that Arabi's force was at least 8,000 strong, with twenty guns. (Wolseley's despatch, 27 Aug, 1882, Goodrich, 130).

† 'Rameses' seems to refer to a position *south* of the canal near Tel el-Maskhuta, an unlikely position for the 4th to have arrived at. Talbot's account of the 4th's and 7th's movements is not corroborated by any other sources. None of them gives any detail at all about the early morning advance. All that is certain is that Major A. Bibby and five troopers of the 7th were wounded at this period of the action.

Life Guards' surgeon] and Spry [?] on their own hook. What our poor fellows suffered unnecessarily I will not say, but it was cruel.

'I rigged up a numnah [saddle pad] and saddle to shade Shepherd, who had his leg shattered, and left a man with him . . . I found in the meantime our guns had been playing upon the enemy and their camp, and had silenced those opposed to us.'[13]

By the time the sun was well up, parts of the 4th and 7th Dragoon Guards had rejoined the Household Cavalry. At this time, too, clouds of dust showed that most of the Egyptian artillery had started to retire, while the smoke from railway engines indicated that the infantry was retreating by rail. Wolseley at once ordered his Assistant Adjutant General, Lieutenant-Colonel William Butler, to

' "gallop to Drury-Lowe. Tell him to take all his cavalry and Horse Artillery forward, and *coute que coute* capture one or more of those trains. An engine would be worth a lot of money to me now." I galloped off without waiting for the order to be written,' wrote Butler, 'and soon overhauled the cavalry, which were moving along the gravelly desert in advance, under a dropping shell fire from some Egyptian guns on lower ground near the railway. I delivered my order to General Drury-Lowe; the cavalry went forward at the best pace they could.'[14]

Sir Baker Russell's Brigade Major, Lieutenant-Colonel Hugh McCalmont of the 7th Hussars, in relaying the order to advance to 'a cavalry commander', was met with 'I am under musketry fire already'. 'Nothing,' retorted McCalmont, 'to what you will be before we are done with these lads!' He noted that the British infantry, though ordered to attack on the left of the line, were 'out of the business . . . They were too beat, owing to the heavy sand, to do much.'[15] Unfortunately the cavalry were only in marginally better form. In his despatch Wolseley noted that 'there was not at this time in the whole cavalry brigade a troop that could gallop, their long march and rapid advance having completely exhausted the horses.'[16] The commanding officer of the 7th told Captain Talbot of the Life Guards at this time that 'his horses were beat, he could not move them; and, indeed, as they struggled up by twos and threes, they did not appear capable of effective action.'[17] Luckily, though, the mounted infantry, with their small Egyptian and Cypriot mounts, were in better shape. 'Employed strictly in their proper function of galloping up into effective positions, dismounting, and bringing close and well-aimed infantry fire to bear,' as the official historian put it, they proved very useful.[18]

'We were just too late,' wrote Talbot, 'to catch an engine and train.'[19] In the pursuit which followed, though its pace was slow due to the horses' condition, the Household Cavalry took a few prisoners, while some of the men who had failed to escape by train were hunted down and killed. One of the prisoners taken by Talbot's troop was Arabi's chief engineer, the ablest of all his generals, who had just arrived to take charge of completing the lines at Tel el-Kebir.[20]

By 10 a.m. Arabi's extensive camp at Mahsama had been reached and taken. There fell into Wolseley's hands seven Krupp guns, quantities of rifles and ammunition and seventy-five railway wagons, but no engine.

> 'We found tents,' wrote Talbot a week later, 'which we are still using . . . and stores of all descriptions – rice, barley, lentils, biscuits, beans, and chopped straw in large quantities, besides clothing and all sorts of odds and ends in their tents, many of them brand new from England. Cigarettes and coffee were found in small quantities, and two splendid hospital tents, fully equipped with medical stores and instruments . . . We also found about twenty camels, which will be and have been a most welcome addition to our regimental transport.'[21]

The providential capture of such vital stores made it unnecessary for the cavalry to withdraw, as at first they were ordered to. By 5 p.m. they had been reinforced by some guns and infantry.

The cavalry horses had been saddled, and for much of the time mounted, for forty hours. With the enemy's complete rout they and their riders could now rest in comfort and amidst comparative plenty. They had deserved it.

In the two actions of Magfar and Mahsama the Household Cavalry had one man killed and twelve wounded, while sixteen were struck down by sunstroke. Eleven horses were killed. The 4th Dragoon Guards suffered, it seems, no casualties. The 7th had one officer and five men wounded, three horses killed and six wounded. The mounted infantry had two officers and one man wounded.

The total casualties were five killed, twenty-eight wounded, forty-two struck by the sun and twenty-seven horses killed and wounded.

One Life Guardsman, on 24 August, found himself separated from his troop. An Egyptian shot his horse and then, as he was getting up, 'cut him over his guard across the arm'. Wolseley, visiting him in hospital, asked: ' "Well, and what became of your friend?" He replied, without moving a muscle, "I cut him in two, sir." In several instances these great giants,' wrote Sir Garnet, 'with their heavy swords cut men from the head to the waistbelt.' The following day one of the Blues, who had dismounted to take an Egyptian prisoner, was attacked by him with a dagger. He was wounded in the hand, but, with 'a single side stroke, *he cut his antagonist in two*, and took the dagger as a souvenir!'[22]

The two days' fighting enabled work to start on removing the formidable obstacles from canal and railway, repairing the railway, and accumulating stores.

Prelude to actions at Kassassin

'General Graham states, in the most emphatic manner, that no message was sent by him about being "only just able to hold his own", an expression for which Lieutenant Pirie is solely responsible.'

Wolseley's despatch after the first engagement at Kassassin

'I could see our brave old General, the
 gallant Drury-Lowe
Meant mischief, if he had the chance, that
 night against the foe.

* * *

The Body Guard of England's Queen have woke
 to life once more,
The glories won at Waterloo in stormy days
 of yore,
Thus answering without anger the tongues
 who cast their sneers
"That we were useless, save for show"; let
 this assail their ears:
We were the foremost in the fight where e'er
 the conflict raged.'

TROOPER TOM FROUDE, 2nd Life Guards, 'The Charge of Kassassin'[1]

(iii)

The Egyptian campaign, 1882: actions at Kassassin, 28 August and 9 September

At daylight on 26 August a troop of the 4th Dragoon Guards advanced to seize the vital lock at Kassassin. This, as well as the bridge, they found undefended and undamaged. Later in the day an infantry brigade took over this advanced position. Though vedettes were posted ahead of it, the bulk of the cavalry remained at Mahsama.

Meanwhile the disembarkation of Wolseley's main force at Ismailia went ahead as speedily as that little port's facilities (all the while being extended by the Royal Engineers) would allow. By 28 August the Indian cavalry brigade had arrived there from Suez. The previous day the first trickle of supplies began to be ferried

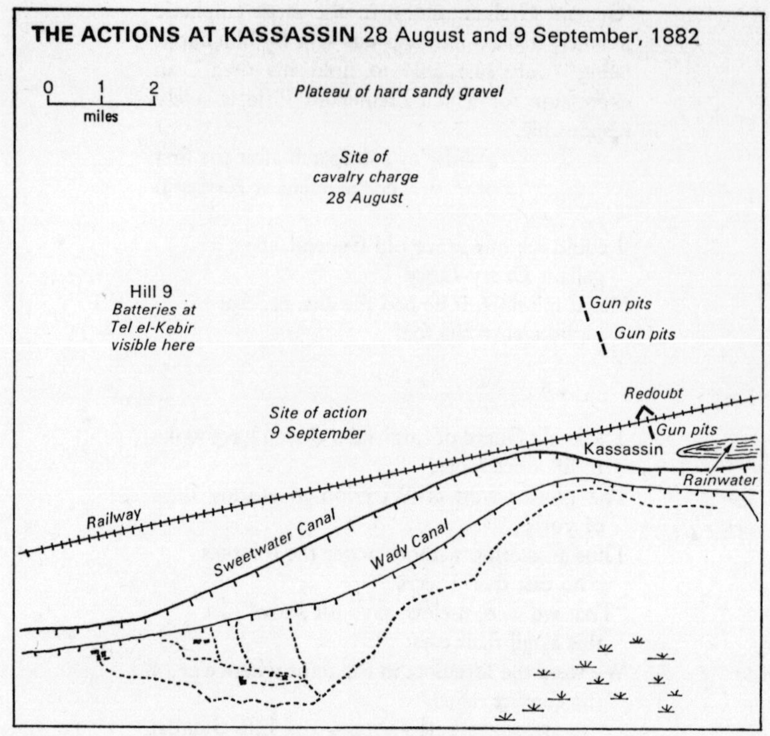

Map 13

westwards along the sweetwater canal.* Except for what had been captured in Arabi's camp, the troops were virtually without food or shelter for three or four days. They, however, looted some pigeons and water-melons from neighbouring villages, and on 27 August, a foraging party brought in fourteen head of cattle as well as some sheep and turkeys: 'all paid for'.[2] On the same day a single locomotive arrived from Suez.

* * *

On 28 August the Egyptians made a serious attempt to regain their lost ground. They threatened Major-General Gerald Graham's

* '27th August . . . After great exertion, we got three boats full of ammunition for the horse artillery and cavalry above the dam, and had them towed by horses up-stream to Mahsameh [Mahsama], while a detachment of cavalry [19th Hussars] kept at bay some brigands [Bedouins] on the south of the canal.' (Molyneux, 243.)

force at Kassassin with something like 8,000 foot soldiers, 1,000 horsemen and twelve guns. Graham commanded 1,700 infantry, fifteen men of the 4th Dragoon Guards, forty-two of the 7th and seventy mounted infantry, with two 13-pounders of the Royal Horse Artillery. When, at about 9.30 a.m., enemy horsemen appeared in force, Graham heliographed to Drury-Lowe at Mahsama to move up his brigade (less the 4th Dragoon Guards, who were at Tel el-Maskhuta), ready for action if required, and to keep in touch by signal. For many hours, however, nothing more than 'an ineffectual and distant artillery fire was attempted by the Egyptians'.[3] At about 3 p.m. the mounted infantry reported that the masses of the enemy, which had been threatening Graham's right flank all day, were retiring. All this time the cavalry had remained dismounted, 'most of the men sitting under their horses to get some shade'.[4] Captain Talbot found this exposed inactivity 'far more trying than working. There was no wind, and it was indescribably hot.' About 4 p.m. the artillery duel ceased and the cavalry returned to camp. 'Many a time has one seen horses mad with thirst,' wrote an officer of the 7th, 'but surely never so mad as on that day, for no sooner was the canal in sight than the horses took charge of their riders, and rushing down the muddy banks, plunged into the water girth-high, and drank as if they had never drunk before.'[5]

> 'We had hardly watered and fed our horses, and the men had not time to get their dinners,' wrote Talbot, 'when the firing recommenced, and General Graham sent a message to send up the Marines in trucks along the Railway, and a request that the Cavalry might move up on the enemy's left, for the enemy was advancing in force upon Kassassin Camp.'[6]

What had happened was that at about 4.30 p.m. the enemy, in the words of Graham's despatch, had 'advanced his infantry in great force, displaying a line of skirmishers at least a mile in length, with which he sought to overlap my front on the left, supported by a heavy and well-directed fire of artillery.'[7]* An heliographic message was immediately sent off to the cavalry to turn out once again. Some

* The enemy, apparently, made persistent efforts to break through the line where were stationed (between two infantry battalions), the 'little band of Mounted Infantry and the detachment of the 4th Dragoon Guards'. These, according to Graham, put up a 'gallant resistance'. 'The services of the Mounted Infantry', he added, 'have been invaluable to me in the absence of a sufficient force of cavalry.' (Goodrich, 135.)

fifty minutes later, Graham, seeing that the enemy's horsemen were beginning to advance on the British extreme right and would soon fully expose themselves to a charge by the cavalry, sent off his extra aide-de-camp, Lieutenant D. V. Pirie of the 4th Dragoon Guards, with a verbal order to Drury-Lowe. This was worded something like this: 'Take the cavalry round by our right . . . and attack the left flank of the enemy's skirmishers.' But Drury-Lowe was much further back than Graham or Pirie supposed. It had seemed to the cavalry commander 'very unadvisable'[8] to hurry out again his exhausted men and horses. Consequently Pirie was not able to deliver the order until his charger had dropped from fatigue and he had borrowed another mount from one of the batteries which was retiring to collect more ammunition. By then he had become so excited and worried at the wasted time that he lost his head. He informed Drury-Lowe that Graham was 'only just able to hold his own'.[9] It was under this false impression that the cavalry commander pushed forward that evening.

The following account of the famous 'moonlight charge' which resulted is by Captain Talbot of the 1st Life Guards. It is the best first-hand one available and it is graphic:

> 'It was just before sunset [about 6 p.m.] that we marched off . . . this time upon no fruitless errand. It was a full moon, and, after the sun set, we had brilliant moonlight. The 7th Dragoon Guards led the way, followed by our R.H.A. Battery, the Household Cavalry in rear in squadron columns in single rank.
>
> 'We marched silently along, getting away to the right, along the line of sand ridges, an occasional order to trot or to change direction alone breaking the silence. We must have marched some five or six miles, when the silence was broken by the boom of a gun, followed by the hissing of a shell which went far beyond us, and then in rapid succession were seen flashes from guns about 1,500 yards distant on the summit of the ridge along which we had been advancing. They were above us somewhat, and firing down a gentle slope. The guns had no doubt been firing on General Graham's Camp, but on our approach, having perceived that we had got round their rear, they were faced about.
>
> 'General Lowe shortly ordered our guns to unlimber and reply, and the 7th Dragoon Guards to clear the front of our

guns, which they did by retiring,* making us the first line. A few shots from ourselves had only been fired, the Household Cavalry continuing to advance at a walk to their right, when in a moment became visible a white line of infantry in our immediate front, which opened a tremendous fire upon us. Not a moment was to be lost: "Front form in two lines," "Draw swords," "Charge," and we were upon them.'

The order to charge was given by Sir Baker Russell, not by Lieutenant-Colonel Ewart, who was in immediate command of the composite regiment. Wolseley was told that 'Baker's word of command: "*Household Cavalry*, *Charge*" was like thunder. He led like a man. I wonder he was not killed as he was a most remarkable object, being the only man with a white jacket on. His horse was killed, but they tell me that when on foot he laid well about him killing two or three of the enemy.'[10]

Talbot's narrative continues:

'Until we got within 100 yards they continued to fire, but in one moment the brilliant light from the firing line, and the rattle of the fire, and the whiz of the bullets ceased: the white line had faced about and was in flight.

'We rode them down in solid rank, but as they dispersed we opened out and pursued. They fell like nine-pins, many of them unwounded, who fired and stabbed our horses as we galloped past them . . . We could give no quarter, for they fired after they were wounded as soon as one's back was turned . . . We charged for some 300 yards; then Ewart, who had led the first line (Home† being in command of the second), called out "Rally," and we set to work to collect our men. This was no easy work, for they in the hot pursuit had become separated, and although the moonlight was brilliant it is very different from daylight.

'I can imagine no more splendid sight than this moonlight charge of our fine fellows on their black horses, against the guns supported by the white line of infantry, whose fire was so brilliant in the night that it looked more like the lighting of some grand pyrotechnic display than anything I can describe, Then the cheer we gave, then the few seconds of silence, and

* 'in column of troops from both flanks, to the rear of the Household Cavalry.' (Maurice, 63.)

† Lieutenant-Colonel D. M. Home, Royal Horse Guards.

> then the havoc and slaughter. The rout was complete, and it was only the want of being able to see that saved their guns.'

Here Talbot touches on a controversial point. In his official despatch, Drury-Lowe says: 'The enemy's infantry was completely scattered, and our cavalry swept through a battery of seven or nine guns, which in daylight must have been captured, but, unfortunately, their exact position could not be found afterwards, and they were no doubt removed during the night, after our retirement.'[11]

Major J. F. Maurice, the official historian, wrote that

> 'All evidence, both Egyptian and our own, is concurrent that the Egyptian artillery was never reached by our cavalry. It is, however, probable that, had it not been for the darkness and the impossibility, in an open desert, of obtaining any points to move on after the artillery had ceased firing, our cavalry could and would have captured the guns, whose escort [the white-uniformed infantry] had been destroyed, seeing that the artillery had limbered up and were out of action at the moment the cavalry charge would have reached them, and that the 7th Dragoon Guards, who had followed in support, were an intact body fully in hand and available.'[12]

Some years later Maurice explained in an article why he believed that the guns were never reached: 'The desert sand is a tell-tale indicator of movements. When many of us visited the scene of the cavalry charge immediately after the action [i.e. at daybreak next day], it was abundantly clear that the tracks of the guns were markedly distinct from the tracks of the cavalry, that it was evidently a mistake to say that the cavalry had "swept through the battery".' When he questioned Drury-Lowe and Lieutenant-Colonel Herbert Stewart, the Assistant Adjutant General of the Cavalry Division (of whom more will be heard in this volume), they both said

> 'what any English gentlemen or honest men would have said under the circumstances: "Really we don't know. A rumour reached us that night from the men that they had been through the guns. Very likely it was not so. The whole charge was so confused from the darkness that mistakes might easily have occurred. We were obliged to report what we believed to be true at the time, but you had better inquire of the regiments." '

43. The Life Guards: Heavy Camel Corps in Egypt, 1885

44. 'Farewell'. Men of the Household Cavalry entraining at Waterloo station for Southampton, 1882

45. 'The Desert March: scene at the Wells of Aboo Halfa'

This Maurice did. 'After careful inquiry, it appeared that the only man who had seen the guns was Captain Sir Simon Lockhart, of the 1st Life Guards . . . The negative evidence on the English side was overwhelming.' Maurice further made enquiries of Arabi and some of his generals who were in exile in Ceylon. They confirmed Maurice's view. They also, incidentally, deposed that the Egyptian infantry had been 'destroyed', not merely 'scattered' as stated by Drury-Lowe.[13]

Why Sir Simon Lockhart was the odd man out is explained by Captain Talbot, whose letter was not known to Maurice:

> 'Simon Lockhart, about whom I was very anxious, re-appeared about a quarter-of-an-hour after the rally, having got away to the left-front by himself. In coming back he found himself amongst the enemy's guns, limbered up. He blazed away with his revolver, but could do no more. Another man,' he added, 'who also was alone, saw a gun being dragged off by two ponies and two camels in front.'[14]

The Egyptian cavalry, which was on the enemy's extreme left, according to Talbot,

> 'never came near us, but fifteen men of our right troop who had got away to the right saw a squadron formed up, and thinking they were part of the Regiment, hailed them, when they were answered by fire from the squadron. Our men charged and the enemy bolted down the hill. Another of our men, who was alone, saw a mounted man going off with one of our horses. He rode at him and cut him down, and recaptured the horse, but could not keep him, as he was attacked by some Cavalry and had to escape.'[15]

The total casualties in the cavalry and mounted infantry in this engagement, known as the first battle of Kassassin, were one officer* and eight men killed (six of these were in the 1st Life Guards),

* This was Lieutenant H. C. Gribble, 3rd Dragoon Guards, who was attached to the 7th Dragoon Guards, and acting as Baker Russell's orderly. That morning he had mentioned to a fellow officer that 'his horse was a troublesome, excitable brute, very difficult to hold . . . The worst sort of charger to be on in a fight, because if he bolted with you to the rear everybody said you were running away, while if he bolted with you to the front you were either killed or captured.' It seems that Gribble was run away with to the front. (McCalmont, 216.)

three officers and twenty-two men wounded, and twenty horses killed and twenty-one wounded.

At daybreak next day some of the bodies of the British dead were recovered, but the Bedouins had already been on the ground and consequently others were not found. Fifty-eight Egyptian corpses were buried. On 30 August, two days after the charge, Major A. B. Tulloch, Graham's Assistant Adjutant General, found to his horror several wounded Egyptians near the ground, 'some in a state of delirium, others very weak but still sensible'.[16]

Whether this famous charge had any real effect upon the fortunes of the day, coming as it did when the main fight was over, may be doubted. It certainly had a good effect upon the morale of the Household Cavalry and it probably lowered the Egyptians'. 'This moonlight charge,' wrote an American naval officer attached to Wolseley's headquarters, 'was the most dramatic as it was one of the most gallant episodes of the campaign. It ended the battle in a brilliant and novel manner.'[17] Wolseley wrote to his wife: 'I shall be curious to see the newspapers about Household Cavalry. They can be laughed at no longer. I believe they will owe the continuance of their existence to my bringing them here and pushing them well to the front. They certainly are the best troops in the world: at least none could be better.'[18]

The triumphant cavalrymen got back to camp at about 1 a.m. A staff officer found the cavalry staff 'carousing over an immense brass bowl of boiling coffee . . . Everybody was jubilant. "Oh, if you had only stopped with us! We got fairly home this time".'[19]

* * *

The next twelve days saw the final removal of all canal and railway obstructions, the gradual build up of supplies at the front and the arrival of more and more troops at Ismailia. Telegraphic communication was re-established between base and front, and by 9 September Kassassin and Ismailia were connected by telephone, the very first time that it was used for military purposes in the field. It had only been invented six years before. 'No doubt,' writes the historian of the Royal Corps of Signals, 'the instruments were part of the civil equipment and it is most unlikely that they were used by anyone other than the telegraph personnel, since the staff in these days and for many years to follow were averse to handling them themselves.'[20]

The first troop of Indian cavalry – from the 13th Bengal Lancers – arrived at Kassassin on 2 September. It was swiftly followed by the rest of the Brigade,* one regiment of which 'mightily astounded us from England', as an infantry staff officer put it, 'by bringing twelve hundred pack-ponies' with it.[21] The 2nd Bengal Cavalry found itself camped alongside the Household Cavalry.

> 'It was amusing,' wrote Lieutenant St G. L. Steele of the Bengal Staff Corps, 'to see the big troopers . . . coming into our lines to have their swords sharpened by the sikhligars, and gladly exchanging clasp knives, etc., for the Indian chupatti to supplement their rations which had been rather short . . .
>
> 'The syces were kept pretty busy, as, after going out with the regimental transport to cut green forage on the cultivated land bordering the canal, they had to make a second daily journey to cut and bring in stuff for the British cavalry . . . The Household Cavalry were carefully located near a field of jowar [millet]. Their officers came and asked us what they were to do for forage, and were astounded when told that it was growing at their doors. Our men turned out and cut the field down for them.'[22]

Much of the incessant patrolling, outpost and reconnaissance work during these days of the build-up for the battle of Tel el-Kebir was undertaken by the three Indian regiments and by the 19th Hussars. Not only Arabi's own patrols but also marauding Bedouins were often encountered. There are in existence carbon copies of some of the orders written by Lieutenant-Colonel Kendal Coghill, commanding the 19th. They are worth quoting as they indicate the sort of matters which exercised a commanding officer in the field:

> 'O.C. 19 H to Adjt. 19 H
>
> Send up Inlying Squadron to Ninth Hill† Picket to support Native Cavalry who are getting it hot.
>
> 6 a.m., 4 Sept.

* From now on Drury-Lowe commanded a Cavalry Division of two Brigades. Baker Russell commanded the 1st – the heavies – while Brigadier-General H. C. Wilkinson commanded the 2nd – the Indian.

† This was a small eminence, some 2,000 yards to the British right front, from which the batteries at Tel el-Kebir could be seen.

Kassassin, 9 September 1882

O.C. 19 H to Q.M. 19 H

Send up hospital litters & water carts to our Left front advanced picket – sharp – also more carbine ammunition.

8.15 a.m., 4 Sept.

O.C. 19 H to Adjt. 19 H

'Send up another Troop to Ninth Hill at a trot and let the rest saddle and stand to.

9.10 a.m., 4th.

O.C. 19 H to Adjt. 19 H

Come up with all available men – Leave Q.M. in charge of camp with dismounted men who must be belted and armed.

10 a.m., 4th.

O.C. 19 H to G.O.C., 2 Brigade [infantry] 9th Hill*

Found Infantry Picket of enemy's in Waddi about 1½ miles W.S.W. of camp – about 50 men – They opened a close but harmless fire. I have encircled them. Shall I clear village?

6 a.m., 6th [?] Sept.'[23]

* * *

On 9 September Arabi, believing the force at Kassassin to be only a weak advance guard, made a combined attack from Tel el-Kebir and Es-Salihiyeh. In fact he came up against 8,000 troops of all arms.

At 4 a.m., Lieutenant-Colonel C. R. Pennington of the 13th Bengal Lancers, who was Field Officer of the day, going out as usual to relieve the vedettes, found masses of Egyptian horse and foot about to advance. He at once dismounted his fifty men behind a ridge and opened fire, thus giving timely warning of the danger. When hard pressed, Pennington's men remounted and charged some massed horsemen, killing ten of them and taking five horses. They lost one sowar.[24]

According to Lieutenant-Colonel Coghill of the 19th Hussars, whose account of the battle follows, at much the same time as Pennington encountered the enemy on the left, a small party of the 3rd King's Royal Rifles, with two guns, was going out to the right to seize some of the enemy's ammunition which they had abandoned in an outpost affair a day or two before. Coghill 'went to look on at this' when he was

* See second footnote, p. 291.

'met,' as he wrote home next day, 'by an officer of Rifles begging me to save his men by galloping to stop their falling into an ambuscade. I rode for a mile and overtook them, and then I rode to the top of the hill and found three regiments of enemy's infantry and two cavalry lining the crest. I raced back to camp for supports & found about 12,000 of the enemy drawn up in three lines, evidently placed there overnight for a morning surprise of our camp. I gave the general [Lieutenant General G. H. S. Willis, commanding the 1st Infantry Division] the alarm, and the trumpets rang out the alarm and the double and by 6.30 we were all in battle order.*

'My regiment is nearest Headquarters so that just as I marched from my Camp, five shells dropped into the place where the horses had left that minute, as the enemy shelled Headquarters. For the first hour they shelled us very hotly and with admirable precision . . . One shell fell between front and rear ranks of one of my troops halted and I thought would have destroyed the troop – but as it didn't explode no one was hurt. In an hour we saw their place of attack, so all the Cavalry and two batteries of RHA went from our Right & by a detour got on left rear of the enemy and rolled them clean back. We went very fast, but we could not catch them, as they are demons to bolt & hate close quarters . . . They overlapped us by quite a mile . . . with a dense mob of Bedouins in rear.

'We had 28 guns engaged & it is said that they had 40 [Wolseley in his despatch says thirty,][25] but that must be guesswork. Their artillery fire is very good, but bursting of shells bad. We are much safer from infantry fire when close than when far as they aim straight but high. By about 9 a.m. our fire, which was good, silenced their guns a bit & then our left (infantry) advanced, driving the enemy back. They recovered for a while, but the Marines and Rifles on our left made a grand charge for 300 yards & took 4 good Krupps guns.

'As the Cavalry, consisting of Life Guards, 4 & 7 Dragoon Guards, 19th Hussars & 2nd Bengal Cavalry, 13th Bengal Lancers, and 2 Batteries, RHA were rolling back the enemy's

* Coghill's message to the general, sent at 5.30 a.m., reads: 'Enemy in 3 lines of all arms advancing in great strength. First line still out of range. They extend about 2½ miles N. to S. & apparently throwing *their* Left up. I have ordered up my Inlying Sqn. & rest to be ready.' (Coghill's Note Book, 7112-39-5, National Army Museum.)

left we received a counter attack from a few thousand enemy's infantry, with 9 guns on our Right. Our extreme Right was Life Guards, so they wheeled out and charged, driving the enemy back and taking a Krupps & a Standard.*

'Our whole line then advanced & drove them back, but the infantry was played out fighting without breakfast, and toiling over hot deep sand – so hot that it is painful to lie down on it.

'. . . Their [the Egyptians'] eventual retreat was a panic, as they cut off their camel packs and chucked away their ammunition boxes freely. The Soudanies were engaged which form their best troops as they like fighting & Egyptians hate it . . . When all was over, 19th H., one Battery of RA & 18th Royal Irish were left to cover the retirement. We remained on the battle field till 7 p.m. So we had a hot & starving day without water.† I lost one officer & one man from sunstroke.

'Feeling famished, I prowled amongst the killed & found plenty of hard black biscuits in their haversacks. I collected these & their water panikins for my men & officers. While gnawing a biscuit I said, "Blow this Gyption, he has left a tooth in it", & it was hard enough to have smashed every tooth in his head. I took the tooth out, and having finished the mouthful found with disgust that it was my own tooth – *the one* bad one which I had had stopped in Florence.

'The water here, which is priceless even in drops or rather gouts, is sheer mud which you can't see the spoon in through a tumbler.

'In going through the dead I came across a good many wounded, all of whom reached out for their rifles to have a dying shot before being killed as they thought . . .

'Just as I was going to charge yesterday and had drawn swords, not being more than 300 yards apart from the enemy, the Assistant Adjutant General, Tulloch, came and said – "Oh, Colonel, do let me join your charge. I have always longed for such a chance all through my soldiering." Unfortunately he was badly mounted & as we charged on, our ranks

* The chief task of the heavy cavalry brigade was to keep the two prongs of the Egyptian attack apart. This they achieved.

† At 3.30 p.m. Coghill sent the following order to his Quartermaster: 'Send up water carts filled again, also officers' & men's food as soon as possible & get men's teas ready by 7 p.m. We should all be back by that.' (Coghill, 7112-39-5, National Army Museum.)

swept over & passed him; but he lost nothing as the enemy wouldn't wait & bolted so that we only caught their slowest & the stragglers, & never got well home into them.'[26]

Just before Major Tulloch joined the charge he had

'found a splendid situation on rising ground from which a great mass of the enemy's retiring infantry was in full view. I galloped to the battery and brought it up to the position I had found, and then a perfect rain of shrapnel was directed on the infantry. As the shells burst over them I could not help feeling unhappy at what I had done, but it was business: the battle harvest had to be reaped when the crop was ready.'

Tulloch's account of the charge in which he joined is very different from Coghill's, which shows how two first-hand accounts by responsible officers can disagree.

'We increased our pace,' wrote Tulloch in his *Recollections*, published twenty-one years later, 'to a steady canter. The enemy, being about 700 yards in front in a great unwieldy square, now began firing. We quickened our pace, and in another minute or two would have charged, when a bugle or trumpet sounded in our rear, and the colonel [Coghill] halted the regiment. On my inquiring why on earth we halted, the colonel said it was his general sounding the halt. I then rode back and besought the general to let us go on. The charge would have been a splendid one; we felt certain we should have broken the square, and that done, my idea was to wheel to the left front and come down on the flank of three or four batteries of the enemy's artillery in front of our main attack. But the general did not think our light cavalry force strong enough.'[27]

By 10.30 a.m. the routed Egyptians had fallen back whence they had come. When the pursuing British arrived within about 5,000 yards of the lines of Tel el-Kebir, (where since as long ago as February, intelligence had learned that Arabi was preparing a fortified position), they came under heavy fire from entrenched breech-loaders. At 1.30 p.m. all arms returned to camp. The second battle of Kassassin was over. The British lost only three killed and seventy-seven wounded.

Now once again Wolseley's army could concentrate on the

continuing build-up which he intended should lead to a decisive victory. Four days later all was ready. Nearly 2,800 cavalry,* over 12,000 infantry and 2,500 artillerymen† with sixty-one guns and six Gatlings had been assembled together with massive supplies.

[The Egyptian army is] 'quite despicable and good for nothing, so I hope the English public will not crow too loud over our success.'

MAJOR J. D. H. STEWART[1]

(iv)

The Egyptian campaign, 1882: battle of Tel el-Kebir, 13 September – the race to Cairo – surrender of Arabi – end of campaign

The formidable but incomplete entrenchments of Tel el-Kebir extended for nearly four miles northwards from the sweetwater canal. They consisted of a dry ditch up to twelve feet wide and nine deep. Behind this was a breastwork up to six feet high, with a firing step in rear. In places salient redoubts broke the lines. The entrenchments were manned by some 8,500 well-disciplined regulars, including 2,000 horsemen. Fifty-eight guns‡ were served by first-class artillerymen. The remaining 11,000 men were a rabble.[2]

What reconnaissance was possible had shown the general line of the works. More important, though, was the discovery that the Egyptian vedettes only emerged just after dawn and that at night there were no outposts. Even before this helpful knowledge came to him, Wolseley had decided upon what he called 'the most deadly but the most difficult of military operations,'[3] a dawn attack after a night march. 'To have turned the enemy's position . . . was

* The 19th Hussars provided three troops at different points between Ismailia and Tel el-Kebir to guard the lines of communication. (Coghill, 10 Sep, 1882). Otherwise the whole of the cavalry and Mounted Infantry were available.

† The proportion of officers to other ranks was exceptionally high: 634 to 16,767. There was also said to be one general to every 900 men!

‡ Arabi stated later that there were seventy-five guns; but only fifty-eight seem to be accounted for.

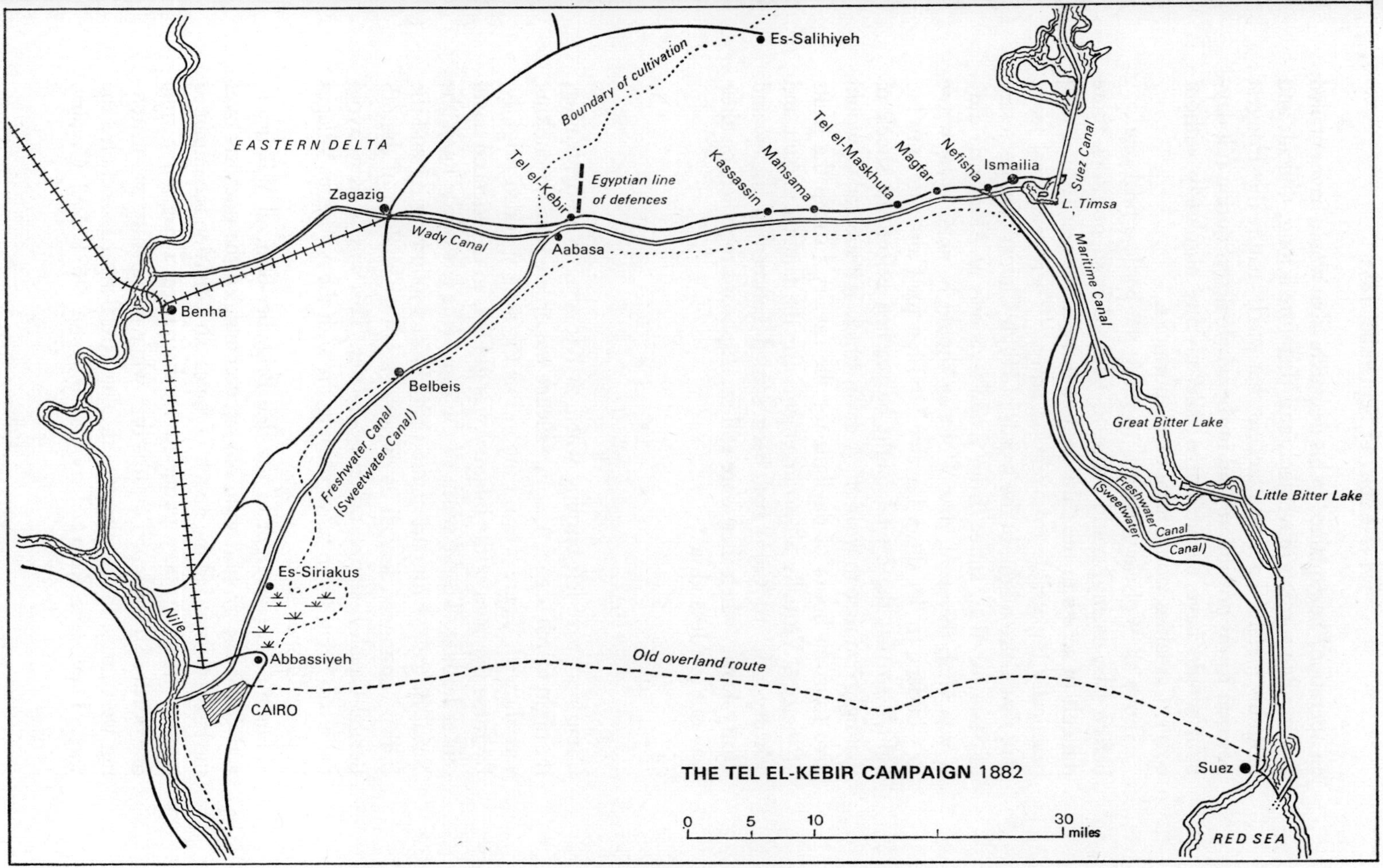

THE TEL EL-KEBIR CAMPAIGN 1882
Es-Salihiyeh
Boundary of cultivation
EASTERN DELTA
Tel el-Kebir
Egyptian line of defences
Kassassin
Mahsama
Tel el-Maskhuta
Magfar
Nefisha
Ismailia
Suez Canal
L. Timsa
Zagazig
Wady Canal
Aabasa
Maritime Canal
Benha
Belbeis
Freshwater Canal (Sweetwater Canal)
Great Bitter Lake
Little Bitter Lake
Freshwater Canal (Sweetwater Canal)
Es-Siriakus
Nile
Abbassiyeh
CAIRO
Old overland route
Suez
RED SEA
0 5 10 30 miles

Map 14

an operation,' he explained in his despatch, 'that would have entailed a very wide turning movement, and therefore a long, difficult and fatiguing march.' To have attacked what was by nature the strongest position it was possible to find in the whole desert during full daylight would have meant a five mile advance absolutely without cover. Casualties would have been enormous.

Above all Wolseley, 'wished to make the battle a final one . . . before [the enemy] could retire to take up fresh positions more difficult of access in the cultivated country in his rear [which was] practically impassable to a regular army.'[4] There were real fears, too, that Cairo might, in the words of Hugh Childers, the Secretary of State for War, suffer 'from Arabi's vandals as Alexandria did'. It was vital, therefore, that Wolseley should be able, as he wrote to Childers, to 'let slip a Cavalry Division for Cairo after my big fight,'[5] so that the capital might be reached before the shock of that fight had time to wear off. A dawn attack, if it succeeded, would give fourteen hours of daylight for the cavalry to reap the fruits of victory. Virtually all arrangements for the famous pursuit and 'cavalry ride' to Cairo had been settled between Wolseley and Drury-Lowe 'when they were still on shipboard together, on their way out to Alexandria'.[6]

* * *

Camp fires were left burning when, at 1.30 a.m. on 13 September, the night march began. Absolute silence was ordered and no smoking was allowed. There was no moon but the stars sparkled brightly. By these the mass of the infantry was guided, an experienced naval officer leading. To the south of the canal (the left of the line), the Naval Brigade, with part of the 19th Hussars following it,[7] and the Indian contingent, less all its cavalry except a squadron of the 6th Bengal Cavalry, started off an hour later. This was so as to avoid the alarm being given when passing through the numerous villages in the cultivated land.

On the extreme right of the line Brigadier-General Wilkinson, who knew the ground well, having commanded the outposts over the last few days, led the march of the cavalry division accompanied by two horse artillery batteries. He had fixed a flagstaff a mile due north of the camp. Towards this, while the infantry was marching westwards, the cavalry set off. The 13th Bengal Lancers led the way. They were followed by the 2nd and 6th Bengal Cavalry.

Then came 'N' Battery of 'A' Brigade, followed by 'G' Battery of 'B' Brigade, Royal Horse Artillery, with the mounted infantry behind them. The heavy brigade, led by the 7th Dragoon Guards, formed the rear of the column. On arriving near the flagstaff, 'which was not found till after the cavalry had been halted, and could not be seen at fifteen yards distance, the Division formed up. At 2.15 a.m.,' according to the official historian, 'the march was resumed in a north-westerly direction. The whole force moved off in column of troops.'[8]

Major Molyneux of the infantry staff learned a lesson in those early hours. 'Mounted men at night,' he observed, 'where silence is necessary, should always go in pairs; for a horse alone on the desert in the dark will neigh enough to waken the dead, and you cannot stop him.' Except for the occasional neighing of the lonely mounts of staff officers and the rare whispering of orders, the silence was generally impressive. The rumble of the guns seemed very loud in comparison with it.[9]

Soon after 3 a.m. the cavalry halted, fronted westwards and waited. At this point the division was nearly two miles[10] from the extreme left of the entrenchments. An hour and a half later, while it was still completely dark, the forward movement started, first at a walk and later at a slow trot. Fifteen minutes later, just as first light began to show behind them, the horsemen found themselves about 2,000 yards from the closest parapet. At the same moment the first shots of the battle, well to their left, gave the long-awaited signal. The pace was at once increased to a swinging trot, and almost instantaneously the leading lancers came under fire from the redoubt on the extreme Egyptian left.

> 'The Horse Artillery galloped forward,' in the words of the official history, 'engaged and silenced the fort, as well as a field battery which showed itself in the open ground in rear of the parapet. The cavalry continued their advance ... in line of squadron columns and at about the time that the two centre regiments of the Highland Brigade had driven back the Egyptians from the front parapet, and were beginning to advance into the interior of the work ... the cavalry passed the line of the entrenchments, and began to swing round on to the left rear of the enemy.'[11]

The attack of the infantry and artillery was well timed. It took the Egyptians completely by surprise. Just before the sun appeared the last few hundred yards were covered at a run under a storm of shot and shell, most of which went high. The first parapet was taken at the point of the bayonet, without a shot being fired till it was topped. Some of the Sudanis fought fiercely for a while, the rest began their flight after little more than a token resistance. Fighting had virtually ceased thirty-five minutes after the first gun was fired. Only sixty British officers and men were killed, and 409 wounded or missing.*

By good fortune the infantry and artillery had veered to the right in the course of their march. Their left (not including the Indians south of the canal, who were well behind) missed, therefore, a large isolated redoubt which was more forward of the Egyptian line than any other – about 1,000 yards. Reconnaissance had failed to detect its existence since it was sited behind rising ground.[12] As it was bypassed, the guns in it came to life and played with some effect on the infantry and upon Wolseley's staff who were not far to the right. Soon, from behind it, a body of enemy cavalry emerged. Lieutenant-Colonel Butler, the Assistant Adjutant-General, remembered years later that

> 'Our big group of staff had been ordered to scatter . . . so as not to draw too concentrated a fire from this redoubt. The commander-in-chief still kept me by him. I called his attention to the movement of the enemy's cavalry. "Order the squadron of the 19th Hussars to meet them," he said. It was not in sight. I galloped back to meet it, and they went forward at a canter in column of troops, passing within 300 yards of the 8-gun redoubt, and offering a splendid target to it. The redoubt fired four or five shots as the squadron passed it, but neither man nor horse was hit.
>
> 'Down the slopes, through the camps, over the railway, and across the canal, the white-clad fugitives were flying south and west in dots, in dozens, in hundreds.'[13]

Even before the rout started and about half-an-hour after the first shots of the battle, some of the artillery from the British centre had to be ordered to cease firing north-westwards, 'because,' as the official history states, 'the Horse Artillery with the Cavalry Division were indicated in the distance by a cloud of dust beyond the enemy's entrenchment, and might be struck by the shell.'[14]

* The cavalry throughout the day suffered only one casualty: an officer of the 19th Hussars was wounded.

This indicates that Drury-Lowe had by that time reached a point well to the west of the northern redoubt and about level with it, and that he was now moving south at considerable speed.

On the left, meanwhile, the artillery was concentrating its fire upon the trains at Tel el-Kebir station, by means of which Arabi was trying to save his intact reserve. At the same time Lieutenant-Colonel Coghill with his squadron of the 19th Hussars, as soon as the infantry had secured the entrenchment in his front,

> 'galloped in and began my rush. I made straight for the rail,' he wrote home next day, 'and succeeded in stopping the advance train by dropping a camel that chanced to be bolting across it at the moment. We therefore boxed three trains with about 130 trucks full of every possible munition of war.'[15]*

The mass of fugitives was now caught between three converging cavalry forces. From the north the advance of the Indian brigade, considerably ahead of the rest of Drury-Lowe's division, towards the bridge of Tel el-Kebir was being 'somewhat retarded'[16] by the flying rabble. It was also, according to McCalmont, 'a good deal hampered . . . in getting clear of the various brigades and units which had been participating in the fight.'[17] From the left-centre Coghill's squadron had already, according to his own account,[18] got well ahead of the Indians, racing due west. South of the canal the squadron of the 6th Bengal Cavalry (three officers and 102 sowars) was pushing forward 'to cut off the fugitives who were now pouring into the village of Tel el-Kebir from the northern side over the bridge.'[19]

At first the flying Egyptians were cut down, 'as rumour had it that they would otherwise lie down and hamstring the horses

* The official history's account differs from Coghill's. Maurice says that 'the first two trains escaped without being hit, but in the third some ammunition was exploded and the train stopped.' (Maurice, 94.) The historian of the Royal Artillery adds that the guns 'had just brought one [train] to a standstill, when its fire was unfortunately masked by the cavalry.' (Headlam, Maj. Gen. Sir John *The History of the Royal Artillery from the Indian Mutiny to the Great War, III – Campaigns (1860–1914)*, 1940, 200.) The historian of the 2nd Bengal Cavalry says that his regiment (near the van of Drury-Lowe's division) reached 'a train full of armed men' just as it was steaming off. This they were unable to stop, but they effectually stopped three more trains which were getting up steam by shooting the engine driver and stoker of the leading train and blocking the line with a dead camel. The large number of armed men on these trains inflicted some casualties on us here.' (Whitworth, 36.) Butler says that a 'fourth train' was captured 'at 6.10 a.m.' to the west of Tel el-Kebir. (Butler: *Journal*, 31.)

passing over them or rise up and shoot our troops in the back. However a staff officer rode up with an order that all Egyptians throwing down their arms were to be spared.'[20]

Wolseley and his generals now met, amidst the acclaim of the infantrymen, on the bridge at Tel el-Kebir. There he gave Drury-Lowe his final orders for the dash to Cairo. A sergeant of the 79th Highlanders records that 'just as we were cheering the General, the cavalry came galloping forward to take up the pursuit, and shouting with many oaths, "You —— jocks haven't left us the chance of a fight!" shot past in a whirl of dust.'[21]

The heavies and the horse artillery crossed the canal and followed its south-easterly bank towards Belbeis. The Indian brigade kept to the north-westerly bank, having captured the lock at Aabasa, and then also made for Belbeis. The horse artillery guns were at once delayed by the difficulties of crossing the narrow bridges over the branch canals which were intended only for pack animals. Thus the Indians won the race to Belbeis, arriving there at about noon, more than four hours before the 4th Dragoon Guards and the mounted infantry. The rest of the heavy brigade were later still, and in fact bivouacked that night some distance short of the town. The telegraph office was at once seized. Messages from Arabi, who had himself only arrived one station ahead, to some of his generals, ordering concentrations of fresh forces from other parts of Egypt, were intercepted. Thus Arabi's attempts at a rally were frustrated by the cavalry's rapid pursuit.

In the meantime Coghill, with his squadron of the 19th,

> 'being a free rover with nobody to give me orders, pursued for about twelve miles [towards Zagazig] when my men and horses were beginning to pack up. The enemy was entirely and completely routed and demoralised, cutting off all weight from camels and horses, throwing away arms and bolting everywhere. Numbers of them died from heat and exhaustion without a wound.
>
> '. . . I turned south again and at last struck off the canal where I watered my men and horses and rested. There is no loot but military stores, camels, ponies, mules, etc. My regiment is utterly broken up in scattered pursuits. Two troops . . . are by this time [late on 14 September] in Cairo with the Heavies. Two troops have gone to support the infantry at Zagazig – two are on the base line and I have two here [at Tel el-Kebir].'[22]

The Indian contingent set off at once for Zagazig. Well ahead of it went the squadron of the 6th Bengal Cavalry. With it rode the contingent's commander, Major-General Sir Herbert Macpherson, VC, with his staff. When within about five miles of the town the squadron broke into a gallop.

> 'It was something like a hunt,' wrote Macpherson, 'and came very near Mr Jorrocks's description of that sport, as the morning lesson at Tel el-Kebir had deprived our pursuit of much of its danger. The Egyptian troops were streaming along the canal bank, while we stuck to the railway within 250 yards of them; but, being intent on railway stock, we could not afford to notice them.'

So exhausted were most of the squadron's horses that only a handful of troopers and one or two staff officers led the way into the town. Undeterred by their small numbers they pushed on right into the railway station.

> 'The scene at the station (there are four junctions),' continued Macpherson, 'was very amusing. Six engines had their steam up. Three trains were puffing and in motion. We managed to stop all three, and a fourth, which we feared had escaped, in the hurry ran on to the wrong line and into a train coming from Benha, blocking both lines, and enabling us to secure these two engines and trains. We had to tear up a rail on the Salahieh [Es-Salihiyeh] line to prevent the inopportune arrival of an Egyptian division that the station-master assured me he expected in a quarter of an hour.'[23]

Before the end of the day the cavalry division and the Indian contingent had reached points fifteen miles from the field of battle. All had gone according to plan. Now the real race for Cairo was on.

* * *

Drury-Lowe's advance over the thirty or so miles which lay between Belbeis and Cairo started at about 4 a.m. on 14 September. The best account of the day's events is given by the Deputy Assistant Adjutant-General, Major Maurice:

> 'The cavalry moved now on firm desert, good marching ground, on the east of the canal. On the other side of the canal the inhabitants crowded down to the banks and received

with acclamations of pleasure a Proclamation previously prepared in Arabic . . . In it Sir Garnet informed them that the war was over . . . The cries of "Aman! Aman!" ("Peace, Peace!") . . . were repeated from village to village.'

At Es-Siriakus, a two hours' halt was made and the cavalrymen on the western side of the canal crossed it, so that the division might move as one body. Since the state of things in Cairo was unknown, Drury-Lowe halted some distance from the Abbassiyeh barracks, which formed a sort of outpost to the capital.

'Thence he sent forward Lieutenant-Colonel [Herbert] Stewart, with a detachment of about fifty men, composed partly of the 4th Dragoon Guards, and partly of the Indian cavalry, with Captain Watson as Arabic interpreter, and two Egyptian officers . . . who had accompanied him throughout the march.

'The little party,' wrote Major Maurice, 'as it approached the barracks saw before them large numbers of Egyptian troops. Soon, from among these, a squadron of cavalry advanced towards them, each trooper having a white flag attached to his carbine. It was 4.15 p.m. Evidently the Egyptians intended to capitulate.'[24]

Indeed by the end of the morning of the next day, 15 September, many thousands of Egyptian troops had marched out of barracks and been disarmed. Not one of them put up even a token resistance, nor was there the slightest disorder in the city. At 10.45 p.m. on 14 September Arabi had given up his sword to Drury-Lowe. The sudden arrival of the small force of cavalry had convinced Arabi's War Committee that capitulation was inevitable.[25] In due course he and his chief collaborators were exiled to Ceylon. By noon on the 15th the entire cavalry division had arrived in the capital. Some of them had marched nearly sixty-five miles in fifty hours. The campaign was over and the occupation of Egypt which was to be such a familiar part of the British army's life for nearly three-quarters of a century had begun. Almost at once the population, 'numbers of whom had only just exchanged their uniforms for their ghalabeahs, treated the cavalry more like a party of Cook's Tourists than an invading force.'[26]

The Household Cavalry soon returned home. So did the 4th Dragoon Guards. The 7th Dragoon Guards and the 19th Hussars remained as part of the garrison of Cairo. The 13th Bengal Lancers travelled by train to Alexandria to escort the Khedive back to his capital. An eye-witness thought that 'the troopers with their rolling eyes, fierce upturned moustaches and beards, their long bamboo lances with red and blue pennons, big-turbanned, jack-booted, and much be-belted' were 'admirable in the way of a picturesque bodyguard.'[27] The 2nd Bengal Cavalry, on duty at a Cairo railway station,

> 'hearing that a horse train was expected, arranged,' according to one of their officers, 'for all the horses to be escorted into the regimental lines . . . and promptly branded them "2 B.C." These horses and those seized on the march to Cairo helped to make good the many casualties the regiment had suffered. The barbs and Egyptian mules which we took were all splendid animals. Most of our trumpeters rode the flea-bitten grey barbs, and the last of them must have died out in the regiment about 1900 or soon after . . . One was playing polo in 1899.'[28]

A 'virulent epidemic' attacked all the horses a few weeks after arrival in Cairo. The 19th Hussars, for example, in an effort to shake it off, were moved to a station outside the city early in November. By then they had lost fifty-six horses, and had 248 sick. By March, 1883, the regiment had lost 141.[29]

Representatives of each of the Indian regiments were sent to England to be presented to the Queen. These were probably the first Indian soldiers ever to visit Britain. By the end of October all the rest of the Indian troops had arrived at Bombay. Wolseley was glad to see them go, as 'their followers,' he told Childers, 'break into houses everywhere, and plunder right and left.'[30] Generally speaking the behaviour of the troops in Cairo was reported as good. Lieutenant-Colonel Butler believed that

> 'drunkenness is rare, and the numerous riding donkeys in the streets afford the soldiers a means of amusement, which, if a little incongruous with the dignity and appearance of the profession of arms, is at least an excellent investment for arrears of pay, and a useful promoter of exercise.
>
> 'The relations between the soldiers and the lower class citizen appear to be friendly and even cordial, nor does the mutual ignorance of language limiting conversation to the fewest possible expressions, seem a bar to intercourse.'[31]

The discipline of 'spit and polish' was speedily restored. The following orders soon appeared:

> 'Officers will be properly dressed with red serge tunics, boots and breeches, or overalls, boots and spurs with either swords or pistols when visiting Cairo.'
>
> 'Soldiers are positively forbidden to sell their old clothing whilst in Egypt. The Commander in Chief cannot allow natives to appear dressed in the uniform of the British Army.'
>
> 'The Chief of Police will post notices in Arabic that any native who is detected selling spirits to soldiers in or near any of the camps will be handed over to the civil Police and flogged on the spot and all his liquor confiscated.'[32]

7

'By the discipline of their armies the Government was triumphant. The tribes of the Red Sea shore cowered before them. But as they fought without reason, so they conquered without profit.'

WINSTON CHURCHILL in 1899

'The cavalry showed all the dash and almost reckless gallantry in action that have characterised that arm in our military record.'

SIR GERALD GRAHAM'S General Order
after the 2nd battle of El Teb

'Well, I've served under Barrow at home
and afar,
Where the pyramids jostle the Nile,
And that day at El Teb, on the road to Tokar,
When he tackled the Fuzzies in style.
Oh! that was the fight I shall never forget.
For things were looking blue;
But Graham held his own, you bet,
The 19th pulled him through!'

From the Song of the 19th Royal Hussars[1]

(i)

The Eastern Sudan – 1st and 2nd battles of El Teb, February, 1884

Having crushed Arabi's rebellion, Britain now proceeded to eject French influence, hoping to put Egyptian affairs right unaided. She intended, in the words of the Earl of Dufferin, ambassador at Constantinople, to enable the Egyptians 'to govern themselves under the uncompromising aegis of our friendship'.[2] The first task was for British officers to create and train the new Egyptian army and police (see p. 363) and to regenerate the administration. As soon as these ends had been accomplished (under the firm hand of Evelyn Baring, later Earl of Cromer, who was appointed Consul-General), the military occupation, it was fondly believed, could be ended. After a year or two Egypt, like Afghanistan and the Transvaal, could be evacuated with safety. But as one Cairene remarked to another as they watched their ruler's re-entry into his capital, 'The Khedive returns like a child in his nurse's arms.'[3] He in reality retained no authority but that which British power could lend him. Gladstone's cabinet intended a speedy withdrawal, leaving British influence supreme. In fact such a withdrawal, it was soon discovered, would create a dangerous vacuum.

Events in the Sudan, that vast territory to the south over which since 1820 Egypt had held shaky sway, quickly tore the wool from British eyes. Even before Arabi's revolt in the north, a Sudanese insurrection was occurring in the south. It was an attempt to supplant Cairo's fragile foreign rule, sometimes oppressive, often inefficient, by a religious regime, 'whose blood-lust,' according to Winston Churchill, 'spread terror everywhere'.[4] This 'holy war' was led by the self-proclaimed 'Mahdi' (a sort of Moslem Messiah), son of a boat builder and a fanatic preacher of extraordinary power and intelligence. He was massively supported by those merchants who resented the efforts of General Gordon as Khedive Ismail's Governor-General to suppress the lucrative slave trade. In spite of some nine defeats of the Mahdi's so-called 'Dervishes' by Egyptian troops (partially counterbalanced by six victories), almost the whole of the country south of Khartoum was in open revolt by the end of 1882.

The demoralization of the 30,000 Egyptian troops who were scattered over enormous areas of the Sudan had been hastened by Wolseley's destruction of the rest of the army at Tel el-Kebir. As early as October, 1882, Sir Edward Malet, Baring's predecessor, had warned London that 'the way lay open for a Dervish advance into Lower Egypt'.[5] In May, 1883, however, a force of 5,000 scratch Egyptian troops led by Colonel William Hicks ('Hicks Pasha'), a retired officer of the Indian army, gained a victory over the Mahdists which seemed decisive enough to make the southern frontier of Egypt safe for some time. But in November, Hicks's army, now doubled in size and certainly the only force anywhere available, was annihilated at the so-called battle of Kashgil. Faced with this major catastrophe, Gladstone's government realized that the Sudan must either be reconquered at unacceptable expense, or be evacuated. Evacuation was therefore chosen.

To bring out the beleagured Egyptian garrisons General Charles ('Chinese') Gordon was sent to Khartoum. 'He is a genius, and of splendid character,' wrote Earl Granville, the Foreign Secretary, adding, 'It is a great pity that there should be some eccentricity.'[6]

It was hoped that this remarkable hero, who between 1877 and 1880 had been employed by the Khedive as Governor-General of the Sudan, could exercise his experience and his magnetic charm so as to secure the frontier against the Mahdi.

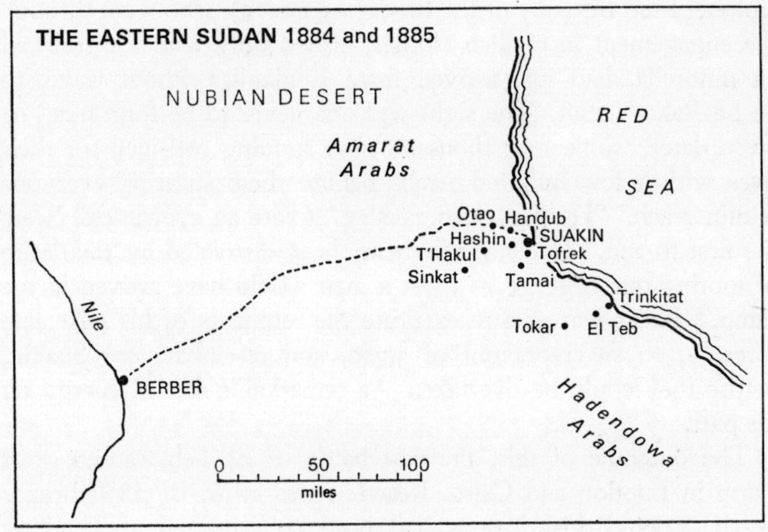

Map 15

But events some 350 miles to the north-east of Khartoum were speedily reducing his chances. There the Mahdi had acquired an astute, resourceful lieutenant called Osman Digna. By December, 1883, this dealer in slaves and ostrich feathers (who was only captured sixteen years later) had amassed a formidable force which, if reinforcements did not arrive soon, would capture the important Red Sea port of Suakin and engulf the whole of the eastern Sudan. Consequently some 2,500 of the raw Egyptian gendarmerie and other odds and ends, including 520 horsemen among whom were some European volunteers, accompanied by six guns, were despatched by sea from Cairo to strengthen the weak garrison of Suakin. They were commanded by General Valentine Baker Pasha, who readers of the second volume of this work will remember as lieutenant-colonel of the 10th Hussars. After a varied career (see p. 116) this outstanding cavalry officer had entered the Khedive's service in 1882, being assigned the task of reorganizing the Egyptian police. Now he was given supreme civil and military command and ordered 'to pacify the country between Suakin and Berber'.[7]

Many of his men were under contract to serve only in Egypt. Some had to be forcibly dragged from their homes and actually arrived in chains and without rifles. It is not surprising therefore that on 4 February, 1884, they were totally defeated in their first action, fought in an attempt to raise the sieges of Sinkat and Tokar. Colonel Fred Burnaby of the Blues (see p. 119), who went through the engagement in civilian clothes, armed only with a pistol and an umbrella, had just arrived from England, without leave, to be on Baker's staff. 'The sight was one never to be forgotten,' he wrote later, 'some four thousand men running pell-mell for their lives with a few hundred Arabs behind them spearing everyone within reach.' 'The Egyptian cavalry,' wrote an eyewitness, 'were the first to run.'[8] Had not the enemy been distracted by 'the desire of looting our baggage . . . not a man would have arrived in the camp.'[9] Baker was able to extricate the remnants of his miserable force, 1,300 survivors out of 3,700, and re-embark for Suakin, before they could be overtaken – a remarkable feat of energy on his part.

The outcome of this, the first battle of El Teb, caused great alarm in London and Cairo. Reaction was swift. By 28 February nearly 4,000 British troops had been concentrated at Trinkitat forming what was known as the Tokar Expeditionary Force. It was commanded by a distinguished Engineer officer, Major-General Sir Gerald Graham, VC, a man, according to Wolseley 'with the courage of a lion and the modesty of a young girl',[10] whose part in the 1882 campaign has already been touched upon. (See p. 284.) His command now included some 750 mounted troops, constituting a cavalry brigade under Brigadier-General Herbert Stewart, whom we last saw securing Cairo after Tel el-Kebir.

Under his command came the 10th Hussars, whose transport, taking them home after eleven years in India, had been diverted to Suakin. There General Baker, their one-time commander, handed over to them 300 of the horses belonging to his three gendarmerie regiments. It was said that the men of these were delighted: 'How kind these English are; they take our horses, groom them, and are, absolutely, going to fight our battles for us.'[11] Many of these horses were quite untrained, and it seemed that those that were understood only one movement, that of retreating in face of the enemy.[12] With them came saddles

'of a rough description, mostly an old French cavalry pattern,

> with no means of attaching the carbines. The bits were of a very severe kind, the Mameluke bit. No heel-ropes and a very few headropes came with the horses, no nose-bags, and altogether,' according to the regimental historian, 'very little kit. Admiral Sir William Hewett and the officers and men of the fleet rendered the greatest assistance in every matter and helped to remedy all the deficiencies. Sailmakers were landed, who set to work to make nose-bags, head- and heel-ropes. The *main-tack* of HMS *Euryalus* was cut up into lengths of long rope for picketing in standing camp, and carbine buckets were improvised by cutting a hole through the shoe cases, through which the carbines were passed, the muzzles fitting into a small leather bucket that the Egyptians had used.'[13]

Among the troops which came from Cairo were the 19th Hussars, 477 in number, with 395 horses, many of which were small Syrian Arabs procured from the Egyptian cavalry.[14] The rest of the brigade was made up of mounted infantry drawn from various regiments of foot.* These, too, were issued with Egyptian army ponies, all stallions, 'such brutes most of 'em to look at,' wrote Lieutenant Percival Marling of the 60th, 'but I fancy they are better than they look.' The ship in which they travelled from Suez

> 'had no horse fittings whatsoever. We just tied the horses up to the ship's rail, where they fought and bit one another . . . Seven horses got loose and galloped up and down the deck. One nearly knocked me over, and another all but jumped overboard. One fell down the companion, and, wonderful to say, was not damaged except for a few bits of skin knocked off.'

In the camp set up at Trinkitat all drinking water had to come from the Red Sea via the condensing plants aboard the ships. Marling saw it, on occasion, pouring into 'the canvas horse troughs so hot that although the horses were almost mad with thirst we had to take them away for ten minutes to let it cool.'[15]

* * *

At about 8.15 on 29 February Graham advanced his force in the

* 'General Stewart loved the MI, and although a cavalry man himself, he always put us in front of the 10th and 19th Hussars; he said he liked our long rifles. In those days, except at close range, the cavalry shooting was rotten.' (Marling, 116.)

formation of a rectangle 'having an interior space of about 200 × 150 yards'.[16] The sides contained the infantry (about 3,000); in the angles were placed the eight seven-pounder and six Gatling machine guns, and in the centre the animals carrying ammunition and medical supplies. The front and left were covered by the first squadron of the 10th Hussars and some 120 of the mounted infantry, marching in a wide semi-circle about a mile in advance. On the right was a troop of the 19th Hussars. The rest of the mounted element was in the rear, forming a compact body, the other squadrons of the 10th in the front line and the rest of the 19th in the second and third. The orders for the cavalry issued the previous day read as follows:

> 'The mounted troops will operate outside the square. In case of attack the cavalry must avoid masking, or galloping in the line of fire in any way, and keeping generally clear of the infantry action. When the enemy is in retreat the cavalry will follow in pursuit at the discretion of the O.C. Cavalry Brigade [Stewart], who will exercise all necessary precautions, keeping his men well in hand and falling back if any serious resistance is made or on reaching any ground difficult for cavalry to move over.'[17]

The enemy, estimated at about 6,000 men, was discovered on a hill a quarter of a mile from the site of the first battle of El Teb, in a strong entrenched position, surrounded in places by high mimosa bush. Well sited in this position were four Krupp guns, two mountain guns and one Gatling gun. These had been taken (together with numerous small arms and much ammunition) from Baker's ill-fated force twenty-five days previously.

As the rectangle came under fire, Graham moved it to the right so as to attack the enemy's left flank. The British guns then came into action, and some forty minutes later, the enemy's guns being silenced, the rectangle lumbered slowly forward again towards the ridge. As it did so, the enemy, armed chiefly with sword and long spear, dashed at it in small groups with reckless bravery, usually being mown down some yards from it, but on occasion actually reaching the British bayonets before succumbing. Thus, fighting at every step, the British infantry eventually captured the whole position with its seven guns.

Well before this moment, probably after the first of the two enemy gun emplacements had been taken by the infantry, Stewart, thinking, it is supposed, that the part of the main body which he now saw retreating from the ridge comprised the sum total of the enemy, gave the order for the cavalry to advance. Without delay the first two lines swept round the south of the ridge, accompanied by cheers from the victorious infantry. For some distance, some say as much as three miles, they drove the enemy before them. The details of what happened next remain obscure. Graham in his despatch says that the enemy 'in large numbers . . . attacked the flanks of the lines, so that they had to change front in order to shake them off' and that 'the charges actually made were upon masses of the enemy not yet engaged with the infantry.'[18] Of this there can be no doubt, but whether Stewart was aware of the presence of these fresh enemy masses when he ordered the advance is not certain. If he was not, he probably ought to have been. If he was, he was clearly disobeying his orders. The historian of the 10th Hussars, Lieutenant-Colonel R. S. Liddell, who was present as second-in-command of his regiment, states that 'the brigade . . . having cleared the position in the front, took a few prisoners and was in the act of driving in some cattle when intelligence was brought that the left squadron of the 19th Hussars, echeloned in rear, had been attacked in flank by a body of Arabs who had suddenly sprung up out of the grass and nullahs.'[19] The historian of the 19th Hussars states that

> 'it was found necessary to return to encounter a large body of the enemy . . . passed in the broken ground and that now interposed between [the brigade] and the infantry. The 10th Hussars, and two squadrons of the 19th under Lieutenant-Colonel Barrow charged a large body of Arabs composed of horsemen [estimated at about 130[20] carrying two-handed swords, and riding bare-backed[21]], men on camels and footmen, and at once became involved in a desperate hand to hand conflict. This body of Arabs had not been engaged with our infantry, and were quite fresh.'[22]

Lieutenant-Colonel Coghill of the 19th (see p. 279) described events as he saw them.

> 'Briefly, the 10th were in 1st line. My wing in 2nd line and [Lieutenant-Colonel A. G.] Webster's wing in 3rd line. Webster's wing got separated – not long after that we wheeled about and by glorious luck we became 1st line and still better came upon a large mass of the enemy. The leader of the 1st line

was not long in communicating his views to the Brigadier [who] you may be sure [was] not long in preparing for attack. There was no hurry or confusion. When we did go the men rode straight and well and deserve all the credit that they have received. My one thought you may be sure was the regiment. We lost rather severely but I think all were ready to lay down their little all.'[23]

Barrow himself nearly laid down his 'little all' for he was very severely wounded in the mêlée. A spear, passing through his arm, entered his side. Surrounded by the enemy as he was, he must have been killed had not Quartermaster-Sergeant William Marshall ridden to his assistance. Marshall took him by the hand and, supported by Sergeant Fenton and Trooper Boseley, 'running in this fashion, in rear of the charging squadrons, Barrow, with the heavy spear swaying to and fro in his side, managed to get free of the enemy before he sank down. His attendant trumpeter, in spite of sixteen terrible wounds, kept his horse going, and escaped from the press, to die of his injuries later.'[24] For his gallantry Marshall was awarded the Victoria Cross. Of those in the regiment who lost their mounts, Barrow and a Corporal Murray were the only two to survive. Murray, it seems, remounted himself three times, but each of his four horses was either speared, clubbed or hamstrung.[25]

The 10th Hussars had experiences similar to those of the 19th. Liddell says that the two regiments charged again and again but that

'the ground in many places was covered with high mimosa bush, the thorns of which the horses avoided, and as this caused gaps in the ranks, opportunities were given to the active enemy of rushing out from their hiding-places and of ham-stringing the horses and stabbing their riders. In this manner Major Slade, 10th Hussars, while wheeling his squadron from the flank, was attacked by several Arabs on all sides and killed. Lieutenant Probyn [a nephew of Sir Dighton Probyn] (attached to the Tenth [from the 9th Bengal Cavalry]), who, as he entered the action, had asked special permission to exchange his position of serrefile to ride in front of the squadron, was also killed; but from the appearance of his sword afterwards it was seen that some of his opponents had paid dearly for their success. Sergeant J. Cox, too, as fine a soldier as ever served in the regiment, who often had carried off the regimental prize for swordsmanship, thinking he saw a good opportunity, left the flank of his squadron, and charged a group of savages, but being overpowered by numbers he lost his life. Three private soldiers of the Tenth were killed in these charges and several wounded.'[26]

There were a number of personal encounters. That of Trooper Hayes, a bandsman of the 10th Hussars and a well known pugilist, stands out particularly. Failing, probably because his horse was too unsteady, to get at his adversaries with their large hippopotamus-hide shields, he coolly dismounted, dispatched some with his sword and others with his fists before mounting again. A year later he received the Distinguished Service Medal from the hands of the Queen herself.[27]

When an enemy failed to hamstring a horse, he often tried to spear it, sometimes throwing his weapon from a distance. The Sudanese spears were rather like the Zulus' assegais (see p. 183), except that they were weighted with a roll of iron at the end of the shaft. This gave them greater momentum. Boomerang-like clubs made of mimosa wood were carried by some of the Arabs. By throwing these at the legs of the British mounts, they were brought, poor, miserable brutes, to their knees.

On Barrow being wounded, his line was taken over by Captain Jenkins, the next senior officer available, but he was almost immediately engaged by three of the enemy at the same time, his horse being wounded thrice and he himself once. This deprivation of its leaders by the 19th's first line, just at the moment when large, fresh bodies of the enemy emerged on its right flank, meant that it swept straight on where Barrow would no doubt have wheeled it round to meet the new threat. Stewart

'who was riding somewhat in advance of the left flank of the second line, noting at once the flaw, drove spurs into his horse, and with his staff galloped hard to bring round the erring squadrons. It was a race between this small band, the General and Staff, and a number of the enemy rushing from the right. The former won, and caught up the first line; but in this conflict,' according to Charles Royle, a contemporary historian of the Sudan campaigns, 'during the sweep of the 10th Hussars, as they followed . . ., the chief casualties of the day occurred . . . Of the General's orderlies one was killed and two were wounded.'[28]

After a considerable time, during which both the 10th and the

19th charged again and again without much effect, largely due to the unsteadiness of the Egyptian horses, each of the three lines was forced to dismount some of its men. It was these, firing volley after volley, who eventually persuaded the enemy to melt away into the bush. At about the same time the infantry were finally putting the main body to flight. Over 2,000 corpses of the indomitable Sudanese were said to have been buried 'in the positions captured, irrespective of those killed in the cavalry operations'.[29]

The infantry and artillery lost only ten killed and ninety-four wounded, while the two cavalry regiments' casualties totalled twenty killed and forty-eight wounded.* This works out at about one man in every eight engaged. Graham in his despatch made it as clear as he possibly could without resorting to actual censure that Stewart committed a major error of judgement. Posterity, from the evidence available, can but concur. It seems very doubtful whether these charges, executed with exemplary dash, contributed anything of real value to the infantry's victory. It appears probable that more damage would have been done if a proper pursuit had been carried out once the infantry had completed their work, and when the enemy was in full flight. Indeed Stewart when that time came had to report to Graham 'that his horses were too much exhausted to pursue the enemy'.[30]

Though the little Egyptian horses, not more than 14.2 hands high, were difficult to control, and though their lack of weight, size and pace limited their efficiency in action, their powers of endurance were remarkable. By the end of the battle they had gone for nearly twenty-four hours without water, and yet they showed little sign of fatigue. This is all the more remarkable since they were carrying weights of seventeen or eighteen stone.[31] Nevertheless they, as well as their riders, were glad to drink at the captured wells of El Teb. When they had thus quenched their thirst, they made their way back to Trinkitat by the quickest route. This unfortunately took them over the field of the first battle of El Teb. The stench was still so appalling from the thousands of decaying Egyptian corpses that several of the hussars were sick over their saddle-bows.[32]

* * *

* *10th Hussars:* killed: 2 officers, 4 other ranks; wounded: 1 officer, 5 other ranks.

19th Hussars: killed: 1 officer, 13 other ranks; wounded: 2 officers, 20 other ranks.

Tamai, 13 March 1884

After the relief of Tokar, which took place without further fighting, Graham's force sailed for Suakin. When the mounted infantry began to disembark, Lieutenant Marling says: 'We just chucked the ponies into the sea, and a dismounted party caught them as they got to shore.'[33]

Graham's next objective was Tamai where Osman Digna was in person. On 13 March he fought a bloody battle in which two infantry brigade rectangles advanced in echelon. He lost 109 officers and men killed and 112 wounded before victory was his. At one moment, due it is believed to orders not being properly heard, gaps occurred in the sides of one of the rectangles. Through these the enemy penetrated.* Stewart at once ordered part of his 700 mounted troops to gallop forward and dismount so as to pour volleys into the flank of the Arabs as they streamed into the rectangle. This action certainly helped to avert what looked like turning into a catastrophe.

Except for a few further skirmishes and the burning of rebel villages, the campaign was over. It had not achieved any permanent result. It had shaken but not destroyed Osman Digna. The beleagured garrisons had been rescued, but the Government's policy of 'rescue and retire' made it too easy for the Mahdi's followers to convince themselves that they had driven the British out of the eastern Sudan, although, of course, the base at Suakin was still retained. By the end of March Graham's force had re-embarked for Cairo on the orders of Gladstone's government. A large number of lives had been lost virtually to no purpose. In the course of the succeeding year the small force of Royal Marines, shut up within their camping lines, were over 300 times under fire. Osman Digna remained master of the entire surrounding district.[34] Charles Royle believed that

> 'after the victory of Tamai Graham could have sent a few squadrons of cavalry through to Berber with ease, and he was anxious to do so. Two squadrons would, in the opinion of all the authorities in the Soudan, have sufficed to open the road and to save Berber, which was the key to the Soudan,

* The Gardner machine gun had jammed, which did not help at this critical moment. The same gun also jammed at Abu Klea ten months later. (See p. 335.) The Gardner machine gun, invented by the American, Captain W. M. Gardner, took various forms. This one had five rifled barrels, each of .45 inch calibre. These were loaded and fired by means of a crank. It was supposed to fire 357 rounds a minute.

and without the retention of which evacuation was hopeless.'[35]

This last statement is open to doubt, but at one time it seems to have been the opinion of Gordon too. Graham always regretted that he had not sent Stewart forward to Berber on his own responsibility instead of telegraphing for approval which was refused. It is the present writer's view, however, that such a dash for Berber, across a waterless desert, would have been far too risky a venture.

In little more than a year Graham was back at Suakin, once again charged with the destruction of Osman Digna. How he fared will be shown in due course.

'The Queen trembles for General Gordon's safety. If anything befalls *him*, the result will be awful.'

QUEEN VICTORIA to Mr Gladstone,
9 February, 1884

'Late, late, so late! but we can enter still.
Too late, too late! ye cannot enter now.'

TENNYSON, *Guinevere*[1]

(ii)

The Gordon Relief Expedition, 1884–1885 (I)

After Tel el-Kebir Lord Wolseley had resumed his duties as Adjutant-General in London. From there, as early as March, 1884, he warned the cabinet that Gordon was in great danger at Khartoum. In this he was strongly seconded by Baring in Cairo. Both men pointed out that he would be unable to evacuate that city since the Mahdists were closing in upon it. He would certainly be unwilling to return alone, without the garrisons he had been sent to rescue. They pressed, therefore, for an expedition to 'relieve' him.*

* Since it was probable that Gordon would refuse to come away, with or without the men, women and children he had been sent to rescue, the Khedive was told to give Wolseley a secret firman allowing him, if necessary, to supersede the reluctant Gordon.

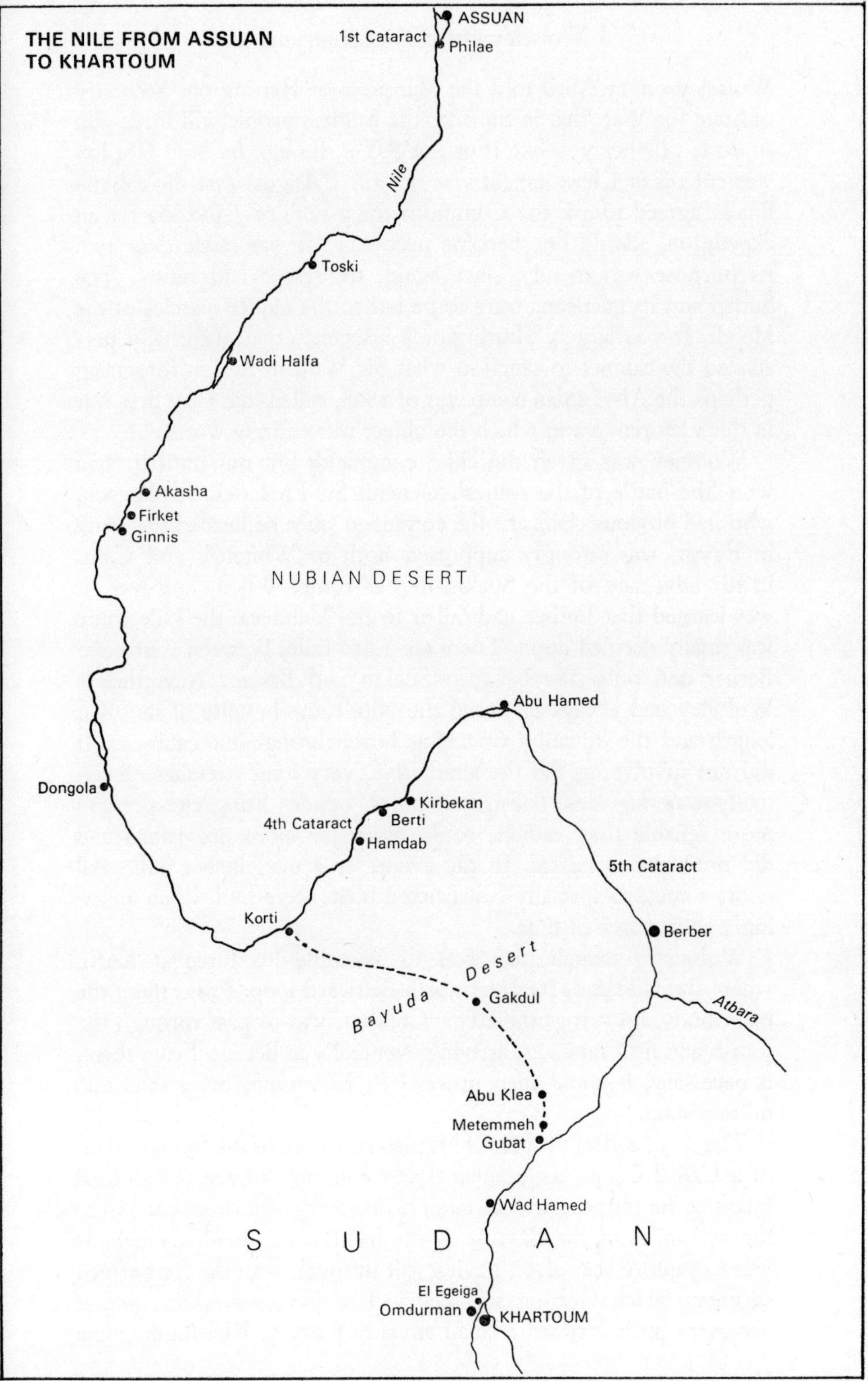
THE NILE FROM ASSUAN TO KHARTOUM
ASSUAN
1st Cataract
Philae
Nile
Toski
Wadi Halfa
Akasha
Firket
Ginnis
NUBIAN DESERT
Abu Hamed
Dongola
Kirbekan
Berti
4th Cataract
Hamdab
5th Cataract
Korti
Berber
Bayuda Desert
Gakdul
Atbara
Abu Klea
Metemmeh
Gubat
Wad Hamed
S U D A N
El Egeiga
Omdurman
KHARTOUM

Map 16

Wolseley on 13 April told the Marquess of Hartington, Secretary of State for War, that in the end 'the English people will force you to do it whether you like it or not'.[2] Yet, though by May Gordon was cut off in Khartoum, it was not till 1 August that the cabinet finally agreed to ask the Commons for a vote of £300,000 for an expedition, should one become necessary. It was made clear that its purpose was merely, once again, to 'rescue and retire'. The Sudan and its garrisons were to be left to the tender mercies of the Mahdi. It was largely Hartington's insistence that eventually persuaded the cabinet to sanction what Sir William Butler, forgetting perhaps the Abyssinian campaign of 1868, called 'the very first war in the Victorian era in which the object was entirely worthy'.[3]

Wolseley was given the chief command, but not until he had won 'the battle of the routes'. General Sir Frederick Stephenson, who had obvious claims to the command since he headed the army in Egypt, was strongly supported both in Whitehall and Cairo in his advocacy of the Suakin-Berber route. When, however, it was learned that Berber had fallen to the Mahdists, the Nile route was finally decided upon. There are 1,650 miles between Cairo and Berber and only 280 between Suakin and Berber. Nevertheless Wolseley had always favoured the Nile route in spite of its great length and the difficulty of taking boats through the cataracts. It did not involve, as did the alternative, very long stretches of virtually waterless desert. Further, boats, besides being cheaper and more reliable than camels, could carry far more provisions and did not have to be fed. In the event, by a magnificent industrial effort some 800 specially constructed boats were built in an amazingly short space of time.

Wolseley's overall plan was to assemble his force at Korti, where the Nile ends its great north-eastward loop. From there the main body, known as the River Column, was to pass through the fourth and fifth cataracts, arriving eventually at Berber. From there, if necessary, it could then proceed to Khartoum, more than 200 miles distant.

The more audacious part of his plan consisted of the formation of of a Camel Corps, as 'a small flying column'[4] to act as mounted infantry. Its purpose was to take, if necessary, the short-cut across the 176 miles of the Bayuda desert from Korti to Metemmeh. It was to capture that place, having got in touch with the four armed steamers which Gordon was believed to have sent there, and if necessary push forward a small advance party to Khartoum, some

46. Egyptian cavalry cleaning their arms on board a transport

47. Captain Lord Charles Beresford, RN

48. Hampshire Carabiniers coming off the chain ferry at East Cowes on their way to mount guard at Osborne House, c. 1895

49. Kitchener: Pastel by C. M. Horsfall, 1899

50. Battle of Omdurman, 2 September 1898: gunboat saving the Camel Corps from destruction

100 miles further on. It could then either move on to Gordon's rescue if the city's fall seemed imminent, or co-operate with the River Column in a longer term assault upon the beseiging Mahdists.

The camel corps was to be 'raised upon the same principle,' wrote Wolseley, 'that was lately adopted when raising a corps of 200 mounted infantry from the line battalions at home, namely, by obtaining so many men and one or two officers as volunteers.'[5] In the event the mixture of units making up what was known as the Desert Column was truly remarkable. Attached, beside small detachments of the medical, commissariat and transport staffs, were others from the Royal Artillery with three mountain guns, from the Royal Navy with one Gatling machine gun and from the Royal Engineers. The only true cavalry consisted of eight officers and 126 men and 155 horses of the 19th Hussars again under Lieutenant-Colonel Barrow. His men had an average of seven years' service. Most of them had been through the Tel el-Kebir and Suakin campaigns.[6]* Their grey Syrian stallions, as at Suakin, were all under fifteen hands in height, 'hardly deserving the name of horses . . . They seemed,' as an officer noted later in the campaign, 'to thrive on desert air and crumble dry grass'.[7] Brigadier-General (now Sir) Herbert Stewart, who commanded the column, described them as 'the acme of Light Cavalry'.[8]

The mass of the 'camelry', forming what came to be vulgarly known as 'the Nile Circus', comprised four camel regiments totalling some 1,789 officers and men.[9] Three of these regiments were sent out from home. The first, known as the Heavy Camel Regiment, was drawn entirely from the regular cavalry. There were ten detachments. These were found from the 1st and 2nd Life Guards, the Royal Horse Guards (Blues), the 2nd Dragoon Guards (Bays), the 4th and 5th Dragoon Guards, the 1st Dragoons (Royals), the 2nd Dragoons (Scots Greys), and the 5th and 16th Lancers. From each came two officers, two sergeants (or, in the case of the Household Cavalry, one corporal-major and *two* corporals of horse),[10] two corporals, one bugler or trumpeter and thirty-eight men, a total of twenty-three officers and 431 men. The second regiment, which was employed almost exclusively on the lines of communication in the forward areas, was the Light Camel Regiment, numbering twenty-one officers and 388 men from

* When the regiment arrived at Assiout a 'stowaway' was discovered. He was a bandboy and he accounted for himself by saying that he was 'the only *man* in the band without a medal, and he could not stand it'. (Biddulph, 247.)

the 3rd, 4th, 7th, 10th, 11th, 15th, 18th, 20th and 21st Hussars. The third was the Guards' Camel Regiment consisting of 421 officers and men drawn from the seven regiments of Foot Guards and the Royal Marines Light Infantry. The fourth was the Mounted Infantry Camel Corps whose personnel came from the mounted infantry companies of battalions either already serving in Egypt or at home and elsewhere. It numbered altogether about twenty-five officers and 480 men. Each of the four regiments had a staff of commanding officer, adjutant, surgeon and quartermaster. Of the officers in the Household Cavalry contingent, it is socially interesting to note that only one was not a peer or the son of a peer.

The men chosen were all volunteers and had to be at least twenty-two years old. They were meant to be marksmen or first-class shots, medically fit and 'of as good character as possible'.[11] Nevertheless Lord Cochrane of the 2nd Life Guards, though he found them 'a magnificent lot', had to admit that the opportunity was taken 'of getting rid of a few who were continually in the guard-room for drunkenness, as the Colonel [John Stephenson Ferguson] said they would be all right out there on the Nile water.'[12]

The Duke of Cambridge, the Commander-in-Chief, when he heard of these proposals (which Wolseley wisely did not send home until he was safely at sea), declared them to be 'outrageous'. Nevetheless, since the government sanctioned them as necessary if Gordon was to be saved, the Duke did not see how they could 'be refused with propriety'.[13] His suggestion that as an alternative a regiment of hussars and a battalion of rifles should be converted into a camal corps was not accepted.[14] The Duke's cousin, the Queen, told Hartington that she believed 'that the system of breaking up regiments had been condemned as unsound, and she would therefore be glad to learn the reasons for reverting to this principle. And whether, if further reinforcements are called for, the regiments at home can furnish the men for service and at the same time maintain their efficiency for duty.' The Secretary of State replied:

> 'The practice which Lord Hartington believes has been condemned as unsound was that of breaking up regiments or battalions for the purpose of raising others about to proceed on foreign service to the necessary strength. The same objections do not appear to apply to forming a special Corps by small drafts under their own officers from regiments at home

which are not likely to be immediately required for active service. There was indeed no other way in which the Cavalry at home, many regiments of which are over their establishment, could be utilised on the present occasion.'[15]

On 9 October Wolseley, who by then had been a month in Egypt, wrote home from Wadi Halfa (nicknamed 'Bloody Halfway' by the troops): 'The great camel corps arrived at Alexandria yesterday. I am anxious to see all the fine gentlemen of H.M. Household Troops dressed in workmanlike fashion moving over the sands of this desert on camels.' Lieutenant Count Gleichen of the Grenadier Guards, one of these 'fine gentlemen', who was adjutant to the Guards' Regiment, thought that the 'workmanlike' uniform 'looked more like the 17th than the 19th century' with the men's 'bandoliers, breeches and stocking-like puttees giving them a look of the last Civil War.'[16]

The brown leather bandoliers, worn over the left shoulder, held fifty rounds of rifle ammunition. The breeches (or pantaloons) were made of yellow-ochre Bedford cord; the puttees (or leg bandages) were dark blue. On the head was worn a khaki-coloured pith helmet, which in the case of the Heavy Regiment had a dark edging to the pagri wound around it. The ends of these pagris came down behind the helmets, forming 'neck-protectors'. A corporal and a trooper of the 2nd Life Guards were not alone in losing theirs. To this carelessness Lord Cochrane attributed their becoming 'affected by the sun. They were never really right afterwards,' he wrote. 'Corporal Kerr when he returned home drowned himself in the Thames at Windsor, and Trooper Smith blew his brains out with a carbine in London.'[17]

In Egypt grey serge jumpers (or loose tunics) were always worn, though the men also had with them red serge ones. A brown waistbelt, with a pouch attached, holding twenty rounds, a haversack and brown ankle boots completed the uniform. The men carried in their valises 'goggles, veil, drawers, cholera-belt, Prayer Book, housewife, spurs (which were never once used), spare pair of boots, shirts, socks, and all the usual paraphernalia of a man's kit.' No greatcoat was taken but a spare rolled blanket and a waterproof sheet were carried on the saddle, as also was a *tente d'abri* – one for every two men. In two canvas and red leather saddlebags (or *zuletahs*) were carried a further 100 rounds, a leather water bottle (or *mussek*) holding three quarts and a six-gallon water-skin (or *gerbah*), which, unless it let 'it all leak out in half-an-hour, made the water beautifully cool'. The arms carried were a rifle in a Namaqua rifle-bucket, 'for attaching to the saddle, the rifle being placed in it butt foremost', as used by the mounted infantry in South Africa at this date. The rifles were Martini-Henrys, which by the mid-1880s were a little old-fashioned. They possessed none of the advantages of 'the powerful Lee-Mitford rifle, with its smokeless powder, its magazine action, and its absence of recoil'.[18] In all, the weight carried by a camel was often not less than 350 lbs.

The officers looked much the same as the men, except that they generally wore long field boots instead of puttees. Their arms, beside their swords, usually consisted of an Enfield or an Adams revolver, or a two- or four-barrelled pistol of larger calibre. This was attached to a brown leather waistbelt with shoulder-braces. During the voyage out, the officers and men amused themselves by cutting out red cloth distinguishing badges with their regimental initials and numbers on them. These they sewed to their jumper sleeves above the right elbow.[19]

'A good deal of amusement was caused and some chaff excited,' one of the headquarters staff recorded, 'by Wolseley's demand for 1,000 white umbrellas to protect the Camel Corps riders against the heat of the coming summer.'[20] Further amusement was caused by the adoption of the old Clan Campbell march. Naturally enough the first line was altered to 'The Camels are Coming'.

With the remarkable feats of organization which brought the expeditionary force, racing against time, nature and the narrowness of the Nile valley, to points from which active operations could begin, we are not concerned. It is enough to say that the addition of the Camel Corps considerably increased the already formidable difficulties of supply. It added nearly 2,000 extra mouths to be fed, the owners of which 'could not do a stroke of work towards carrying their own food to the fighting base.'[21] The first major difficulty encountered by the Corps concerned the provision of camels. The Desert Column was to suffer much hardship from an insufficiency of animals. Colonel Sir Charles Wilson, chief of the Intelligence department, the star member of which was young Captain Herbert Kitchener, was blamed for the muddles which stopped the buying of camels prematurely.[22] But there is little doubt that Major-General Sir Redvers Buller, as he had now become, Wolseley's chief of staff, must shoulder the largest part of the blame, if, indeed, the problem was ever solvable in the time available. The provision of enough camel forage, too, proved difficult. Owing to its bulk, it could not be brought from lower Egypt, while local sources in the Korti area were 'far from being abundant'.[23] In the end, for the whole force, nearly 8,000 camels of all types were bought. They cost on average £13 6s 11d each,[24] really good ones being bought for £16 and more. Captain Lord Charles Beresford, RN, for instance, paid £24 for his famous racing camel 'Bimbashi'. He claimed that it could trot sixteen miles in an hour.[25] Such first-class specimens as this, of which only a very few were available, came from Arabia. They were extraordinarily swift.

> 'Their pace is so smooth,' wrote Gleichen, 'that the test at the Mecca Tattersall's is for the rider to carry a full cup of coffee at full trot; if he spills any it is considered that the animal is under-bred. The Delta camels were the weakest, though not the smallest, whilst the steeds selected for us came mostly from the parts round about. They were a nice-looking set of beasts, and we were of course very particular to have the pick of the lot; sore-backed ones were exchanged and camel after camel sent back for (sometimes imaginary) weaknesses, till the officer in charge vowed he'd exchange no more.'[26]

The home authorities were abysmally ignorant about camels. Nor, apparently, did they try to remedy this by asking those who were not, such as the authorities in India. Had they bothered to do so Lieutenant Percival Marling of the Mounted Infantry would not have written, 'The War Office are a weird lot. They have sent us out two farrier sergeants and two shoeing smiths to shoe the camels!!! and two rough-riding sergeants from the cavalry to teach us how to ride camels. One of them told me he had never seen a camel, not even in the Zoo, till he got to Egypt.'[27]

The difference between a 'baggager' and a riding camel (known as a dromedary or a *hygeem*)* was enormous in every respect – as much, according to Lieutenant Adye, who was on Wolseley's staff, 'as there is between a thoroughbred and a dray horse'. He found a really good riding camel 'far preferable to a horse' for a long-distance ride at five or six miles an hour.[28] But an officer who had to ride a camel at least as much as Adye declared at the end of

* Dromedary is the name for a light, fleet breed of camel, specially trained for riding. The term is usually applied to the Arabian or one-humped riding camel, but is also sometimes used to describe a particularly agile type of the only other species, the Bactrian or two-humped camel.

the campaign: 'If you ever want to know the pleasure of being on a horse try 1,000 miles on a camel!'[29]

A cavalry officer who knew the camel well in India thought that little could be said to his advantage.

> 'He is not a lovable beast,' wrote Robert Baden-Powell. '"'E's a devil an' an ostrich an' a orphan-child in one." He has, however, one supreme quality – philosophy. He is the most stolid of beings, apparently entirely indifferent as to what is going on round him so long as he can chew the cud and curl his lips in contempt at men. Wounds he will accept with philosophic calm, merely giving expression to a grunt or an annoyed gurgle when he finds that his inside has been perforated by a bullet, and this is the only sign he makes. Such an animal is extremely useful in war.'

Gleichen found that camels were 'really delicate animals' who suffered from

> 'all sorts of unknown ailments if carelessly looked after. When taken down to the river, some would look aimlessly about, exhausting the patience of the men by not drinking for ten minutes, or more, and sometimes not drinking at all if the least jostled. They used to get colds in their noses, too, at night, especially the flank ones; sometimes they caught colds if the saddles were removed too soon; sometimes, also, they fought in the lines; and got their ropes into fearful confusion. They used to break away at times, and wander all over the lines, causing great sorrow to their riders, who came to seek them, and they were not. Besides this, on the march a camel would occasionally go slower and slower, and at last kneel down without warning, refusing to get up; no examination would discover the seat of the sickness or injury (if any), so he was whacked till he did go on. Altogether they were a sad trouble.'[30]

Another problem which early faced the Camel Corps was the provision of riding saddles. The Egyptian war department was quite unable to produce the number required in the time. Ready-made saddles for sale hardly existed. To make the approved, long-lasting, but rather heavy 'mounted infantry' pattern, which required iron as well as wood, skilled artificers were needed. These were few in number, but there were just enough to make sufficient saddles for the officers. For the men the lighter, all-wooden, cheaper and easier to manufacture 'knifeboard' pattern was constructed in adequate numbers by the Egyptian ordnance department. This saddle had no regular seat, but a blanket placed under the covering pad made it comfortable enough. Being narrower than the mounted infantry saddle it allowed a better grip to be taken by the legs. Its chief drawback was that the rawhide girths and straps became very brittle in the dry climate. They could only be 'kept going by a liberal application of grease.' In due course the bindings too gave way. These were soon replaced by telegraph binding wire. This 'turned out excellently, and in no case,' according to the expedition's official historian, 'did a saddle during the campaign require rebinding.'[31]

Camel harness consisted of a black leather headstall. There was no bit in the mouth. The rein, made of rope, was about seven feet long, attached to an iron curb-chain under the lower lip, not in the mouth. It also served for tethering or for knee-lashing. This was achieved by tying one of the kneeling animal's forelegs to its neck. In double knee-lashing both forelegs were thus fettered.

Lord Cochrane found the first mounted parades most amusing to watch. He observed 'two or three of the camels going off with their riders, who soon succeeded in getting into laughable positions, hanging on by one leg with heads down.'[32] Count Gleichen gave advice to beginners as to how to effect the 'exciting work' of mounting a frisky animal. 'Having made your camel kneel by clearing your throat loudly at him and tugging at his rope, shorten your rein till you bring his head round to his shoulder, put your foot in the stirrup, and throw your leg over. With his head jammed like that, he cannot rise, and must wait till you give him his head.'[33]

The basis of the 'Camel Drill' which Stewart had evolved after much trial and error, was, of course, that of the infantry. Some of the cavalry officers 'said they would be d——d if they would learn infantry drill, and I'm afraid,' wrote Cochrane, 'they did not like doing it, but they did it all the same. Cavalry dismounted drill is too loose a formation for working in a square, also when mixed up with infantry one drill is advisable, and that must necessarily be the one practiced by infantry.'[34] The principle of the drill was, as Gleichen put it, 'to jam the camels into a square mass, and flank them by squares of men at one or two opposite corners; if necessary to act away from the camels, to leave simply enough men to defend them, and manoeuvre freely as Infantry.'[35]

Considerable proficiency in camel drill was gained during the two weeks of waiting at Korti. At one field day, with Wolseley looking on, two regiments were marching in columns of companies, extending over 500 yards in length. On being given the 'command "close order, right front, left rear", the front halted, the rear companies closed up, the camels [were] knee-lashed, two squares [were formed] flanking the camels, in one minute and a half, the time being taken,' reported one young sublatern, 'by several watches on the ground.'[36]

To test the reaction of camels, they were fired *into* with blank cartridges and *over* with ball. There were 'no visible results'. At one brigade drill, the 19th Hussars charged a mass of unprotected animals, cheering and yelling.

> 'Everybody,' wrote Gleichen, 'expected to see them break their ropes and career wildly over the desert. The only result was that one solitary camel struggled to his feet, looked round, and knelt down again; the others never moved an eyelid . . . The general opinion was that they would stand charging niggers or anything else in creation with equanimity . . . We came to the conclusion that it was want of brains, *pur et simple*, that caused our steeds to behave thus docilely; any other animal with a vestige of a mind would have been scared to death, but, as it was, no one regretted their deficiency.'[37]

The days of waiting were occupied with field days on camel-back and by 'stables' three times a day. This consisted chiefly 'in picking the ticks out of the camel's hide'. When Wolseley inspected the Corps at least ten men fell off at the trot. On that occasion the Mounted Infantry element, 'thinking no small beer' of themselves, as Lieutenant Marling put it, 'wore the largest possible spurs'. Wolseley would have none of it. He ordered them to be removed at once. 'There was nearly a mutiny at the order. Fancy,' commented Marling, 'wearing spurs on a camel!!'[39]

* * *

Based on what little information was percolating through from Khartoum, the Commander-in-Chief decided at the end of December that the Desert Column must be employed in the emergency for which it had been created. Gordon's danger seemed too great to await the River Column's lengthy progress over 400 miles of the rapidly falling Nile. The idea was that Captain Lord Charles

Beresford and about thirty Royal Navy seamen who had been ordered to accompany the Column, were to man Gordon's armed steamers. When they reached Metemmeh they would dash the ninety-six miles to Khartoum, where it was fondly believed (chiefly by Gordon), the sight of a few redcoats would frighten off the besiegers. When the River Column eventually arrived at Metemmeh it would be able to replenish the Desert Column's supplies and effect the final relief of Khartoum.

At three o'clock in the afternoon of 30 December the Desert Column set off, moving forty camels abreast. The force was neither as complete nor as self-sufficient as had been planned. Some of the units had not yet reached Korti, and, as has been shown, there was a grave lack both of camels and of camel forage. Because of this, it was impossible for the Column to march direct to Metemmeh in a body with the necessary supplies. Instead, the body to which Wolseley, standing alone on a little knoll, now waved goodbye, was a mere convoy, sent to the wells of Gakdul, there to form the most important of a number of staging posts. The camels which carried the men there were to return to bring on more men and supplies.

Indeed, for the whole duration of the enterprise, there were camel trains continually passing to and fro across the desert. A typical convoy was that which left Korti for Gakdul on 7 January, escorted by three sections of the Light Camel Regiment. 790 camels carried general supplies; 100 were laden with small arms ammunition, eighty with medical and thirty with artillery stores.[40] Had the Column been able to press straight on, it is clear that Metemmeh would have been entered virtually unopposed. As it was, all the shuffling back and forth necessary to the build-up of the force gave time for news of its approach to spread and for the concentration not only of the local tribesmen but also of reinforcements sent by the Mahdi from the Khartoum area.

Six local guides had left earlier in the day, escorted by a small party of the 19th Hussars. The rest of the regiment's contingent, consisting of two officers and thirty-two other ranks with forty horses, after providing a rearguard of twelve men, preceded the main body of the column. 'Coming to a plain with hills in the distance,' observed Gleichen, 'you'd see various specks on the tops of the furthest hills, and with the help of your glasses discover them to be the 19th, scouting quite magnificently.'[41] For artillery there were three seven-pound screw guns. Three powerful camels carried one gun and its ammunition between them. 100 rounds per gun were taken. With the Naval Brigade were a Gardner gun and 1,000 rounds.

Of the 2,195 camels, over 650 carried the commissariat and medical stores, including litters and cacolets for the sick and wounded. The 'natives' – in fact mostly Aden and Somali boys 'clothed in a red turban, a blue jersey, a haversack, and a brass ticket – nothing more'[42] – numbered over 200, while, including the staff, the Europeans numbered seventy-eight officers and 1,029 other ranks.

The Heavy and Light Camel Regiments acted as transport, each camel carrying 230 lbs and one man leading three camels.[43] Each officer's and man's baggage was limited to what he could carry on his camel. This was not to exceed forty pounds. It included, as Gleichen pointed out,

> 'a change of tunic, pair of boots, sponge, towel, soap, pair of socks, and a shirt; what more *could* you want? If you were extravagant enough to want a bath, a hole in the sand lined with your waterproof sheet made a beautiful one; with that and one blanket rolled on the near side, and another blanket and your great-coat on the off-side, you had heaps of room in your zuleetahs for any amount of luxuries in the shape of French novels, sketch-books, and other articles of toilet. Half-a-dozen spare camels carried the men's cooking pots, rations, water and our mess saucepans, and *voila tout*.'[44]

On the second day out, according to Lieutenant Marling, 'officers and men had *one pint* each of water served out to them. It was measured out like liquid gold. Also one pint for their dinners at 1.30.' Four days later he wrote: 'We lie out every night just like animals, in the open. The only preparation we made was to scratch a hole in the sand to fit one's hip and thigh into.'[45]

Eleven days later Marling reported that the camels were 'breaking down in all directions, and the native drivers falling down and shrieking for water.' By 16 January the camels had fearful sores on their humps. 'I could put my fist into some of the holes, and they get full of the most loathsome maggots . . . As the camels lost condition . . . their humps got smaller and smaller, and the saddles didn't fit.' It is said that Beresford's naval bosun reported to him: 'I've caulked all them sick camel seams, sir'. Asked what this meant, Lord Charles replied, 'Oh, he's been stuffing oakum and tar into the camels' sore backs.'[46] Beresford's own way with an exhausted camel was to treat it 'as I would a tired hunter, which, after a long day, refuses its food.' He would feed the beast 'by handfuls, putting them upon a piece of cloth or canvas, instead of throwing the whole ration upon the ground at once.' An officer of the 5th Lancers noticed that 'a camel would be going slower and slower until the tail of the animal in front, to which he was tied, looked like coming off; then he would stop for a second, give a mighty shiver and drop down stone dead.' Beresford, realizing that it was 'a case of a man's life or a camel's suffering,' when he came across a fallen camel, 'had it hove upright with a gun-pole, loaded men upon it, and so got them over another thirty or forty miles' until the poor beast finally died.[47]

Life with the Desert Column, however, was not all grim. A lieutenant of artillery met at one halting-place a cavalry officer: 'One Captain Brabazon, known to many as "Bwab", a very fine specimen of the military dandy . . . He amused me very much by pulling a beautiful handkerchief from the sleeve of his khaki jacket, upon which a strong odour of "Ess Bouquet", or something like it, floated away on the desert air. In a place and at a time when water was so scarce and transport limited . . . a supply of scent seemed startling.'[48]

* * *

The ninety-eight miles to the Gakdul wells were covered in just sixty-four hours, thirty-three of them employed in actual marching. This was good going, particularly since 'ever and again', as Gleichen reported, 'came a faint bugle sound from the rear, intimating that the baggagers were lagging. The sound was passed on from bugler to bugler, and the order given to halt the column till the rearguard came up.'[49]

With the help of pump and hose, the wells proved adequate. In the days during which the second convoy travelled to and from base, two forts were constructed and a regular camp was laid out. Young Captain Kitchener of the Intelligence Staff failed to obtain news of any Arab force lying between Gakdul and Metemmeh.

Prelude to Abu Klea, 16 January 1885

'I'm pushing Stewart forward as I did I went to the extreme limits of the risks to which a commander should expose his troops.'

WOLSELEY TO HARTINGTON, 16 March, 1885[1]

(iii)

The Gordon Relief Expedition, 1884–1885 (II): Abu Klea – The River Column

By 14 January sufficient supplies had been built up at Gakdul for the Column, now about 1,800 combatants strong, to start the forty-three mile march to the wells of Abu Klea. At about 9 a.m. on 16 January the leading detachment of the 19th Hussars, commanded by Major John French (see p. 78), observed a small party of Arabs on camels two or three miles to his right front. These he chased up to the wadi which led to the wells. As he rode ahead to reconnoitre, accompanied only by a corporal, more and more Arabs, mostly on foot, came into sight. One of these he managed to seize, whereupon bodies of both mounted and foot Arabs began to converge upon him. 'We had to drop our prisoner and bolt,' said the future Field-Marshal. He had come across the enemy's main position.

Lieutenant-Colonel Barrow, quickly on the scene, as soon as he saw that the Arabs intended to occupy the hills commanding the wells, disposed his small force of horsemen to prevent them doing so. In this, attacked on both flanks by mounted men, the Hussars, by their dismounted fire, were partially successful. The main body some miles behind was immediately informed of the situation by flag signals.[2] 'Well, gentlemen,' said Stewart, 'the enemy is ahead of us! Barrow has exchanged shots with his outposts, and I am going to attack him at once.' One of the war correspondents who heard him, noted 'the tone of quiet determination in which this was uttered,' adding, 'He had that carriage peculiar to cavalrymen when on foot which gives them an air, at any rate, of being bandy-legged. In his hand he carried a short stick with which he sketched in the sand for the direction of his aides-de-camp the formation in which he intended to advance, and they hurried off to carry out his orders.'[3] With his staff he then went forward to reconnoitre. By the time his glasses had revealed to him hundreds of enemy banners barring his way to the wells, it was nearly 2 p.m. Though the need for water was pressing, he decided to wait till morning, forming a zariba meanwhile.

Sleep that night was not easy, for 'as the darkness thickened, there arose that maddening noise of tom-toms, whose hollow and menacing beat, endlessly and pitilessly repeated, haunts those who have heard it to the last day of their lives. Swelling and falling, it sounds now hard at hand, and again far away.'[4] This was accompanied throughout the night by long-range rifle fire whenever any sort of light was shown. Though it did little damage, the Hussar sentries nearest to the hill from which it came (one of whom was hit) wisely retired into the zariba.

At dawn on 17 January the fire increased in intensity and accuracy.

> 'In our front,' wrote Stewart in his despatch, 'the manoeuvring of their troops in line and in column was apparent, and everything pointed to the probability of an attack upon our position being made. Under these circumstances no particular hurry to advance was made, in the hope that our apparent dilatoriness might induce the enemy to push home.'

But the enemy wisely refrained from attacking and before long their rifle fire, combined with the need for water, forced Stewart to advance 'to seize the Abu Klea Wells'.[5]

The square in which the force now moved forward was composed thus:

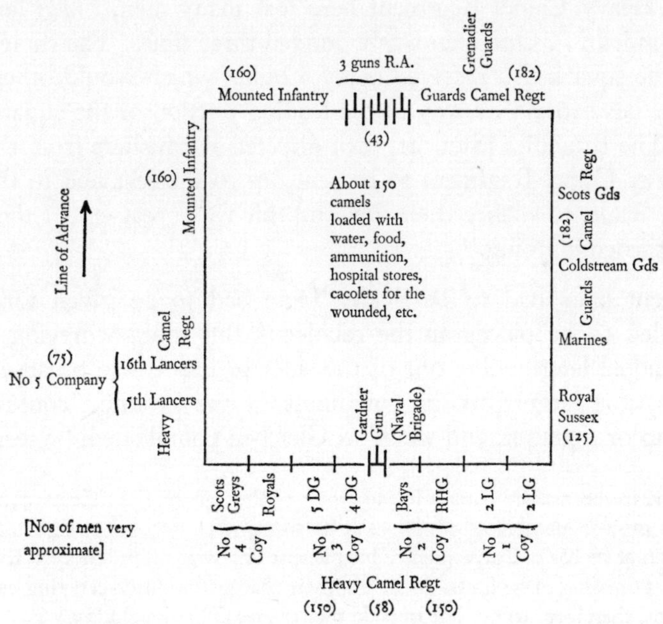

While the square was forming the 19th Hussars seem to have been sent out to head off 'a body of some 500 of the enemy, horsemen and footmen combined'. Where the Hussars were during the following engagement it is impossible to establish, though they were said to have 'helped the square with dismounted fire'.[6] It is most likely that they only returned just as the action was finishing.

The route taken by the square was parallel to, and a few hundred yards from, the wadi which ran to the square's left towards the wells. In this shallow ravine 'grew stunted trees, and thick high grass concealing deep watercourses, giving admirable cover for the enemy.'

> 'Our course,' wrote Lieutenant-Colonel the Hon. R. A. J. Talbot of the 1st Life Guards, commanding the Heavy Camel Regiment, 'was up and down, and across steep hillocks of hard sand, which sloped towards the wadi, and it was commanded by hills to the right and rear occupied by Arab riflemen. It was trying ground for camels, hardly a yard of it being level, and also for the Gardner gun [placed centrally in the rear face of the square], which was hauled by the bluejackets with an energy and activity that deserve all praise.
>
> 'Immediately after leaving the zariba, the enemy's sharpshooters commenced firing . . . chiefly upon the right rear, and the Heavy Camel Regiment here lost many men, killed and wounded . . . One man was wounded three times. The camels in the square also received many a bullet which would otherwise have found its way to the leading portion of the square.
>
> 'The Brigadier [Stewart] then directed skirmishers from the Heavy Camel Regiment to be sent out to the rear and to the rear flanks to silence their fire, and this to a great extent they succeeded in doing.'[7]

Frequent halts had to be made. Time had to be given for the wounded to be placed in the cacolets.* But more worrying was the gradual lengthening out of the sides of the square because the camels, due largely to the roughness of the ground, 'could not keep up or together, and were,' as Gleichen complained, ' a terrible

* Due to the massed camels in the centre of the square, the officers controlling its movements, being of course at its front, were unable to see what was going on at its back. Consequently insufficient time was often left even for the roughest dressing of wounds. Surgeons, their charges and litter-carrying camels were apt, therefore, to get left outside the square. (Dundonald, 37.)

trouble, sometimes throwing the rear face into great confusion.'[8] The impossibility of keeping the rear properly closed up much impaired the formation and therefore the strength – indeed the whole point – of the square. The situation was made worse because the camels, or rather their drivers, tended to sidle away from the enemy's fire on the right rear. They thus pushed out the left corner of the square. To fill up the gap caused there No. 4 Company of the Heavy Camel Regiment (Royals and Scots Greys) had to be moved in part from the rear to the left face. Lord Cochrane noticed (a fact which he later verified) that, as there were were more men on the right than on the left face, the latter was considerably shorter. 'The numbers of companies composing both faces,' he wrote, 'was the same, but they were of different regiments and varied largely in strength; this was a very serious drawback.'[9] Talbot describes what happened next:

> 'After marching for about two miles at a very slow rate, the enemy's flags, which had been visible since leaving the zariba, suddenly became animate, and a large force of Arabs, distant some 500 to 700 yards, sprang up, and advanced as if to attack the left leading corner of the square. The square was at once halted, but immediately afterwards was moved to the right on to a slightly elevated knoll – a simple movement for men, but difficult for camels, many of which remained outside the square when it halted.'[10]

Several of these with their loads of wounded were abandoned by their drivers, who, failing to get them on to their legs, 'bolted into the square to save their own skins. It looked,' wrote Gleichen, 'like certain death for the wounded, and would no doubt have proved so' had not an officer and one or two privates 'gallantly rushed out and hauled several of the camels in by main force just as the Arabs reached the square.'[11]

Beresford, seeing 'the appalling danger' of the opening in the left rear corner (some sixty to eighty yards wide),[12] 'ordered the crew of the Gardner gun to run it outside the square to the left flank.'[13] After firing about seventy rounds the Gardner jammed, just as this very same gun had jammed at Tamai ten months before (see p. 317). Only one of its crew, as well as Beresford himself, survived.

'At this moment,' records Talbot, 'the wadi to our left became alive with Arabs, from which a solid column was seen emerging;

but our skirmishers were still out, and their attention being concentrated upon the enemy's sharp-shooters, with whom they were exchanging shots, they did not soon enough perceive the attack upon the main body.'[14] The skirmishers' tardiness in re-entering the square prevented the men both on the left and in the rear from firing at the dense mass of fast-moving Arabs. 'We in the square,' remembered Marling, 'shouted to the skirmishers to lie down and we would fire over them – as if anyone would lie down with 4,000 —— fuzzy-wuzzies prancing behind them with 6-foot spears. Old Johnny Campbell shouted, "No, no, run like hell," and he was quite right too.

'The skirmishers came running in [crawling on their hands and knees to avoid the bullets of their comrades][15] and only got into the square about 250 yards in front of the enemy.'[16]

Colonel Burnaby, at about this point, in an attempt, it seems, partly to give covering fire for the return of the straggling, hard-pressed skirmishers, and partly to assist Beresford's gun crew, ordered no. 3 Company (4th and 5th Dragoon Guards) to wheel outwards. But no sooner had the gallant Colonel* seen

> 'that, not only on our flanks, but on our rear, the attack was being developed, than he rode in front of the company and shouted to the men to wheel back'.[17] Talbot records that 'the order was obeyed, the men stepping steadily backwards. Before they had got back into their original place, the Arabs were in through the interval thus created and through the gap already existing at the left rear corner of the square.'[18]

Burnaby himself seems to have made no effort to get back inside the square. His biographer relates what happened next:

> 'A furious sheikh charged at him on horseback, spear outstretched, but a bullet from the ranks brought him headlong to the ground before they closed. Tribesmen followed close behind and one dashed at him, pointing a long spear at his throat. Checking his pony and slowly reining back, Burnaby leaned forward in the saddle and parried with his sabre. He fenced calmly and smartly as if he was playing in an assault-at-arms,

* No longer carrying a shotgun as he had at the second battle of El Teb because, as he put it, 'the sentimentalists and their friends at home had made such an outcry on account of it.' (Bennet Burleigh, quoted in Alexander, 195.)

> but the length of his opponent's spear – over eight feet – prevented him from striking back. At that moment another Arab came from the right and with a sudden spring ran his spear-point into Burnaby's shoulder. It was only a prick, but it caused him to turn in his saddle and defend himself from this new quarter. Seeing his Colonel in danger, Corporal Macintosh of the Blues ran out from the square and drove his bayonet into the man's back, but was himself almost immediately speared by the oncoming horde.
>
> 'Burnaby's brief sideways glance gave his opponent the opening he had been waiting for; a heavy spearpoint was driven into his now unguarded throat. He held on for a moment, then fell to the ground. Half a dozen Arabs were immediately upon him, but he somehow got to his feet and with blood spurting from his jugular vein laid about him with desperate sword-strokes.'[19]

Another cavalry officer, Captain C. P. Piggott of the 21st Hussars, known as 'Bloody-minded Piggott', was seen to be creating havoc with a shotgun charged with buskshot, being less concerned than Burnaby with the sentimentalists at home. 'Here's another joker, sir!' a soldier would shout as an Arab popped up from the ground and tried to stab someone in the back, and Piggott would loose off at the emergent head, 'riddling it "like the rose of a watering-can" '.[20]

Running 'as fast as a pony could gallop'[21] the Arabs now hurled themselves 'with terrific rapidity and fury'[22] into the opening of the square. They advanced in dense, oblong columns of spearmen, led by 'either an Emir or Shiek on horseback carrying a flag, and accompanied by mounted attendants'.[23] On the right face of the square, Gleichen, unable to see what was going on at the left rear, assumed that the enemy had been repulsed there, when

> 'suddenly a terrific shock was felt, accompanied by redoubled yells and firing. I found myself lifted off my legs amongst a surging mass of Heavies and Sussex, who had been carried back against the camels by the impetuous rush of the enemy. I forced my way through the jam to see what had happened. Heavies, Sussex, and camels of all sorts were pressing with terrific force on our thin double rank, and it seemed every moment as if it must give; but it didn't.
>
> 'On getting through to the other side of the press, a grue-

some sight was seen. Immediately in front were swarms of Arabs, in desperate hand-to-hand fight with our men, hacking, hewing, hamstringing, and yelling like a crowd of black devils on a ground literally piled up with dead and dying. On the right the Mounted Infantry were pouring in their fire with deadly effect, the niggers falling in hundreds . . . I shouted myself hoarse trying to get the men to aim carefully, but my voice was lost in the din. A rain of bullets whizzed dangerously close past my head from the rifles behind . . . Numbers of the Arabs went down in that hail, and I fear several Englishmen too. Everything depended on the front and right faces standing fast. And well did they stick to it. With the rear rank faced about, the men stubbornly withstood the pressure, and, do what they would, the Arabs could not break the solid masses of men and camels.'[24]*

Indeed it was the camels who largely saved the situation. But for their solid, impassive mass, over and around which the action now raged, there would have been nothing to stop the enemy penetrating straight through and speedily to the inside faces of the square. There is evidence that a number of the British rifles, unlike the .43 Remington single-loaders used by the Madhi's men,† jammed and that some of the bayonets bent.‡ These faults had very little influence upon the outcome of the battle. The organized volleys from the turned-round rear ranks of Mounted Infantry and the Guards on the front and right sides of the square had a devastating effect upon the Arabs. 'They wavered, turned and retreated, not in total flight but slowly and sullenly, so that the riflemen picked many of them off before they disappeared behind the hills.'[25] Thus came to an end what Winston Churchill called 'the most savage and bloody action ever fought in the Sudan by British troops.'[26]

* Lord Cochrane's batman, 'David Gilligan of the 2nd Life Guards, the best and truest man ever born,' as his master wrote, 'was close to me all this time; a Downpatrick man from the north of Ireland, before joining he had been a riveter in Harland & Wolff's yard at Belfast; his bayonet, covered with blood, was twisted like a corkscrew.' (Dundonald, 39.)

† These rifles had all been taken from Hicks' ill-fated Egyptian force.

‡ Beresford says that during the action 'the officers were almost entirely employed in clearing jammed rifles passed back to them by the men', and that the bayonets twisted as a 'result of a combination of knavery and laziness on the part of those who were trusted to supply the soldier with weapons upon which his life depends. The bayonets were blunt, because no one had thought of sharpening them.' (Beresford, 267.)

It became firmly established in the minds of the Mahdi's men that the square had been deliberately opened so as to let them in, and then closed so as to facilitate the killing of every one of them. Certain it is that not one who entered remained alive in it.

Lieutenant Lord Binning, a young Blues officer, as soon as the Arabs had slunk off, made his way to the spot where he had last seen Burnaby:

> 'But I was not the first to find him. A young private in the Bays, a mere lad, was already beside him, endeavouring to support his head on his knee. The lad's genuine grief, with tears running down his cheeks, was as touching as were his simple words: "Oh! Sir; here is the bravest man in England dying, and no one to help him." It was too true, a glance showed that he was past help. [Beside his throat wound] his skull had been cleft by a blow from a two-handed sword – probably as he fell forward on his pony's neck . . . The marvel was that he was still alive. As I took his hand, a feeble pressure, and a faint look of recognition in his eyes, told me he still breathed, but life was ebbing fast, and it was only a matter of a few moments before he was gone. Amid the slain Arabs he lay there, a veritable Colossus, and alone of the dead his face wore the composed and placid smile of one who had been suddenly called away in the midst of a congenial and favourite occupation; as undoubtedly was the case . . .
>
> 'In my own detachment many of the men sat down and cried . . . His colossal strength, and the tales of his prowess and recklessness, whether ballooning or fighting in distant lands, appealed vividly to the imagination of the big troopers.'[27]

Punch, when the news reached Britain, published a commemorative ode:

> 'Brave Burnaby down! Wheresoever 'tis spoken
> The news leaves the lips with a wistful regret.
> We picture the square in the desert, shocked, broken,
> Yet packed with stout hearts and impregnable yet.
> And there fell, at last, in close mêlée, the fighter
> Who death had so often affronted before,
> One deemed he'd no dart for his valorous slighter
> Who such a gay heart to the battle-front bore.
> But alas! for the spear-thrust that ended a story,
> Romantic as Roland's, as Lion-Heart's brief!

Yet crownéd with incident, gilded with glory,
And crowned by a laurel that's verdant of leaf.
A latter-day Paladin, prone to adventure,
With little enough of the spirit that sways
The man of the market, the shop, the indenture!
Yet grief-drops will glitter on Burnaby's bays.
Fast friend and keen fighter, the strife-glow preferring,
Yet cheery all round with his friends and his foes;
Content through a life-story, yet soul-stirring
And happy, as doubtless he'd deem in its close.'[28]

Hero though he was, it is difficult to acquit Burnaby of committing a serious error when he ordered his Company out of the square. It is safe to say that only a very poor infantry officer would have given such an order, for his training would have drummed into his head that an unbroken front was the very essence of the square formation. There is something in Sir Charles Wilson's comment:

'A cavalry man is taught never to be still, and that a square can be broken. How can you expect him in a moment to forget all his training, stand like a rock, and believe no one can get inside a square . . . ? Those who were near the Heavies told me that as the men fired they moved back involuntarily – not being taught, as infantrymen are, to stand in a rigid line . . . A cavalry man,' he added, 'has a short handy carbine; he is given a long rifle and bayonet, and uses them for the first time in his life when a determined enemy is charging him.'[29]*

Wolseley himself was

'very sorry about this Heavy Cavalry Camel Regiment. The men and officers were magnificent, but not being drilled as infantry, they did not have that confidence in their rifles that an infantry regiment would have had. It is a dangerous experiment, using cavalry as foot soldiers under such a trial, but

* During the voyage out, sixty rounds per man had been allotted for practice, which was hardly enough to make efficient the handling of a rifle and bayonet by cavalrymen whose previous training on the short light carbine had been little more than perfunctory. Most of the Mounted Infantry on the other hand would have been receiving an allowance of ten rounds a week on colonial stations. The Martini was supposed to stop an attack at 400 yards, but at Abu Klea the Arabs ran so fast that some of them came in to 150 yards before being shot down. (Tylden: *CC*, 30; Henderson, G.F.R. *Stonewall Jackson*, I, 140.)

being picked men they ought to have done better. I confess I am somewhat disappointed in them.'[30]

To set against all this is the fact that a number of enemy horsemen, at the same moment as the main attack, threatened to charge the right rear angle of the square, where the Household Cavalry were stationed. They were greeted with volleys which left thirty dead horses 'on the spot where the advance was made, which tends to show,' as Talbot proudly states, 'that the shooting of the Heavy Cavalry Regiment was not so indifferent as had been implied.'[31]

Stewart, whose horse was shot under him at one stage of the battle, (which lasted little more than ten minutes), estimated the enemy's strength 'from 8,000 to 14,000 men' of which some 3,000 took part in the main attack. He says that 'not less than 800 lay dead'.[32] The Column's casualties were eleven officers (seven of whom were cavalry officers) and sixty-five other ranks killed; seven officers and eighty-five other ranks wounded. This represents about ten per cent of the whole column. The loss of eleven killed and seven wounded from the detachment of the 5th Dragoon Guards was nearly 50 per cent of its total numbers.[33]

* * *

'Why don't the 19th Hussars charge?' asked Stewart impatiently as he watched the slow, reluctant retreat of the dervishes.[34] The answer lay in the fact that, as one subaltern put it, the horses were 'too starved, small, thirsty and weak to be of much use in charging'. In fact, the Hussars were of more use firing their carbines dismounted, though some of them did manage to follow and cut down a few stragglers.[35]

Their next task, as the re-formed square moved slowly onwards, the men suffering agonies of thirst, was to find the wells of Abu Klea some four miles off. This they eventually did, but it was late at night before the exhausted men and camels got their first taste of water. It was 'yellow and of the consistency of cream; but,' wrote Beresford, 'it was cool, sweet and delicious.'[36]

A party was now sent back to bring on the men and supplies from the zariba. These did not arrive till dawn, leaving those in the square without food, coats or blankets. Gleichen said it was the coldest night he had ever experienced.[37]

At 4 p.m. next afternoon, the force, reduced by nearly a quarter of its strength, started off towards the Nile. The moonless night march which followed was hindered by untrustworthy guides and thick mimosa. It took fourteen hours to cover eighteen miles. Next day the enemy in increasing numbers harried the square. Stewart himself was shot in the groin and had to hand over the command to Sir Charles Wilson who made no pretence of being a fighting soldier.

In consultation with Stewart, Wilson formed another zariba and prepared to fight his way to the river. This time there were no skirmishers to mask the disciplined volleys from the square. At the action of Gubat, the dervishes were dispersed with fearful casualties in half the time it had taken to defeat them at Abu Klea. As the moon rose that evening the Nile was at last attained. Next day contact was made with Gordon's converted steam gunboats.

A history of the cavalry is not concerned with the details of the rest of the story, with how Wilson wasted three vital days attempting to take Metemmeh, sending back a convoy to Gakdul, writing his despatch and unnecessarily reconnoitring the river northwards; nor with how he eventually set off towards Khartoum only to find that he was too late, getting himself wrecked and rescued on his return. All that is necessary to say here is that when Wolseley heard of Stewart's wound (which proved fatal) and even before he learned of Gordon's death and the fall of Khartoum, he at once sent off his Chief of Staff, Major-General Redvers Buller, with reinforcements. But Buller found that his only task was to extricate the remnants of the Camel Corps as best he could. This, with the camels dying in thier hundreds and the men worn out, dispirited and 'many of them almost shoeless',[38] was achieved, astonishingly enough, without serious interference by the enemy. The last troops to reach Korti from the desert did not do so till 16 March. More than a fortnight before that Buller, on arrival at Gakdul, had reported:

> 'Having barely camels to move my stores and supplies, all the men and officers had to march; this, in this weather, on three quarts of water per man per day, was most exhausting, but nothing could have been better than the spirit shown by all ranks . . . I wish expressly to remark on the very excellent work that has been done by the small detachment of the 19th Hussars, both during our occupation of Abu Klea and during our retirement. Each man has done the work of ten, and it is not too much to say that the force owes much to Major French and his thirteen troopers.'[39]

The strength of the Heavy Camel Regiment had shrunk from 411 of all ranks on its departure from Korti on 7 January to 296 on its return two months later. A memorial to the ten officers and ninety-two men who had been killed or had died was later inscribed by order of its commander upon the walls of the temple of Philae.[40]

* * *

What had happened in the meantime to the River Column? Wilson had already set off in his steamer from Metemmeh when Major-General William Earle started out from his base at Hamdab forty miles up-Nile from Korti. The Column had got no further than Berti when, on 5 February, the General learned that Khartoum had fallen. Three days later he was ordered to push on to Abu Hamed and there to await further instructions. This unexpected order resulted from the Government's reaction to the news of Gordon's death. It had been decided under the shock of this news that the campaign against the Mahdi was to be continued – vigorously. Wolseley was given *carte blanche* and all the troops he required. Delighted though he was, he had to point out that it was impossible to do anything till the autumn when the hot weather had passed.

Earle, whose force included a squadron of the 19th Hussars, initially numbering ninety-one sabres and 107 horses under Major Hanford-Flood, as well as an Egyptian Camel Corps, pressed slowly onwards till he reached Kirbekan. Here the first serious Arab resistance was encountered and on 10 February there was fought an entirely successful action which young Ian Hamilton, who was present, described as 'a gem amongst battles'. Since it was fought exclusively by infantry, the temptation to describe it here must be resisted. Towards its end Earle was killed and Colonel Henry Brackenbury, a promiment protégé of Wolseley's, assumed command. On 24 February, with Abu Hamed still not reached, the Column was ordered to retreat to Korti since it was now known that Buller was making his way there. When the squadron of the 19th Hussars returned Major Hanford-Flood proudly stated that not a single man had been on the sick list since leaving Korti and that only three horses had died: a remarkable record.[41]

* * *

Thus ended in total failure the Gordon Relief Expedition. It probably never had a chance of success because, simply, it started too late. For this no one but Gladstone was to blame. Had there been fewer difficulties and delays on the way up the Nile, especially respecting camel supply, and had Stewart not been wounded, it is possible that contact would have been made with Khartoum some days earlier. But it seems very unlikely that 'a few redcoats' in an armed steamer would have cowed the Mahdi into withholding the *coup de grâce* which he had been poised to administer for some time past.

All this is still controversial and will ever remain so. What is not in doubt is that Stewart's death, at the age of forty-two, deprived the army of an outstanding general. He was the son of a parson and a descendant of the 7th Earl of Galloway. Backward as a scholar at Winchester, but an accomplished cricketer, Stewart entered the army as an infantry ensign when aged twenty. Ten years later, having served on the staff in Bengal, he exchanged into the 3rd Dragoon Guards and in 1877 went to the staff college, at the same time being admitted a student of the Inner Temple, where he kept twelve terms – an uncommon thing for a Victorian cavalry officer to do. In 1880 he became Military Secretary to Wolseley in South Africa. In the first Boer War the following year, on Colley's staff, he was made prisoner after Majuba. As we have seen, in 1882 he was Brigade Major to the Cavalry Brigade in the Tel el-Kebir campaign. At that time Wolseley said of him that he was one of the best staff officers he had ever known. To his widow after his death he wrote: 'I feel as if my right arm has been amputated . . . If I were a woman, I would sooner be his widow than the wife of half the men I know.'[42]

* * *

From the cavalry point of view one of the most interesting, indeed astonishing, aspects of the campaign was the endurance of the Arab ponies ridden by the 19th Hussars. Lieutenant-Colonel Barrow made a special report upon them. They were all stallions, he wrote to the Principal Veterinary Surgeon, averaging fourteen hands in height. Their ages were usually between eight to nine years, though some 15 per cent were over twelve. They had been bought, chiefly in Syria, for around £18 each.

About half of them had served in the Eastern Sudan in early

1884 'and returned in a very exhausted state'. Some 10 per cent had been in the Tel el-Kebir campaign in 1882. In September, 1884, they had marched 210 miles to Wadi Halfa, where 350 had been handed over to the 19th. From Wadi Halfa to Korti, about 360 miles, they averaged sixteen miles a day, receiving only six pounds of grain, barley or dhurra and ten pounds of dhurra stalk.

135 officers and men, with twelve spare mounts, performed all reconnaissance duties for the Desert Column as well as marching back and forth as escorts between Korti and the Gakdul wells time and again. At one point some of them were ridden for 83 out of 141 hours. Over the first ten days their forage ration averaged 5 to 6 lbs of grain and two gallons of water, 'the horses performing thirty-one miles daily, and not counting one day's halt.

'When the first advance was made on Matammeh, the horses marched to the Nile without having received a drop of water for 55 hours, and only 1 lb of grain. Some 15 or 20 horses received no water for 70 hours.' Whilst halted at Gubat between 20 January and 14 February, they 'received no grain, but were fed on dhourra stalk, about 10 lbs daily, or green bean stalk, or green dhourra stalk, about 12 lbs daily. Two days before marching they received 6 lbs of grain.'

For the first seventy-five miles of the return journey to Korti, 'the horses performed the whole distance on 4 lbs of grain and three gallons of water; the remainder of the journey water was plentiful and 8 lbs of grain were supplied. Two marches of over 40 miles were performed, which shows that the horses were still able to march.'

As the hot season advanced, they travelled back to Wadi Halfa, mostly by night, but 'generally exposed to a hot sun all day, as there was not much shelter for them under the palm trees. Except two fractures from kicks, no horses were lost or left on the line of march.' After a fortnight's rest at Assuan they 'were handed over to the 20th Hussars in quite as good order as when they left Wadi Halfa nine months previously.'

Out of the 350 horses only twelve died from disease throughout the whole campaign. 'The distance actually marched from point to point, not taking any account of reconnaissance, etc., was over 1,500 miles. The weight carried was reduced to the minimum, but averaged fourteen stone.'

The casualties between 13 November, 1884, and 5 July, 1885, totalled seventy-one of which twenty were killed in action and thirty-seven had to be destroyed. Several horses which were 'very severely wounded . . . recovered rapidly, though in a very exhausted state.

'I venture,' concluded Barrow, 'to think that the performance of the Regiment on these Arab ponies will compare with the performance of any horsemen on record.'

He added some 'practical hints':

'1. When water was limited to 2 gallons, or less, it was given in small quantities, not all at once. Even 1 pint given to the horses, or just enough to moisten their mouths, enabled them to come up to time again.

'On one occasion, late at night, the horses were much exhausted, we were 35 miles from water, and less than 1 pint left per horse. The horses could not eat, their mouths were so parched. I had a sack of dhourra meal, and with water made a number of moist balls of meal. These balls revived the horses, and they marched their 35 miles next morning. I obtained this hint previous to the campaign from General Valentine Baker, who told me that the Turkomans used to carry, in skins, balls of grease or oil, and meal.

'2. The horses were saved on every possible occasion, and by every possible device. The men never sat on their horses' backs a moment longer than necessary. Marches in column were avoided, extended line being used, so that each horse had pure air to breathe. When picketed, horses always had plenty of room, and their heads to the breeze.

'When possible, they were washed two or three times a week, which tended much towards their healthy condition.

'The horses were allowed to graze, on every possible occasion, on the grass of the Bayuda Desert, but it was very dry. They chewed the grass, but ate very little. During the last few days of the march to Matammeh, there was no opportunity for even giving the horses grass. On several occasions I obtained from the Commissariat tins of mouldy biscuit, unfit for issue to the men; the horses ate it greedily, and worked on this food.'

There were 107 horses of the 19th Hussars with the River Column. Only four of these died between 1 January and 8 March.[43]

* * *

On 22 March Wolseley wrote to the Queen that if she was 'satisfied with the conduct of her troops I don't think our men care very much what Mr Gladstone may think of them: *they* certainly don't think much of *him*.'[44]

It was to be thirteen years before Gordon's death was avenged. The reasons for the change of plan which occasioned this long delay will appear in Chapter VIII.

'From a military point of view, of the two insurrectionary leaders, the Mahdi's lieutenant [Osman Digna] was really the more dangerous. From a critical and difficult position, the Nile Expedition withdrew without serious interference from an enemy who seemed chary of descending below the Nile junction, but on the Red Sea littoral, the rebel chief was able to threaten both the British position at Suakin and the Suakin-Berber route.'

WILLIAM GALLOWAY, *The Battle of Tofrek*

'This mighty display of strength put forward by a powerful nation to subdue a few thousand lean-shanked savages armed with shields and spears.'

A transport officer on arrival at Suakin[1]

(iv)

The Suakin campaign, 1885: engagement at Hashin

It will be remembered that in the eastern Sudan the power of Osman Digna had not been crushed in early 1884 because Gladstone had withdrawn Graham's troops before that general could effect his object. Now, while the determination to overthrow the power of the Mahdists as soon as practicable was still strong, everyone agreed that something must be done, if only to satisfy public opinion and restore the army's prestige.

Consequently a force more than twice the size of that of a year before was speedily assembled at Suakin where a much harrassed garrison had survived Osman's pinpricks and the hot season more or less intact. Once again Graham was appointed to command it. He was ordered first to crush Osman Digna and then to make it possible to begin a railway across the desert to Berber. When this project was first agreed upon after the fall of Khartoum had become known, it was still hoped that Berber would in due course be captured by the River Column.* Some people considered the building of this railway an essential adjunct to the eventual advance on Khartoum.

By the beginning of April Graham had under his command some 13,000 troops with 11,000 followers, formed into the Suakin Field Force. They were carried in more than sixty steamships. There were two British infantry brigades, comprising seven battalions, four batteries of artillery, including one from New South Wales,† and one of horse artillery, as well as numerous supporting troops and services, including even a balloon detachment.

The cavalry brigade, commanded by Colonel H. P. ('Croppy') Ewart, consisted of two squadrons of the 5th Lancers (248), two of the 20th Hussars (261), a squadron[2] of the 19th Hussars, probably not more than 130 in number,‡ and four companies of mounted infantry (196). These last comprised men from thirty-five different units, including cavalry, engineers and Royal Marines.[3]

There was also a brigade of 3,000 men from the Indian Army. This included three battalions of native infantry and the 9th Bengal Cavalry, which we last heard of in action as Hodson's Horse in the Mutiny, nearly three decades earlier (see Vol II, 176). The regiment was en route to Ambala from Peshawar in the ordinary course of relief, when, on 10 February, having reached Wazirabad, a telegram was received ordering an immediate move by rail to Cawnpore where it was to be converted to a lancer regiment whilst

* This second Eastern Sudan expedition had first been thought of as early as mid-November 1884. Its purpose then was to secure the flank of the Nile column by keeping Osman Digna occupied. (Graham, 285.)

† There was also an Australian infantry battalion. Never before in British history had white colonial troops been used outside their own part of the world.

‡ The 19th Hussars had received 310 recruits in the last eighteen months. Between 15 October, 1883, and 14 October, 1884, eighty-two soldiers, fully trained and with over five years' service, but who had not completed their full engagement term, were allowed to leave the regiment for the reserves. (Major-General Charles C. Fraser, in a letter to *The Morning Post,* 10 March, 1885.)

retaining, of course, its carbines. As each squadron arrived it was at once supplied with lances and all items necessary for three months' field service. Considering that there were in India at this time a number of lancer regiments, and since it was generally agreed that to make a lancer proficient required two years' training, it is extraordinary that the 9th should have been selected. As one officer put it: 'Beyond a certain amount of tent-pegging at regimental sports, not one of them had ever had a lance in his hand before.' The sole practice they had before going into action came from a few days' instruction from some of the 5th Lancers. It was alleged that at Hashin the sowars actually threw away their lances and drew their swords.

Between 6 and 10 March the whole regiment, 582 strong, complete with its 426 followers, 308 baggage mules and ponies and two camels, camp equipment and ammunition, arrived at Suakin from Bombay.[4]

The Indian government also sent out, to quote the official history:

> '6,000 Camels (for baggage only, equipped with zuletahs and proper proportion of headmen and drivers), in two corps of 3,000 each. [The second of these was not in fact completed.]
>
> '500 Riding camels (complete with saddles and proportion of attendants).
>
> '150 Ponies for mounted infantry (complete with saddles, bridles, and spare materials for repairs).
>
> 'Corps of camel drivers, 1,500 (or rather 2,050, allowing for proportion of headmen and percentage for replacement of casualties), for camels purchased at Suakin.
>
> 'Corps of muleteers, 300 strong.
>
> 'Corps of bhistis, 300 strong.
>
> 'Corps of dhooly bearers, 500 strong, with 100 Lushai dandies. [A dandi was a kind of litter consisting of a cloth hammock hung from a bamboo pole.]
>
> 'Corps of labourers, 900 strong, of whom 400 were to be specially adapted for railway work.
>
> 'The requisitions for these various corps were received by the Government of India between the 11th and 21st February, 1885, and with so good effect was exertion made for expediting the collection of animals, and recruiting men, that by the

5th April the whole force had been embarked and despatched from India [the majority of it much earlier].'[5]

This astonishing feat is recorded here to show how efficient the Indian authorities had become by this date. The fact that most of the Indian contribution was not in the event employed does not detract from the excellence of the achievement.

Indeed, nearly all the arrangements for this long forgotten campaign, undertaken in a country virtually destitute of supplies of any kind, were admirable.* Historians have hitherto neglected them, largely, perhaps, because the campaign itself was so short-lived. The chief requirement was for water to supplement the small quantities procurable from the local wells. To meet it, nine ships were used as 'extemporised condensers'. By 1 April these were producing a daily average of between 65,000 and 85,000 gallons of drinking water. To convey these to the piers, three steam pumping lighters were necessary. To distribute the water (and other supplies) to the various camp depôts, narrow gauge railways were constructed. Along these

> 'water trains, composed of 400-gallon tanks, mounted on railway trollies, were employed . . . The immediate distribution of water to the troops was carried out by means of regimental water carts, non-commissioned officers being appointed to attend at the different depôts, to see that no water was taken except on production of a ticket signed by the Commissariat Officer who issued the ration, specifying the number of gallons to which each corps was entitled according to the following scale:
>
> 'Officers and men, 2 gallons daily
> 'Natives, 1 gallon daily
> 'Hospital patients, 6 gallons daily
> 'Working parties, 1½ pints per man, each relief.'

When, later, it came to conveying water to the advanced zaribas, camel convoys carrying water kegs, india-rubber bags, 'which proved a complete failure', galvanized iron tins, closed by screw stoppers which could only be opened by a special key,[6] and skins, were organized by the Transport Department. All this imposed

* Private enterprise at Suakin flourished too. 'It is a curious fact,' remarked one officer, 'that you could get an iced brandy and soda at the little Red Sea port, for exactly the same price you have to pay for it in a London hotel.' (De Cosson, 79.)

an enormous extra burden upon the department because whereas the food ration's gross weight was under four pounds, the water ration weighed twelve.

At the height of the campaign, the daily consumption of food reached 160 tons, of which 110 were for forage. Fresh meat, 'chiefly the produce of cattle supplied from Odessa', was often provided, so were fresh vegetables.

> 'The tinned meat, at first sent out, was mostly all corned, and in 6 lb. tins; but this was found to occasion excessive thirst, and the size of the tins to cause waste. Later on sufficient supplies of 2 lb. tins of preserved fresh meat were received, to enable it to be issued to the troops on the march . . .
>
> 'The forage for horses was chiefly obtained from England, in the shape of compressed hay, compressed forage, hay cake, and grain cake.
>
> 'Camel forage was obtained from Egypt and India.
>
> 'Wood was obtained from Egypt, Cyprus, India and locally.'[7]

Most of the camels came from Egypt or India, but some came from Berbera and from Aden. The mules were brought from Gibraltar, Malta and Cyprus.

The Suakin Field Force was one of the first to dispense almost entirely with field forges and their accompanying plant and fuel, for 'the new pattern machine-made shoes and nails' were so malleable that the horse-shoes could be fitted cold.

The medical and veterinary arrangements seem to have been made on a generous scale. There were, for instance, sixty-seven medical officers, ranging from Deputy Surgeon-General O. Barnett, the Principal Medical Officer, to thirty-nine plain surgeons. There were also three hospital ships. For the animals there were eleven veterinary officers headed by Inspecting Veterinary Surgeon W. B. Walters. At base a sick horse depot with shelter sheds for eighty horses was established. Many of the camels arrived with contagious skin diseases. These had to be isolated in 'a camel lazaretto zariba'. According to the official history this was so successful that by 14 April 'parasitic mange was practically stamped out'.[8]

* * *

Graham made his first objective the area near Hashin, seven miles west of Suakin, where, around the foothills which terminate the open coastal plain, enemy forces were known to be. These, thought Graham, might threaten the flank of his projected main advance upon Tamai, where Osman Digna's headquarters were believed to be. On 19 March the cavalry brigade reconnoitred the area to examine the wells there and try to discover the enemy's strength. The historian of the 9th Bengal Cavalry describes how the brigade moved: 'The front was covered by a screen of scouts, supported by "cossack parties" of one squadron of the Ninth, followed by the two other squadrons of the regiment, in line of squadron columns. The two squadrons each of the 5th Lancers and 20th Hussars formed the second and third lines, echeloned respectively on the right rear and left rear of the Ninth.'[9]

Next day Graham took the bulk of his troops, (accompanied by 500 camels carrying 13,000 gallons of water)[10] so as to establish a strong zariba near Hashin, and if possible to bring the enemy to battle. While the zariba was being established and redoubts were being formed on the hills which overlooked it, most of the infantry advanced towards Hashin and the Dihilibat hills to the south of the village, where the enemy was awaiting them. They moved in the formation of three sides of a square, the cavalry covering its front and flanks, the advanced scouts with 'cossack' parties in support being furnished by the 9th Bengal Cavalry.

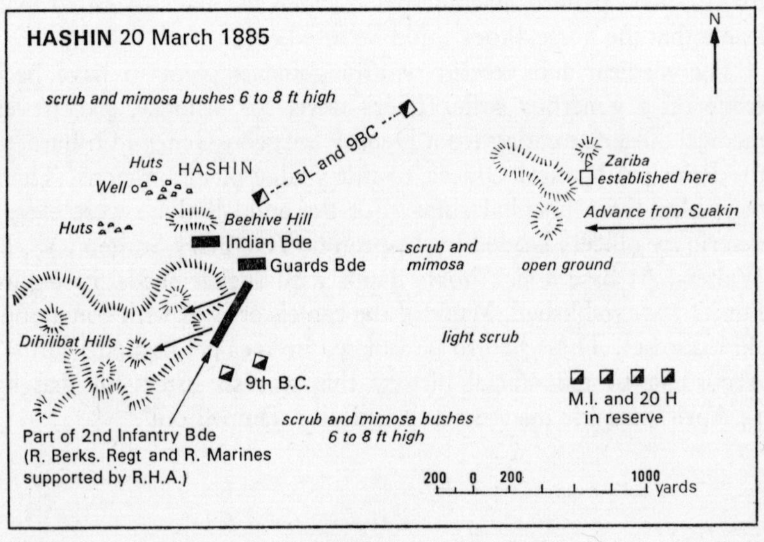

Map 17

51. Colonel Broadwood

52. Battle of Omdurman: charge of the 21st Lancers

53. James Collins, Principal Veterinary Surgeon, Army Veterinary Department, from 1876 to 1883

54. Dr George Fleming, Principal Veterinary Surgeon, Army Veterinary Department, from 1883 to 1890

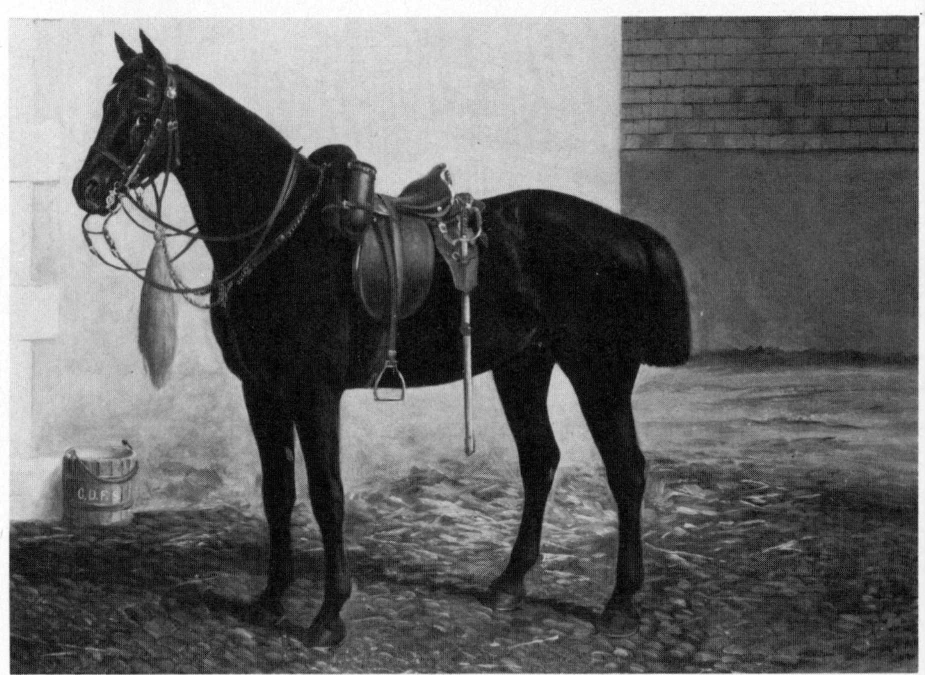

55. The charger of Major G. D. F. Sulivan, 15th Hussars, 1891

Part of one of the infantry brigades, supported by horse artillery now drove the enemy from Dihilibat hills. At about 9.40 a.m. Colonel Ewart, seeing a number of them making off southwards, took two squadrons of the 9th Bengal Cavalry to cut them off. The regimental historian tells what happened next:

> 'As they passed along the south-east face of Dihilibat Hill a large body of Arabs on the hillside threatened their right flank. One squadron, under Major D. H. Robertson, dismounted and opened fire with their carbines. Whilst so occupied they were suddenly charged by a crowd of spearmen, who creeping through and under the thick bushes with extraordinary speed, threw themselves on the dismounted men almost before the threat of attack was realised. For some minutes there was a wild hand-to-hand mêlée. The sowars regained their horses as best they could and cleared the front of the Guards Brigade which had been brought up in support; but a good many casualties occurred in the first rush, during which in several instances remarkable coolness and courage were displayed by officers and men. Major Robertson, in saving the life of a sowar who was attacked by two Arabs, received a severe spear wound in the thigh. Captain Garstin [later to become Commandant of the regiment] was twice hit by spears, but escaped serious injury. In fact all the officers had narrow escapes, including Risaldar Hukm Singh, who, together with nine non-commissioned officers and men, was awarded the Order of Merit for gallantry on this day.'[11]

Graham, in his despatch written next day, stated that 'Colonel Ewart ordered two squadrons to dismount* and fire volleys. These squadrons were charged by the enemy in considerable strength, and retired with loss.'[12]

Osman's men had certainly lost none of their daring. Instead of fleeing before the Bengal lancers, they had actually attacked them and forced them to retire. The 9th's casualties were very high: twelve men and seven followers killed and Major Robertson and fourteen men and one follower wounded. Some of these were occasioned before the main attack. When the 9th first entered the dense bush, at least two men were killed. The method used was for one Arab to engage the lancer's attention in front, and while

* Later, Graham amended this sentence so that it started: 'Colonel Ewart ordered part of one of these squadrons to dismount . . .' (*Graham*, 418.)

'thus occupied in playing his lance at the enemy before him, two other Arabs, equally stealthy in their approach, would spring upon the man from behind, drag him off his horse, and stab him to death in a few moments.'[13]

It was a mistake to use cavalry – particularly lancers – in country totally unsuited for it. Formed bodies obviously could not move in thorny mimosa scrub* between six to eight feet in height, through which the stealthy, speedy spearmen were expert at crawling in silence. Graham telegraphed Wolseley to say that Ewart was responsible for the heavy losses 'owing to the very bad way in which he handled the cavalry. The fact is,' wrote Wolseley in his diary, not, of course, fully seized of what actually happened, 'that cavalry charges except when the enemy is broken and running away are a mistake with these Arabs.' Graham even went so far as to ask Wolseley to withhold the rank of Brigadier-General from Ewart.[14]

About an hour after this unfortunate engagement, the 5th Lancers and two squadrons of the 9th Bengal Cavalry, again fighting amongst tall scrub, kept off a considerable enemy force which seemed to want to turn the British right flank. Major Alfred Bissel Harvey of the 5th, in action for the first time since joining the regiment twenty-one years before,

> 'charged the Arabs on the flank,' according to the regimental historian, 'going right through them, and then, wheeling about, riding them down a second time. The Arabs practised their usual tactics, and lay flat on the ground when they saw the Lancers approaching, doing their best to hamstring the horses as they passed. But on this occasion [unlike on the earlier Suakin campaigns] they had the Queen of weapons to reckon with, and the lance put an end to many a Mahdiist before he could put his plan into execution.'

Harvey himself was wounded by a lance wrenched by an Arab from a sowar of the 9th Bengal Lancers.

> 'Kneeling on the ground, the fellow kept himself in front of Harvey, who was somewhat perplexed to know what he was going to do, so he went straight at him with his drawn sword. The Arab suddenly jumped on one side, and as Harvey passed him, endeavoured to run him through with the lance. So quick

* Chiefly *Acacia Arabica*, 'the thorn bush', known locally as *Kittar*.

> was the Arab that the sword was too late to parry the point, and the spear was lodged deeply in the rider's thigh, so deeply indeed as to wrench it from the Arab's grasp. With the bridle in one hand and his sword in the other, there was no possibility of Harvey withdrawing the lance, which caught in a bush and nearly unhorsed the gallant major.'[15]

The 5th Lancers lost a troop sergeant-major and four troopers killed as well as a total of eight wounded: rather a large number for so insignificant an engagement.

Graham now withdrew his whole force, leaving only enough men to man the zariba and redoubts. The futility of the whole operation can be judged by the fact that the enemy at once re-occupied the Dihilibat hills and that only five days later the zariba and redoubts were dismantled and the place abandoned.[16]

The action at Hashin is chiefly remembered in the cavalry for being the last in which lance-flags were used attached to the lances.

> 'The attack of the rebels was conceived and carried out with all the astuteness of a Red Indian tribe. They sprang from behind the bushes, from inequalities of ground, and seemingly from the very ground itself, as if by magic.'
>
> *Daily Chronicle*, 23 March, 1885

(v)

The Suakin campaign, 1885: engagement at Tofrek

Two days later on 22 March, 'a broiling red-hot day',[1] the 2nd infantry brigade, commanded by Major-General Sir J. C. M'Neill, VC, and part of the Indian contingent under Brigadier-General J. Hudson, set out towards Osman's supposed headquarters at Tamai, fifteen miles from Suakin. Their first object was to establish an intermediate zariba (leaving the 2nd brigade to garrison it, whilst the Indians returned to Suakin). From the point of view of supplies, especially of water, this was an essential step. Whilst the zariba was being built in the form of a triple square in a clearing at Tofrek, some six miles from Suakin, the force was surprised by a large number of Arabs. It suffered enormous losses. The very minimum estimate puts them at 298 soldiers and followers killed or missing and 174 wounded, with over 700 camels and mules slaughtered or missing.

Part of the reason for this shocking business lies in the fact that the only mounted men accompanying the force were those of a weak squadron of the 5th Lancers. At most they numbered four officers, twenty non-commissioned officers and seventy-six lancers.* This was under one-seventh of the cavalry force employed in the advance on Tamai in the previous year (see p. 317), and contrasts surprisingly with the use of the entire cavalry brigade at Hashin. Perhaps the ill-management of that force was a reason for depriving M'Neill of an adequate scouting screen. Yet however large the mounted force, there would still have been some difficulty in giving sufficient warning. The zariba site was closely surrounded by thick mimosa trees, 'just low enough for a horseman to see over their flat-spreading tops, but so thick that he could not see under or through them'.[2] These made it, as Graham had written in his Hashin despatch, 'impossible to follow the movements of an enemy on foot, who can conceal himself perfectly within a short distance of our vedettes.'[3]

To protect the work of cutting the mimosa and building up the zariba, small infantry piquets of four or five men each were thrown out about 150 yards all round. In front of these a quarter of a mile or so further out and quite invisible from the zariba area were the lancers arranged in 'cossack' posts of four men each (that is, one vedette and three men in reserve). Another 'cossack' post, also of four men, was employed as a connecting link. Captain Llewellyn H. Jones, who commanded the squadron, says that he had over three miles of frontage to cover. This would mean that the distance between each post was quite likely to have been as much as a quarter of a mile. This certainly would have given, as one description of the action puts it, 'but an open mesh for a dense bush, within which an enemy might freely operate unperceived'.[4] Graham's despatch indicates that part of the squadron – he does not state what proportion – was 'being held in support on some

* And possibly far less. General Hudson is believed to have stated that there were only forty-three, while *The Times* says: 'eighteen cavalry vedettes'. (Galloway, 193; *Times*, 25 Mar., 1885.)

open ground about 500 yards to the south-west of the zariba area.'*

A few minutes before 3 p.m. a lancer galloped up to report to M'Neill that the enemy was 'collecting in front'.[5] A second followed a minute or two later, but he never reached the general.

> 'Having jumped his horse over the west side of the large zariba, [he] cantered up to an officer who was standing there and said, "Can you tell me, sir, where I shall find Capt. Jones?" The officer replied, "Who is Capt. Jones?" And the man answered, "He is the captain of my picket, and I want to report the enemy coming on in force." "Oh," said the officer, who, like most of us,' wrote the officer in charge of transport, 'had not the slightest idea that the enemy could be very near, "then you had better go out there," pointing due South; "there are some of the Staff officers, and I think General M'Neill also; you should report at once to him." The man trotted off to obey, and tried to jump his horse out of the zariba, but it refused the fence; the few moments when warning might have been of value slipped by, and he was still trying to make his horse face the hedge, when the enemy were upon us.'[6]

Just before this another lancer had ridden in to say that the Arabs were 'advancing rapidly', upon which M'Neill shouted 'stand to arms'; but before the men who were outside the zariba zone could obey,† the rest of the vedettes, according to an officer of the Berkshires 'galloped through us with the enemy alongside'. 'The black swarm of Arabs seemed rising up like the sands of the desert all round us; indeed,' wrote another eye-witness 'so numerous were they that the very stones might have been transformed by the stroke of a magician's wand into swarthy warriors armed with spear and sword.' In Suakin a gigantic column of dust was seen to rise into the air. 'The whole of our little force,' according to Captain De Cosson, the officer in charge of the transport, 'appeared

* Early in the day, Lieutenant J. B. Richardson with an officer's patrol of four men had been sent off to the left of the line of advance. About midday, his horse 'getting knocked up', he rode into Suakin to get a fresh one before returning to his reconnoitring duties. The patrol was never heard of again. It was caught, presumably, in the great Arab wave which swept down from Tofrek. (Willcox, 197.)

† The official historian states that though 'men were out on all sides cutting and dragging in the materials for the zaribas . . . more than two-thirds of the force remained by their arms.' (Colvile, II, 203.)

to burst asunder, amid smoke and fire, like an exploding shell.' Within moments there was 'a roaring plunging rush of camels, riderless horses, carts without drivers, pack mules chained three together, with loose ammunition boxes clattering behind them, all bolting in mad panic towards Suakin. The Arabs were running among them, cutting and stabbing, nimble as cats.'[7]

The enormous loss of transport animals came about, according to Graham's despatch, because some of them stampeded and 'the enemy being amongst them in all directions, they were shot in large numbers by our own men.'[8]

Most of the troops behaved with great sang froid, but a part of the 17th Bengal Infantry broke in panic as the 5th Lancers, closely followed by the Arabs, galloped in on them. So also did the followers and transport drivers. Nevertheless, within twenty minutes the Arabs were driven off and, by M'Neill's orders, the bugles sounded the cease fire. It is said that over 1,000 enemy bodies were counted after the engagement.*

* * *

Largely so as to protect the telegraph line which had been rolled out as the force went forward,† a squadron of the 20th Hussars had been ordered to patrol all day between Suakin and M'Neill's force. Its commander, Major Frank Graves, reported to the general at about 1 p.m. He had seen, he said, a few parties of the enemy, but they had all melted away on his approach. Half-an-hour later he took his men back towards Suakin. On the way he was met by a squadron of the 9th Bengal Cavalry, some 150 strong, commanded by Lieutenant Algernon Peyton, which had been sent out to relieve him. Almost as they met they heard the firing from the zariba. Graves at once hastened back there with both squadrons. Within a mile or so, according to De Cosson,

'they met a great number of the baggage animals, together

* Two of the four Gardner guns of the Royal Navy detachment were not set up for firing at the time of the attack. The other two were in action from the start. They only fired 400 rounds but apparently did great execution. The detachment was commanded by Lieutenant (later Admiral Sir) Alfred W. Paget, a grandson of Lord Uxbridge, Wellington's cavalry commander at Waterloo.

† This was possibly the first time that the telegraph had ever been carried right into the fighting line.

It is an extraordinary fact that it was not cut during the action, though it was three-and-a-half hours after it.

with many camp-followers, some Native Infantry, and a few English soldiers, pursued by the Arabs, who were cutting them down and killing numbers without resistance. Half the cavalry were then dismounted and some volleys fired, which checked the pursuit: mounting again, they pushed forward, occasionally repeating the same tactics, so as to drive the Arabs before them.'[9]

As was their custom some of the Arabs lay down, feigning death. At one point, as described by William Galloway, who wrote a lengthy volume devoted to the action,

'Major Graves having gone out in front with his trumpeter, two of the Arabs who had lain down suddenly sprang up and rushed at him. Before the Major could disable him, one of them succeeded in wounding Troop Sergeant-Major Mobbs, who was riding at this assailant. He fell before the revolver, and, pinned to the ground by one of the 9th Bengal Cavalry [with his lance] was promptly killed. Captain Bellasis, noticing the incident, bore down on the second Arab, who, turning, threw his spear at his assailant, when Major Graves fortunately shot him down. Captain Bellasis very narrowly escaped, the spear passing within an inch of his neck.

'This skirmish over, Major Graves noticed that the enemy were trying to turn his left flank towards the sea, with the object no doubt of again falling upon the Transport, and ordered Lieutenant Peyton to take a troop of the 9th Bengal Cavalry and intercept them. This he did most effectually, bringing some twenty wounded and stragglers safe to Suakin. When Major Graves saw that his flank was safe, and being joined by a troop of the 5th Lancers, under Lieutenant Goodair, to the number of forty [part, no doubt, of Captain Jones's squadron], he brought up his left flank and, pursuing on, drove the enemy by dismounted fire in front of the left or sea face of the zeriba, from which they were enfiladed so effectually that they were dispersed towards the sea and did not again assemble in any numbers.

'He then formed a strong cordon round the Transport and baggage, and, sending out some patrols, came into the zeriba and reported his return.'[10]

* * *

Unlike his conduct in 1884, Osman Digna, not slow to learn the lessons of that earlier campaign, never in 1885 risked a full-scale confrontation with a British fighting square. The action at Tofrek (also known as 'the battle of M'Neill's zariba') showed that his new tactics of attacking Graham's cumbersome apparatus whilst at its least prepared, were, though costly, far more successful. In 1884 the convoys between Suakin and Baker's zariba had gone back and forth not only not in square formation, but with scarce even an escort. They had not once been disturbed by a single enemy attack. This experience may account for, if it does not excuse, the lack of cavalry for M'Neill's force a year later.

It seems, too, that a considerable amount of intelligence had been gathered about Osman's intention to attack the convoy on 22 March. This, it appears, was not communicated to M'Neill or to Major Graves. Had it been, the feeling of absolute security which prevailed might have been shaken.

That the 5th Lancers should have given more warning than they did was suggested in an anonymous pamphlet entitled 'Arab Warfare' which appeared soon after the campaign: 'Had the Lancer vedettes broken through their regimental tradition, and fired at the enemy, sufficient time might perhaps have been available for the labouring infantry and pioneers to prepare to meet the coming onslaught'.[11] In other words, would not the carbine have been more useful than the lance?!

By others the state of training of the men was called in question. It is a fact that of the regiment's establishment of 469 men, 252 were recruits who had only joined in the previous year and a half.[12] What proportion of these was included in the two squadrons in Graham's army is not clear.

* * *

During the rest of March, beyond occasional long-range firing in the bush, no further fighting took place. On 3 April Graham reached Tamai against virtually no opposition, burned its huts and two days later was back in Suakin. There had been no sign of the elusive Osman. On 6 April M'Neill's zariba was evacuated.

Meanwhile the railway building proceeded. By the end of April it had reached Otao. On 6 May a large expedition set off with the help of a newly formed Camel Corps and an armoured train, towards the T'Hakul valley, eighteen miles from Suakin, to disperse what was believed to be the only remaining formed body of Osman's followers. This it did at the cost of three wounded.

At this point the government, especially Gladstone, wanted an excuse to evacuate the Sudan altogether. It came when a small Russian force entered a remote village on the ill-defined northern Afghan frontier. On the pretext that an invasion of Afghanistan was imminent and that every soldier would be needed to defend India's frontier, the Eastern Sudan was evacuated, the railway was broken up* and, as in 1884, only a garrison was still retained at Suakin. In 1888 Osman Digna again became active. Consequently, strengthened Egyptian forces, led of course by British officers, including some troops of cavalry, were kept busy for three testing years until in 1891 Osman's base at Tokar was captured. This dealt his influence a serious blow.

* * *

The Conservatives, when they took office in June, 1886, despite their criticism when in opposition of the Liberals' decision to evacuate the Sudan, did nothing towards reconquering it.

In the same month the Mahdi died. The Khalifa Abdullahi, who succeeded him, now made his first attempt at invading Egypt. On the last day of the year, two Anglo-Egyptian brigades, under Lieutenant-General Sir Frederick Stephenson, soundly beat him at Ginnis. In this action, believed to be the last in which some of the British infantry wore red coats, the mounted element consisted of the 20th Hussars, some mounted infantry (under Barrow), one British and one Egyptian Camel Corps and a regiment of Egyptian cavalry. It was a straightforward, old-fashioned engagement (except for the infantry's long-range rifles), in which the Khalifa's men had little chance. Once the infantry's volleys had broken them, they were charged and pursued by the cavalry. Their casualties were said to be 800, while the Anglo-Egyptians lost no more than forty-one. Nineteen months later an Egyptian force, led by British officers, wiped out a strong Sudanese army at Saras. This was the first action in which the dervishes had been beaten without the help of British troops. A squadron of the 20th Hussars and a force of Egyptian cavalry commanded by Lieutenant-Colonel H. H. Kitchener were also engaged in an action near Toski on 3 August,

* The villagers of Handub used the rails in constructing their dwellings. (Wingate, 494.)

1889. Otherwise, during the following nine years, the dervishes were kept at bay in the valley of the Nile almost exclusively by Egyptian troops, whose self-confidence increased as their training under British officers progressed.[13]

8

'War should be long in preparing in order that you may conquer the more quickly.'

PUBLILIUS SYRUS, in the 1st century, B.C.

'The diplomatist said: "It is to please the Triple Alliance." The politician said: "It is to triumph over the Radicals." The polite person said: "It is to restore the Khedive's rule in the Soudan." But the man in the street . . . said: "It is to avenge General Gordon."'

WINSTON S. CHURCHILL in *The River War*

'In the Sudan . . . the galloping instinct, bred in the hunting field, was still the enemy of good order. Even Broadwood . . . would abandon control to lead a charge; Haig, who did not greatly care for hunting, preferred to spend his energies in preserving order.'

JOHN TERRAINE in *Douglas Haig, the Educated Soldier*[1]

Rebuilding the Egyptian army 1883–1896 – the Omdurman campaign 1896–1898

'It appeared easier,' wrote the young Winston Churchill in 1898, 'to draw sunbeams out of cucumbers than to put courage into the *fellah*.'[2] Yet, to a remarkable degree, this is just what a devoted band of British officers did in the decade which followed Tel el-Kebir. First under Major-General Sir Evelyn Wood, as he had now become, who was the first Sirdar or Commander-in-Chief of the Egyptian army; then for seven years from 1885, under Brigadier-General Francis Grenfell and after 1892 under Major-General H. H. Kitchener, there was forged an army capable of defending Egypt's border and of contributing substantially to the re-conquest of the Sudan.*

At the start it was limited to 6,000 of all arms and designed solely for the maintenance of internal order, the newly recruited

* An early task was the translating into Egyptian-Arabic the almost universal Turkish words of command, as well as the English drill books. This last, surprisingly, was undertaken by Count Della Sala Pasha! (Wood, 177.)

police forming the first reserve. The organization was modelled to a considerable degree upon the Indian army system. Gradually, as the lengthy frontier warfare against the Mahdists developed, the army's strength was increased, so that by 1897 it numbered over 20,000. In the beginning there were only twenty-five British full-pay staff and regimental officers, including, incidentally, Captain Kitchener as second-in-command of a cavalry unit. By the time he became Sirdar there were nearly 140 officers, including a good proportion of Egyptians. These latter were selected initially from those in the old Turco-Egyptian army, but before long a military school, somewhat on the Sandhurst lines, was set up, to which potential officers were admitted by competition.

The ranks were filled by conscription, the majority of recruits being drawn from the Delta *fellahin*, 'the most domestically inclined individuals in the world',[3] to whom in the pre-1882 days 'the corvee, or forced labour gangs, were . . . a sort of relative paradise, contrasted with entering the army.'[4] Under the old dispensation they would commit almost any crime or grievously mutilate themselves so as to escape the call to the colours. Once conscripted, sometimes driven in chains by police, they would look upon themselves as doomed never to see their families again. Now, for the first time in modern Egypt's long history, the men found themselves respected and cared for by their officers, regularly and handsomely paid, well clothed and, in Churchill's words, 'treated with justice. Their rations were not stolen by the officers. The men were given leave to go to their villages from time to time. When they fell sick, they were sent to hospital instead of being flogged.'[5] In his report for 1886 the Adjutant-General wrote of a man telling his commanding officer that when a soldier in the old army returned to his village, 'he used to sneak back like a dog, glad if our sheikh did not strike him. When I come back,' said the man, 'the sheikh asks me in to have coffee, and begs me to tell him the news.'[6]

The mounted establishment of the Egyptian army in the late 1890s consisted of a camel corps, some 600 to 800 strong,* with five British officers, and sometimes eight but later usually ten independent cavalry squadrons of about 100 men each. Six or seven of these were commanded by British officers with the local rank of

* Four of the six companies were Sudanese, recruited often, as was also the case in the infantry, from prisoners or deserters. These were always more warlike than the peasants of Egypt. The corps was equipped with the Martini and the bayonet. The men sat astride the regulation mounted infantry saddle.

major, each exercising wider powers than the colonel of a British regiment. 'Each squadron leader,' wrote one of them, 'has a free hand entirely, and can train his men as he likes.'[7] There was also one horse artillery battery with another of 'galloping' Maxim machine guns. The cavalry horses were usually stout, hardy animals of about thirteen hands, capable of very hard work. The cavalry had the pick of the conscripts, all of them Egyptian, many coming from the Fayum oasis. Their physique, according to Sir Evelyn Wood, was 'superior to any European army, and their aptitude for the perfunctory parts of drill was remarkable.'[8] They were equipped with sword, Martini carbine and, in their front ranks, lances. Generally poor horsemen, they treated their horses kindly, while their uniforms, saddlery and arms claimed their ceaseless care, for being strangers to such valuable things, they regarded them, in Churchill's words, 'with awe and wonder'. They were 'obedient, quiet and docile'. Their only serious troubles arose from opium smoking

> 'or through some dusky beauty . . . Initiative [the trooper] did not possess, high resolve he did not know, but he would ride out boldly into the desert on patrol, would fire steadily when dismounted, would charge – if not with dash, at least with discipline . . . No matter what the danger, he would, though fearful, obey the white officer. And when I met the officers, I no longer wondered. The certainty of war had attracted the best; the field of selection had been large; the choice had justified itself.'[9]

* * *

Lord Salisbury's Conservative-Liberal Unionist coalition government came to power with a large majority in 1895. Many and various were the motives which induced it to invade the Sudan in the following year. In the minds of the cabinet the desire to avenge Gordon after more than a decade was given a low priority, though it would certainly help to rally the support of public opinion. So also would the suppression of the revived slave trade. When in March, 1896, the Prime Minister announced the sudden decision to advance 200 miles south of the Egyptian frontier to Dongola, he was largely prompted by fears that certain of the European powers might attempt to gain possession of part of the Nile Valley and thus, among other unpleasant consequences, tamper with the flow of the river. This was part of Britain's over-riding concern, in the interests of imperial defence, to control those parts of Africa which seemed vital to the security of the Mediterranean and therefore of the world. For some years past the Foreign Office had been trying to exclude other powers from the Nile area. It had never quite succeeded. It had come to realize that ultimate occupation of the whole Nile Valley was the only truly safe course. For this Salisbury had had, for a very long time, half-formed plans. The Sudan would have to be invaded from Egypt sooner or later. He only looked for the diplomatic opportunity. Whether, when it came, he could take it, would of course depend in some degree upon how strong the Madhist power still was, and even more upon the state of Egyptian and British finances.

The diplomatic opportunity came as a result of the defeat on 1 March, 1896, of an Italian army by the Emperor Menelek of Abyssinia at Adowa assisted by French arms. This was the immediate occasion of the abrupt determination to send the Egyptian army southwards. In London it was appreciated that the Madhists, who now threatened the Italians in Kassala, would be much strengthened by joining the victorious Ethiopians. Further, if Menelek was to be the tool of France, the threat to the Nile must increase. For many months, too, it had been known in London that the French intended to try to obtain a foothold on the Nile not only from the east but also from the west by sending a force right across the continent to Fashoda, where it was wrongly believed the river could be easily dammed.

The plight of the Italians was only, of course, the pretext for the Sudan adventure. It could be represented as a diversion designed to take the pressure off them. On this ground, Germany and Austria, being attached to Italy by the Triple Alliance of 1882, were bound to support it. For the same reason, too, whatever slight opposition there might be in the House of Commons could be overborne.

As to finance, though Egypt could not afford to pay all the costs of recovering her lost provinces, it so happened that the British Exchequer at this time had a sufficient surplus to be able to pay for a great deal of it.

There remained only the question of how much and what sort of force was necessary to smash the Madhists' power. At all costs there must be no more ignominious defeats of the Egyptians such as had occurred in the 1880s. Thus it was decided that the military might of the Madhists was to be probed only gradually and with maximum caution.

* * *

On 18 March, 1896, there began from Wadi Halfa the laborious advance which, two and a half years later, was to result in Kitchener's momentous meeting with the French Colonel Marchand at Fashoda, over 1,000 miles to the south.*

The earliest engagements were fought at Akasha on 1 May (chiefly a cavalry skirmish) and at Firket on 7 June (where it was claimed that some 800 dervishes were killed). Neither action was important militarily, but both much boosted the morale of the Egyptian troops, especially that of the mounted arm. This was commanded, as it was to be throughout the war, by Lieutenant-Colonel Robert George Broadwood, a 12th Lancer. He, according to one of the newspaper correspondents, was 'a rapid, adroit and daring leader: long-legged, light, built for a horseman, never tired . . . the ideal of a cavalry general.'[10]

By September the province of Dongola had been retaken against no great opposition. Eleven months then elapsed before the advance was resumed. The success of this second phase was to depend chiefly upon logistical and engineering factors rather than upon purely military ones. Kitchener, with his experience in the Royal Engineers, was the ideal commander for the operations which it entailed. He it was who took the all-important decision to build a railway all the way from Wadi Halfa to the junction of the Nile with the Atbara, which nearly everyone said was impossible. For more than half of its 400 miles – between Wadi Halfa and Abu Hamed – it was laid across open desert, thus, by cutting out the enormous Dongola loop of the river, shortening the route by hundreds of miles. It was one of the greatest engineering enterprises of modern times.

Gunboats for blasting whatever enemy forts might be encountered were the Sirdar's other chief requirement. These he either inherited or had sent out in packing cases for assembly on the

* Early in May, since Kitchener required all the Egyptian troops he could muster, the garrison at Suakin was replaced by a brigade from India, which included the 1st (Duke of Connaught's Own) Bombay Lancers. After six broiling months of inactivity, having suffered enormous casualties from disease, this brigade returned, disgruntled, to India.

river bank. As ever Thomas Cook and Son saw to the rapid passage of troops and supplies along the Nile.

On 5 September, 1879, the advance guard occupied Berber, which since he could not count upon the loyalty of the local tribes, the Khalifa had decided to abandon. By 1 November the Sudan Military Railway had reached Abu Hamed which had been captured three months earlier. The second instalment of what Churchill named 'The River War' was now complete. Again, though there had been minor engagements, opposition had been slight.

The Khalifa, realizing that the invaders did not intend to advance further till the next Nile flood, conscious that only 2,000 men held Berber, but naturally unable to appreciate the speedy concentration made possible by the railway, despatched a force of 16,000 men northwards. By the beginning of April these were established in a well fortified zariba on the banks of the Atbara.

On 5 April, 1898, the Sirdar ordered a strong reconnaissance of this entrenchment. Broadwood, with eight squadrons, the horse artillery battery and four Maxim guns, got within 1000 yards of it and made careful note of the enemy's dispositions. Whilst thus engaged, he found himself about to be enveloped by enormously superior mounted forces, supported by quick-moving infantry. The horse guns and Maxims were speedily brought into action, preceded and followed by two charges delivered by two separate portions of the Egyptian cavalrymen. These were pressed home with great verve, but left the squadrons in considerable disarray. Others rapidly dismounted and employed their carbines to good effect.

There seems little doubt that Broadwood was extricated from a potentially disastrous situation by his recently arrived acting 'Chief Staff Officer of Cavalry'. This was Captain Douglas Haig, aged thirty-six, seconded from the 7th Hussars, who was here for the first time under fire. By quick thinking, quick riding and not waiting for orders, he co-ordinated the movements of the various squadrons and guns amidst a minor dust storm which much restricted visibility.

> 'This I hear,' he wrote home, 'is the *first time* the Gyppe Cavalry has ever had anything in the way of fighting to do.*

* This was not strictly true for, (beside the action at Akasha), on 21 March part of the reconnaissance, sent out to discover for which part of the Atbara the enemy was making, had been surprised. One squadron, getting entangled in thick scrub, lost ten men killed and eight wounded before it could be extricated. The want of the Maxim guns was much felt, and subsequently the cavalry never moved without them. (*Egyptian Cav.*, 62–64.)

This accounts for the delight at Hd. Qrs. at discovering that they don't run away. Broadwood was much obliged to me for my assistance and told the Sirdar so. He, Broadwood,' added Haig characteristically, 'was wrong to charge as he did with the first line for the whole Brigade then passed from his control. But he is a sound fellow and is excellent at running this show.'[11]

In what was the sole example of a rearguard action in the war, six troopers were killed and ten wounded. Over twenty horses were killed and many wounded. The dervish loss was put at over 100. One officer who witnessed the action declared that it was 'Maiwand again, only properly done'.

Nevertheless, Lieutenant-Colonel John Maxwell, a contemporary of Haig's, who was present as a member of Kitchener's staff thought

'the cavalry day was very nearly being a very serious affair for us, and at one time it looked uncommonly as if they would bag the lot of us; we were completely surrounded by their horsemen and could not see a yard for dust, bullets fizzing about, and had a real attack been pushed home, they would undoubtedly have got the lot of us, as we were too far out in the desert for any of us to have got away.'[12]

However that might be, the information gained was just what Kitchener wanted, and everyone seemed to think that 'the dogged, up-hill, back-breaking, heart-breaking work of fifteen years had come to bear fruit,' and that by showing 'his indifference to cold steel' the Egyptian trooper had been vindicated. 'The cavalry mess,' according to one who visited it, 'was a hum of cheerfulness that night' and 'the troopers riding their horses down to the pool moved with a swing that was not there before.'[13]

Three days later, on Good Friday, the Sirdar launched a frontal attack on the zariba. Within half an hour it was overrun. Many dervishes lay dead, but the British casualty list was not many short of 600. The country through which the routed dervishes fled up the Atbara after the battle was so dense and tangled that no effective pursuit proved possible.

* * *

For the third and final phase of the war Kitchener now waited till the Nile should be navigable up to Khartoum, and the railway should be completed to the Atbara. This last was accomplished by 3 July. Amongst the reinforcements asked for and received were a second British infantry brigade, an howitzer battery and the 21st Lancers.

This regiment had been raised as the 21st Light Dragoons in 1759 and disbanded sixty-one years later, as part of the post-Waterloo reductions (see Vol I, p. 75). In 1862 the regiment was re-born in India out of the 3rd Bengal European Cavalry, and called the 21st Hussars (see Vol II, p. 346). During nineteen years in India and fifteen at home, partly in Ireland, it had never seen any sort of action, though it had provided a contingent for the Light Camel Regiment which guarded the lines of communication for the Gordon Relief Expedition of 1884–5 (see p. 321). In 1896 it arrived in Cairo to relieve the 2nd Dragoon Guards (Queen's Bays). During the following year it was converted into a regiment of lancers. Before the men left Cairo for the south they exchanged their large troop horses, which they had brought with them from India, for light Syrian and country-bred stallions. Both officers and men were extraordinarily anxious to deserve no longer the unkind regimental motto some wit had awarded them. It read: 'Thou shalt not kill'. An infantry officer, perhaps rather apprehensively, remarked of the lancer officers at this time, 'These men are regular Thrusters'.[14]

On first seeing the regiment ready for the field, G. W. Steevens, correspondent of *The Daily Mail*, thought the troopers 'looked less like horsemen than Christmas trees'. Indeed they referred to themselves as being in 'Christmas Tree Order'. Churchill describes how, as they entrained, there dangled from every part of their bodies, 'haversacks, canteen-straps, cloaks, swords and carbines'. To these last, as Steevens noted, picketing pegs were lashed, while from the saddles hung 'feeds of corn, canvas buckets opposite them, waterproofs behind, bulky holsters in front, . . . water-bottles in nets under the horses' bellies, khaki neck screens flapping from helmets and blue gauze veils hooding helmets and heads and all. The smallest Syrian,' he adds, 'had to carry eighteen stone; with a heavy man the weight was well over twenty.'[15]

Lieutenant Winston Spencer Churchill of the 4th Hussars was one of a number of young officers attached to the regiment. He had obtained a troop upon the death of its commander. This did not prevent him from also acting as unofficial war correspondent for *The Morning Post*. 'The 21st Lancers,' he told his mother, 'are not on the whole a good business and I would much rather have been attached to Egyptian cavalry staff.' He was pleased, though, that the campaign was to be conducted, so far as officers were concerned, 'in a luxurious manner. We are allowed 200 lbs baggage in contrast to the very strict Indian "80 lb scale" . . . I cannot help realizing how much is superfluous. However the sound policy is to "take as much as you can as far as you can".'[16]

The regiment left Cairo on 2 August. Thirteen days later it arrived in the Atbara camp. The horses, after being cramped all that time in trucks and barges (where they had been so tightly packed that 'biting was the sole expression they could give to their feelings'), found the forced marches which followed a severe trial. They travelled nearly thirty miles daily throughout the midday heat of each of the nine days it took to reach Wad Hamed. Nearly fifty had to be destroyed. This was chiefly because they went lame with 'a peculiar form of *laminitis* . . . caused partly by the hard, hot ground and partly by the sand wearing away the frog of the hoof . . . The unfortunate horse,' noticed Churchill, 'can hardly walk, and doubtless takes every step with agony . . . All the cripples among the horses who gave any hopes of getting well if they had a day's rest, were relieved of their loads. To carry the men and saddles twenty donkeys and a dozen camels were borrowed from the infantry transport.'[17] This, unlike the river-borne infantry itself, formed part of the unwieldly mass of men, guns and supplies which the cavalry and the Camel Corps were escorting along the river banks.

Churchill considered this forced marching 'a gross piece of mismanagement and miscalculation on the part of the Sirdar'.[18] Kitchener, however, in his tough, insensitive way, said to Haig: 'They have mismanaged their march.' In a letter home Haig, now commanding a comparatively veteran Egyptian squadron, commented: 'But I *thought* it would be hard for fresh troops!!'[19]

On arrival at Wad Hamed an extraordinary operation took place. Out of the 21st Lancers' three squadrons, each nearly 130 strong, their commanding officer, Lieutenant-Colonel Rowland Hill Martin, now proceeded to form four.

> 'The method,' according to the young Churchill, 'was as follows: One of the four troops was taken from each of the three squadrons and formed into a new and separate squadron, making a regiment of four squadrons of three troops each,

> instead of a regiment of three squadrons of four troops each. Then one section was taken from each of the three troops of every squadron and formed into a fourth troop for each squadron, making four squadrons of four troops of three sections each. Then the three sections of each troop were told off as four sections . . . This took place five days before the regiment was actually in contact with the enemy.'

Churchill gives the reason for this 'appalling internal convulsion' thus: 'The Sirdar has said that he wanted a regiment of four squadrons, and rather than run the risk of being left behind the 21st Lancers would have formed forty. Colonel Martin had no choice.'[20] Kitchener's desire to alter the established system of three field squadrons and one depot squadron may have arisen from a feeling that squadrons of 130 men were unwieldy or a belief that lancer regiments required a stronger front rank, so that as many men as possible should be able to use their lances in the charge. Whatever his motives, a more unsettling disturbance can hardly be imagined, coming on top of the recent conversion to lancers and the even more recent exchange of horses.

* * *

The final advance began on 24 August, 1898. For five days the mounted arm patrolled ahead finding virtually no enemy, until on 31st, reaching the northern foot of the Kerreri ridge, some seven miles from the sprawling mass of Omdurman, the lancers came across a dervish outpost. While the regiment withdrew to report, the adjutant and another officer rode out alone, unofficially and rather recklessly, to draw the enemy's fire and return it. Soon afterwards a gunboat lobbed some shells at the outpost, drawing the day's activities to a close.

From 1 to 9 a.m. on the following day, 1 September, there occurred, most unexpectedly, 'a terrific storm of rain and wind'. Long before it had come to an end, the cavalry, in Haig's words,

> 'pushed on ahead; the 21st Lancers kept near the river, working independently of us, and (I thought) somewhat recklessly, knowing, from what I saw on the Atbara, what a foxlike enemy the dervish is. The Egyptian cavalry and horse [battery] and four maxims reached the west end of Kerreri ridge about 8 o'clock. From the top of the ridge, Omdurman was visible,

some five or six miles off, with the Mahdi's tomb standing high above every other building . . .

'On reaching the round [topped] hill a most wonderful sight presented itself to us. A huge force of men with flags, drums and bugles was being assembled to the west of the city; the troops formed on a front some three miles long, and as each body or "roob" was complete, it commenced to move northwards. With my glass I saw that they were moving very fast indeed. To my mind we were wasting time where we were . . .

'There were about some 30,000 men extending across the plain, and all in movement before we left the round hill. I acted as rear guard with my squadron to five companies of camel corps and two machine guns. The [rest of the Egyptian] cavalry preceded us in the retirement – a faulty disposition: the more mobile arm (cavalry) should have all been in the rear of the slow moving camelry . . . The ground being open, I kept all my squadron together except three small groups which I left out towards our right rear. Some dervish horsemen galloped forward and engaged these – two dervishes were disabled; my fellows still all right and full of pluck . . . The dervish infantry was coming on in lines, running and shouting and beating drums; it seemed to me still a race, though of course we could always pass to the north of the Kerreri hill if cut off from passing south of it . . .

'Some of their cavalry were coming uncomfortably near . . . As soon as my squadron reached the hill I dismounted a few men behind it, and (taking a carbine myself) fired as rapidly as possible at those of the enemy nearest to us. We disabled several, and they delayed for those following to join them; then they opened a hot fire against the ridge, evidently thinking it was our main position. By the time they discovered their error, we were well on our way to camp.'[21]

The 21st Lancers had also brushed with the enemy patrols, losing, according to Churchill, 'about a dozen' horses from exhaustion in the course of the day.[22]

Kitchener's main force, in the meantime, had established camp in the form of a semi-circular, partially entrenched, zariba on the bank of the Nile at El Egeiga. At about 1.45 p.m. the dervish advance ceased.

During this day the gunboats had shelled Omdurman inflicting extensive damage on many buildings including the greatest of all dervish symbols, the tomb of the Mahdi. It seems likely that the Khalifa's original intention was to fight the invader in Omdurman itself. Had he stuck to it, the resultant street fighting would have vastly diminished the ability of Kitchener's infantry to deploy its superior fire-power. As it was the gunboats' fifty-pound Lyddite shells seem to have persuaded the Khalifa to move his shell-shocked troops out of the city to join their comrades on the plain of Kerreri. The opposing armies lay during the night less than four miles from each other. Some 50,000 Mahdists, some armed with modern small bore rifles, mostly Italian obtained in Abyssinia, others with Remingtons, more with even less sophisticated firearms, and most with spears and swords, lay facing an Egyptian army of 25,800, of which 8,200 were British, supported by, on land, forty-four pieces of artillery and twenty Maxims, with over 7,000 animals. Aboard the gunboats were sixty more guns, including twenty-four Maxims.

* * *

Against a night attack Kitchener took every conceivable precaution, including the constant use of the gunboats' searchlights. His very real fears were not, in the event, realized.

At about 5 a.m. Captain the Hon Everard Baring, seconded from the 10th Hussars, led his squadron of Egyptian cavalry out of camp. As soon as it was light enough he established that the enemy was still encamped in the Kerreri plain.*

> 'By a quarter to six a.m.,' recorded Haig in his diary, 'Baring reported in person to the Sirdar that the whole dervish army [divided into five main sections covering a front of some four miles] was in movement northwards, its right two miles from the river . . . By this hour I had my squadron deployed as an advanced guard for the infantry between Signal† and Kerreri Hills . . . Going forward to my advanced parties, I could see the vast masses of the enemy going for the Kerreri Hills (that is northwards) and not moving east.'[23]

In other words, the Khalifa, for some unexplained reason, seems

* A short time later Churchill with an advanced patrol of the 21st Lancers had confirmed the enemy's presence. The text of his messages sent direct to Kitchener is given in *Companion*, 972.

† Jebel Surgham was also known as Signal or Heliograph Hill.

to have assumed that the Sirdar had abandoned his riverside camp and was drawn up along the Kerreri range.

As the dervish masses advanced, Kitchener realized that his adversary, although marching in the wrong direction, was on the offensive. Much relieved, he ordered his infantry, which at dawn had been paraded outside the roughly formed zariba, to take up position behind it.

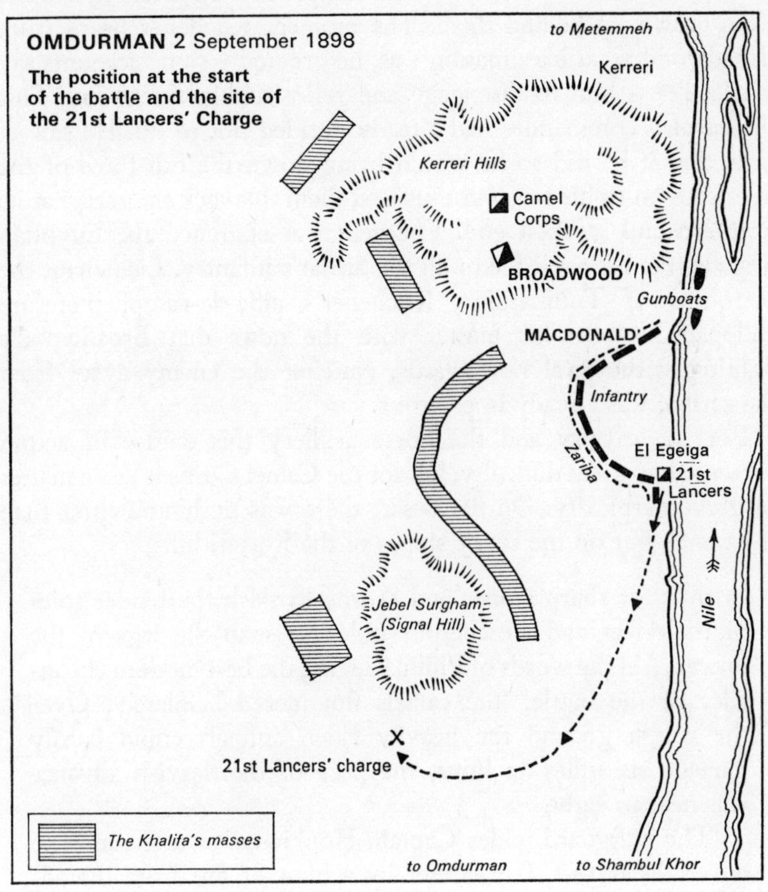

Map 18

At about the same time Broadwood ordered Haig to clear the front in good time so as to allow the guns to open fire. This they did, with very good effect. But their target was only a comparatively small, and by no means the best, part of the Khalifa's army. It numbered perhaps 18,000. These fanatical men, having wheeled to the right, disregarding the gaps torn in their ranks, advanced, unshaken, till the fire of the British infantry in the centre of the zariba mowed them down. Only a few got closer than 800 yards.

Meanwhile a far greater dervish mass, perhaps 25,000 strong, was clambering up the Kerreri hills, as Haig reported, 'at a great pace'. To meet them were the horse artillery, whose antiquated 9 lb Krupp guns had 'not the slightest effect in checking them', the four 'galloping' Maxims* and the Camel Corps. The Egyptian squadrons were drawn up behind them. The moment Kitchener heard from Broadwood what his situation was, he ordered – some accounts say 'advised'[24] – him to disengage and retire within the zariba. This the cavalry commander had already decided not to do. He saw at once that if he did so he would bring down the full force of the dervishes on to his tail, and thus lead them to attack the zariba at its northern and weakest end. For here was stationed the Egyptian brigade, the least reliable of all the Sirdar's infantry. Lieutenant the Marquess of Tullibardine, Kitchener's aide-de-camp, therefore galloped back to his master with the news that Broadwood's fighting withdrawal northwards, enticing the enemy away from the zariba, was already in progress.

For the cavalry and the horse artillery this course of action presented no great difficulty, but for the Camel Corps it was a matter of grave perplexity. On flat desert there was nothing swifter than the camel, but on the rocky slopes of the Kerreri hills,

> 'with razor sharp stones and thorns to slash the tender soles of their feet and treacherous holes to snap the legs of the unwary,' in the words of Philip Ziegler, the best modern chronicler of the battle, 'the camels floundered helplessly. Over the rough ground the heavily laden animals could hardly manage six miles an hour, the pace of the dervish advance was near to eight.
>
> 'The rearguard under Captain Hopkinson swung round to cover the retreat. It was met by a blast of fire from the advancing dervishes. "There was a thud [wrote Hopkinson], like a fist sinking into flesh, and I felt my beast lurch under me. It sank down on its knees and twisted round its neck, so that its huge brown eyes flecked with a septic yellow seemed to be staring reproachfully at me. Its mouth was open in a grimace of

* These, at this critical moment, were sent for by Kitchener, to assist the infantry in the zariba. (*Haig*, 118.)

pain and a thick trickle of black blood oozed from the corner and smeared the brown of its hide. It uttered a despairing 'grunk', half groan, half wail, and keeled slowly over till it lay twitching feebly on its side." '[25]

The horse artillery attempted to cover the retreat of the Camel Corps, but they stayed too long. As they started to move off, with the enemy almost upon them, a lucky dervish shot killed one of the horses. While the gun crew tried to free the corpse, the wheel of a second gun became entangled in the wreckage of the first. Hotly pursued by the dervishes, who were by now within a hundred yards of them, the artillerymen, 'two on a horse or clinging on to the stirrup of a friend', fled from the scene, leaving two of their six guns abandoned. The Camel Corps eventually reached the haven of the zariba, saved by the guns of the *Melik* gunboat commanded by General Gordon's nephew, which Kitchener had ordered downstream for the purpose. The Corps' casualties numbered over sixty.[26]

While this drama was being enacted, the men of Haig's squadron, supported by others, were doing their best to distract the bulk of the enemy, dismounting, firing their carbines, remounting and again and again repeating the process.* Captain Sir Henry Rawlinson, bart, the Sirdar's Deputy Assistant Adjutant-General, arriving from headquarters to see what was going on, observed Haig's confident bearing which 'seemed to have inspired his fellaheen, who were watching the dervish advance quite calmly'.[27] Haig, himself, noted that the enemy followed him

'with a very hot fire, and large parties, moving further from the river, tried to get round our flank. We halted about eight o'clock . . . some three to four miles north of the Kerreri ridge. We now saw that the enemy had discovered his mistake (viz. that he had attacked *en l'air*) and that he was moving back over the west portion of the Kerreri Ridge very fast. [A portion of the cavalry now went back to recover the two abandoned guns, while the rest] trotted south and rejoined the infantry . . .'[28]

* * *

* When, a little later on, a group of enemy horsemen joined in the pursuit, Major B. T. Mahon, Broadwood's second-in-command, charged them, and put them to flight.

Kitchener, once the first attack on the zariba had been repulsed, believed that whatever further Mahdist forces remained in the field, it was of paramount importance that he should occupy Omdurman before they could reach it and perhaps commit him to costly street fighting. With this object in mind he now sent forth the 21st Lancers to reconnoitre from the southern extremity of the zariba up to the city's outskirts. A little while later, as will be seen, he ordered the infantry and guns to leave the zariba and prepare to march towards the city.

As the lancers passed the eastern slopes of Signal Hill, they saw, in Churchill's words, 'a broad stream of fugitives, of wounded' flowing 'from the Khalifa's army to the city . . . Only the scattered parties in the plain appeared to prevent a glorious pursuit . . . The skirmishers among the rocks . . . soon began to fire at the regiment and we sheltered among the mounds of sand, while a couple of troops replied with their carbines.' The regimental signals officer now, it seems, heliographed a message to headquarters reporting that there were still formed bodies ahead. It took some time before Lieutenant-Colonel Martin received further instructions to advance. At 8.30 a.m. he received an heliographed order from Kitchener which said: 'Annoy them as far as possible on their flank and head them off if possible from Omdurman.'[29]

Two strong patrols now went forward. That which rode south-westwards along the base of Signal Hill soon reported to the colonel that 'in a shallow and apparently practicable *khor* [dry water course] . . . between the regiment and the fugitives, there was drawn up a formed body of Dervishes'. This body appeared to be about 700 strong.

In *The River War,* his incomparable account of Kitchener's campaign, Churchill records what happened next: 'As the 21st Lancers left the ridge, the fire of the Arab riflemen on the hill ceased. We advanced at a walk in mass for about 300 yards. The scattered parties of Dervishes fell back and melted away, and only one straggling line of men in dark blue waited motionless a quarter of a mile to the left front.'[30] In a letter written to his friend Colonel Sir Ian Hamilton a fortnight later Churchill says that this line of men numbered 150.*

> 'We all thought these spearmen. They let us get within 250 yards in silence. We proposed – at least I think this was the idea

* In his book, though, he says 'scarcely a hundred strong'. (*River War*, 134.)

> – to move round their flank and slip a squadron at them and then on to the better things beyond. The ground looked all right and besides we did not intend doing anything from that direction.
>
> 'We trotted in column of troops across their front from right to left. As we did so the enemy got down on their knees and opened a very sharp fire.'[31]

Several men and horses came crashing to the ground. 'Bullets,' wrote Lieutenant R. N. Smyth, 'seemed to be whistling and splashing all round.'[32]

Churchill told Ian Hamilton that there seemed to be only two courses now open to Colonel Martin:

> 'Left wheel into line and gallop off – coming back for wounded – a bad business [or] Right wheel into line and charge . . . While the trumpet was still jerking we were all at the gallop towards them. The fire was too hot to allow of second lines – flank squadrons or anything like that being arranged. The only order given was Right Wheel into Line. Gallop and and charge were understood.'[33]

Thus 'on the instant all the sixteen troops swung round and locked up into a long galloping line, and the 21st Lancers were committed to their first charge in war.'[34]

Before this famous charge is described, a look must be taken to see what was happening on 'the other side of the hill'. No one on the British side seems to have been aware that beside the comparatively small dervish groups which had attacked the zariba and the much larger ones which had been futilely chasing Broadwood northwards,* the Khalifa had kept back some 21,000 of his finest troops. These had so far remained out of sight of the British behind Signal Hill. The 700 men seen by the lancers, who had apparently so surprisingly dwindled to 150 by the time the charge started, were merely a force stationed in the *khor* to keep open the Khalifa's line of retreat to Omdurman. What Colonel Martin could not know was that, in Churchill's words, 'as soon as the 21st Lancers left the zariba the Dervish scouts on the top of [Signal Hill] carried the news to the Khalifa. It was said that the English cavalry were coming to cut him off from Omdurman. Abdullahi thereupon . . . immediately ordered four regiments, each 500 strong',[35] drawn from his

* Of which, incidentally, over 5,000, having swung leftwards, had never been engaged at all.

reserve of 21,000, to reinforce the men in the *khor*. These and the unseen remainder of the 700 had concealed themselves in this dry water course whilst the lancers were awaiting their orders. As Philip Ziegler has written: 'It was one of the oldest and favourite tricks in the Arab repertoire; Broadwood would have been immediately suspicious, Martin had no such qualms. His only regret was that . . . there were hardly enough enemy to give the Lancers' coming victory any real distinction.'[36]

As the regiment charged, the bullets of the thin line of dervishes struck the ground, throwing up stinging particles of sand. To shield their faces the men 'bowed their helmets forward, like the Cuirassiers at Waterloo. The pace,' wrote Churchill, 'was fast and the distance short. Yet, before it was half covered, the whole aspect of the affair changed.' What had been supposed to be a mere shallow depression was now seen to be a twenty-foot-wide *khor* with sides sloping down to a depth of between four and six feet. From it there now

> 'sprang, with the suddenness of a pantomime effect and a high-pitched yell, a dense white mass of men nearly as long,' Churchill noted, 'as our front and about twelve deep. A score of horsemen and a dozen bright flags rose as if by magic from the earth. Eager warriors sprang forward to anticipate the shock. The rest stood firm to meet it. The Lancers acknowledged the apparition only by an increase in pace. Each man wanted sufficient momentum to drive through such a solid line.'[37]

Of his own part in the charge, Churchill, who was riding 'a handy, surefooted, grey Arab polo pony',[38] wrote to Hamilton:

> 'I went through the first 100 yards looking over my shoulder to see what sort of effect the fire was producing. It seemed small. Then I drew my Mauser pistol – a ripper – and cocked it.* Then I looked to my front . . .

* 'Before we wheeled and began to gallop', wrote Chruchill twenty-five years later, 'the officers had been marching with drawn swords . . . I had always decided that if I were involved in hand-to-hand fighting, I must use a pistol and not a sword. I had purchased in London a Mauser automatic pistol, then the newest and the latest design. I had practiced carefully with this during our march and journey up the river. This then was the weapon with which I determined to fight. I had first of all to return my sword into its scabbard, which is not the easiest thing to do at a gallop. I had then to draw my pistol from its wooden holster and bring it to full cock.' (*Early Life*, 204.)

'I thought – capital – the more the merrier . . . I was right troop leader but one. I saw we overlapped. I was afraid we would charge into air. I shouted to Wormald 7th Hussars (an excellent officer), [commanding the right troop], to shoulder and we actually struck the enemy in a crescent formation. Result of our shoulder was this – my troop struck [the *khor*] diagonally and their decreasing slope enabled us to gallop through not jump it. Result we struck faster and more formed than the centre troops.

'Opposite me they were about four deep. But they all fell knocked A.O.T. [arse over tip] and we passed through without any sort of shock. One man in my troop fell. He was cut to pieces. Five or six horses were wounded by back handers etc. But otherwise unscathed. Then we emerged into a region of scattered men and personal combats. The troop broke up and disappeared. I pulled into a trot and rode up to individuals firing my pistol in their faces and killing several – three for certain – two doubtful – one very doubtful. Then I looked round and saw the Dervish mass reforming . . . I realized that this mass was about twenty yards away and I looked at them stupidly for what may have been two seconds. Then I saw two men get down on their knees and take aim with rifles – and for the first time the danger & peril came home to me. I turned and galloped. The squadron was reforming nearly 150 yards away. As I turned both shots were fired and at that close range I was grievously anxious. But I heard none of their bullets – which went Heaven knows where. So I pulled into a canter and rejoined my troop – having fired exactly ten shots & emptied my pistol – but without a hair of my horse or a stitch of my clothing being touched. Very few can say the same.'[39]

Writing to his mother two days after the battle Churchill said that the charge 'passed like a dream and some part I cannot quite recall. The Dervishes showed no fear of cavalry and would not move unless you knocked them over with the horse. They tried to hamstring the horses, to cut the bridles – reins – slashed and stabbed in all directions and fired rifles at a few feet range.'[40]

Another who came through unscathed was the commanding officer, although he drew neither sword nor revolver. Major W. G. Crole Wyndham's horse was shot under him, yet he managed to fight his way out of the savage crowd on foot, uninjured. Lieutenant Wormald's sword, made 'by a well-known London maker', bent double. He kept hold of it as a souvenir, and perhaps with the intention of lodging a complaint. Captain Fair's sword snapped on striking a dervish spear. He only survived the spear owner's thrust by flinging the hilt into his face.

Strongly contrasted in style with Churchill's account is that of Lieutenant Smyth, the left troop leader of the right squadron, who was therefore two troops nearer the centre:

> 'Find myself at [*khor*]. Man bolts out leaving two donkeys in my way, catch hold of horse hard by head, knowing to fall would be fatal. He blunders against donkey, recovers and scrambles out; am met by swordsman on foot, cuts at my right front, I guard it with sword. Next man, and a face, all in white, having fired and missed me, throws up both hands. I cut him across both hands, he cuts at me, think this time I must be done but pace tells and my guard carries it off. Duck my head to sword thrown, just misses me, another cut at my horse, miss guard but luckily cut is too far away and only cuts through my breastplate and gives my horse a small flesh wound in the neck and shoulder. Then I remember no more till I find myself outside with four or five of my troop . . . Rally my troop as well as I can. Horrible sights. Everyone seems to be bleeding including my own horse . . . It seems to be blood, blood, blood everywhere. Horses and men smothered [with it].'[41]

In the centre of the line some of the lancers' mounts were actually forced to jump on to the spears of the massed dervishes, whose heads in places were scarcely level with the horses' knees. In a letter published in *The Morning Post*, Churchill wrote that 'many horses pecked [pitched forward] on landing and stumbled in the press, and the man that fell was pounced on by a dozen merciless foes.'[42]

One of the troops near the centre was that of Lieutenant Robert Grenfell. It fared worst of all, having a high bank of boulders to scramble up before it could escape from the *khor*. Grenfell himself fell dead, struck by a sword in the back and pierced in the wrist by another. His helmet when recovered was seen to have received eleven separate cuts or thrusts. The troop also lost its centre guide, both flank guides, ten killed and eleven wounded. After the charge Sergeant Freeman was seen trying to collect and rally the troop with his face cut to pieces, his nose, cheeks and lips flapping 'amid red bubbles'.[43] 'Fall in, No. 2; fall in,' he shouted. 'Where are the devils? Show me the devils!' No. 2 fell in – four whole men out of twenty.[44]

Lieutenant the Hon Raymond Hervey de Montmorency commanded the next troop to the left. He, having come out of the *khor* safely, at once returned to look for his troop sergeant, found his bleeding body and hauled it on to his horse. This animal, before he could remount, bolted. Captain P. A. Kenna seeing de Montmorency surrounded by a screaming horde, fought his way to him, while Corporal Swarbrick caught the horse and restored it to its master. All three men then somehow hewed and chopped their way to safety. The two officers were later awarded the Victoria Cross, while the corporal received the Distinguished Service Medal.

The horse of Lieutenant the Hon R. F. Molyneux, attached from the Blues, was killed under him. At the moment of firing his pistol it was knocked from his hand by a sword cut across his wrist. Beset on all sides he saw a single lancer from his troop not far off. To him he called out for help. Though Private Thomas Byrne's right arm had received a bullet and his chest a spear thrust, he had kept his seat. 'All right, sir,' he shouted. 'I won't leave you,' and without hesitation he forced his way to his officer. As he did so a spear just missed his face. '—— the ——! He's broken my pipe,' he exclaimed in his strong Irish brogue. He then shepherded Molyneux to safety and rode to join his troop. There he was ordered to fall out but insisted upon remaining to have 'another go at them'. Soon afterwards he fainted from loss of blood. He was the third member of the regiment to be awarded the Victoria Cross for bravery in the charge.[45]

One corporal found the 'whole charge was a blank. He knew nothing until he reached the other side, and then he found his sword-arm red to the shoulder with blood and thought he must be wounded, but found himself unhurt – the blood was that of other men.'[46] But Churchill describes the most astonishing escape of all those recorded. Lieutenant C. S. Nesham's experience, he wrote,

> 'was that of the men who were killed, only that he escaped to describe it. He had scrambled out of the *khor* when, as his horse was nearly stopping, an Arab seized his bridle. He struck at the man with his sword, but did not prevent him cutting his

> off-rein. The officer's bridle-hand, unexpectedly released, flew out, and, as it did so, a swordsman at a single stroke nearly severed it from his body. Then they cut at him from all sides. One blow shore through his helmet and grazed his head. Another inflicted a deep wound in his right leg. A third, intercepted by his shoulder-chains, paralysed his right arm. Two more missing him narrowly, cut right through the cantel of the saddle and into the horse's back. The wounded subaltern – he was the youngest of all – reeled. A man on either side seized his legs to pull him to the ground. The long spurs struck into the horse's flanks, and the maddened animal, throwing up its head and springing forward, broke away from the crowd of foes, and carried the rider – bleeding, failing, but still alive – to safety among the rallying squadrons.'[47]

Churchill reckons that the charge was over in 120 seconds. He also claims that 'in less than five minutes'[48] the regiment had re-formed and was ready to charge back. A quarter of a century later he wrote that his men were 'ready, though they looked serious. Several asked to be allowed to throw away their lances and draw their swords. I asked my second sergeant if he had enjoyed himself. His answer was, "Well, I don't exactly say I enjoyed it, Sir; but I think I'll get more used to it next time." At this the whole troop laughed.'

But for Colonel Martin it was no laughing matter. One officer and twenty men had been killed, four officers and forty-six men wounded out of a total of little over 300, and 119 horses killed or wounded.* Not more than twenty-three of the dervishes were killed. The number of their wounded, though not great, will never be known. As riderless horses careered across the plain and as others limped and staggered with their wounded riders, the colonel decided against a further charge. He

> 'remembered for the first time that we had carbines,' wrote Churchill. 'Everything was still in great confusion. But trumpets were sounded and orders shouted, and we all moved off at a trot towards the flank of the enemy. Arrived at a position from which we could enfilade and rake the watercourse, two squadrons were dismounted and in a few minutes with their fire at three hundred yards compelled the Dervishes to retreat.'[49]

* The total casualties of the army numbered only 482.

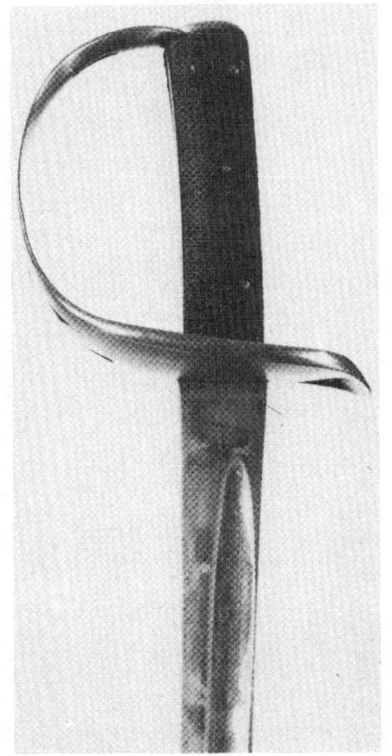

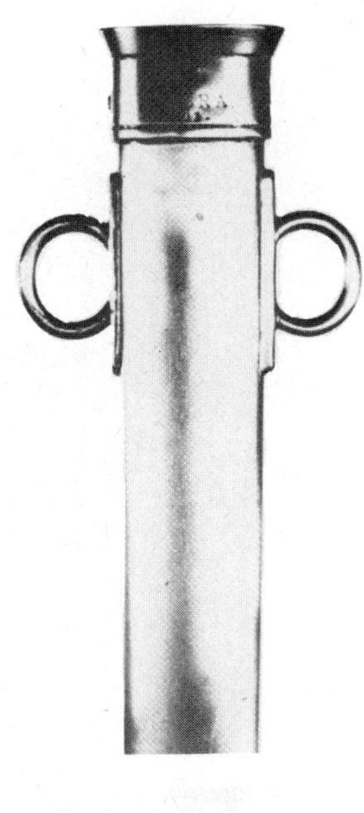

56. Cavalry troopers' sword, 1882 pattern, 'Long and Short, Mk. 1'

57. Cavalry troopers' scabbard, 1885 pattern, Mk. 1

58. A troop horse, 1899. This fifteen-year-old mare served for eleven years without a day's sickness or lameness

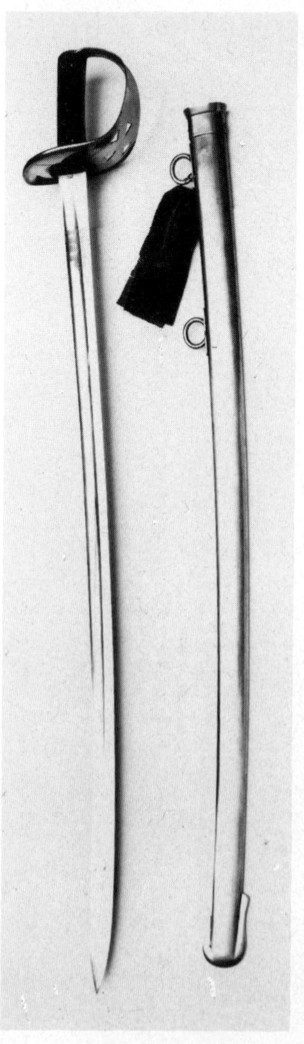

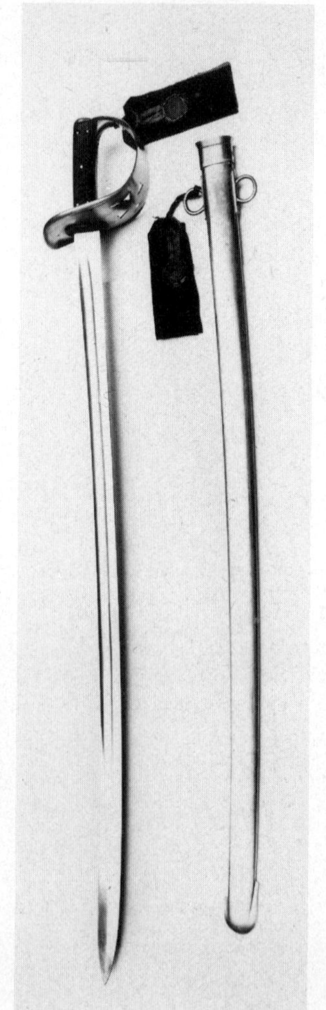

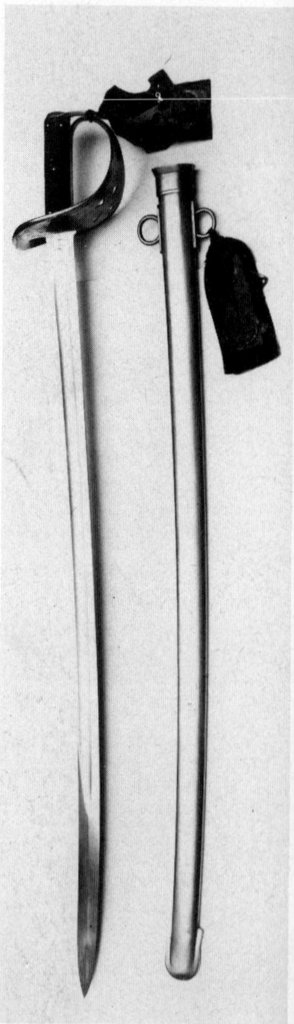

59. Cavalry troopers' sword, 1882 pattern, 'Long (New)'

60. Cavalry troopers' sword, 1885 pattern

61. Cavalry troopers' sword, 1890 pattern

The dervishes in fact advanced in very good order against the dismounted lancers, but the carbine fire they met was too much for them, and they wheeled off to rejoin their comrades behind Signal Hill.

This successful use of firearms at this late stage by only half the regiment points up the comparative uselessness of the charge. It is hard to believe that Churchill was right to conclude that Colonel Martin had but two choices before him when he was first fired upon. There was a third course which one might suppose that an experienced cavalry commander would have adopted. He could, surely, have dismounted a portion of his force and returned the fire, meanwhile sending on a patrol to work round the enemy's flank so as to see what was beyond. Then, if necessary, as he moved closer to the *khor*, he could have used the carbines of nearly the whole regiment against the 2,000 or so dervishes he would have discovered there. Yet it is easy and dangerous to be wise after the event. There is no doubt, though, that the Sirdar was much displeased. In his despatch he hardly mentioned the incident. When the news of it reached England, however, there was no stopping the exorbitant encomiums lavished upon the regiment. As with the charge of the light brigade at Balaklava forty-four years before, the most futile and inefficient part of the battle was the most extravagantly praised. This, of course, as in the earlier case, was chiefly due to the splendid gallantry and discipline of both officers and men. Though equalled in numerous obscure and unsung engagements, especially in India, these were without doubt of the very highest order.

What is also certain is that, as Churchill puts it in *My Early Life*, 'Everyone expected that we were going to make a charge. That was the one idea that had been in all minds since we started from Cairo. Of course there would be a charge. In those days, before the Boer War, British cavalry had been taught little else.'[50] Equally undeniable is the fact that the charge had been costly without obtaining any sort of compensating result. Indeed it had prevented the carrying out of the regiment's set task. Further, and more important, it had removed any possibility of the lancers discovering the Khalifa's massive reserves which were even now beginning to debouch from behind Signal Hill north-eastwards.

The Sirdar's infantry and guns were still marshalling for their southward march when the full weight of the Khalifa's attack from the west fell upon the rear brigade. This consisted of Sudanese and Egyptian battalions, and was commanded by the undoubted hero of the battle, Lieutenant-Colonel Hector Macdonald. First he had to repel a charge of some 100 horsemen, who, in Haig's words, 'charged boldly till all were shot down – the last at about forty yards or less from the line. Mass upon mass of dervish footmen then attacked; they were beaten back.' Almost immediately after this Macdonald had to face the enemy forces which had earlier attacked the Egyptian cavalry and Camel Corps, augmented by the 5,000 who, having veered westwards, had not so far been in action. To Haig the enemy

> 'seemed to come on in countless numbers and in rank after rank. Their order and maneouvring power was wonderful. Macdonald's Brigade was supported by the Camel Corps on his right hand . . . The dervishes rushed on, heedless of the hail of bullets – many of them were killed about 100 yards from the firing line. After some twenty minutes the dervishes began to draw off, seeing Macdonald being reinforced with more troops.
>
> 'The Egyptian cavalry now galloped out in pursuit . . . Many wounded men still rose up and fired at us as we approached, and spearmen tried to hurl a spear. As we proceeded westwards, many little groups of men dropped down on their knees in submission, though some firmly resisted till killed by our lances. I saw, too, men beg for pardon, and then, when we had passed, treacherously assault some unsuspecting trooper from the rear. My squadron was on the left of the line and I directed the line . . .
>
> 'We came under a hot fire from thick crowds of fugitives . . . It was clear that the enemy, tho' flying, was not routed. I dismounted my squadron and fired volleys by troops waiting for the other squadrons to come up. We could not charge towards Omdurman; there were too many resolute men intervening. So it was decided to charge about E. by south, towards the mouth of the Shambul Khor.
>
> 'We commenced our gallop; my squadron on the left, the centre one directing and a third squadron on the right. The fire increased as we advanced, and men on my left who had flung down their arms in submission picked them up again – so that we were enveloped with a cross fire from all directions. The squadron on my right passed in rear of mine to my left, and the right one did likewise, its leader galloping right across

my front. My men seemed to bend their heads to the right as one does to escape a storm of rain. I had seen eight horses go down in my front rank, and being unsupported on my right flank, I, too, brought up my right and moved now directly on Signal Hill. Our three squadrons had attacked some ten or more thousands resolute and armed men all scattered across the plain.

'I lost only five men wounded, but 19 horses. Our horses were now dead beat and we moved to the hill after dressing our wounded. We reached the Nile at about 3 o'clock – at mouth of Khor Shambul.'[51]

Here the whole army, at the height of the midday heat, slaked its thirst. Soon afterwards the infantry entered the city, and Kitchener received the keys from the principal Emir. At about 5 p.m. the cavalry marched round the west side of Omdurman until, as Haig wrote in his diary, they found themselves

'about S.W. of the Mahdi's tomb. Here we saw vast multitudes leaving the town far away to the south – camels, donkeys, horsemen, footmen, men, women and children and armed fugitives. Some came out from the city to surrender. When opposite the West gate Slatin* galloped from the city very excited and said Khalifa had just escaped . . . Our orders were to pursue at once. It was then about 7 p.m., almost dark. We got two guides mounted on camels of the camel corps and we went into the dark – horses dead beat, biscuit till to-morrow morning in the men's haversacks and feeds for horses till noon. A steamer was to bring up further supplies. We could not take the river road; too many armed men on it for safety in the dark, so we struck south towards some hills. The going soon became very soft, and our horses floundered occasionally up to the knees in wet sand. At 11 o'clock we could go no further and drew off to as dry a spot as we could find. Here we halted for the night . . .

'*September 3rd.* At 3 a.m. we moved on, there being a good moon, and by 7 o'clock we saw steamer close to the river bank. On reaching her we found she was 300 yards from the

* Rudolf Slatin Pasha, an Austrian adventurer, who had become Governor of Darfur and been taken prisoner by the Mahdi. He purchased his life by becoming a Moslem. In 1895, after ten years' confinement, he had escaped. He was with Kitchener throughout the campaign as an invaluable adviser.

> shore [unable to approach nearer] and stores could not be landed.'

After going on a further seven miles, Broadwood's men were still unable to find a place where the steamer could get the provisions ashore. By 3 p.m. on the day after the battle, therefore, 'no feed for man nor beast' remaining, and learning from fugitives that the Khalifa had

> 'pushed on all night, we decided to return and camp where we had struck the river in the morning. We got there about 6 o'clock and spent another night in the desert. The camel corps gave us a few pounds of dhurra for the horses and a little biscuit for the men. They also gave us officers some soup and MacConaghie's rations for dinner. This seemed to us a most luxurious dinner, for we had not had a proper meal since dinner on night of 1st September. The fatigue of the horses was extreme. Several had to be shot. Anticipating this we had taken three led horses per squadron.
>
> '*September 4th.* We marched at 5 a.m. and coming by the river road reached the S. end of Omdurman by 8 o'clock . . . A most unpleasant ride through the town on an empty stomach. Many unburied corpses, dead donkeys, etc. strewed the road . . . We passed the Mahdi's tomb much battered with shells . . . Camp was reached about 10 o'clock and right glad were we all to have a wash and a sleep!'[52]

A more ineffective pursuit it is difficult to imagine. 'The name of Omdurman,' wrote Churchill, 'must be added to the long list of battles in which the victorious army failed to take advantage of their triumph.'[53] The Khalifa was not finally tracked down and killed till November, 1899.

The longer term result of the battle was the establishment of firm, enlightened Anglo-Egyptian control of the whole of the Sudan – undoubtedly a good thing for the happiness of its people.

9

'The horse was first an animal of war, and it is inconceivable that war will ever be waged without him.'

From an article in the *Cavalry Journal* of 1929[1]

Horses: Army Remount Establishment founded – registration system started – veterinary reforms – regimental establishments – forage supply – increase in numbers of walers in India

As the nineteenth century drew to a close there came about something approaching a professional, almost scientific, attitude towards the question of providing horses for the cavalry. Two revolutionary steps were taken in the 1880s. The more far-reaching was the founding in 1887 of the Army Remount Establishment, as a separate department. No longer would the buying of horses for the cavalry be subject to the whims of individual commanding officers and the wiles of dealers. No longer would it be necessary as it had been in 1871 and 1872 to buy, so as to be able to take part in manoeuvres, more than 1,000 old horses for a few weeks' work at £38 to £42 each, plus £1 to £2 for travelling expenses.[2]

From now onwards a single policy would be pursued with respect to the quality, prices and ages of horses and also for the production of remounts required for mobilization. The Quartermaster-General now became responsible for the provision of all army remounts. Under him the new department was headed by the Inspector-General of Remounts, who was usually a major-general. This officer was assisted by a Deputy Assistant Adjutant-General whose office consisted of four clerks and a copyist. There were three assistant inspectors operating from London, Woolwich (chiefly for artillery horses) and Dublin. These were normally full colonels and between them they had a staff of 130 non-commissioned officers and men. Five veterinary surgeons were employed full-time travelling in the horse breeding districts buying horses without the intervention of middle men. The annual cost of the establishment was about £16,500.

The normal peacetime purchasing policy was to buy something

like 2,200 horses a year for the whole of the home army. Mares were bought from four years old at about £40 apiece. In 1898–9, for instance, 961 troop horse remounts were bought for the cavalry of the line at an average price of £39 15s each.[3] These were then generally sent to the Remount Depots at Dublin or Woolwich where they spent a few months before being 'issued' to units. The instructions were that they were to be employed on light work until they were mature. In 1898 it was laid down in *Cavalry Drill* that no remounts were to be 'placed in the ranks until the spring of the year in which they become five-year-olds, and then only if well developed and thoroughly trained. They will not be ridden at any manoeuvres of all arms until they are six years old,' though in purely 'cavalry concentrations' they might sometimes be allowed to take part.[4] Britain was the only country of importance where horses under five years of age were until that date considered part of the cavalry establishment. In 1890 there were 392 under that age in the seven regiments of the 1st Army Corps.[5]

It was also laid down that all purchases had to reach a standard of fifteen hands. Whether this was always adhered to is doubtful. Horses which were cast due to advanced years or disease were sold by the Remount Establishment. In 1896–7, for example, 1,200 were sold. Their average age was thirteen and a third years, and their average price was £9 3s each.

* * *

The second revolutionary innovation came about in 1888. Under the National Defence Act of that year a system of registration was started. The Act gave government powers to requisition all the horses and means of transport in the country in time of national danger or when the Militia was being mobilized. Owners of large numbers of the right type of horse, such as livery stable keepers and omnibus and railway companies, were asked to register a percentage of their horses voluntarily. The Remount Establishment then classified the horses and their owner signed a contract which bound him on the declaration of a national emergency to supply within forty-eight hours a certain number of horses for military use. Terms of prepayment were stipulated, and, of course, the horses had to be in good condition and of defined age and breed. Ten shillings a year was paid to owners when the scheme first came into effect. It was not in fact an outstanding success, but it was certainly an important step forward. In 1896–7 there were over 14,500 horses registered. 10,000 of these were draught horses. It was calculated at that date that a Cavalry Division required on mobilization 3,720 horses for the eight regiments of which it would be made up.[6]

When in 1895 the 8th Hussars were mobilized as an experiment (see p. 36), 250 registered horses were drawn from the North Metropolitan Tram Company and from various cab proprietors. 'They were,' according to the regimental historian, 'of a very good stamp, in good condition, wonderfully tractable, perfectly quiet in the ranks after five days. In order, however, to render them equal to trained cavalry, they would require at least a month in the School. They were quieter in the lines than the troop horses, both by day and night, and did not mind shackles.'[7]

* * *

Other important improvements affected the care and health of horses. During 1877 for instance the first Veterinary Statistical Report on the horses of the British army was published.[8] Three years later there was opened at Aldershot the Army Veterinary School. This was the result of the reforming zeal of James Collins, who had become Principal Veterinary Surgeon of the Army in 1876 (see p. 115). The school was designed to instruct combatant officers in such matters as the management of animals and in the veterinary treatment of simple cases when no professional was available. Further, probationary veterinary officers were to be trained in their military duties, while farriers and shoeing smiths were to be taught their tasks as horse hospital assistants. The school became in due course an important centre for research. In this, as in many other excellent reforms, Collins was much helped by that remarkable soldier, Lieutenant-General Sir Frederick Fitzwygram, bart, who commanded the Cavalry Brigade at Aldershot at the time. This rich gentleman had actually qualified as a vet when a captain in the 6th Dragoons as far back as 1854 (see Vol II, p. 384). His books, pamphlets and lectures, such as *Notes on Shoeing, Horses and Stables* and *Hints for the Selection of Remounts,* exercised a considerable influence upon the education of combatant officers in the craft of horsemastership, and in the prevention of disease in horses. Both Collins and Fitzwygram did a greal deal to lessen the most frequent causes of disease: improper diet, bad grooming and careless shoeing. By 1896, for example, no case of glanders, which in the past had been a major curse, had occurred in the army for over eight years.

Collins was succeeded in 1883 by Dr George Fleming, one of whose achievements was to secure the abolition of the contract system of shoeing which had been in existence from the army's earliest days. It is astonishing that this relic of the past should have survived until 1888, only twenty-six years before the First World War. The contract was between the individual farriers and the state. The farrier, who otherwise received no more than a private's pay, was given an allowance of a halfpenny a day per horse shoed. With this sum, which probably seldom reached £12 a year, he was required to provide iron, nails, tools, coal and much hard work, the state finding a forge and shoe-turning appliances. Needless to say, when government relieved the farriers of their contracts and bought their stock, it compensated them very illiberally, causing intense discontent.

Dr Fleming was also responsible for introducing against much opposition from commanding officers and farriers, machine-made shoes which could be put on cold, using machine-made nails. This new method was first tried on service in Suakin in 1885, where it proved highly successful (see p. 351). By 1888 it had crept into the more progressive cavalry regiments. No longer would it be essential to drag heavy forge carts over unmade roads, and no longer would forging capacity in the field fail, as it nearly always had done in the past, to meet the need for horseshoes occasioned by wear and tear.[9]

* * *

Some interesting facts about the number of horses actually available for duty emerged from evidence given to the Wantage Committee in 1891. Lieutenant-Colonel MacGeorge of the 6th Dragoon Guards, for instance, said that at home there were on average ten horses sick at any one time. He added that twenty-eight out of his total of 270 horses belonged to the regimental band, while another forty were young horses. For drill purposes, therefore, he was left with only 192. At that time his regiment was on the low establishment, which meant that each of his four squadrons should have consisted of ninety-eight other ranks with (not counting sick, young and band horses) sixty-seven animals. As things were, however, no more than forty-eight could be mustered, an 'absurdly small' number as the colonel pointed out.[10]

* * *

At home forage was supplied either by contract or by direct purchase. The daily allowance was 12 lbs of hay, 10 lbs of oats and 8 lbs of straw. It was usual to feed the troop horses three times and to water them four times a day. The regulations stipulated that feeding should always follow watering.[11]

Both to stop wastage and to improve the horses' health, a move was made in the 1890s to 'feed for work'. This entailed reducing the ration of oats and hay during the winter so as to have a reserve for the drill season, when, instead of standing or lying idle in stables, the horses 'would have to pay for their keep'. Then, when they were called upon for extra work, they got extra rations of from two to six pounds of oats a day, according to the economy which had been exercised and the nature of the tasks to be undertaken. The extra was found out of 'what used to be simply wasted in stable, or "missing" in other ways'.[12]

Modern industrial techniques were being increasingly employed in the provision of forage. During the Egyptian campaign of 1882, for example, a compressed grain cake, composed mainly of oats, with small proportions of beans, hay and crushed linseed was tried out with considerable success.[13]

* * *

Modern techniques were also coming into use in veterinary science. Captain Western of the Punjab Cavalry used to find in the 1870s that in India

> 'a morning in the operation ward of a horse hospital was a harrowing experience. Horses bought for native cavalry at the fairs in India comprised and still comprise many entire horses. The native is rather fond of noisy, screaming stallions, and a very few young horses are altered before they are brought to the market. With the pure-bred Arab the proceeding [of gelding] is in most cases unnecessary; many Arab stallions are as gentle as the mares, but the price of a pure-bred Arab is outside the troop-horse figure, and these animals are only found amongst the officers' chargers.'

Captain Western's commanding officer was Lieutenant-Colonel Corrie Bird,

> 'a humane and kind-hearted man from whom, when I first approached him with a suggestion that anaesthetics should be used, I received sympathetic co-operation. In fact,' says Captain Western, 'for some period of time this gallant officer defrayed all expenses for anaesthetics out of his own pocket. We speedily discovered that the light outlay (I think in those days the average cost of chloroforming a horse for a gelding operation was about three or four rupees) was more than compensated for by the immunity from death casualties and the speedy convalescence of the animals operated upon, and and when this was certain, the cost was regarded as a fair charge against horse funds.'[14]*

* * *

From the late 1870s onwards the traditional supply of Indian country-bred horses was for a number of reasons drying up.† In consequence increasing numbers of walers (known to the men as 'bounders', for obvious reasons)[15] were being imported from New South Wales. Sergeant-Major Mole found himself in charge of the young horse stables of the 14th Hussars. The first draft of fifty remounts from Australia with which he had to deal were 'from four to five years old each, rather heavier in build and tone than English ones, and lacking blood and breeding. The majority of them were mares, and they were of all colours except grey.' Mole found them extraordinarily frightened.

> 'It took months,' he discovered, 'to get over this timidity, and in some horses it proved quite incurable, for no matter how kindly and gently treated, they never ceased to dread the approach of the rider. All were more or less addicted to buck-jumping, and it was a very long and tedious job to get the worst ones to take the saddle quietly, for the moment they felt the girths tighten they would bound like a ball some feet into the

* Chloroform had been invented in 1831. It was first used as an anaesthetic on humans in 1847.

† One reason was that the Afghan War had taken an enormous toll of the horses from the Deccan. By the early 1880s breeding stock no longer existed. The breed, which had had a high reputation, never really recovered. (Tylden: *H. & S.*, 51.)

> air, trying to make their heads and tails meet between their legs. But trained they had to be, though it caused many practiced riders to experience a nasty fall, generally preluded by a somersault in the air.'

Mole was appointed a member of a government commission sent out to Australia to see what could be done to improve this fecund source of remounts. The commission was received by

> 'a deputation of breeders. The points urged were the advisability of importing good sires from England; the necessity of stabling and handling the young stock, instead of letting them run wild like mustangs; and, above all, the discontinuance of the barbarous practice of branding them with such enormous irons, which not only disfigured the horses, but seemed to give them a shock they never got over. The advice was readily adopted, and its fruits became apparent in two or three years. In 1874–5 the wretched skeletons of beasts that were bundled ashore at Madras, more dead than alive, were often sold at ten pounds a head. In 1879 the Government price was sixty pounds a horse.'[16]

When the 5th Dragoon Guards arrived in India in 1893 they found that 'owing to trouble in Egypt', the regiment which they were replacing had taken their mounts with them. The 5th had, therefore, to be mounted on about fifty horses from each of the regiments in India that had walers, as well as by raw remounts straight from Australia. The regiment soon discovered, as Mole had a couple of decades earlier, that the waler 'is a peculiar animal. He is landed in India, as a rule, in the autumn, having just shed the coat that he has grown during the Australian winter, and has to start immediately to grow a fresh one. A certain number never get over this very drastic change of habit and diet, and contract a most malignant skin disease which is practicably incurable.'[17] An officer who served in the 15th Hussars in Afghanistan says that the regiment lost 2 per cent of its Arabs, 15 per cent of its country-breds and 25 per cent of its 'Australian-breds'.[18]

10

'The history of the British cavalry trooper's sword in the nineteenth century is largely one of complaints. How far these complaints genuinely arose from defects in the swords and how far they were due to deficiencies in the users is difficult to determine.'

BRIAN ROBSON in *Swords of the British Army*, 1975

'A sword, it is generally admitted, must be carried by every mounted man as the best means of protection against a sudden charge . . . Controversy is thus confined to the lance, and it may be said at once that the lance is undoubtedly a far more formidable weapon, even if it is not in reality more deadly, than the sabre or the revolver.'

COLONEL HENDERSON in 1902[1]

Small arms: development of the cavalry sword – increased use of the lance – the new patterns of carbine – pistols and revolvers – saddles

When in 1897 Colonel Baden-Powell took command of the 5th Dragoon Guards believing that the British regiments in India ought to keep their swords sharp for immediate use, he ordered them to be sharpened. 'I only then,' he wrote, 'realized that with the plant available it took nearly three weeks to get the weapons of the whole regiment made effective. I had no sooner got the work completed than a peremptory order came from HQ directing me to have them blunted again, as the sharpening of the blades would reduce the natural life of a sword, which in the estimates was expected to last some twenty-five to fifty years!'[2] This was typical of the official attitude towards the cavalryman's chief weapon. Unfortunately the attitude of many cavalry officers was not much better. Very little attention was paid to the care of swords, let alone to the principles of the weapon. Unlike much of the native cavalry in India, the study and practice of the art of mounted swordsmanship were generally neglected in the European regiments. As will be shown in the next volume of this work, it was not until the shock administered by the Great Boer War that the basic problem of cavalry sword design was seriously tackled. Not until just before the First World War was the summit of development reached.

In the 1870s the 1864 pattern of sword was used by other ranks in all cavalry regiments, except those of the Household Cavalry which had their own designs. The 1864 pattern was basically the same as the 1853 pattern which had come into use during the Crimean War.* Many complaints about its weight and unwieldiness led eventually to two new patterns of sword being introduced in 1882. They were handier but proved less durable, many of the blades being too soft and brittle. In 1885, therefore, yet another pattern was introduced, but bending and breaking were again complained of. Consequently in 1890 yet another new sword was produced. This, ironically, was even heavier than the 1864 pattern.† Thus was carried on a fruitless search for a truly satisfactory sword.

* On p. 410 of Vol II it is stated that 'there is no evidence that [the Pattern 1853 cavalry sword] was used in the Crimea'. Recent research by Mr Brian Robson shows that this is not so. By the end of the war virtually all the cavalry regiments in the Crimea carried the Pattern 1853 sword, and, indeed, numbers of them were in use by the Heavy Brigade at Balaklava. As they were in short supply, regiments at home were deprived of theirs and re-armed with obsolete swords. (P.R.O., W.O. 3/143, quoted in Robson, 179.)

The statements concerning the progression of cavalry sword patterns between 1821 and 1864 on p. 409 of Vol II are also inaccurate. They were based in part on Wilkinson-Latham, J. *British Cut and Thrust Weapons*, 1971, whose chief source seems to have been ffoulkes, C. and Hopkinson, E. C. *Sword, Lance and Bayonet*, 1938. The facts as now established by Mr Robson are, briefly, as follows: (1) Both the Heavy and Light Cavalry sword patterns were adopted in 1821, although actual issues were protracted; (2) The blades of the 1853 and 1864 patterns were, in fact, identical; (3) There was no sword common to the three Household Cavalry regiments, nor is there evidence, beyond that of Valentine Baker, that any of the Household Cavalry patterns were 'much more efficient' than those issued to regiments of the line. Further, the chief reason why the Household Cavalry patterns were not adopted by the line regiments was their great length.

I am grateful to Mr Robson for pointing out my errors in correspondence. His excellent *Swords of the British Army* was published after my Volume II.

† The 1864 sword was 35½ inches long in the blade and weighed 2 lbs 7¾ ozs. The blades of the two 1882 patterns were 33 and 35½ inches and the swords weighed approximately 2 lbs 1 oz and 2 lbs 3 ozs respectively. The 1885 pattern had a blade 34½ inches in length and weighed 2 lbs 6 ozs, while the 1890 pattern was the same in length, but weighed as much as 2 lbs 9 ozs. (Robson, 57.)

In the course of evolution of the 1890 sword an experiment was made with dead horses slung in a riding school. These were ridden at by a Farrier Quarter-

Committees, questionnaires, more stringent testing and careful comparisons with foreign armies' swords, characterized the last two decades of the century. Yet no serious attempt was made to face the fact that no one sword was good for both cutting and pointing. The battle between the cut and thrust schools had not yet been decided and until it was the sword problem could not be satisfactorily solved.

* * *

Scabbards underwent no major changes during the three last decades of the century, though they became lighter in weight. The 1864 scabbard weighed 2 lbs 1¼ ozs, while the 1885 pattern weighed 1 lb 8 ozs and the 1890 pattern ('Pattern 1885 Mark II') weighed 1 lb 14½ ozs. All were made of steel, but the 1882 patterns had a solid wood lining. From 1885 onwards all scabbards had two fixed sling loops fixed on either side about 2¼ inches from the mouth, instead of the two loose rings fixed on one side to take an upper and lower sling of earlier models. The new arrangements which involved two equal-length slings prevented the scabbard tilting over when an upper sling broke which sometimes meant that the sword fell out.

* * *

In 1896 the differences that had existed since the late eighteenth century between the types of sword carried by heavy and light cavalry officers were terminated. This reform took place forty-three years after *troopers'* swords had been standardized. The standard cavalry officer's sword was now the heavy officer's scroll-hilted pattern of the early 1860s.

Not until 1899 were leather scabbards for officers officially introduced. This happened because, since the early 1890s, the Sam Browne belt had been gradually coming into use. The Sam Browne used a frog which overcame the allegedly awkward problem of fixing carrying rings to a leather scabbard.* No longer would it

master Sergeant who was known as a very fine 'man-at-arms'. He inflicted some remarkable wounds, including a fracture of the tibia from a cut. (H.R.A.V.C., 185.)

* Nevertheless native regiments in India had found no difficulty in using leather scabbards for many years before the introduction of the Sam Browne belt. (See p. 161.)

be necessary on active service to find ways of camouflaging the bright steel of scabbards, such as, for instance, the browning which was applied to them in Egypt in 1882, or the brown leather coverings which the 6th Dragoon Guards devised in Afghanistan two years earlier.[4]

The swords of the men of the Household Cavalry had always differed from those of the cavalry of the line. Until 1882 they were bought direct from private manufacturers, unlike those of the line regiments which were controlled through the Adjutant-General's office and manufactured either at the Enfield Royal Arms Factory or by private firms. They were heavier and straighter than these and sometimes more elaborate in design. Until 1882 the 1st Life Guards were still using their 1820 pattern, while the 2nd Life Guards and the Royal Horse Guards were still using their 1848 pattern. Wolseley reported that at Magfar in 1882 (see p. 275) the Household Cavalry 'with their heavy swords, cut men from the head to the waistbelt'.[5] Whether this was strictly true it is difficult to gauge, but for very big men on very big horses, these swords seem to have been not unsatisfactory, though in 1881 the Chief Inspector of Small Arms at Enfield had formed a poor impression of their strength. However, in 1882, 1888 and 1892 new patterns were introduced.[6] There is little evidence that they were much preferable to those of 1820 and 1848.

* * *

During the fighting in South Africa of 1852 (see p. 175), an artist who was present wrote: 'The superiority of the lance over all other weapons was now evident, for the men, striking two of them in the ground and with another passed horizontally through the loops and a blanket stretched over it, formed most excellent and convenient tents.'[7] The irony of this extract from Thomas Baines's *Sketches in Southern Africa* points up the continuing controversy in cavalry circles about the value of the lance. Two centuries earlier, in 1680, the Austrian general, Count Raimund Montecuccoli had called the lance '*la reine des armes blanches*'.[8]*

In the last quarter of the nineteenth century, many students of the mounted arm agreed with Montecuccoli. Even more of them,

* Both Marshal Saxe in 1751 and General Warnery in 1781 held Montecuccoli's high opinion of the lance. (Saxe, Marshal Maurice, *Mes Reveries*, 1751; Warnery, Maj.-Gen., *Remarks on Cavalry*, 1781, (trans., 1798).)

as they expressed in numerous articles in the military journals, gave qualified support for at least an element of lancers in the line cavalry. There was also a following for the views of Lieutenant-Colonel George Denison who had written in his *Modern Cavalry* in 1868 that, though an efficient weapon when used by a thoroughly trained man, the lance 'in the hands of raw levies' was worthless. Admitting that in the charge it had 'a terrible moral effect upon the enemy,' in the *mêlée* it was, he wrote, 'awkward and cumbersome'.[9] As late as 1902 so thoughtful an authority as Colonel Henderson (see p. 113) could doubt 'whether a cavalry armed only with swords and revolvers, if opposed by one armed with lances, would not absolutely decline to cross weapons in the saddle'.[10] Nevertheless there are numerous instances of swordsmen charging lancers without reluctance: in the Peninsula, at Waterloo, in Bohemia in 1866, in the Franco-German War of 1870, as well as in France in 1914 and, particularly, in 1918 during the Palestine campaign. Other authorities argued that the lance was more liable to break than the sword, that it tangled in wooded terrain, that it hindered rapid mounting and dismounting (indeed the lancer could never act as mounted infantry), that it increased the weight carried by the horse, that it was conspicuous and inconvenient in scouting and detached duties and that its killing power was not always great, since it depended entirely on the horse's momentum.

An example of the successful use of the lance was the 17th Lancers' charge at Ulundi, the final battle of the Zulu War in 1879. The enemy there were unbroken spearmen, some of whom were armed with rifles and muskets, and the lance took a heavy toll of them.[11] (See p. 201.) In the Indian native cavalry, of course, the lance was a favourite weapon, though even against 'natives' occasions arose when the sword overcame it. Such an occasion was the action at Ahmedkhel on 19 April, 1880, during the Afghan War, when the lances of the 19th Bengal Lancers were no match at close quarters for the Ghazis' tulwars.[12]

Marshal Marmont, at the beginning of the century, had suggested that lances should be added to the swords of the front rank only.[13] He argued that they were useless in the hands of the second, reinforcing rank, which was better equipped to follow up the irresistible shock occasioned by the front rank with sword and carbine. This view gained popularity in the 1880s. In 1888 the front ranks of numbers of French dragoon regiments were given the lance. Two years later the British decided to experiment in the same way. The first regiment chosen was the 5th Dragoon Guards. That regiment's historian says that 'instructors were obtained from the 12th Lancers, but the use of the lance presented no difficulties to the men, it having been used by the regiment, for training in equitation, ever since 1817,'[14] as it had been by many other regiments. From 1892 the front rank of all regiments except hussars were thus equipped.

For over forty years from 1829 the British cavalry lance was usually about nine feet in length and its staff was made of ash. It weighed 3 lbs 11 ozs. In the 1860s and 1870s bamboo gradually, but only partially, replaced ash. The difficulty of selecting suitable bamboos (see Vol I, p. 100) led in 1884 to experiments being made with lancewood from the West Indies and with other woods. Though these were less heavy than bamboo they were apt to break and splinter under strain. Consequently where bamboo was unobtainable, ash was again resorted to. It seems that all the lances carried by the 21st Lancers at Omdurman were made of bamboo and weighed about 4 lbs 12 ozs.

* * *

Many cavalry officers remained reluctant to take seriously any sort of weapons except the sword and lance. In the early 1880s 'Wully' Robertson found that in the 17th Lancers 'little or no attention was paid to the art of shooting in the field, and the total amount of ball ammunition expended was restricted to forty rounds per man.'[15] At the same date, however, the 14th Hussars seem to have been an exception to the rule, for after Majuba in 1881 a team of Boers was defeated by men of that regiment firing at targets at known ranges.[16] Lancers in peacetime usually carried no carbine at all, the old horse-pistol being their sole firearm. The 9th Lancers when ordered to join the Kurram Field Force in 1879 had carbines served out to them and the men had to be put through a hurried musketry course[17] (see p. 228).

* * *

The last four decades of the nineteenth century saw an enormous technical advance in small arms. In spite of much cavalry indifference, numbers of improved rifled carbines (short-barrelled versions of the infantry rifle) speedily succeeded each other. In 1866 the Commander-in-Chief recommended that the 20,000 Westley Richards breech-loading, 'monkey-tailed', 22-inch barrelled carbines (see Vol II, p. 419), which had only been ordered two years before, should be sold abroad.[18] Their place was taken by converted carbines using the system invented by Jacob Snider, an American. With these were used Boxer metallic cartridges which for the first time prevented the escape of gas and flame from the breech. The Snider was widely distributed from 1867 onwards, though it was not until 1874 that some of the Indian native regiments were issued with it.[19] By the start of the Afghan War it was in general use. Though an improvement in many respects upon its predecessor, the Snider had its faults. The breech block was apt to jam,[20] and as an officer of the Central India Horse complained, 'after firing a dozen rounds or so, one's shoulder was pounded to jelly. It was quite impossible to expect the recruit to "press the trigger gently". He just shut his eyes, turned his head away, and pulled; and the bullet very often hit the ground nearer to the man than to the target.'[21]

In 1869 a new carbine, the famous Martini-Henry, was favourably reported upon. Nine years later it replaced the Snider in most regiments of the line, though it took another ten years to reach the Indian native cavalry, who found it 'a God-sent novelty. With what alacrity did we pack up the old Sniders,' wrote one officer, 'and send them off to the arsenal. They were dreadful weapons. The calibre was .577 inch, almost as large as a 12-bore gun.'[22] The Martini-Henry's calibre was only .45 inch, and it was correspondingly lighter. Its extraction proved its chief weakness, while its ballistic properties were not up to those of several of its rivals abroad. Consequently a committee sat in 1883 to consider an improved patten. The result in due course was a magazine-loading, repeating weapon which, in its essentials and after certain alterations in the mid-1890s, was almost identical with the .303 inch rifle which became the mainstay of cavalry and infantry alike during the first half of the twentieth century. In 1892 a carbine of this sort known as the Martini-Metford replaced the Martini-Henry. This in its turn was superseded in 1896 by the Lee-Metford magazine carbine.*

The most important difference between these two and their predecessor was due to the work of the French engineer Paul Vieille who had produced in 1884 the first really satisfactory smokeless

* The Bays (2nd Dragoon Guards) were the first regiment to receive the Lee-Metford. (Whyte and Atteridge, 166.)

For a list of cavalry carbines produced at the Royal Small Arms Factory, Enfield Lock, 1867–1896, see Appendix, p. 428.

powder. With the Martini-Metford the army had for the first time in its history a weapon which dispensed with the old black powder. This development coupled with the vastly increased range and the flat trajectory of the new types of small arms completely revolutionized warfare.[23]

* * *

Some regiments, as late as 1878, still carried the ancient, large calibred, muzzle-loading, smooth-bore, flintlock horse-pistols which differed little in essence from those used in Charles II's reign. Since the mid-1850s officers had been arming themselves with five- and six-chambered breech-loading, self-extracting revolvers, and these by the 1890s were commonly issued to warrant officers, staff-sergeants, trumpeters and all other ranks who did not carry carbines. (See Appendix, p. 428, for a list of the Enfield revolvers made in the 1880s).

* * *

Of the numerous alterations in horse furniture which characterized the three final decades of the nineteenth century, the most important affected the cavalry saddle. In 1872 a new Universal Pattern, known as the 'Flat Iron Arch Saddle', partially replaced the wooden arch universal pattern which had been introduced in 1856. It was a failure, since among other things, it was not of strong enough construction. In 1878, as a result of two commissions which sat in 1873 and 1874, a new saddle, known as the 'Universal Pattern, Angle Iron Arch', was brought out. The King's Dragoon Guards and the 17th Lancers used this in the Zulu War. Both regiments reported very unfavourably on many aspects of it.

Consequently various patterns with steel arches were experimented with in the 1880s, but it was not until the revolutionary saddle known as the 'Universal Pattern 1890 Steel Arch' appeared that a more or less satisfactory article at last came on the scene. It was sufficiently excellent for many of its predecessors to be converted by the substitution of steel for iron arches. Other parts of these older saddles, such as the girth attachments, were also altered.

Two marks of the 1890 pattern were tried before Mark III was made a general issue in 1898. What it was like and why it was better than its predecessors will be shown in the next volume of this work. It is enough to say here that the painful search for a satisfactory type of modern cavalry saddle which for many decades had occupied committee after committee was now virtually over. The major problems had always been those connected with strength *versus* weight. As Major Tylden, the leading authority, has said, 'strength, great strength' had at last been attained, combined with 'as little weight as was consistent with the heavy loads still considered necessary for the troop horse to carry. Generations of cavalry officers had fulminated against the overloading of their horses. Now the new steel arch saddle was to be tried out in a war of mounted men [the Great Boer War of 1899 to 1902], who either had to reduce the weight on their horses or fail to carry out the tasks allotted to them.'[24]

EPILOGUE

> 'The rash of European conflicts between 1859 and 1870 and, even more significantly, the American Civil War, suggested to all but the most tradition-bound soldiers that the cavalry's capabilities had undergone a profound and permanent change. Though the connection was only slowly realized and accepted, these campaigns showed that firepower had increased enormously and that cavalry, in so far as it applied shock tactics . . . had suffered a corresponding eclipse.'
>
> BRIAN BOND in 'Doctrine and Training in the British Cavalry, 1870–1914', 1967

As early as 1864 Colonel Patrick MacDougall, an intelligent writer on military affairs, wrote that the influence 'of the improved weapons . . . on cavalry must be nearly to destroy its utility altogether as an offensive arm on the field of battle . . . It can hardly be expected that cavalry can manoeuvre on the ground which separates two hostile armies, without running the risk of utter destruction.' Later, in his *Modern Warfare as influenced by Modern Artillery*, he wrote;

> 'It is principally during a retreat that the advantage of superiority in cavalry is especially felt. Possessed by the beaten army, it may retreat at leisure; but if the preponderance be on the side of the pursuer, the retreating infantry may be compelled, wherever the ground favours cavalry movements, to halt frequently and form squares, thereby keeping it under the fire of the enemy's guns and allowing time for his infantry to come up; and thus the retreating army may be forced either to witness the capture of some of its divisions, or to engage in a battle at great disadvantage to support them.'

In spite of the limitations which modern weapons placed upon it, Colonel MacDougall pointed out that cavalry would still have a vital task in protecting the flanks and rear of a military position, and in 'acting on the communications of an enemy'.[1]*

* Indeed, under the new conditions there can be no doubt that strategically, that is in reconnaissance, raids and protective duties, since cavalry was still, as

All these views turned out to be correct prophecies. Similar ones were expounded by better known military writers. Nevertheless one of these, Colonel George Denison, an officer of the Canadian Militia, writing four years after MacDougall, disagreed with him that heavy cavalry designed for the shock tactics of knee-to-knee, close-order charging had 'received its death-blow'. He advocated the retention of at least a quarter of the mounted arm as 'real cavalry, armed as such, educated as such, and taught that nothing can withstand a well-executed charge'. However, Denison agreed with Major Sir Henry Marsham Havelock, writing in 1867, that the advent of increasingly efficient rifled arms and the evidence of the American Civil War had made pure shock tactics obsolescent.[2] All three writers were well ahead of their time.

Yet for a wide variety of reasons it took many years before their ideas percolated into the minds of any but a select few senior officers. Similarly the various lessons, sometimes conflicting, which emerged from the American Civil War, from the Austro-Prussian War and from the Franco-Prussian War, were mostly either ignored or misinterpreted by those who gave thought to the future of cavalry. For a time, because the Germans defeated the French in 1870–71, British official doctrine was apt to copy very closely everything German. In the five years between the end of the Civil War in America and the Franco-Prussian War there were those, like Denison and Havelock, who took to heart the numerous successes produced by the American 'amateur soldiers' who had accepted the notion that the rifle and dismounted action should replace the traditional role of cavalry in tactical fighting. But the highly professional Germans' continuing devotion to shock tactics, soon emulated by the defeated French, obliterated the trans-Atlantic experience.* To most British cavalry officers it was not necessary to discover whether the German shock tactics had really been a vital factor in the Prussian victory. It was enough that the winning side believed in them. For men whose whole way of life was bound up with the

it always had been, the chief means of mobility, its utility was likely to be enhanced. This was especially so with the expansion both of armies and of battle fronts.

* Unfortunately Von Bredow's famous 'Death Ride' at Vionville-Mars-la-Tour in 1870 gained enormous renown as a successful cavalry action. The fact that it was virtually the only one of any importance during the Franco-Prussian War, and that there were numerous occasions when cavalry catastrophes occurred, such as at Morsbrunn and Sedan, was conveniently overlooked by those who wished to prove that cavalry was not an anachronism.

glory of the charge, here was comfort indeed. As we have seen in the behaviour of the 21st Lancers at Omdurman, the average cavalry colonel's views as to how to use his regiment was no different in 1898 from what it had been a century before.

It is easy to criticize this attitude today, but was it not very understandable at the time? Not only had the leading military nation of Europe appeared to succeed with the old ways, but these had also seemed, in the eyes of most cavalry officers, to have been adequate for the needs of the numerous small wars in which Britain had been engaged. It is impossible for us living towards the end of the twentieth century to appreciate fully what Brian Bond, a leading writer on the doctrine of the British cavalry in Victorian times, has called that combination of factors which

> 'gave the cavalry national as well as service prestige out of all proportion to its size [which in 1889 was only 22,000 out of 266,600]. Over its real historical achievements there had accumulated an aura of glamour and romance [which] was distilled into "the cavalry spirit", an essence said to be found in no other corps and of practical value as a foil to unwelcome reforms.'[3]

One can only manage a tiny glimmering of understanding of the intense dismay with which cavalrymen of all ranks contemplated the loss of their traditional role. One can perhaps nevertheless find some sympathy with their stubborn, unyielding fight to retain it.

Readers of this volume will have realized that actual experience in the field, particularly in South Africa, had on numerous occasions shown that some sort of mounted infantry or at least irregular cavalry was generally more useful than the *arme blanche* pure and simple. Further, unlike the senior officers of the great continental armies, the leading lights of the British army, men such as Wolseley, Roberts, Buller and Wood, were already in the 1880s and 1890s urging a greater emphasis upon training for the use of the carbine on foot. In the final volumes of this work the progress of the battle between these reformers and the cavalry die-hards, and its consequences, will be fully chronicled.

APPENDIX

1. *Pay of the rank and file of a cavalry regiment.* (See p. 68.)

Comparative rates of daily pay, 1866 and 1893, showing ranks which had ceased to exist by the latter date and those which had been added:

	1866		1893	
	s.	d.	s.	d.
Regimental sergeant-major	3	8	5	4
Bandmaster	3	8	5	6
Quartermaster-sergeant	3	2	4	4
Troop sergeant-major	3	2		—
Squadron sergeant-major (none before 11 February, 1892)		—	4	4
Squadron quartermaster-sergeant (none before 11 February, 1892)		—	3	4
Ditto, (if a troop sergeant-major before 11 February, 1892)		—	3	10
Squadron sergeant-major rough-rider		—	3	10
Sergeant-instructor in gymnastics and fencing	2	4	3	3
Trumpet-major or sergeant-trumpeter	2	4	2	8
Armourer-sergeant:				
in regiments armed with interchangeable arms	5	0		—
in regiments *not* armed with interchangeable arms	2	4		—
Farrier-major or farrier quartermaster-sergeant	3	8	4	0
Saddler-sergeant	3	4	3	8
Staff sergeant-farrier (none before 11 February, 1892)		—	3	4
Farrier sergeant or sergeant-farrier	2	6	2	10
Sergeant-instructor of musketry	3	0		—
Paymaster sergeant	2	4		—
Paymaster sergeant after three years' service	2	10		—
Regimental orderly-room clerk	2	4		—
Regimental orderly-room clerk after three years' service	2	10		—
Hospital sergeant	2	4		—
Hospital sergeant after seven years' service	2	10		—
Sergeant	2	4	2	8
Corporal, if paid as lance-sergeant		—	2	4

	1866 s.	1866 d.	1893 s.	1893 d.
Corporal shoeing-smith		—	2	2
Corporal saddler		—	2	0
Corporal saddletree-maker		—	2	0
Private, if paid as lance-corporal		—	1	7
Private	1	3	1	2
Kettle-drummer (when authorized)	1	10	1	9
Trumpeter	1	5	1	4
Shoeing-smith	1	11	1	8
Saddler	1	10½	1	9½
Saddletree-maker	1	10½	1	9½
Boys, till they attain age of fifteen	0	10		—
Boys, till they attain age of eighteen		—	0	8

(Pomeroy, 189, 190)

2. *Establishment of cavalry officers.* (See p. 91 and p. 123.)

The total number of officers in the three regiments of Household Cavalry and the twenty-eight line regiments on a peace footing varied with the changes in establishment, but it averaged over the three last decades of the century something like 850. In 1875, for instance, it was as follows:

	At Home			*In India*	
	H. Cav. (3 regts)	Cav. of Line (19 regts)	Depots	Cav. of Line (9 regts)	Totals
Lieutenant-Colonels	1	1	3	1	34
Majors	1	1	1	1	32
Captains	8	8	—	7	239
Lieutenants	12	13	—	14	409
Adjutants	1	1	1	1	32
Riding masters	1	1	1	1	32
Quartermasters	1	1	1	1	32
Veterinary surgeons	1	1	1	1	32
Totals per regiment	26	27	8	27	842

(*A.P.R.C.*, 95)

3. *Some examples of alterations to the establishments of regiments of cavalry of the line, 1872–1898.* (See p. 123.)

(1) *7th Hussars*

1872	(a) Officers:	1	captain added
		12	lieutenants and sub-lieutenants in place of 7 lieutenants and 3 cornets
	(b) Rank and file:		the following added: 1 troop sergeant-major; 1 farrier; 1 trumpeter; 1 shoeing-smith; 1 saddler; 3 sergeants; 11 corporals
	(c) Total:	28	officers
		59	NCOs and trumpeters
		447	privates
		534	(+ 320 troop horses]
1878	(a) Officers:	4	second-lieutenants added
	(b) Total:	652	rank and file [+480 troop horses]
1886	On transfer to India:	21	officers
		587	rank and file

(2) *13th Hussars*

1874	On transfer to India:	25	officers
		1	schoolmaster
		1	bandmaster
		1	quartermaster-sergeant
		1	farrier-major
		1	orderly-room clerk
		1	saddler sergeant
		1	paymaster sergeant
		1	sergeant-instructor of fencing
		1	hospital sergeant
		1	armourer
		6	troop sergeant-majors
		16	sergeants
		29	corporals
		6	farriers
		5	trumpeters
		358	privates
		455	

1881	Rank and file:		
		414	[+419 troop horses]
	Drafts from the depot at Canterbury and volunteers from regiments going home between 1874 and the regiment's return home totalled		
		7	officers
		487	rank and file
	In 1885, on the regiment being ordered home, volunteers to six regiments remaining in India totalled		
		80	rank and file
1885	Total:	17	officers
		377	rank and file
1886	6 troops:	3	field officers
		6	captains
		13	subalterns
		3	staff
		508	rank and file [+294 horses]
1894	Total:	395	rank and file [+274 horses]
1895	4 squadrons:		rank and file:
		1	regimental sergeant-major
		1	bandmaster
		1	armourer
		8	staff-sergeants
		4	squadron sergeant-majors
		4	squadron quartermaster-sergeants
		8	farriers
		24	sergeants
		4	lance-sergeants
		28	corporals
		8	trumpeters
		1	orderly-room clerk
		8	shoeing smiths
		4	saddlers
		1	saddle-tree maker
		24	paid lance-corporals
		8	unpaid lance-corporals
		467	privates
		604	[+350 horses]
1897	3 service and 1 reserve squadrons (increase due to abolition of Canterbury depot):		
	rank and file:	668	[+465 horses]

(3) *15th Hussars*

1875 In India, rank and file:

566

1891 rank and file establishment raised from:

498 [+325 horses]

to: 603 [+350 horses]

1894 rank and file establishment raised to:

658 [+410 horses]

(4) (See p. 268.) When three regiments (beside the Household Cavalry) went to Egypt in 1882, their establishment on a war footing was:

Officers		Horses		
		Chargers	Troop	Draught
Lieutenant-Colonels	2	8		
Majors	3	12		
Captains	5	15		
Subalterns	16	48		
Adjutants	1	3		
Paymaster	1	2		
Quartermaster	1	2		
Medical Officer	1	2		
Veterinary Surgeon	1	2		
Total	31	94		

NCOs and Men		Horses		
		Chargers	Troop	Draught
Sergeant-major	1			
Quartermaster Sergeant	1			
Band Sergeant	1			
Paymaster Sergeant	1			
Armourer Sergeant	1			
Saddler Sergeant	1			
Farrier Sergeant	1			
Sergeant Cook	1			
Trumpet Major	1			
Orderly-Room Clerk	1			
Transport Sergeant	1			
TSMs	8			

Continued

NCOs and Men		Horses		
		Chargers	Troop	Draught
Sergeants	24			
Farriers	8			
Saddlers	4			
Shoeing Smiths	8			
Wheelers & saddletree makers	2			
Trumpeters	8			
Corporals	32			
Bandsmen	15			
Privates	480		480	
Drivers (transport)	22			44
Totals	622		480	44

(5) *11th Hussars*

1886 Rank and file establishment increased from:
467 [+300 horses]
to: 599 [+400 horses]

1890 On transfer to South Africa:
20 officers
476 rank and file
Left at Canterbury depot:
198 of all ranks

(6) *14th Hussars*

1886 On return home from India:
17 officers
405 rank and file

(Barrett, II, 79, 87; Barrett: *XIII H*, 43-108; Wylly, 293, 329; Goodrich, 222; Williams: *XI H*, 264, 267; Oatts, 259.)

4. *Dress regulations for rank and file, 1898.* (See p. 49.)

ORDER OF DRESS

REVIEW ORDER

Full dress headdress
Tunic

Gauntlets (gloves for Hussars)
Sword-belt
Girdle (lancers only)
Pouch-belt
Pouch

When mounted

Sword
Carbine
Lance (for services in possession)
Pantaloons
Knee-boots
Jack-spurs

When dismounted

Trousers
Wellington boots
Spurs
Sword
Carbine or lance

Horse furniture

Saddle and bridle, complete, with head-rope, and wallets unpacked
Breastplate
Cape, in front, in cape protector
When ordered, Cloak, rolled, behind the saddle, and nose-bag

MARCHING ORDER

(In Mounted services, Marching Order for Guard will be the same as Review Order dismounted, but with frock instead of tunic, and no girdle for Lancers. The cloak will be carried, *en banderolle*, over the right shoulder (to be taken off when the guard has mounted), and the sword on the belt.

On the man

Field-Cap (Helmet for service abroad, and full dress headdress when on guard, and on change of station)
Frock
Jersey (in cold weather)
Pantaloons
Knee-boots
Jack-spurs
Gauntlets (gloves for Hussars)
Sword-belt
Pouch-belt
Pouches

MARCHING ORDER—*cont.*

Haversack
Water bottle
Revolver and pouch (for ranks in which carried)
Flannel belt,
Field dressing,
Pocket-knife and lanyard,
Description card
Ammunition
} On Active service only

On the horse

Saddle and bridle, complete with head-rope and wallets packed
Breast-plate
Breast-harness
Pioneer equipment
} Regulation proportion
Hoof-picker
Nosebag
Small corn-sack
Forage-net
Mess-tin
Heel-rope
Carbine in bucket
Sword, in frog on shoe-case, edge to the rear
Carbine sling (on Field Service only), on carbine
Lance (for services in possession)
Cape, in front of wallets
Cloak, rolled, in rear of saddle
Field cap, if not worn, in pocket of the cloak, when woollen cap is not carried (Helmet for service abroad, and full dress headdress when on guard, and on change of station)
Surcingle pad
Cape protector

In the wallets (weight to be evenly distributed)

2 Iron picketing pegs, with rings
Horse-brush and curry-comb
Horse-rubber
Sponge
1 pr. socks
1 shirt
Holdall, complete
Towel and soap
Spare bootlaces

For Active Service only

Tin of grease

Emergency ration
Woollen cap

For 'Home Marching Order (on change of Quarters only)':
In the wallets

Horse-brush
Curry-comb
Sponge
Oilcan
1 shirt
1 pr. socks
Towel and soap
Holdall, complete
Tin blacking
Polishing-brush
Cloth-brush
Blacking brush
Brass-brush
Hair-brush
Horse-rubber
Pipe-clay and sponge
1 pr. trousers, authorized for grooming
Head-dress plume
Spare bootlaces

5. *Dress regulations for cavalry officers, 1898.* (See p. 101.)

REVIEW ORDER

Full dress head-dress
Tunic
Sword
Dress sword-knot
Dress sword-belt
Dress shoulder-belt
Dress pouch
Gauntlets (gloves for Hussars)

When mounted

Pantaloons
Knee boots
Steel jack spurs
Sabretache (dress for Hussars)

When dismounted

Undress trousers
Wellington boots

REVIEW ORDER—*cont.*

Steel box spurs
Dress sabretache (Hussars only)
Note: When dismounted on State occasions, and in the evening when Review Order is worn, Hussars will wear Hessian boots and dress pantaloons; other regiments dress trousers.

Horse furniture

Saddle
Bridle, complete, with head-rope
Breastplate
Wallets
Leopard or sheepskin
Cape, in front of saddle
Throat ornament (in 1st & 2nd Dragoons and Hussars)
The cloak to be worn behind the saddle when ordered
Lance buckets (except Hussars)

MARCHING ORDER

Field Cap (Helmets for service abroad and full dress headdress when on guard, and on change of stations)
Frock
Pantaloons
Knee boots
Steel jack-spurs
Sabretache (undress for Hussars)
Haversack
Sword
Whistle
Sword-knot
Sword-belt
Shoulder-belt
Pouch
Note: Undress belts etc, for those regiments permitted to wear them.

On Active Service or when ordered:

Field Dressing
Revolver
Water-bottle
Pocket compass
Pocket Book and Army Message Book 153

Horse furniture

As in Review Order, but no leopard or sheepskin or throat ornament

Field glasses on off side of saddle
Cloak, rolled, behind the saddle

On Active Service or when ordered:
Mess-tin
Nose-bag
Picketing pegs
Heel rope
Spare shoes and nails, as carried by the men

DRILL ORDER

Field Cap,* or other headdress (without plume) according to climate
Other articles as in Marching Order
Brown gloves when men do not wear gloves
No haversack unless ordered

Horse furniture
As in Marching Order, but no cloak, unless ordered
Throat ornaments to be worn

MESS ORDER

Mess Jacket
Waistcoat (Kamarband worn in hot climates)
Dress trousers
Wellington boots
Brass spurs

* Helmets for service abroad, and full dress headdress when on guard, and on change of station.
(*Cav. Drill*, 21–24.)

6. *Cavalry units of the Indian Army as in 1888*. In order of precedence. (See p. 147.)

1. *BENGAL*

Regular:

Governor General's Body Guard:	Commandant	Subadar
	Adjutant	2 Jemadars
	Medical Officer	7 Havildars
		7 Naiks
		3 Farriers
		2 Trumpeters
		98 Sowars

Appendix

Silladar:

Regiments	Officers	Native ranks
1, 2, 3, 4, 5, 6 (Prince of Wales's), 7 and 8 Bengal Cavalry (8 troops each)	Commandant 4 Squadron Commanders 4 Squadron Officers Medical Officer	4 Risaldars 4 Ressaidars Wurdi-Major 8 Jemadars 8 Kote Daffadars 56 Daffadars 8 Trumpeters 536 Sowars

*Punjab Frontier Force**

Regiments	Officers	Native ranks
1, 2, 3 and 5 Punjab Cavalry (8 troops each)	(Establishment the same as for Bengal Cavalry Regiments)	
Corps of Guides (Queen's Own) (Cavalry) (6 troops)	Commandant 3 Squadron Commanders 3 Squadron Officers Medical Officer	3 Risaldars 3 Ressaidars Wurdi-Major 6 Jemadars 6 Kote Daffadars 42 Daffadars 6 Trumpeters 394 Sowars 8 Camel sowars Native doctor
9†, 10 (Duke of Cambridge's Own)† 11 (Prince of Wales's Own)† 12†, 13 (Duke of Connaught's), 14†, 15 (Cureton's Mooltanee),† 16, 17 Bengal Cavalry, 18 Bengal Lancers and 19 Bengal Cavalry†	(Establishment the same as for 1 to 8 Bengal Cavalry)	

The Central India Horse

Regiments	Establishment	
1 and 2 Regiments (8 troops each)	(Establishment the same as for Bengal Cavalry Regiments)	

* Until 1886 the P.F.F. was under the Government of the Punjab. In that year it was placed under the Commander-in-Chief, India.

† (Lancers). 9 and 18 were converted to lancers in 1886, 15 in 1890.

Deolee Irregular Force		
(Cavalry (lancers) element)	Commandant	2 Risaldars
(2 troops)	Squadron	2 Jemadars
	Commander	18 Daffadars
	Medical Officer	2 Trumpeters
		138 Sowars
		2 Camel Sowars
Erinpoorah Irregular Force		
(Cavalry element)	(Establishment the same as for Deolee Irregular Force except for 136 Sowars and 4 Camel Sowars)	
(2 troops)		
Hyderabad Contingent		
1, 2, 3 and 4 Hyderabad	Commandant	14 native officers
Cavalry	Squadron	48 Daffadars
	Commander	4 Camel Gunners
	2 Squadron Officers	7 Trumpeters
	Medical Officer	478 Sowars
2. *MADRAS* (all regular)		
Governor's Body Guard	Commandant	2 Subadars
	Adjutant	4 Jemadars
	Medical Officer	Havildar Major
	Sergeant-Major	7 Havildars
	Hospital Assistant	6 Naiks
		Farrier Major
		2 Farrier Havildars
		2 Shoeing Smiths
		2 Trumpeters
		100 Sowars
		10 Recruit and Pension Boys
	Native artificers:	Superintendent Smith
		2 Chucklers (shoemakers)
		Hammerman
		Bellows Boy

1*, 2 Madras Lancers*, 3 and 4 (Prince of Wales's Own) Madras Light Cavalry (6 troops each)	Commandant	6 Subadars
	3 Squadron Commanders	6 Jemadars
	4 Squadron Officers	Havildar Major
	Medical Officer	30 Havildars
	2 Hospital Assistants	30 Naiks
		Trumpet Major
		6 Trumpeters
		Farrier Major
		6 Farrier Havildars
		3 Shoeing Smiths
		3 Veterinary Pupils
		396 Sowars
		40 Recruit and Pension Boys
		Second Tindal (foreman)
		3 Regimental Lascars
		6 Puckallies (water-carriers)
		1 Choudry
		2 Toties
	Native artificers:	Superintendent
		Maistry Smith
		Maistry Chuckler
		Smith
		Hammerman
		Bellows Boy
		3 Chucklers

3. *BOMBAY*

Regular:

Governor's Body Guard:	Commandant	Risaldar
		Ressaidar
		Jemadar
		Kote Daffadar
		5 Daffadars
		Trumpeter
		Farrier
		60 Sowars

* Converted to lancers in 1886.

Silladar:		
1, 2,* 3, 4 Bombay Lancers 5 (Sind Horse), 6 (Jacob's Horse), 7 (Beluch Horse) Bombay Cavalry† (8 troops each)	Commandant 4 Squadron Commanders 4 Squadron Officers Medical Officer	Risaldar Major 3 Risaldars Wurdi-Major 4 Ressaidars 8 Jemadars Kote Daffadar Major Farrier Major 8 Kote Daffadars 32 Daffadars 8 Trumpeters 40 Naiks 518 Sowars
Aden Troop	Commandant	Risaldar 2 Ressaidars Kote Daffadar Pay Daffadar 8 Daffadars Trumpeter 2 Farriers 83 Sowars

Note: There were a number of alterations of all sorts in the three last decades of the century, but 1888 is taken as a typical year. (*The New Annual Army List . . . 1889* (*Hart's Army List*), 431–2, 444–5, 448, 449–449a, 495, 522–3.)

7. *Mounted units of the Indian States Forces*. (See p. 148.)

Baroda: 1st Cavalry, raised 1886
Baroda Lancers, raised 1886

Bhavnagar Lancers, raised 1892

Bikaner Dungar Lancers, raised 1455

Dhar: Maharaj Kumari Kamla Raje's Own Light Horse, raised 1864

Gwalior: 1st Jayaji Gwalior Lancers, raised 1833
2nd Alijah Gwalior Lancers, raised 1852
3rd Gwalior Maharaja Madho Rao Scindia's Own Lancers, raised 1868

Hyderabad: 1st (Nizam's Own) Hyderabad Imperial Service Lancers raised 1864

* Converted to lancers in 1883.

† Raised 1885

	2nd (Nizam's Own) Hyderabad Imperial Service Lancers, raised 1893
	3rd (Nizam's Own) Golconda Lancers, raised 1873

Jodhpur Lancers, raised 1888

Junagarh Lancers, raised 1891

Mysore:	Mysore Lancers, raised 1799. Mysore Local Service Regiment, raised 1892
Patiala:	1st Patiala (Rajindra) Lancers, raised 1889
	2nd Patiala Lancers, raised 1824
Rampur:	(Rohilkand) Lancers, raised 1840

(Jaipur, H. H. Maharaja of *The Indian State Forces . . .*, 1967.)

8. *Class composition of Indian cavalry regiments.* (See p. 155.)

(1.) In 1864 a General Order laid down rules as to the classes whose enlistment in the Bengal Army was permitted or otherwise, stating in detail the caste constitution of each regiment. In 1883 and 1889 new General Orders revising the rules were issued. In the 1889 Order only two of the Bengal cavalry regiments were designated Class *Regiments* (1 B.C., all Hindustani Mahomedans, and 14 B.L., all Jats). All the other regiments became units consisting of Class *Troops*. Four examples are given below:

3 B.C.:	3 tps,	Hindustani Mahomedans
	2 tps,	Sikhs
	1 tp,	Rajputs
	2 tps,	Jats
7 B.C.:	2 tps,	Hindustani Mahomedans
	1 tp,	Sikhs
	1 tp,	Dogras
	1 tp,	Rajputs
	2 tps,	Jats
	1 tp,	Brahmans
11 B.L.:	1 tp,	Punjabi Mahomedans
	1 tp,	Trans-Indus border tribes (not more than a quarter to be Afridis)
	4 tps,	Sikhs
	2 tps,	Dogras
2 Punjab C.:	1 tp,	Hindustani Mahomedans
	1½ tps,	Punjabis
	1½ tps,	Trans-Indus border tribes
	3 tps,	Sikhs
	1 tp,	Jats

(Cardew, 408.)

(2.) Examples of the class composition of the Bombay cavalry regiments in 1895 are:

3 B.L.C.:	2 tps,	Jats
	2 tps,	Kaimkhanis
	2 tps,	Jat Sikhs
	2 tps,	Rangers
5 B.C. (Scinde Horse):	2 tps,	Trans-Indus Pathans
	2 tps,	Sikhs
	4 tps,	Derajat Pathans
6 B.C. (Jacob's Horse):	3 tps,	Hindustani and Derajat Mahomedans
	2 tps,	Sikhs
	2 tps,	Pathans
	1 tp,	Rangars and Mewatis

(Cadell, 335.)

9. *List of Indian ranks with their British equivalents.* (See p. 152.)

Daffadar	Sergeant (silladar (or irregular) cavalry)
Daffadar-major	Sergeant-Major (silladar (or irregular) cavalry)
Havildar	Sergeant (regular cavalry and infantry)
Havildar-major	Sergeant-Major (regular cavalry and infantry)
Jemadar	Lieutenant or Second-Lieutenant
Kot- (or kote-) daffadar	Troop sergeant-major (silladar (or irregular) cavalry)
Lance-daffadar	Corporal (silladar (or irregular) cavalry)
Lance-naik	Lance-corporal (regular cavalry and infantry)
Naib-risaldar	Brevet captain or troop commander (silladar (or irregular) cavalry)
Naik	Corporal (regular cavalry and infantry)
Ressaidar	Junior captain or troop commander (silladar (or irregular) cavalry)
Risaldar	Captain or troop commander (silladar (or irregular) cavalry
Risaldar-major	Senior captain (silladar (or irregular) cavalry)
Subadar	Captain (regular cavalry and infantry)
Subadar-major	Senior Captain (regular cavalry and infantry)
Wurdi (or Woordie) Major	Native adjutant (silladar (or irregular) cavalry)

10. *Note on the cavalry strength at Maiwand.* (See p. 250.)

The figures of non-commissioned officers and men in the two cavalry regiments engaged at Maiwand, 27 July, 1880, are taken from Major Hogg's narrative in which he noted 'the exact strength of both corps, as given by the officers commanding on approaching the field of battle, the returns having been called for by me under instructions from General Burrows' Brigade Major, having expressed his astonishment to me that the cavalry force in point of numbers appeared exceedingly small.' These are worth quoting in full, not only because it is seldom indeed that a detailed strength state is known a few hours before a major engagement, but also because they show the sort of proportion of men not available for fighting purposes. In the case of these two regiments, out of a total of 508 men, something like sixty-three appear to have been non-combatants.

'*3rd Sind Horse.* [Five European and eight Native officers]

Lieutenant Smith's troop	50
Lieutenant A. M. Monteith's troop	51
Camel sowars	4
(Sick and lame horses with baggage and rear guard	36)*
Sick men	4
Pustoo-speaking orderlies	6
Ammunition guards	6
Farrier-major and farrier with sick horses	2
With Colonel Malcolmson	96
	255'

'*3rd Light Cavalry.* [Six European and thirteen Native Officers]

1st Squadron	76
2nd Squadron	72
3rd Squadron	74
Orderlies with baggage	8
Dismounted men	4
Sick men	12
Colonel St John's [Political Officer] orderlies	5
General Nuttall's orderly	1
General Burrows' orderlies	7
Baggage guard	26
Ammunition	4
(Lame horses	11)*
	300'

(*Reports*, 5)

* Though these two items appear to refer to horses, it is not unlikely that they refer in fact to men in charge of unfit horses. If this is so, it argues that

These figures differ from those given in the *Official Account* where the total of non-commissioned officers and men is given as 544 on p. 500 and 576 on p. 501. Neither of these figures is as likely to be correct as Hogg's.

11. *The Maiwand Courts-Martial.* (See p. 251 and p. 261.)

(1.) The charges against Major Albert Purcell Currie, commanding 3rd Bombay Light Cavalry at Maiwand, which were preferred against him at a General Court-Martial in Bombay on 1 March, 1881 were:

> '*First Charge* – With misbehaviour before the enemy in such manner as to show cowardice during the action and in the retreat from the field of battle . . . in the following instances:
>
> '*First* – In having, when ordered by Brigadier-General Nuttall to charge the enemy so as to relieve the Infantry, then hard pressed, failed to deliver the charge directly to his front upon the mass of the enemy, but instead charged to the right and rear avoiding the mass of the enemy and falling upon merely a small band of men, so that the charge had no effect.
>
> '*Second* – In having, when ordered by Brigadier-General Burrows shortly after the foregoing occasion to charge across the front and save the Infantry from total defeat, made no effort to comply.
>
> '*Third* – In having, when the Cavalry were ordered to return to succour the Rear Guard, remained with a troop required for other duty at a distance from the enemy, instead of himself proceeding to the Rear Guard.
>
> '*Second Charge* – With conduct to the prejudice of good order and military discipline during the action and in the retreat from the field of battle . . . in the following instances:
>
> '*First* – In having failed to exert himself to execute the order of Brigadier-General Nuttall to charge the enemy and retrieve the fortune of the day when the Infantry were thrown into confusion.
>
> '*Second* – In having thereafter failed to exert himself and by a display of soldier-like spirit to arouse his men to a sense of their duty, in order to comply with the order of Brigadier-General Burrows to charge the enemy and clear the front at the time when the Infantry were sorely pressed by the enemy.
>
> '*Third* – In having, when ordered to detach a troop to succour the Rear Guard, detailed Lieutenant Geoghegan for this duty, instead of going himself to the post of honour nearest to the enemy, and himself proceeded with the only remaining troop of his Regiment which was required for other duty at a distance from the enemy.'

a very considerable number of horses were unfit. If each man was needed to look after, say, two unfit horses, this would mean that there were, in the two regiments, as many as ninety-four such horses.

(2.) The charges preferred against Lieutenant-Colonel 'and Brevet-Colonel' John Henry Porter Malcolmson, C.B. 'of the Bombay Staff Corps, Commandant of the 3rd Regiment Sind Horse' at his Court-Martial on 7 April, 1881 were:

'*First Charge* – With misbehaviour before the enemy in such a manner as to show cowardice . . . during the retreat from the field of battle . . . in the following instances:

'*First* – In having, at the commencement of the retreat near Khusk-i-Nakad, while Brigadier-General Nuttall was with the Rear Guard employed in placing wounded and tired men on horses and camels, proposed to retire at once, assigning as a reason that he saw a strong body of Cavalry moving towards them, which was not the fact.

'*Second* – In having, at a later period of the retreat, when commanding his Regiment, among which were the guides, upon whom the retreating force depended for the direction of the night march, marched away to Ata Karez, and for the time abandoned the wounded and tired men; so that he, with his Regiment, reached Ata Karez some two hours before the Rear Guard, although he had been ordered by Brigadier-General Nuttall to march slowly, being told that an orderly and slow retirement was requisite to hold the enemy in check, as well as to conform with the slow progress of the wounded and tired men of the force.

'*Third* – In having, at a period of the retreat later than the foregoing . . . openly expressed to Brigadier-General Burrows his desire to abandon the guns, which were laden with wounded officers and men, and to push on to Kandahar, giving as one reason that the Artillery of the enemy were pursuing, and that the whole of the force yet surviving would be destroyed, and as another that three Companies of Native Infantry in advance . . . required aid.

'*Fourth* – In having . . . outmarched the rest of the retreating force and placed a distance of some three miles between himself and the guns laden with wounded officers and men, although he had been ordered by Brigadier-General Burrows not to lose the touch of the guns [*sic*].

'*Second Charge* – With having by word of mouth spread reports calculated to create unnecessary alarm . . . during the retreat . . . in the following instances:

'*First* – In having, at different intervals of the night, magnified the report of jezails and matchlocks discharged from villages that were passed, into the sound of Artillery of the enemy in pursuit, and represented that clumps of trees passed were Cavalry of the enemy threatening the flanks.

'*Second* – In having, towards dawn . . . raised the alarm that the Cavalry of the enemy were upon them, saying "Here they come at a gallop;" the fact being that the Cavalry seen was the rear guard of the retreating force, consisting of a weak troop.

'*Third Charge* – With having used words calculated to create despondency . . . during the retreat . . . in the following instances:

'*First* – In having, on an occasion when rebuked by Brigadier-General Burrows, and by him asked if he wanted a stampede into Kandahar, openly replied: "It will end in that yet."

'*Second* – In having . . . openly remarked that he thought any further delay on the part of the Cavalry unnecessary, and that not one of the force would reach Kandahar alive.'

(*General Orders*, Poona, 18 March and 6 May, 1881, kindly made available by the Registrar of the Judge Advocate General, London.)

12. *List of cavalry carbines produced at the Royal Small Arms Factory, Enfield Lock, 1867–1896.* (See p. 402.)

1. 1867 Carbine Cavalry, Snider, Pattern I, .577″ (Converted from Carbine Cavalry, Pattern 1861).
2. 1877 Carbine Cavalry, Martini-Henry, .45″
3. 1892 Carbine Cavalry, Martini-Metford, Mark I, .303″
4. 1892 Carbine Cavalry, Martini-Metford, Mark II
5. 1892 Carbine Cavalry, Martini-Metford, Mark III
6. 1893 Carbine Cavalry, Martini-Metford, Mark I*
7. 1893 Carbine Cavalry, Martini-Metford, Mark II*
8. 1894 Carbine Cavalry, Magazine Lee-Metford, Mark I, .303″
9. 1896 Carbine Cavalry, Martini-Enfield, Mark I, .303″
10. 1896 Carbine Cavalry, Magazine, Lee-Enfield, Mark I*, .303″

Note: Nos 3 to 9 were all converted from No. 2

(Cottesloe, Col Lord 'Notes on the History of the Royal Small Arms Factory, Enfield Lock'. *JAHR*, XII (1933), 209–10).

13. *List of pistols (revolvers) made at the Royal Small Arms Factory, Enfield Lock, 1860–1889.* (See p. 403.)

1. 1860 Pistol, 10″, Pattern No. 2 (Muzzle-loading), .577″
2. 1880 Pistol, Revolver, Enfield, Mark I, .455″
3. 1882 Pistol, Revolver, Enfield, Mark II, .455″
4. 1887 Pistol, Revolver, Enfield, Mark II, with safety catch, Mark I, .455″
5. 1889 Pistol, Revolver, Enfield, Mark II, with safety catch, Mark II, .455″

Notes: Nos 2 to 5 were breech-loading and self-extracting. The 1889 pattern was not superseded till 1921 when the Webley was introduced. (Cottesloe, Col Lord 'Notes on the History of the Royal Small Arms Factory, Enfield Lock', *JAHR*, XII (1933), 211).

Household Cavalry and Line Cavalry

	1872	1873	1874	1875	1876	1877	1878	1879	1880	1881	1882
Household Cav. (1660)	H	H	H	H	H	H	H	H	H	H	H/E
1st D.G. (1685)	H	H	H	H	H	H	H	H/A	A	A	I
2nd D.G. (1685)	H	H	H	H	H	H	H	H	H	H	H
3rd D.G. (1685)	H	H	H	H	H	H	H	H	H	H	H
4th D.G. (1685)	H	H	H	H	H	H	H	H	H	H	H
5th D.G. (1685)	H	H	H	H	H	H	H	H	H	H	H
6th D.G. (1685)	H	H	H	H	H	H	I	I	I	I	I
7th D.G. (1688)	H	H	H	H	H	H	H	H	H	H	H
1st D. (1661)	H	H	H	H	H	H	H	H	H	H	H
2nd D. (1678)	H	H	H	H	H	H	H	H	H	H	H
6th D. (1689)	H	H	H	H	H	H	H	H	H	A	A
3rd H. (1685)	I	I	I	I	I	I	I	I/H	H	H	H
4th H. (1685)	I	I	I	I	I	I	I/H	H	H	H	H
5th L. (1858)	I	I/H	H	H	H	H	H	H	H	H	H
7th H. (1690)	H	H	H	H	H	H	H	H	H	H/A	A
8th H. (1693)	H	H	H	H	H	H	H	I	I	I	I
9th L. (1715)	H	H	H	H/I	I	I	I	I	I	I	I
10th H. (1715)	H	H/I	I	I	I	I	I	I	I	I	I
11th H. (1715)	I	I	I	I	I	I	H	H	H	H	H
12th L. (1715)	H	H	H	H	H	H	H	H	H	H	H
13th H. (1715)	H	H	H/I	I	I	I	I	I	I	I	I
14th H. (1715)	H	H	H	H	H/I	I	I	I	I	I/A/I	I
15th H. (1759)	I	I	I	I	I	I	I	I	I	A	H
16th L. (1759)	I	I	I	I	I	H	H	H	H	H	H
17th L. (1759)	H	H	H	H	H	H	H	H/A/I	I	I	I
18th H. (1759)	I	I	I	I	H	H	H	H	H	H	H
19th H. (1759)	H	H	H	H	H	H	H	H	H	H	H/E
20th H. (1861)	I/H	H	H	H	H	H	H	H	H	H	H
21st L. (1861)	I	I/H	H	H	H	H	H	H	H	H	H

Key:
A: South Africa
E: Egypt and the Sudan
I: India
H: Home (i.e. U.K.)

Regiments: Stations from 1872–1898

1883	1884	1885	1886	1887	1888	1889	1890	1891	1892	1893	1894	1895	1896	1897	1898
E	E	E/H	H	H	H	H	H	H	H	H	H	H	H	H	H
I	I	I	I	I	I	I	I	I/H	H	H	H	H	H	H	H
H	H	H/I	I	I	I	I	I	I	I	I	I	I/E	E/H	H	H
H	H	H	H	H	H	H	H	H	H	H	H	H	H	H	H
H	H	H	H	H	H	H	H	H	H	H	H/I	I	I	I	I
H	H	H	H	H	H	H	H	H	H	H/I	I	I	I	I	I
I	I	I	I	I	I	H	H	H	H	H	H	H	H	H	H
H	H	H	H	H	H	H	H	H	H	H	H	H	H	H	H
H	H	H	H	H	H	H	H	H	H	H	H	H	H	H	H
H	H	H	H	H	H	H	H	H	H	H	H	H	H	H	H
A	A	A	A	A	A	A	A/H	H	H	H	H	H	H	H	H
H	H	H	H	H	H	H	H	H	H	H	H	H	H	H	H/I
H	H	H	H	H	H	H	H	H	H	H	H	H	H/I	I	I
H	H	H	H	H	H/I	I	I	I	I	I	I	I	I	I	I/A
A	A	A/H	H/I	I	I	I	I	I	I	I	I	I/A	A	A	A/H
I	I	I	I	I	I	I/H	H	H	H	H	H	H	H	H	H
I	I	I/H	H	H	H	H	H	H	H	H	H	H	A	A	A/I
I	I/E/H	H	H	H	H	H	H	H	H	H	H	H	H	H	H
H	H	H	H	H	H	H	H/A	A	A/I	I	I	I	I	I	I
H	H	H	H	H	H	H	H	H	H	H	H	H	H	H	H
I	I/A	A/H	H	H	H	H	H	H	H	H	H	H	H	H	H
I	I	I	I/H	H	H	H	H	H	H	H	H	H	H	H	H
H	H	H	H	H	H	H	H	H	H	H	H	H	H	H	H
H	H	H	H	H	H	H/I	I	I	I	I	I	I	I	I	I
I	I	I	I	I	I	I	I/H	H	H	H	H	H	H	H	H
H	H	H	H	H	H/I	I	I	I	I	I	I	I	I	I	I/A
E	E	E	E	E	E/H	H	H	H/I	I	I	I	I	I	I	I
H	H	H	E	E	E	E	H	H	H	H	H	H/I	I	I	I
H	H	H	H	H	H/I	I	I	I	I	I	I	I	I/E	E	E/H

ABBREVIATIONS USED IN THE FOOTNOTES AND SOURCE NOTES

Only those sources which occur more than once in the footnotes or source notes are included in this list.

A 0821	W.O. Confidential Paper, A 0821 (Memorandum on officers' retirements, pay, etc.) [the Lawson Committee], 1881
Acland-Troyte	[Acland-Troyte, J. E.] *Through the Ranks to a Commission*, 2nd ed., 1881
Adams	Adams, W. J. *The Narrative of Private Buck Adams, 7th Dragoon Guards . . . 1843–1849*, (ed.) Gordon-Brown, A., 1941
Adye	Adye, Sir John *Soldiers and Others I have Known*, 1925
Airey	*Report of the Army Organization Committee*, [the Airey Committee], 1880
Aitken	Aitken, Sir William *On the Growth of the Recruit and Young Soldier . . .*, 2nd ed., 1887
Alexander	Alexander, Michael *The True Blue: the Life and Adventures of Colonel Fred Burnaby, 1842–1885*, 1957
Allenby	Gardner, Brian *Allenby*, 1965
Anderson	Anderson, Maj. M. H., Anderson, Lt.-Col. E. S. J. and Molloy, Col. G. M. *The Poona Horse (17th Queen Victoria's Own Cavalry) 1817–1913*, I, 1933
A.P.R.C.	*Report of the Royal Commission on Army Promotion and Retirement*, 1876
Ardagh	Malmesbury, Susan Countess of (Lady Ardagh) *The Life of Major-General Sir John Ardagh*, 1909
Arthur	Arthur, Capt. Sir Geo. bt *The Story of the Household Cavalry*, 1909
Arthur: *Maxwell*	Arthur, Sir Geo. bt *General Sir John Maxwell*, 1932
Ashe	Ashe, Maj. W. *Personal Records of the Kandahar Campaign, by officers engaged therein*, 1881
Aston	Aston, Maj.-Gen. Sir George *His Royal Highness the Duke of Connaught and Strathearn: A Life and Intimate Study*, 1929
Atkinson	Atkinson, C. T. *History of the Royal Dragoons, 1661–1934*, 1934
Baden-Powell	Baden-Powell, Lt.-Gen. Sir Robert *Memories of India: Recollections of Soldiering and Sport*, [1915]
Barnett	Barnett, Correlli *Britain and Her Army, 1509–1970, A Military, Political and Social Survey*, 1970

Abbreviations

Barrett	Barrett, C. R. B. *The 7th (Q.O.) Hussars*, 2 vols., 1914
Barrett: *XIIIH*	Barrett, C. R. B. *History of the XIII Hussars*, 2 vols., 1911
Beresford	*The Memoirs of Admiral Lord Charles Beresford, Written by Himself*, 2 vols., 1914
Biddulph	Biddulph, Col. John *The Nineteenth and Their Times . . .*, 1899
Birdwood	Birdwood, F-M Lord *Khaki and Gown: An Autobiography*, 1941
Bisset	Bisset, Maj.-Gen. *Sport and War or Recollections of Fighting and Hunting in South Africa . . . 1834 to 1867 . . .*, 1875
Blatchford	Blatchford, Robert *My Life in the Army*, n.d. [1910?]
Blunt	Blunt, Wilfred Scawen *Secret History of the English Occupation of Egypt . . .*, 1907
Bolitho	Bolitho, H. *The Galloping Third*, 1963
Bond	Bond, Brian 'Recruiting the Victorian Army, 1870–1892', *Victorian Studies*, 1962, V, 334
Bond: *Effect*	Bond, Brian 'The Effect of the Cardwell Reforms on Army Organization, 1874–1904', *J.U.S.I.*, vol. 105, 1960
Bond: *Prelude*	Bond, Brian 'Prelude to the Cardwell Reforms, 1856–68', *JUSI*, vol. 106, 1961
Bond: *VA & SC*	Bond, Brian *The Victorian Army and the Staff College, 1854–1914*, 1972
Burleigh	Burleigh, Bennet *Desert Warfare, being the Chronicle of the Eastern Soudan Campaign*, 1884
Burnaby	Wright, Thomas *The Life of Colonel Fred Burnaby*, 1908
Butler: *Autobiography*	Butler, Sir William F. *An Autobiography*, 1911
Butler: *Campaign*	Butler, Sir William F. *The Campaign of the Cataracts . . .*, 1887
Butler: *Journal*	Butler, Sir William F. *Journal of Operations, Expeditions to Egypt, 1882*, 1882
Cantlie	Cantlie, Lt.-Gen. Sir Neil *A History of the Army Medical Department*, 2 vols., 1974
Cardew	Cardew, Lt. F. G. *A Sketch of the Services of the Bengal Native Army to the year 1895*, 1903
Cav. Drill	[Official] *Cavalry Drill*, 1898
Childers	Childers, Erskine *War and the Arme Blanche*, 1910
Churchill	Churchill, W. S. *A History of the English-Speaking Peoples, IV, The Great Democracies*, 1958
Churchill: *Companion*	Churchill, Randolph S. *Winston S. Churchill, Companion Volume I, Part 2, 1896–1900*, 1967
Coghill: letters	Coghill, Lt.-Col. Kendal J. W. MS letters home, Sept., 1882, 7112-39-4, National Army Museum
Coghill: notebook	Coghill, Lt.-Col. Kendal J. W. MS notebook, Sept., 1882, 7112-39-5, National Army Museum
Colley	Butler, Lt.-Gen. Sir William F. *The Life of Sir George Pomeroy-Colley, 1835–1881 . . .*, 1899

Colvile — Colvile, Col. H. E., *History of the Sudan Campaign*, 2 vols., 1889

Combe — *Letters from B. A. C. (Afghanistan 1878–80)* [Capt. Boyce Albert Combe to his brother Charles Combe], privately printed, 1880. The property of Edmond Combe, Esq.

Crane — Crane, B. P. *The Ninth Lancers in Afghanistan, 1878–1879–1880. The Second Afghan War . . . being a Diary kept daily by Private B. P. Crane, Ninth Q.R. Lancers*, 2nd ed., n.d.

Crawford — Crawford, Surg.-Gen. Sir T. *Special Report on the Hospital Organisation, Sanitation and Medical History of the Wars in Afghanistan 1878–1880* (Appx 3 to *Army Medical Dept Report* for 1880), 1882

Cunynghame — Cunynghame, Gen. Sir Arthur Thurlow *My Command in South Africa, 1874–1878*, 1879

Curtis — Curtis, S. J. *History of Education in Great Britain* [1957]

Dawson — Dawson, Douglas 'Sir Herbert Stewart's Desert March', *The Nineteenth Century*, Nov., 1885

De Cosson — De Cosson, Maj. E. A. *Days and Nights of Service with Sir Gerald Graham's Field Force at Suakin*, 1886

Duke — D[uke], J. [medical officer to Gen. Roberts] *Recollections of the Cabul Campaign, 1879 and 1880*. Privately printed, [1882]. (The copy used, annotated by Roberts and in places corrected by him, is the property of John P. Saunders, Esq.)

Dundonald — Dundonald, Lt.-Gen. The Earl of *My Army Life*, 1926

Early Life — Churchill, W. S. *My Early Life: A Roving Commission*, 1930

Egyptian Cav. — [Anon.] 'From the Unpublished Diary of an Officer.' 'A Short Account of the Work of the Egyptian Cavalry during the Atbara and Omdurman Campaigns', [attributed to Haig], *The Cavalry Journal*, V, 1910

Emery — Emery, Frank *The Red Soldier: Letters from the Zulu War, 1879*, 1977

Erickson — Erickson, Arvel B. 'Edward T. Cardwell: Peelite', *Transactions of the American Philosophical Society*, 1959

E.T.O.C. — *Report of the Committee appointed to consider the Education and Training of the Officers of the Army*, 1902 [The Akers-Douglas Committee]

Forbes — Forbes, Archibald 'Bill Beresford and his Victoria Cross', *Barracks, Bivouacs and Battles*, 1891

Fortescue — Fortescue, the Hon. J. W. *A History of the British Army*, 13 vols., 1899–1930

Fortescue: *17L* — Fortescue, the Hon. J. W. *A History of the 17th Lancers*, 1895

Fuller — Fuller, Maj.-Gen. J. F. C. *Memoirs of an Unconventional Soldier*, 1936

Abbreviations

Galloway	Galloway, William *The Battle of Tofrek fought near Suakin, March 22nd, 1885, under Major-General Sir John Carstairs M'Neill, VC, in its relation to the Mahdist Campaigns of 1884 and 1885*, 1887 (limited edition)
Gerard	Gerard, Lt.-Gen. Sir M. G. *Leaves from the Diaries of a Soldier and Sportsman . . . 1865–1885*, 1903
Gleichen	Gleichen, Lt. Count, Grenadier Guards, *With the Camel Corps up the Nile*, 1888
Goodrich	Goodrich, Lt.-Comm. C. F. (U.S. Navy) *Report of the British Naval and Military Operations in Egypt, 1882*, 1885
Gough	Gough, Gen. Sir Hugh H., VC 'Old Memories: Afghanistan, 1878–1880', *Pall Mall Gazaette*, May, 1898, 1899
Graham	Vetch, Col. R. H. *Life, Letters and Diaries of Lt.-Gen. Sir Gerald Graham, VC, GCB, RE*, [1901]
Grant	Wolseley, Lord 'Memoir of General Sir Hope Grant, GCB', *United Service Magazine*, 1893
Haggard	Haggard, H. Rider *The Last Boer War*, 1899
Haig	Haig, Countess (ed.) *Douglas Haig: His Letters and Diaries*, I. 'Advance Proof Copy' of a work which was never published. The property of the 2nd Earl Haig.
Hamilton	Hamilton, Col. H. B. *Historical Record of the 14th (King's) Hussars*, 1901
Hanna	Hanna, Col. H. B. *The Second Afghan War, 1878–1879–1880: Its Causes, its Conduct and its Consequences*, 3 vols, 1899, 1904, 1910
Hansard: (C)	*Hansard's Parliamentary Debates*, House of Commons
Henderson	Henderson, Col. G. F. R. *The Science of War: A Collection of Essays and Lectures, 1891–1903* (ed.) Col. N. Malcolm, 1st ed., 1905; 2nd ed., 1933
Henderson: *Cav*	Henderson, Col. G. F. R. 'The Tactical Employment of Cavalry', *Encyclopaedia Britannica* (Supplement), 1902, in Henderson, 51–69
Hensman	Hensman, Howard *The Afghan War of 1879–1880, being a Complete Narrative of the Capture of Cabul, the Siege of Sherpur, the Battle of Ahmed Khel, the Brilliant March to Candahar, and the defeat of Ayub Khan, with the Operations on the Helmund, and the Settlement with Abdur Rahman Khan*, 1881
Hodson's Horse	Cardew, Maj. F. G. *Hodson's Horse, 1857–1922*, 1928
H.R.A.V.C.	Smith, Maj.-Gen. Sir Frederick *A History of the Royal Army Veterinary Corps, 1796–1919*, 1927
Hudson	Hudson, Gen. Sir H. *History of the 19th King George's Own Lancers . . . 1858–1921*, 1937
I.L.N.	*The Illustrated London News*
I.O.L.	India Office Library
J.A.H.R.	*The Journal of the Society for Army Historical Research*
J.U.S.I.	*The Journal of the United Services Institution*

Abbreviations

J.U.S.I.I.	*The Journal of the United Service Institution of India*
Kirchhammer	Kirchhammer, Alexander (Capt., Gen. Staff, Imp. Royal Austrian Army) 'The Military Impotence of Great Britain', *The Nineteenth Century*, April, 1881
Leigh Maxwell	Maxwell, Col. Leigh, MS of *My God, Maiwand!*, kindly made available before publication
Le Messurier	*Kandahar in 1879: being the Diary of Major Le Messurier, R. E., Brigade-Major R. E. with the Quetta Column*, 1880
Liddell	Liddell, Col. R. S. *The Memoirs of the Tenth Royal Hussars (Prince of Wales' Own), Historical and Social*, 1891
Life	[Anon. official] *Life in the Ranks of the English Army*, [1883]
McCalmont	Callwell, Sir C. E. (ed.) *The Memoirs of Major-General Sir Hugh McCalmont . . .*, 1924
McCourt	McCourt, Edward *Remember Butler . . .*, 1967
Macdonald	Macdonald, Alex. *Too Late for Gordon and Khartoum: the Testimony of an Independent Eye-Witness . . .*, 1887
MacGregor	(ed.) MacGregor, Lady *The Life and Opinions of Major-General Sir Charles Metcalfe MacGregor . . ., Quarter-Master-General in India*, II, [1888]
Maguire	Maguire, Capt. C. M. 'Organisation and Employment in War of Native Cavalry', Prize Essay, *J.U.S.I.I.*, 1890
Male	Male, Rev. Arthur *Scenes through the Battle Smoke*, 1901
Marling	Marling, Col. Sir Percival, bt, VC *Rifleman and Hussar*, 1931
Masters	Masters, Capt. A. 'Organisation and Employment in War of Native Cavalry', 2nd Essay, *J.U.S.I.I.*, 1890
Maunsell	Maunsell, Col. E. B. *Prince of Wales's Own, The Scinde Horse, 1839–1922* (privately printed), 1926
Maurice: 'Critics'	Maurice, Col. J. F. 'Critics and Campaigns', *Fortnightly Review*, July, 1888
Maxwell	Maxwell, Capt. E. L. *A History of the XI King Edward's Own Lancers (Probyn's Horse)*, 1914
Midshipman	Wood, F-M Sir Evelyn, VC *From Midshipman to Field Marshal*, 1906
Mitford	Mitford, Maj. R. C. W., 14 Bengal Lancers, *To Cabul with the Cavalry Brigade: a Narrative of Personal Experiences with the Force under General Sir F. S. Roberts, GCB . . .*, 2nd ed., 1881
Molyneux	Molyneux, W. C. F. *Campaigning in South Africa and Egypt*, 1896
Moodie	Moodie, D. C. F. *The History of the Battles and Adventures of the British, the Boers and the Zulus, etc, in Southern Africa . . .*, 1888
Morris	Morris, Donald R. *The Washing of the Spears: A History of the Rise of the Zulu Nation under Shaka and its Fall in the Zulu War of 1879*, 1965

Morrison	Morrison, Maj., Royal Dragoons, *Notes on Military Law, Organization and Interior Economy (for use at the R.M.C.)*, 1898
Mossop	Mossop, George *Running the Gauntlet: Some Recollections of Adventure*, 1937
Munro	Munro, Surg.-Gen. William *Records of Service and Campaigning in Many Lands*, 2 vols., 1887
Murray	Murray, Rev. R. H. *The History of the VIII King's Royal Irish Hussars, 1693–1927*, 2 vols., 1928
Nalder	Nalder, Maj.–Gen. R. F. H. *The Royal Corps of Signals, A History of its Antecedents and Development (circa 1800–1955)*, 1958
Narrative	[Rothwell, J. S. (compiler)] *Narrative of the Field Operations connected with the Zulu War of 1879 prepared in the Intelligence Branch of the Quartermaster-General's Department, Horse Guards, War Office*, 1881
Norman	Norman, Lt. W. W. 'Organisation and Employment in War of Native Cavalry', 3rd Essay, *J.U.S.I.I.*, 1890, 284
Norris-Newman	Norris-Newman, C. L. *In Zululand with the British throughout the War of 1879*, 1880
Oatts	Oatts, Lt.-Col. L. B. *Emperor's Chambermaids: the Story of the 14th/20th King's Hussars*, 1973
Official Account	[Anon.] *The Second Afghan War 1878–1880: Abridged Official Account. Produced in the Intelligence Branch, Army Headquarters, India*, 1908
Pomeroy	Pomeroy, Maj. Hon. R. L. *The Story of the 5th Princess Charlotte of Wales' Dragoon Guards*, 2 vols., 1924
Preston	(ed.) Preston, Adrian *In Relief of Gordon: Lord Wolseley's Campaign Journal of the Khartoum Relief Expedition 1884–1885*, 1967
P.R.O.	Public Record Office
Q.R.	*The Queen's Regulations and Orders for the Army*
Razzell	Razzell, P. E. 'Social Origins of Officers in the Indian and British Home Army: 1758–1962' *British Journal of Sociology*, XIV, (Sept., 1963)
Repington	Repington, Lt.-Col. Charles à Court Repington, *Vestigia*, 1919
Reports	India. Army HQ. Intelligence Branch. *Reports and Narratives of Officers who were engaged at the Battle of Maiwand, 27th July, 1880*, n.d.
River War	Churchill, W. S. *The River War: an Historical Account of the Reconquest of the Soudan*, (ed.) Col. F. Rhodes, 2 vols., 1900
Roberts	Roberts of Kandahar, F-M Lord, VC *Forty-One Years in India: From Subaltern to Commander-in-Chief*, II, 1897
Roberts: Desp.	*Afghan War, 1879–1880. Despatches of Lt.-Gen. Sir F. S. Roberts, KCB, CIE, VC, 8th to 24th December 1879.* Reprinted from *The Gazette of India*, 1880

Robertson — Robertson, F-M Sir William, bt *From Private to Field-Marshal*, 1921

Robinson — Robinson, R., Gallacher, J. and Denny, Alice *Africa and the Victorians: the Official Mind of Imperialism*, 1961

Robson — Robson, Brian *Swords of the British Army: The Regulation Patterns, 1788–1914*, 1975

Royle — Royle, Charles *The Egyptian Campaigns 1882 to 1885. New and Revised Edition continued to December, 1899*, 1900

Sandhurst — Smyth, Brig. Sir John, VC, *Sandhurst . . . 1741–1961*, 1961

Sheppard — Sheppard, Maj. E. W. *The Ninth Queen's Royal Lancers, 1715–1936*, 1939

Simmons — Simmons, Gen. Sir L. 'The Critical Condition of the Army', *Nineteenth Century*, XIV (1883)

Skelley — Skelley, A. R. *The Victorian Army at Home: The Recruitment and Terms and Conditions of the British Regular, 1859–1899*, 1977

Smith — Moore Smith, G. C. (ed.) *The Autobiography of Sir Harry Smith*, 2 vols., 1901

Smith-Dorrien — Smith-Dorrien, Gen. Sir Horace *Memories of Forty-Eight Years' Service*, 1925

Smithers — Smithers, A. J. *The Kaffir Wars, 1779–1877*, 1973

Smith: Malcolmson — Lt. E. D. N. Smith's evidence, European General Court Martial, trial of Lt.-Col. and Brevet Col. J. H. P. Malcolmson, C. B., Commandant, 3rd Regt. Sind Horses, Bombay, 18 April, 1881, I.O.L. L/MIL/3/915

Smyth — Smyth, Lt. R. N. 'A Letter from Omdurman [4 Sept., 1898]', *The Yeoman*, 1900

Social Life — 'A British Officer' *Social Life in the British Army*, 1899

Steele — Steele, Col. St G. L. 'The Egyptian Campaign of 1882', Whitworth, 33–7

Steevens — Steevens, G. W. *With Kitchener to Khartum*, 1898

Stewart — Stewart, Capt. P. F. *The History of the XII Royal Lancers (Prince of Wales's)*, 1950

Stewart — (ed.) Elsmie, G. R. *Field-Marshal Sir Donald Stewart: an account of his Life, mainly in his own words*, 1903

Stewart's March — [Anon.] 'Sir Donald Stewart's March from Kandahar to Kabul' *Macmillan's Magazine*, 1881

Suakin — [Anon.] *Suakin, 1885, being a Sketch of the Campaign of this Year by an Officer who was there*, 1885

Swinnerton — Swinnerton, Rev. C. *The Afghan War: Gough's Action at Futtehabad*, 1880

Talbot — Talbot, Lt. & Capt. (later Lt.-Col.) Hon. R. A. J., 1st Life Guards, to Col. Keith Fraser, Ismailia, 2 Sept., 1882. Privately printed letter, Household Cavalry Museum, Windsor

Talbot (2) — Talbot, Lt.-Col. Hon. R. A. J. 'The Battle of Abu-Klea', *The Nineteenth Century*, Jan., 1886

Thompson	Thompson, Col. C. W. *Seventh (Princess Royal's) Dragoon Guards: The Story of the Regiment (1688–1882)*, 1913
Tomasson	Tomasson, W. H. *With the Irregulars in the Transvaal and Zululand*, 1881
Tulloch	Tulloch, Maj.-Gen. Sir Alexander *Recollections of Forty Years' Service*, 1903
Turner	Turner, E. S. *Gallant Gentlemen: a Portrait of the British Officer 1600–1956*, 1956
Tylden: *AFSA*	Tylden, Maj. G. *The Armed Forces in South Africa*, 1954
Tylden: *BAT*	Tylden, Maj. G. 'The British Army and the Transvaal, 1875 to 1885', *J.A.H.R.*, XXX (1952), 159–71
Tylden: Berea	Tylden, Maj. G. 'The Affair at the Berea Mountain, 20th December, 1852', *J.A.H.R.*, XIV (1935), 33–45
Tylden: *CC*	Tylden, Maj. G. 'The Camel Corps and the Nile Campaign, 1884–1885', *J.A.H.R.*, XXXVII (1959), 27–32
Tylden: *CMR*	Tylden, Maj. G. 'The Cape Mounted Riflemen, 1827–1870', *J.A.H.R.*, XVII (1938), 227–31
Tylden: *H. & S.*	Tylden, Maj. G. *Horses and Saddlery . . .*, 1965
Tylden: *Inhlobane*	Tylden, Maj. G. 'Inhlobane Mountain and Kambula, Zululand, 28th/29th March, 1879', *J.A.H.R.*, XXXI (1953), 3–9
Tylden: *ORC*	Tylden, Maj. G. 'The British Army in the Orange River Colony and Vicinity, 1842–1854', *J.A.H.R.*, XVIII (1939), 67–77
Tylden: *PCF*	Tylden, Maj. G. 'The Permanent Colonial Forces of Cape Colony', *J.A.H.R.*, XIX (1940), 149–59
Victoria	Buckle, G. E. (ed.) *The Letters of Queen Victoria . . ., III, 1879–1885*, 1928
Vogt	Vogt, Lt.-Col. Hermann *The Egyptian War of 1882*, 1883
Wantage	*Report of the Committee appointed by the Secretary of State for War to consider the Terms and Conditions of Service in the Army* [The Wantage Committee], 1892
Watson	Watson, Maj.-Gen. W. A. *King George's Own Central India Horse*, 1930
Western	Western, Col. J. S. E. *Reminiscences of an Indian Cavalry Officer*, 1922
Whitworth	Whitworth, Capt. D. E. (ed.) *A History of the 2nd Lancers (Gardner's Horse) from 1809 to 1922*, 1924
Wickenden	Wickenden, James 'With the Gunners at Tel-el-Kebir', Small, E. Milton *Told from the Ranks: Recollections of Service during the Queen's Reign by Privates and Non-Commissioned Officers of the British Army*, n.d. [1890s?]
Willcox	Willcox, W. T. *The Historical Records of the Fifth (Royal Irish) Lancers . . .*, 1908
Williams: *XI H*	Williams, Capt. G. T. *The Historical Records of the Eleventh Hussars Prince Albert's Own*, 1908

Wilson	Wilson, Col. Sir C. W. *From Korti to Khartum: A Journal of the Desert March from Korti to Gubat, and of the Ascent of the Nile in General Gordon's Steamers*, 1886
Wingate	Wingate, F. R. *Mahdiism and the Egyptian Sudan*, 1891
Wolseley	Wolseley, Gen. Viscount 'The Army', Ward, T. H. *The Reign of Queen Victoria*, 1887
Wolseley: *L & SS*	Wolseley, Lt.-Gen. J. Garnet 'Long and Short Service', *The Nineteenth Century*, 1881
Wolseley: *papers*	The papers of F-M Viscount Wolseley, letters to Lady Wolseley, August–September, 1882, W/P11, The Area Library, Hove, Sussex
W.O.	War Office
Wood	Williams, Charles *The Life of Lieutenant-General Sir Henry Evelyn Wood, VC*, 1892
W.O.P.	*War Office Papers*
Wylly	Wylly, Col. H. C. *XVth (The King's) Hussars, 1759 to 1913*, 1914
Ziegler	Ziegler, Philip *Omdurman*, 1973

SOURCE NOTES

CHAPTER I (p. 29–87)

(i)

1 *Armed Forces and Society*, (1975), I, 4; Airey, 3; *Punch*, 61:30, 1871; Wantage, 5
2 Fortescue, XIII, 1930, 579
3 *Report of the Commissioners appointed to inquire into the Recruiting for the Army*, 1867, 105
4 See Clode, Charles M. *The Military Forces of the Crown . . .*, 1869, II, 291 for background to the Reserve question. See, also, Bond: *Prelude*, 231–2
5 Arnold-Foster, H. O. *The War Office, the Army and the Empire*, 1900, 34; 'Stanhope Memorandum', 1 June, 1891, Dunlop, J. K. *The Development of the British Army, 1899–1914*, 1938, 307
6 Wantage, 422
7 Bond, 332
8 Airey, 379, 380; Mole, 290, 293, 303; Marquess of Hartington, *Hansard: (C)*, CCLXXXVI, (1883), 83
9 Wantage, 6, 163, 77
10 Lt.-Col. Logan's evidence, Airey, 139, 140
11 Wantage, 21
12 Airey, 370–1, 474
13 Wantage, 431
14 Airey, 474
15 Wantage, 23
16 Memo. for S. of S. by Lieut.-Gen. R. C. H. Taylor, D. A. G., 20 Aug., 1877, Appx. I, Airey, 459
17 Wantage, 76; Barrett: *XIII H*, 76–7
18 Wantage, 450; Mole, 336
19 Wantage, 533
20 Murray, II, 503
21 Wantage, 14
22 Wantage, 82
23 Wantage, 14
24 Evidence of Lieut.-Col. W. H. MacGeorge, Wantage, 422
25 Wantage, 164
26 Wantage, 75, 80
27 Airey, 425
28 Morrison, 179
29 *Q.R.*, 1883, 200

30 Quoted in Lord, John *Duty, Honour, Empire . . . R. Meinertzhagen*, 1971, 155
31 Wantage, 75
32 *Hansard* (*C*), CCCL (1891), 1105, 1415
33 Southerne, T. *The Loyal Brother* [a play], 1682

(ii)

1 *W.O.P.*, 1867, (Confidential Paper 0312, para. 152), Bond, B. 'Prelude to the Cardwell Reforms, 1856–68; *J.R.U.S.I.*, vol. 106 [1961], 234; Arthur, 678; Mole, 333; Airey, 137; Wantage, 429
2 Parl. Papers (1886), LXVII (c. 5447), 481; (1901), XXXIX (c. 521), 303
3 Butler: *Campaign*, 174
4 Airey, 131, 134–5
5 Evidence of Deputy Inspector-General of Military Hospitals, Airey, 335, 337
6 Evidence of Maj.-General J. H. Rocke, Inspector-Gen. of Recruiting, Wantage, 17, 18 ,19
7 Evidence of Col. E. A. Wood i/c Hounslow depot, Wantage, 181
8 Rocke, Wantage, 17, 18, 34; evidence of Lord Wolseley, Wantage, 154; evidence of Maj.-General J. K. Fraser, Inspector-Gen. of Cavalry, Wantage, 444
9 Bond, 336
10 Wantage, 13, 18
11 *Gen. Order 30*, May, 1878
12 Airey, 406; see also Wantage, 184
13 Airey, 323
14 Evidence of Lieut.-Gen. E. A. Whitmore, Airey, 132
15 Fraser, John *Sixty Years in Uniform*, 1939, 42; Airey, 295
16 Question put by Lord Napier and answered by Col. W. Mure, M.P., Airey, 260
17 Wantage, 49
18 Evidence of Maj.-Gen. J. K. Fraser, Wantage, 446
19 *Gen. Order 73*, 1876; *Gen. Order 13*, 1877; *Gen. Order 82*, 1881; Aitken, 41
20 *Report of Commission of officers on Army Reorganisation*, 1881, C.2791, paras. 46 *et seq.*
21 *Standard*, 8 June, 1883
22 Wantage, 444
23 Aitken, 167
24 Wolseley, quoted by Gathorne-Hardy in moving Army Estimates, *The Times*, 3 Mar., 1870
25 Airey, 226, 228; Wantage, 423
26 Simmons, 170, 187
27 Wantage, 26
28 Aitken, 140
29 *Gen. Order 88*, 1881
30 Evidence of Lieut.-Col. Joseph Logan, Airey, 137, 139
31 Wantage, 73
32 Evidence of the Adjutant-General, Wantage, 3, 10; Aitken, 168–9

33 Aitken, 164–5, 166
34 Wantage, 429
35 Wantage, 431
36 Wantage, 116
37 Airey, 145
38 *Gen. Order 73*, Sep., 1876
39 Mole, 334
40 Evidence of Lieut.-Gen. E. A. Whitmore, Airey, 129
41 Airey, 25, 139
42 Evidence of Lieut.-Col. Robert Law, Staff Officer of Pensioners, Plymouth, Airey, 151
43 Willcox, 165
44 Kirchhammer, 608; Parl. Papers (1881), XXI (C.2791), 209; Bond, 334
45 Wantage, 159; evidence of Sgt.-Maj. Thompson, Airey, 371
46 Wantage, 21, 183
47 Airey, 336
48 Blackburn, D. and Cadell, W. W. *Secret Service in South Africa*, 1911, 124

(iii)

1 Blatchford, 23
2 Wantage, 116; *Social Life*, 71
3 Wantage, 8; *Life*, 10
4 Wantage, 46, 54
5 Wyndham, Horace *Soldiers of the Queen*, 1889, 31; *Annual Reports of the Army Medical Dept.* (Parl. Papers), 1857, 1875, 1895; Skelley, 54
6 Forbes, Archibald 'Soldiers' Wives', *Memories and Studies of War and Peace*, 1895, 320; Wolseley to E. Stanhope, 1891, *Stanhope MSS*, quoted in Skelley, 40
7 Robertson, 2–12
8 Forbes, Archibald *Camps, Quarters and Casual Places*, 1896, 104–119; Robertson, 10
9 23 Feb., 1880, Combe, 139
10 Morrison, 174, 176
11 Mole, 181–2, 187
12 Smyth, Brig. Sir John, Bt, VC *In This Sign Conquer: The Story of the Army Chaplains*, 1968, 112, 118–19, 127; see also Roberts, 275
13 Watkins, Owen Spencer *With Kitchener's Army, being a Chaplain's Experience with the Nile Expedition, 1898*, 1899, 167

(iv)

1 Wantage, 430
2 Gladstone to Cardwell, *Cardwell Papers*, 30/48/2–8: 152–76
3 *Army Circular*, 1 Oct., 1873, 3; *W.O. Historical Survey of Pay, 1660–1891*, 206
4 *The Times*, 25 Feb., 1873, 9
5 Wolseley, 209
6 Wantage, 168

7 Mole, 351–2
8 Roberts, Lord, 'Free Trade in the Army', *Nineteenth Century*, XV (1884), 1061; Cairnes, W. E. *The Army from Within*, 1901, 7, 61, 111; Tucker, A. V. 'Army and Society in England, 1870–1900 . . .', *Journal of British Studies*, 1963, 136
9 Morrison, 197
10 Mole, 194–5; Morrison, 136, 137, 155, 161, 162
11 Morrison, 178; *Q.R.*, 709; Wantage, 184, 449
12 Morrison, 195–6
13 Wantage, 447; *W.O. Special Circular, Supplemental Despatches*, Suakin, 1884, quoted in Burleigh, 319
14 Wolseley, 208
15 See the various Royal Pay Warrants

(v)

1 Hamilton, 358; See Vol II, 288; *Life*, 19
2 Wolseley, 208–9
3 Curtis, 593
4 White, 40
5 *Q.R.*, 1883, 232
6 *Fifth and Sixth Reports on Army Schools*, 1893, quoted in Hawkins, T. H. and Brimble, L. J. F. *Adult Education: the Record of the British Army*, 1947, 36, 38; White, 40–1
7 Curtis, 593, 594; Willcox, 170
8 Wantage, 447
9 *Q.R.*, 1883, 233–4
10 *E.T.O.C.*, 1, 2

(vi)

1 Wolseley to S.o.S. for War, 15 June, 1885, Colvile, II, 225
2 Alexander, 190
3 Wolseley: *L & SS*, 570
4 Morrison, 17–19, 28; *Army Acts* and *Q.R.*
5 Robertson, 12–13
6 *The Broad Arrow*, 27 Oct., 543–4; *The Army and Navy Gazette*, 27 Oct., 676; *The Times*, 3 Nov.; *The Irish Times*, quoted in *The Naval and Military Gazette*, 19 Sep., 1877, 234
7 *Early Life*, 133
8 Pomeroy, I, 207
9 P.R.O. W.O./86/43, p. 109; Gore, Capt. St John *The Strange Case of W. Craven: How I appeared as Counsel, by the Prisoner's Friend* (Unpublished MS), 1893, the property of Home HQ, 5th Inniskilling Dragoon Guards; *The Army and Navy Gazette*, 27 May, 1893; Johnston, S. H. F. *The History of the Cameronians . . .*, I, 1957, 290–1; Pomeroy, I, 207–8
10 Information kindly supplied by the Curator, Household Cavalry Museum, Combermere Barracks, Windsor, based largely on reports in *The Windsor and Eton Express*

(vii)

1 Mole, 354; Acland-Troyte, 114–15; Wantage, 411
2 Airey, 140
3 Evidence of Dr Donald, Airey, 337
4 Quoted by Wolseley in Wolseley: *L & SS*, 570
5 Evidence of Lieut.-Gen. A. J. Herbert (retd.), Airey, 348; evidence of Lieut.-Col. W. Egerton Todd, Staff Officer of Pensioners, West London District, Airey, 14
6 Mole, 354–5
7 Memo., 6 Jun., 1893, W.O.32/1089/101/432
8 Wolseley, 210; *Parliamentary Papers* (1894), LII (189), 289
9 Wantage, 410–11
10 Churchill: *Companion*, 956
11 *Allowance Regulations*, 1890, paras. 654, 657, p. 187
12 Wantage, 448
13 Birdwood, 55

CHAPTER II (p. 88–120)

1 Quoted in Featherstone, D. F. *All for a Shilling a Day*, 1966, 126; Wolseley: *L & SS*, 562; *Hansard* (*C*), 206, 689–92, 1871; *Early Life*, 50, 78
2 *Report on Select Committee on Army* (*System of Retirement*), 1867, s.6
3 Appx. C, *A.P.R.C.*, 223–6
4 *A.P.R.C.*, viii, xxiv
5 A 0821, 5
6 *Pay Warrant*, 1878, 46
7 *Pay Warrant*, 1884, 61
8 [Anon.] 'Promotion by Purchase' *North British Review*, vol. 23, 523 (1855); *Early Life*, 170
9 *E.T.O.C.*, 1, 2
10 Marling, 156; *W.O. Special Circular, Supplemental Despatches*, Suakin, 1884, quoted in Burleigh, 319
11 A 0821, 2
12 A 0821, 2
13 Adye, Gen. Sir John *Recollections of a Military Life*, 1895, 324–8
14 Erickson, 84
15 *A.P.R.C.*, 23
16 *A.P.R.C.*, 261–2
17 *E.T.O.C.*, 50
18 *A.P.R.C.*, 24; The Denne case was the subject of a booklet published by his friends and relations: *The Garnet Ring: Promotion by Selection: Lt.-Col. Denne, 1882–1886*, [1886]. The resumé here given is taken solely from this booklet
19 *W.O. Committee on Reserve of Officers* (Maj.-Gen. R. B. Hawley), 1879, 1–4
20 *Army Circular*, Aug., 1879, Clause 164, 6. See also *Pay Warrant*, 1899, 147–50

21 *E.T.O.C.*, 79
22 Barrett: *XIII H*, 66
23 *Q.R.*, 1883, 558
24 A 0821, 1
25 *A.P.R.C.*, xiii, xli, 157, 159, 161, 282
26 Daniell, 231; *Q.R.*, 1883, 52–3
27 Gallagher, T. F. '"Cardwellian Mysteries": The Fate of the British Army Regulation Bill, 1871' *The Historical Journal*, 1975, 348; Razzell, 253–5
28 *Sandhurst*, 262
29 Vogt, 169
30 Goodrich, 337
31 Fortescue, II, 569
32 *River War*, II, 8; Churchill: *Companion*, 962
33 Wolseley, *L & SS*, 562; *H.R.A.V.C.*, 172
34 *Allenby*, 8
35 Barnett, 314
36 *Social Life*, 1899, 27, 29, 31, 32; *Q.R.*, 1883, 158–63
37 *Early Life*, 75
38 Quoted in Turner, 240
39 Quoted in Turner, 241
40 *McCalmont*, 38–9
41 Combe, 134
42 *Early Life*, 77
43 *Early Life*, 42, 43, 49
44 Gen. Sir H. Gough *Soldiering On*, 1954, 27
45 Fuller, 4; Western, 30, 31
46 *E.T.O.C.*, 79
47 Cooper, Duff *Haig*, 1935, I, 32
48 Marling, 21
49 Repington, 33, 37
50 De Sales la Terrière, Col. B. *Days that are gone*, 1924, 56, 59, 90
51 Callwell, Maj.-Gen. Sir C. E., *Field-Marshal Sir Henry Wilson . . . His Life and Diaries*, 1927, I, 2–4; Baden-Powell, 4
52 *Sandhurst*, 98–102
53 Farrar-Hockley, A. *Goughie*, 1975, 11
54 *Allenby*, 6–7
55 Repington, 38–9
56 Fuller, 5–6
57 *Early Life*, 57–9, 63, 73
58 *A.P.R.C.*, 33
59 Bond: *VA & SC*, 168
60 Gleichen, Lord Edward (Count Gleichen) *A Guardsman's Memories*, 1932, 118
61 Bond: *VA & SC*, 133
62 *A.P.R.C.*, 41
63 To his father, 9 Jan., 1884, Hamilton, I. B. M. *The Happy Warrior*, 1966, 64; to Capt. A. Haldane, 11 Aug., 1898, Churchill: *Companion*, 964

64 Bond: *VA & SC*, 135, 138
65 *Report of Committee on the Working of the Staff College*, 1880
66 Bond: *VA & SC*, 136; Col. J. F. Maurice's evidence, *Report of the Committee on Military Educational Establishments*, 1888, paras. 3608, 3611, 3618–19, 3682
67 Maude, Col. F. N. *War and the World's Life*, 1907, 171
68 Bond: *VA & SC*, 155
69 Appreciation by Lieut.-Gen. Sir Henry Hildyard, in Roberts, F-M Lord 'Memoir', Henderson, xxix
70 Note by Gen. Sir George Barrow in Allenby Papers, quoted in *Allenby*, 1965, 17
71 Terraine, J. *Douglas Haig, the Educated Soldier*, 1963, 12
72 *Allenby*, 1965, 14, 16
73 Robertson, 89, 90
74 Cantlie, 278–9
75 Cantlie, 276–80
76 15 Mar., 1898, *Haig*, 82
77 *H.R.A.V.C.*, 162
78 *H.R.A.V.C.*, 175
79 Fulford, R. *Darling Child: Private Correspondence of Queen Victoria and the Crown Princess of Prussia, 1871–1874*, 1976, 189
80 *Grant*, 783
81 Pearse, Col. H. W. 'Sir Hope Grant', *Cavalry Journal*, V, 1910, 424
82 *Grant*, 779
83 *Grant*, 791
84 21 Jan., 1885, Preston, 122

CHAPTER III (p. 121–166)

(i)

1 Wantage, 1, 15
2 Aitken, 23; Kirchhammer, 600
3 Bond: *Effect*, 521
4 Wantage, 1
5 Wantage, 4
6 Wantage, 448; Mole, 332–3
7 Report of *Cavalry Organisation Committee*, (Gen. Wardlaw), 7; Wantage, 433
8 Wantage, 18, 431, 433
9 Barrett: *XIII H*, 75
10 Murray, II, 497; Sheppard, 179; Wantage, 422
11 Wantage, 421
12 *Cav. Drill*, 19
13 Wantage, 442
14 Wantage, 443
15 Wantage, 42
16 Mole, 334
17 Wantage, 442–3

(ii)

1 Quoted from Croker in Glover, M. *Wellington as Military Commander*, 1968, 49; *J.U.S.I.I.*, 1971, 357–89; Robinson, 12; Mole, 342
2 Oatts, Lt.-Col. L. B. *I Serve: Regimental History of the 3rd Carabineers* . . ., 1966, 164
3 *River War*, II, 64
4 Oatts, 257
5 Airey, 429
6 Mole, 180
7 Daniell, 215
8 Mole, 342
9 Airey, 427
10 Wantage, 229
11 Mole, 156, 161
12 Crawford, 273–5; Mole, 158
13 Mole, 160
14 Bolitho, 177
15 Willcox, 202
16 Bolitho, 176
17 Baden-Powell, 74; Wantage, 34; *Report of the Departmental Committee on Venereal Disease among British Troops in India* (Earl of Onslow), C.8379, 1897; *Cantonments Act, 1897* (C.8919) and *Instructions of Govt of India thereon* (C.9017)
18 Butler: *Campaign*, 260
19 Mole, 156–7, 301
20 Roberts, Maj.-Gen. Sir F. *Correspondence with India while C-in-C, Madras, 1881–1885*, 1890; Roberts, Gen. Sir F. *Speeches 1878 to 1893* (No. 59, 1884, No. 76, 1888), 1895, quoted in 'S.C.W.' 'Temperance and its Rewards in the British Army' *Annual Report, Nat. Army Museum*, 1976–7
21 Biddulph, Brig.-Gen. M. A. S. *Summer Homes for Soldiers' Children in the Himalaya*, 1876, 9, 12
22 Roberts, 410–11; Cantlie, 345–7; Bradshaw, Surg.-Maj.-Gen. Sir A. F. *Memoirs of Catherine Grace Lock*, 1905, 11
23 Wantage, 430; Mole, 145
24 Sir E. Wood's evidence, Wantage, 45
25 Mole, 161–3, 169, 302
26 Airey, 425
27 7 July, 1879, Combe, 61
28 Airey, 425, 427; Mole, 166
29 Mole, 155, 169, 305, 326

(iii)

1 *Early Life*, 117; Combe, 34
2 Goodrich, 302, 303
3 Baden-Powell, 284, 287
4 *Early Life*, 119
5 24 Oct., 1878, Combe, 7
6 Goodrich, 304–6

7 Baden-Powell, 17
8 Pomeroy, 191–2; 8 Mar., 1879, Combe, 34; *Early Life*, 118–19, 122
9 Anon., quoted in Baden-Powell, 36
10 For an excellent account of contemporary pig-sticking see Baden-Powell, Sir R. S. S. *Pig-Sticking or Hog-Hunting*, 1889; Baden-Powell, 36–9
11 Birdwood, 60
12 *Cav. Journal*, IV, 1909, 122–6
13 Liddell, 552
14 Quoted in Brander, M. *The 10th Royal Hussars*, 1969, 52
15 Liddell, 553
16 Baden-Powell, 31
17 *Early Life*, 120
18 Birdwood, 35–6
19 Baden-Powell, 33, 36

(iv)

1 8 Apr., 1878, *The Times*; Baden-Powell, 269; quoted in Hudson, 58
2 Jaipur, H. H. Maharaja of *The Indian State Forces . . .*, 1967, xv
3 Hanna, II, 142
4 Cardew, 376, 402–3
5 Watson, 209
6 Birdwood, 69
7 Birdwood, 38
8 Western, 247
9 Watson, 197–8
10 Quoted (under Nolan) in Elliot, Maj. G. H., 3 Bengal Cavalry, *Cavalry Literature*, 1893, 29
11 Norman, 285
12 Cardew, 404
13 Maguire, 237, 240
14 Anderson, 247
15 Maxwell, 91
16 Gerard, 286–7
17 Cardew, 376
18 Anderson, 250
19 Masters, 256
20 Masters, 257
21 Memorandum by Maj.-Gen. Sir John Hudson, Suakin, 1885, quoted in Galloway, 112
22 Norman, 292
23 Goodrich, 309
24 Birdwood, 64, 90
25 Maguire, 242; Norman, 300
26 Ashe, 62
27 Ashe, 63; Mitford, 4
28 Norman, 289
29 Hudson, 72
30 Anderson, 152

31 Baden-Powell, 271
32 Masters, 256
33 Baden-Powell, 269
34 Ashe, 63
35 Baden-Powell, 270–1
36 Birdwood, 41; Western 171, 172
37 Anderson, 251–2
38 Maunsell, 36
39 Hudson, 67
40 Western, 60–1
41 Maj. Daniel, 1879, quoted in Anderson, 240
42 Hudson, 68–9
43 Goodrich, 327, 328, 332

CHAPTER IV (p. 167–208)

(i)

1 Cunynghame, 1879, 52
2 Smithers, 274
3 Smithers, 18
4 *Smith*, II, 25, 67
5 Amery, L. S. (ed.) *The Times History of the War in South Africa, 1899–1902*, 1902, II, 55
6 Munro, I, 205
7 Tylden; *CMR*, 227–8
8 Fortescue, XI, 399
9 Munro, I, 205
10 Adams, 271, 275
11 Cole, *The Cape and the Kaffirs*, 1852, 110
12 Munro, I, 205–6
13 Tylden: *ORC*, 67–9; Thompson, 63
14 Bisset, 86
15 Thompson, 67
16 Bisset, 90, 91
17 Adams, 154–5
18 Hook, Maj. D. B. *With Sword and Statute on the Cape of Good Hope Frontier*, 1905, 11, 12
19 Munro, I, 139
20 Newman, W. A. *Memoir of J. Montagu*, 1855, quoted in *Smith*, II, 262
21 Wellington to Miss A. Burdett-Coutts, 30 Dec., 1851, Wellington, 7th Duke of *Wellington and His Friends*, 1965, 286–7
22 *W.O.P.* 4/722/236–7 (augmentation)
23 Sir H. Smith to Earl Grey, C.O.48, quoted in Stewart, 117–18
24 Lieut. Jary, quoted in Stewart, 121
25 Tylden: *Berea*, 35
26 Fortescue, XII, 558
27 Anon. Quoted in Cunynghame, 87

28 Napier's Report, 21 Dec., 1852, Moodie, 1888, 79–80
29 Young, P. J. *Boot and Saddle: a Narrative record of . . . the British Cape Mounted Riflemen . . .*, [1955], 59
30 Anon. Quoted in Cunynghame, 87–8
31 Cunynghame, 84
32 Tylden: *Berea*, fns 36, 39, p. 43
33 Henderson, 400
34 Tylden: *PCF*, 149
35 Tylden: *AFSA*, 60–1
36 Tylden: *AFSA*, 33–215
37 Tylden: *AFSA*, ix

(ii)

1 Melville, Col. C. H. *Life of General the Right Hon. Sir Redvers Buller, VC*, 1923, I, 95
2 *Narrative*, 13
3 Morris, 279
4 Tylden, Maj. G. 'Some Aspects of the Zulu Wars', *J.A.H.R.*, XVII (1938), 127–8
5 *Narrative*, 18
6 Tomasson, 128
7 Morris, 302
8 Wood, 374
9 Morris, 330
10 Norris-Newman, 1880, 80–81

(iii)

1 Forbes, 140–1
2 Parr, Capt. H. H. *A Sketch of the Kafir and Zulu Wars*, 1880, 259
3 Forbes, 137
4 Tomasson, 41
5 Tylden: *Inhlobane*, 3
6 Mossop, 38–9; Wood, F. M. Sir E. VC *Winnowed Memories*, 1917, 287
7 Forbes, 137, 142; Mossop, 34, 38
8 Morris, 431
9 Wood, 366
10 Tomasson, 50
11 *Narrative*, 160; Norris-Newman, 289–9; letter of Capt. Henry Vaughan, RA, *I.L.N.*, 31 May, 1879, quoted in Emery, 164; Lieut. A. Blaine to a cousin, 31 Mar., 1879, Moodie, 1888, 279
12 Henderson, 400; Airey, 406
13 Butler, L. *Sir Redvers Buller*, 1909, 38; Airey, 406
14 Wood, 380
15 Tylden; *Inhlobane*, 9; Mossop, 67
16 Tomasson, 58–9
17 Tylden: *Inhlobane*, 9; Mossop, 74; Pte. J. Snook, 1/13 L.I., *North Devon Herald*, 29 May, 1879, quoted in Emery, 173

18 Tomasson, 64
19 Molyneux, 137

(iv)

1 Lehmann, Joseph *All Sir Garnet*, 1964, 255
2 Morris, 502
3 Tomasson, 83
4 Montague, Capt. W. E. *Campaigning in South Africa: Reminiscences of an Officer in 1879*, 1880
5 *Narrative*, 92
6 Tomasson, 125
7 Tomasson, 127
8 Blood, Gen. Sir Bindon *Four Score Years and Ten*, 1933, 203
9 Tomasson, 115
10 Molyneux, 183–4

(v)

1 Mossop, 96
2 Mossop, 93
3 Tomasson, 176
4 Molyneux, 186
5 Wood, 400
6 Morris, 567
7 Tomasson, 191
8 Fotescue: *17L*, 176
9 Molyneux, 188
10 Mossop, 94–5
11 *North Devon Herald*, 18 Sep., 1879, quoted in Emery, 232–3

(vi)

1 Tomasson, 24; Colley to his wife, 28 Jan. 1881, *Colley*, 291; Colley to S. of S. for War, quoted in Bond, B. 'The South African War 1880–1', Bond, B. (ed.) *Victorian Military Campaigns*, 1967, 218
2 Tylden: *BAT*, 162
3 MS *Chief of Staff's Journal, Transvaal, 1879*, Ministry of Defence Library, 58
4 Haggard, 117
5 Haggard, 124
6 Blackburn, D. and Cadell, W. W. *Secret Service in South Africa*, 1911, 123
7 [F-M Sir] George White to his wife, 23 Dec., 1880, White Papers, I.O.L., MSS Eur. F.18
8 Colley to Wolseley, 30 Jan., 1881, *Colley* 287–9
9 *Colley*, 291–2
10 Buchan, John *The History of the Royal Scots Fusiliers, 1678–1918*, 1925, 244
11 See Colley, Lady 'Sir George Colley in South Africa' *The Nineteenth Century*, March, 1904, 408, and Haggard, 141

CHAPTER V (p. 209–267)

(i)

1 Durand, Sir H. *The First Afghan War, and its Causes*, 1879; Wellington to Ellenborough, 1842, quoted in Hanna, III, 551; Trollope, Anthony, *Ayala's Angel*, World Classics ed., 596
2 Cowling, Maurice 'Lytton, the Cabinet, and the Russians, August to November, 1878' *English Historical Review*, 1961, 59
3 10 Dec., 1878, Combe, 16
4 11 Feb., 1879, Combe, 27
5 Combe, 36
6 Gerard, 255–6; Maxwell, 70
7 Hanna, II, 284
8 Maxwell, 70–1
9 Hanna, II, 285
10 Combe, 38–9
11 Liddell, 401–2
12 Kipling, R. *Verses 1889–1896*, 1898, 66
13 Combe, 40–1
14 Hanna, II, 291
15 Combe, 43
16 Sir S. Browne's despatch, *Guides*, 86
17 7 Oct., 1879, *London Gazette*
18 Swinnerton, 59–61
19 Combe, 42
20 Gough, 207
21 Gough's Report, 9 Jan., 1879, quoted in Hanna, II, 208
22 [Anon.] *Regimental Records, 5th Regiment, Punjab Cavalry*, 1886, 37
23 *Official Account*, 333–4; [Anon.] *History of the Second Punjab Cavalry from 1849 to 1886*, 1888, 42–4
24 Stewart to Mrs Stewart, 13 Nov., 1878, *Stewart*, 220
25 Diary of T. C. Hamilton, 15H, Wylly, 298
26 Wylly, 298
27 *Official Account*, 165
28 See Hanna, II, 233–7, for a full account of this action
29 4 Jan., 1879, Le Messurier, 55–6, 58
30 Diary of Capt. Hon. R. Leigh, Wylly, 302
31 Maunsell, 23
32 *Official Account*, 173

(ii)

1 Combe, 50; Hensman, 25
2 6 June, 1879, Combe, 55–6; Hanna, III, 7–8; Cantlie, 303
3 7 Aug., 25 Aug., 1879, Combe, 65, 66; Airey, 403
4 Crane, 22
5 Hanna, III, 44; Mitford, 3; [Anon.] *Regimental Records, 5th Regiment, Punjab Cavalry*, 1886, 43

6 27 Sep., 1879, Crane, 23
7 MS note in Roberts's hand in margin of copy of Duke, 139
8 Hamilton, Gen. Sir Ian *Listening for the Drums*, 1944, 125–6
9 Roberts, 235
10 Gough, 389; Combe, 90; Roberts's 'Introduction' to Childers, vi
11 3 Nov., 1879, Crane, 34

(iii)

1 Hanna, III, 160
2 23 Jan., 1880, Roberts: *Desp.*, 6
3 23 Jan., 1880, Roberts: *Desp.*, 8
4 Crane, 38–9
5 Combe, 109; Hensman, 191
6 Sheppard, 167–8
7 Crane, 39
8 Sheppard, 167–8
9 Crane, 39
10 Roberts, 272
11 MacGregor, 160–1
12 Roberts, 273–4
13 MacGregor, 161
14 Sheppard, 168–9
15 Roberts in his 'Introduction' to Childers, xi; Roberts, 275; *Army Order*, 1 June, 1902
16 Hanna, III, 183
17 Macpherson's despatch, 27 Dec., 1879, quoted in Hanna, III, 184–5
18 MacGregor, 161
19 Combe, 125
20 Sheppard, 169
21 Crane, 42–3
22 Quoted in Hanna, III, 206
23 Combe, 114
24 Combe, 113
25 Crane, 43
26 Gough, 398
27 Roberts, 292
28 Roberts: *Desp.*, 19
29 Col. Money to Maj. Williams, quoted in Hanna, III, 210–11
30 [Anon.] *Regimental Records: 5th Regiment, Punjab Cavalry*, 1886, 53
31 Combe, 114–15
32 Hensman, 247
33 Roberts, 305, 307
34 13 Jan., 1880, Roberts to C-in-C, *Official Account*, 368
35 Hanna, III, 277; *Official Account*, 380

(iv)

1 Chapman, Gen. E. F. 'Two Years under Field-Marshal Sir Donald Stewart in Afghanistan, 1878–80', *Blackwood's Magazine*, Feb., 1902, 261–2

2 Roberts, 321
3 *Stewart's March*, 54
4 *Stewart's March*, 58
5 Hanna, III, 328
6 Hudson, 45
7 Diary, 19 Apr.; Letter to Lady Stewart, 20 Apr., 1880, Stewart, 331, 333
8 Hudson, 46–7
9 Stewart to Lady Stewart, 21 Apr., 1880, Stewart, 335
10 Combe, 188
11 Hudson, 46
12 Brig.-Gen. J. Doran's despatch, quoted in Watson, 149
13 Watson, 150
14 *Official Account*, 410–11; Hanna, III, 368–9

(v)

1 Hills, Maj.-Gen. Sir J., RE *The Bombay Field Force*, 1880, 1900
2 Leigh Maxwell, 110
3 Leigh Maxwell, 99–100
4 Lieut. E. D. N. Smith's evidence, *Reports*, 59; Maunsell, 26; Maunsell, Lieut.-Col. E. B. 'Maiwand: A Cavalry Study of "How not to do it"', *Cavalry Journal*, Oct., 1924, 403–4
5 *The Times*, 16 Oct., 1880
6 Hanna, III, 407
7 *Reports*, 6–7
8 Lieut. J. H. E. Reid's evidence; Lieut. E. D. N. Smith's evidence, *Reports*, 50, 58
9 Nuttall's despatch, quoted in Hanna, 412
10 *Reports*, 48
11 *Reports*, 7
12 Leigh Maxwell, 214
13 Hanna, 413
14 *Reports*, 7–8; Smith: Malcolmson, 48
15 *Reports*, 52
16 Surgeon A. W. F. Street, 3 B.L.C., *Reports*, 54
17 *Reports*, 8
18 *Reports*, 17–18
19 *Reports*, 23; Combe, 200
20 Smith: Malcolmson, 48
21 Hanna, III, 424
22 Hills, Maj.-Gen. Sir John *The Bombay Field Force, 1880*, 1900, 29
23 For an excellent account of the battle see Robson, Brian 'Maiwand, 27th July 1880', *J.A.H.R.*, LI, (1973), 194–224
24 Roberts, 337
25 21 Aug., 1880, Combe, 188
26 Gerard, 299
27 Gerard, 301
28 Sheppard, 171
29 Roberts, 349

30 Gerard, 301
31 Roberts, 349
32 Crane, 63–5
33 Combe, 189
34 Combe, 198
35 Sheppard, 175
36 Benians, E. A. 'Finance, Trade and Communications, 1870–1895', *The Cambridge History of the British Empire*, III, 1959, 187

CHAPTER VI (p. 268–306)

(i)

1 Robinson, 81
2 Churchill, 265
3 Robinson, 87
4 Robinson, 103
5 Halberg, C. W. *The Suez Canal: Its History and Diplomatic Importance*, 1931, 266
6 Maurice, 6
7 Vogt, 136
8 Adjt.-General's Memorandum for Os.C., Household Cavalry, 11 Jul., 1882, Household Cavalry Museum, Windsor; Coghill: notebook, 3 Sep., 1882
9 Arthur, 673; Goodrich, 224; Wickenden, 98; Wolseley to Lady Wolseley, 11 Aug., 1882, W/P ii/8iii, Wolseley: *papers*
10 Adye, Maj.-Gen. Sir John *Soldiers and Others I have Known*, 1925, 70
11 Maurice, 12; Smith-Dorrien, 37–8; *Wood*, 471
12 Goodrich, 225
13 Dawson, Brig.-Gen. Sir D. *A Soldier Diplomat*, 1927, 74
14 Tylden, Maj. G. 'Mounted Infantry', *J.A.H.R.*, XXII (1944), 178
15 Arthur, II, 673; Male, 314

(ii)

1 4 Sep., 1882, *McCalmont*, 211–12
2 Wolseley's despatch, 26 Aug., 1882, Goodrich, 127
3 Maurice, 44; Butler: *Journal*, 7
4 Wolseley's despatch, 26 Aug., 1882, Goodrich, 128
5 Butler: *Autobiography*, 226
6 Talbot, 1
7 Maurice, 47
8 Talbot, 1–2
9 Wolseley's Despatch, 26 Aug., 1882, Goodrich, 127
10 Tulloch, 303; Wickenden, 98, 99; Corban, Laurence, Surg.-Maj. *Experiences of an Army Surgeon during the Egyptian Expedition of 1882*, 1882, 3
11 Coghill: letters, 10 Sep., 1882
12 Talbot, 3; Wickenden, 98
13 Talbot, 2
14 Butler: *Autobiography*, 227

15 *McCalmont*, 211
16 Wolseley's despatch, 27 Aug., Goodrich, 130
17 Talbot, 2
18 Maurice, 51
19 Talbot, 2
20 Blunt, 415–16; Talbot, 2
21 Talbot, 2
22 Wolseley to Duke of Cambridge, 28 Aug., 1882, quoted in Arthur, II, 675; Macaulay, Pte., Scots Guards 'With the Guards in Egypt', Small, E. M. *Told from the Ranks* . . ., 1897, 49

(iii)

1 3 Oct., 1882, quoted in *Graham*, 242; Froude, Tpr. Tom, 2 LG, 'The Charge of Kassassin', n.d., Household Cavalry Museum
2 Royle, 159
3 Maurice, 60
4 Molyneux, 244
5 Thompson, 70
6 Talbot, 3
7 Graham to Wolseley, 29 Aug., 1882, Goodrich, 133
8 Maurice, 62
9 Drury-Lowe to Lt.-Gen. Willis, 29 Aug., 1882, Goodrich, 136
10 Wolseley to Lady Wolseley, 31 Aug., 1882, W/P 11/13, Wolseley: *papers*
11 Drury-Lowe to Lt.-Gen. Willis, 29 Aug., 1882, Goodrich, 136
12 Maurice, 64
13 Maurice: 'Critics', 116–19
14 Talbot, 4
15 Talbot, 3–4
16 Tulloch, 309
17 Goodrich, 136
18 Wolseley to Lady Wolseley, 31 Aug., 1882, W/P 11/13 ii, Wolseley: *papers*
19 Molyneux, 247–8
20 Nalder, 25–6
21 Molyneux, 254
22 Steele, 34, 35
23 Coghill: notebook, Sep., 1882
24 Goodrich, 142
25 Wolseley's despatch, 10 Sep., 1882, Goodrich, 141
26 Coghill: letters, 10 Sep., 1882
27 Tulloch, 315–16

(iv)

1 Letter quoted in Chenevix Trench, C. 'Gordon's Staff Officer', *History Today*, March, 1975
2 Blunt, 419
3 Quoted in Burne, Lieut.-Col. Alfred H. *The Battlefields of England*, 1951, 275

4 Wolseley's despatch, 16 Sep., 1882, Goodrich, 150
5 Wolseley to Childers, 8 Sep., 1882, and Childers to Wolseley, 8 Sep., 1882, Childers, II, 122, 125
6 Maurice: 'Critics', 114
7 Biddulph, 237
8 Maurice, 84
9 Molyneux, 264
10 Butler: *Journal*, 31
11 Maurice, 88–9
12 Tylden, Maj. G. 'Tel-el-Kebir, 13th September, 1882', *J.A.H.R.*, XXXI (1953), 53
13 Butler: *Autobiography*, 234–5
14 Maurice, 90
15 Coghill: letters, 14 Sep., 1882
16 Maurice, 90
17 McCalmont, 220
18 Coghill: letters, 14 Sep., 1882
19 Maurice, 96
20 Steele, 36
21 [Palmer, A. V.] 'A Battle Described from the Ranks', *The Nineteenth Century*, March, 1890, 403
22 Coghill: letters, 14 Sep., 1882
23 Macpherson to Childers, 24 Sep., 1882, Childers, 135–6
24 Maurice, 98
25 Blunt, 424
26 Thompson, 71
27 Richards, W. *Her Majesty's Army, Indian and Colonial Forces*, n.d. [1896?], 67
28 Steele, 37
29 Biddulph, 238
30 Wolseley to Childers, 17 Sep., 1882, Childers, 132
31 Butler: *Journal*, 44
32 *4th/7th Royal Dragoon Guards Regimental Magazine*, XXII, Dec., 1970, 87–8

CHAPTER VII (p. 307–362)

(i)

1 *River War*, I, 79; quoted in Liddell, 445; Maitland, F. H. *Hussar of the Line*, 1951, 71
2 Dufferin to Granville, 6 Feb., 1883, C.3529, Parl. Papers (1883), LXXXIII, 89
3 Capt. Cameron's report, *The Standard*, quoted in Vogt, 222
4 Churchill, 266
5 Malet to Granville, 2 Oct., 1882, C.3461, *P.P.* (1883) LXXXIII, 401
6 Granville to Sir H. Ponsonby, 15 Jan., 1884, Buckle, G. E. (ed.) *The Letters of Queen Victoria . . . III, 1897–1885*, 1928, 472
7 Colvile, I, 19

8 John Macdonald, special correspondent, *Daily News*, 5 Feb., 1884, telegram quoted in Burleigh, 16
9 Alexander, 157–8
10 Male, 444
11 Wright, 222
12 Biddulph, 286
13 Liddell, 432
14 Biddulph, 241
15 Marling, 99–101
16 *Graham*, 375
17 Quoted in Marling, 102
18 Graham to Sec. of State for War, 2 Mar., 1884, *Graham*, 377, 380
19 Liddell, 438
20 Burleigh, 66
21 Royle, 285
22 Biddulph, 242
23 Barrow to Coghill, 11 Apr., 1884, 7112-39-4, Nat. Army Museum
24 Biddulph, 243; see also Burleigh, 303
25 Royle, 285
26 Liddell, 438–9
27 Liddell, 442; Royle, 289
28 Royle, 286
29 Colvile, 22
30 Graham to Sec. of State for War, 3 Mar., 1884, *London Gazette*, 27 Mar., 1884
31 Marling, 118
32 Alexander, 166
33 Marling, 9 Mar., 1884, 109
34 Galloway, xviii
35 Royle, 307

(ii)

1 Q. Victoria to Gladstone, 9 Feb., 1884, *Victoria*, 477; Tennyson, Alfred, Lord, *Guinevere*, 1859
2 Wolseley to Hartington, 13 Apr., 1884, Wolseley: *Papers*
3 Butler to Lady Butler, quoted in McCourt, 168
4 Wolseley to Hartington, 11 Sep., 1884, Colvile, I, 56
5 Wolseley to Hartington, 11 Sep., 1884, Colvile, I, 55
6 Biddulph, 248
7 Gleichen, 104
8 Tylden: *CC*, 28
9 *General Order*, 26 Oct., 1884
10 Arthur, II, 684
11 Gleichen, 3
12 Dundonald, 21
13 Sheppard, Edgar (ed.) *George, Duke of Cambridge: A Memoir of his Private Life based on the Journal and Correspondence of His Royal Highness*, 1906, II, 135

14 Arthur, II, 682
15 Q. Victoria to Hartington, 22 Sep., and Hartington to Q. Victoria, 24 Sep., 1884, *Victoria*, 540–2
16 W/P 13/24 ii, Wolseley: *papers*; Gleichen, 4
17 Dundonald, 27
18 *River War*, I, 97
19 Gleichen, 4; Tylden: *CC*, 24, 25, 29
20 Adye, 112–13
21 Colvile, I, 33
22 Magnus-Allcroft, P. *Kitchener: Portrait of an Imperialist*, 1958, 59
23 Colvile, II, 1
24 Colvile, I, 198
25 *Beresford*, I, 222, 238
26 Gleichen, 26–7
27 Marling, 125
28 Adye, 115–16
29 McCalmont, 236
30 Baden-Powell, 235; Gleichen, 40
31 Gleichen, 25; Colvile, I, 202
32 Dundonald, 23
33 Gleichen, 28
34 Dundonald, 28
35 Gleichen, 47
36 Dawson, 723
37 Gleichen, 64
38 Willcox, 174
39 Marling, 126
40 Colvile, II, 5
41 Gleichen, 72
42 Gleichen, 106
43 Barrett, 99
44 Gleichen, 70
45 Marling, 128, 129
46 Marling, 130, 131
47 Willcox, 176; *Beresford*, I, 255, 256
48 Adye, 120
49 Gleichen, 75

(iii)

1 Colvile, I, 77
2 *Beresford*, I, 257
3 Macdonald, 213–15
4 *Beresford*, 258
5 Stewart to Chief of Staff, 18 Jan., 1885, Colvile, II, 255
6 Biddulph, 250–1
7 Talbot (2), 155
8 Gleichen, 128
9 Dundonald, 36

10 Talbot (2), 155
11 Gleichen, 130
12 Binning's Narrative in *Burnaby*, 301
13 *Beresford*, I, 263
14 Talbot (2), 155
15 *Burnaby*, 302
16 Marling, 132–3
17 Macdonald, 235
18 Talbot (2), 156
19 Alexander, 202–3
20 *Burnaby*, 202
21 Marling, 133
22 Talbot (2), 156
23 Macdonald, 236
24 Gleichen, 131–2
25 Symons, J. *England's Pride: the Story of the Gordon Relief Expedition* 1965, 200
26 *River War*, 63
27 *Burnaby*, 303, 305
28 *Punch*, 31 Jan., 1885, 49
29 Wilson, 33–4
30 Wolseley's campaign journal, 21 Jan., 1885, Preston, 122
31 Talbot (2), 157
32 Colvile, I, 257
33 Pomeroy, 223–4
34 Dundonald, 41
35 Biddulph, 251
36 *Beresford*, I, 270
37 Gleichen, 140
38 Buller to Wolseley, Colvile, II, 72
39 Buller to Wood, 26 Feb., 1885, Colvile, II, 74
40 Arthur, 694, 697
41 Biddulph, 260
42 9 Mar., 1885, Wilkinson O. and J. *The Memoirs of the Gemini Generals*, 1896, 423
43 Lt.-Col. P. H. S. Barrow to Principal Veterinary Surgeon, Nile Expeditionary Force, 13 Aug., 1885, *Official Reports on the Campaign*, W.O. (VIII(5)), 321
44 *Victoria*, 631

(iv)

1 Galloway, xx; De Cosson, 31
2 Biddulph, 261
3 Smith-Dorrien, 55
4 *Suakin*, 128–9; *Hodson's Horse*, 119–20
5 Colvile, II, 184, 312
6 Galloway, 36, 345
7 Colvile, II, 186–9

8 Colvile, 192–4
9 *Hodson's Horse*, 125
10 De Cosson, 86, 91
11 *Hodson's Horse*, 126–7
12 *Graham*, 418
13 Galloway, 57
14 22 Mar., 1885, Preston, 174
15 Willcox, 192–3
16 Royle, 416

(v)

1 De Cosson, 131
2 De Cosson, 131
3 *Graham*, 416
4 Galloway, 55–6
5 *Graham*, 422
6 De Cosson, 154–5
7 Capt. C. Mackenzie Edwards, Berkshire Regt., in a letter home, 27 Mar., 1885, Petre, F. L. *The Royal Berkshire Regiment*, 1925, I, 331
8 *Graham*, 423
9 De Cosson, 161
10 Galloway, 80
11 Quoted in Galloway, 199
12 Letter from Maj.-Gen. C. C. Fraser in *The Morning Post*, 10 Mar., 1885
13 Wingate, F. R. *Mahdism and the Egyptian Sudan . . .*, 1891, 275–9, 423–33; Smith-Dorrien, 60–5; Ardagh, 203–9; *Memoirs of F-M Lord Grenfell*, [1925], 84–8; Arthur: *Maxwell*, 26–8

CHAPTER VIII (p. 363–388)

1 *Sententiae*, no. 145; *River War*, I, 173; Terraine, J. *Douglas Haig the Educated Soldier*, 1963, 17
2 *River War*, I, 151
3 Wingate, 205
4 *Wood*, 172
5 *River War*, I, 152
6 Wingate, 224
7 *Haig*, 82
8 *Midshipman*, 476
9 *River War*, I, 410, 412
10 Steevens, 59
11 *Haig*, 94
12 Steevens, 137; Arthur: *Maxwell*, 53–4
13 Steevens, 138. The best accounts of this reconnaissance are to be found in *Haig*, 91–4 and *Egyptian Cav.*, 82–6
14 Quoted in Ziegler, 43
15 Steevens, 219; *River War*, II, 5

16 5 Aug., 24 Aug., 1898, Churchill: *Companion*, 970
17 *River War*, II, 6, 41
18 19 Aug., 1898, Churchill: *Companion*, 968
19 22 Aug., 1898, *Haig*, 111
20 *River War*, II, 341–3
21 *Haig*, 112–17
22 *River War*, II, 104
23 *Haig*, 117–18
24 e.g. Sandes, Lt.-Col. E. W. C. *The Royal Engineers in Egypt and the Sudan*, 1937, 264
25 Ziegler, 137–8
26 Ziegler, 137–8
27 Quoted in Ziegler, 139
28 *Haig*, 119
29 The original of this order was sold by Wallis and Wallis of Lewes in 1972, *The Daily Telegraph*, 24 Nov., 1972, and is now on display at the Military Heritage Museum, Lewes
30 *River War*, II, 134
31 Churchill: *Companion*, 977–8
32 Smyth, 31
33 Churchill: *Companion*, 978
34 *River War*, II, 135
35 *River War*, II, 133–4
36 Ziegler, 148–9
37 *River War*, II, 135–6
38 *Early Life*, 204
39 Churchill: *Companion*, 978–9
40 Churchill to Lady R. Churchill, 2 Sept., 1898, Churchill: *Companion*, 973–4
41 Smyth, 31
42 6 Sep., 1898, *Morning Post*
43 *River War*, II, 139
44 Steevens, 274
45 *River War*, II, 140–1; Ziegler, 153–5
46 Watkins, O. S. *With Kitchener's Army, being a Chaplain's experiences with the Nile Expedition, 1898*, 1899, 175
47 *River War*, II, 141–2
48 *River War*, II, 137
49 *Early Life*, 208
50 *Early Life*, 203
51 *Haig*, 120–1
52 *Haig*, 122–4
53 *River War*, II, 194

CHAPTER IX (p. 389–395)

1 Caldwell, Capt. George L., United States Veterinary Corps, 'History of Cavalry Horses', *Cavalry Journal*, XIX, July, 1929, 402

2 Hozier, Capt. H. M., 'The Breeding of Horses for Military Purposes', *JUSI*, July, 1872, 738
3 Tylden: *H. & S.*, 27
4 *Cav. Drill*, 20
5 Wantage, 449
6 Tylden: *H. & S.*, 25, 27
7 Murray, II, 503
8 *H.R.A.V.C.*, 164–5
9 *H.R.A.V.C.*, 152, 170, 173, 177–9, 197
10 Wantage, 421–2
11 Morrison, 194
12 *Wood*, 234–5
13 Goodrich, 224
14 Western, 163
15 Birdwood, 44
16 Mole, 190, 194
17 Pomeroy, 228–9
18 Wylly, 307

CHAPTER X (p. 396–404)

1 Robson, 34; Henderson: *Cav.*, 67
2 Baden-Powell, 286
3 Robson, 33–45
4 Robson, 78–81
5 Wolseley to Cambridge, 28 Aug., 1882, Royal Archives, Windsor
6 Robson, 94–105
7 Baines, Thomas *Sketches in Southern Africa: Journals of Residence in Africa from 1842 to 1853* MS in the library of Sir Ernest Oppenheimer, bt, in Johannesburg, I, 282
8 Montecuccoli, Count R. *Memorie sull' Arte de la Guerra*, 1680
9 Denison, Lt.-Col. T. *Modern Cavalry . . .*, 1868, 39
10 Henderson: *Cav.*, 68
11 Molyneux, 188
12 May, Maj. E. S. *Achievements of Field Artillery*, quoted in Tylden, Major G. 'Lancers', *J.A.H.R.* XXIII, (1945), 45
13 Marmont, Marshal Auguste de, Duc de Raguse, *Modern Armies* (trans. Capt. Lendy, 1865), quoted in Foulkes, Charles 'The Lance', *Army Quarterly*, XVII (1928), 94
14 Pomeroy, 212
15 Robertson, 23
16 Molyneux, 157
17 Roberts's intro. to Childers, E. *War and the Arme Blanche*, 1910, vi
18 Roads, C. H. *The British Soldier's Firearm, 1850–1864*, 1964, 297
19 Cardew, 334
20 See, for example, Blatchford, 140
21 Watson, 205
22 Watson, 205

23 Tylden, Maj. G. 'Use of Firearms by Cavalry', *J.A.H.R.*, XIX (1940), 12, 13; XXVIII (1950), 181–2

24 Tylden: *H. & S.*, 142–50

EPILOGUE (p. 405–407)

1 MacDougall, Col. *Modern Warfare as Influenced by Modern Artillery*, 1864, 15, 260

2 Denison, Lt.-Col. G. T. *Modern Cavalry*, 1868, 7, 20, 29–31, 73; Havelock, Sir H. M. *Three Military Questions of the Day*, 1867, 33–65

3 Bond, B. 'Doctrine and Training in the British Cavalry 1870–1914', Howard, Michael *The Theory of War: Essays presented to Captain B. H. Liddell Hart on his Seventieth Birthday*, 1967, 100

INDEX

Battles, Regiments and Wars appear under these headings

Index

Index

Index

Swarbrick, Cpl, DSM, 21 L, 383
Swinburn-Martini carbines, 184

Talbot, Maj.-Gen. Hon. Sir Reginald Arthur James (1841–1929), 277, 279, 280, 285, 286, 288, 289; at Abu Klea, 17 Jan., 1885, 334, 335, 336
Tantia Topi (1819?–1859), 194
Tennyson, Alfred, 1st Baron (1809–1892), 318
Terraine, John, 363
Tewfik Pasha, Mohammed, (The Khedive) (1852–1892), 268, 273, 308, 309
Thomas, Capt., 4 Bombay Cav., 162
Todd, Lt-Col Egerton, 50
Tokar Expeditionary Force, 310
Tomasson, Capt. W. H., Frontier Light Horse, 197, 200
Tottenham, Lt-Col William Heathcote, 12 L (1815–1857), 176
Trollope, Anthony (1815–1882), 209
Tullibardine, Maj. John George, Marquess of (8th Duke of Atholl) (1871–1942), 376
Tulloch, Maj.-Gen. Sir Alexander Bruce (1838–1920), 290, 294, 295
Tylden, Maj. G., 170, 180, 183, 404

Vickers, Pte, 5 DG, 82
Victoria Adelaide Mary Louise, The Princess Royal (1840–1901), 117
Victoria, Queen (1819–1901), 30, 65, 128, 134, 143, 273, 318, 322
Vieille, Paul Marie Eugène (1854–1934), 402
Vogt, Lt-Col Hermann, 98
Vousden, Maj.-Gen. William John, VC (1845–1902), 241–2

Wali, the, of Kandahar, 250
Walters, Vet.-Col W. B. (1839–1929), 351
Wantage Committee (Committee on Terms and Conditions of the Army), 37, 43, 44, 46, 49, 54, 73, 86, 87, 124, 126, 130
Wantage, Robert James Lindsay, Baron (1832–1901), 37, 122
Warde, Lt-Col Henry Murray Ashley (1850–1940), 78
Warden, Capt., CMR, 170

WARS (*including campaigns, expeditions, etc.*)
- Afghan (1st), 1838–1842, 209, 211
- Afghan (2nd), 1878–1880, 43, 62, 87, 130, 141, 149, 150, 153, 154, 155, 158, 159, 209–67, 394, 400, 402
- American Civil, 1861–1865, 406
- Ashanti, 1874, 271
- Austro-Prussian, 1866, 406
- Basuto Rebellion, 1880–1881, 179
- Boer (1st), 1881, 206–8, 273, 344
- Boer (2nd or Great), 1899–1902, 31, 35, 40, 385, 397, 404
- China, 1860, 119
- Crimea, 1854–1856, 30, 31, 63, 70, 95, 120, 208, 397
- Egyptian, 1882, 36, 111, 116, 165, 268–307
- Franco-German, 1870–1871, 117, 400
- Gordon Relief Expedition, 1884–1885, 40, 318–47, 370
- Indian Mutiny, 1857–1859, 70
- Kaffir (6th), 170
- Kaffir (7th), 172
- Kaffir (8th), 174–5
- Kaffir (9th) (Galeka Gaika), 1877, 180, 196
- Northern Border Rebellion, May, 1878, 181
- Pokwane Expedition, Jan., 1878, 181
- Russo-Turkish, 1877–1878, 117
- Sekukuni (2nd), Feb., 1878, 181, 190
- Suakin, 1884–1885, 43, 69, 91
- World War I, 1914–1918, 397
- Zulu, 1879, 35, 43, 167, 181–203, 273, 400, 403

Watson, Capt., 304
Weatherley, Lt-Col Frederick (k. 1879), 190
Webb, QM, 1 D, 114
Webster, Col Arthur George (1837–1916), 313
Wellington, Arthur Wellesey, 1st Duke of (1769–1852), 127, 175, 209
Western, Col John Sutton Edward (1857–1931), 105, 393–4
Westley-Richards carbine, 401–2
Whalley, Capt. Watt, Natal Light Horse, 196
White, F-M Sir George Stuart, VC (1835–1912), 226
Wickenden, Driver James, RHA, 278
Wilkinson, Lt-Gen. Sir Henry Clement (1837–1908), 273, 291; at Tel el-Kebir, 13 Sep., 1882, 298
Williams, Maj. B., 5 Punjab Cav., 219
Willis, Gen. Sir George H. S. (1823–1900), 293
Wilson, Col, a 'crammer', 106
Wilson, Maj.-Gen. Sir Charles William (1836–1905), 324, 340, 342

Index

Wilson, F-M Sir Henry Hughes bart (1864–1922), 106
Wiltshire, Lt H., 20 H, 86
Wolfram, Mr, a 'crammer', 105
Wolseley, Sir Charles Michael, 9th bart (1846–1931), 240
Wolseley, F-M Sir Garnet Joseph, Viscount (1833–1913), 33, 37, 47, 52, 65, 66, 69, 71, 74, 86, 94, 99, 110, 118, 120, 206, 208, 287, 290, 293, 295, 296, 298, 302, 304, 305, 308, 340, 342, 343, 344, 347, 354, 399, 407; succeeds Chelmsford in S.A., 1879, 203; i/c Egyptian Expedition, 1882, 271, 273–75, 277, 280–3; warns cabinet of Gordon's danger, 318; i/c Gordon Relief Expedition, 320–2, 324–5, 328, 329
Wood, Maj.-Gen. Edward Alexander (1841–1898), 42, 52
Wood, F-M Sir Evelyn (1838–1919), 35, 45, 46, 54, 80, 115, 126, 273, 363, 365, 407; i/c left column in Zulu invasion, 1879, 184, 187; attacks Inhlobane Mountain, 26 Mar., 1879, 188, 190; at Kambula, 29 Mar., 1879, 191–2, 194; i/c Flying Column, 196, 198; at Ulundi, 4 July, 1879, 200–2; i/c in 1st Boer War, 1881, 206; negotiates Pretoria Convention, 1881, 208
Wormald, Maj. Frederick William, 7 H, (1869– ?), 381, 382
Wright, Rev. Henry Press (1814?–1892), 63
Wyndham, Horace, 54
Wyndham, Col Walter George Crole (1857–1948), 381

Yakub Khan, Mohammed (1849–1923), 223, 225, 227
Yorke, Col P. S., 19 BL, 245, 247
Young, Capt., 4 Bombay Cav., 162
Young, Lt E. A., 19 BL, 247
Ypres, 1st Earl of (see French)

Ziegler, Philip, 376, 380